T0331256

TRUCKING IN THE AGE OF INFORMATION

*In memory of Albert A. Belman (1916-2005),
a wise and loving adviser who introduced me
to the study of labor*

Trucking in the Age of Information

Edited by

DALE BELMAN
Michigan State University, USA

CHELSEA WHITE III
Georgia Institute of Technology, USA

Routledge
Taylor & Francis Group

LONDON AND NEW YORK

First published 2005 by Ashgate Publishing

Reissued 2018 by Routledge
2 Park Square, Milton Park, Abingdon, Oxon, OX14 4RN
605 Third Avenue, New York, NY 10017

First issued in paperback 2021

Routledge is an imprint of the Taylor & Francis Group, an informa business

A Library of Congress record exists under LC control number: 2005014183

ISBN 13: 978-0-815-39864-6 (hbk)
ISBN 13: 978-1-351-14396-7 (ebk)
ISBN 13: 978-1-138-35782-2 (pbk)

DOI: 10.4324/9781351143967

Contents

List of Contributors

Dale L. Belman is a Professor of Labor and Industrial Relations at Michigan State University. He is an Associate Director of the Sloan Foundation Trucking Industry Program and directed a survey of over-the-road drivers for the Trucking Industry Program. His work on trucking has appeared in *Industrial and Labor Relations Review, Transportation Labor Issues and Regulation* and *Applied Economic Letters. Sailors of the Concrete Sea*, a book on truck drivers' work and lives, was published by Michigan State University Press in 2005.

Elyce A. Biddle is the Chief of the Methods and Analysis Team within the Division of Safety Research, National Institute for Occupational Safety and Health (NIOSH). Her work focuses on economic cost models and health outcome measurements for occupational injuries and fatalities. She chairs the NIOSH Economics Interest Group, serves on the steering committee for the CDC Health Economics Research Group, and chaired the National Occupational Research Agenda Social and Economic Consequences of Workplace Illness and Injury team. Her work has been published in the International Labor Organization's Encyclopedia of Occupational Health and Safety, the American Journal of Industrial Medicine, Contemporary Economic Policy, Human and Ecological Risk Assessment, the Journal of Occupational and Environmental Medicine, the Injury Control and Safety Promotion, and the Monthly Labor Review.

Stephen V. Burks is Associate Professor of Economics and Management at the University of Minnesota, Morris (UMM). His interest in trucking dates from the era of deregulation, when he left the study of philosophy to spend several years working in the industry. When he returned to the academy to acquire a Ph.D. in economics at the University of Massachusetts-Amherst he became associated with the Trucking Industry Program (then at the University of Michigan), which led to the current book chapter. He has a parallel research interest in applying behavioral and experimental economics to the workplace. Recently he has organized an ongoing cooperative research relationship between a large trucking firm and UMM faculty and students, focused on driver productivity and turnover.

Enrique Canessa is an associate professor at the Industrial Engineering School of the Universidad Adolfo Ibáñez, Chile. Professor Canessa specializes in Computer Information Systems (CIS), focusing on the organizational impact of Information Technology (IT). He applies survey research and Agent-based Modeling to analyzing the impact of IT on organizations.

Michael E. Conyngham has been in the research department of the International Brotherhood of Teamsters since 1985, beginning as an assistant to the Chief Economist and then as a Senior Research Analyst. He was appointed as Research Director in June, 1999. His primary responsibilities include the Carhaul, United Parcel Service, and National Master Freight Agreement, agreements that cover more than 400,000 transportation workers. The department supports bargaining and the administration of these agreements with the collection of corporate and employment data, contract-costing, and member surveys and is responsible for developing and analyzing economic proposals. Michael Conyngham grew up in the Washington D.C. area and holds an undergraduate degree in Sociology from University of Notre Dame (1982), and a masters' degree in Social Work from the National Catholic School of Social Service, The Catholic University of America (1985).

Professor **Thomas M. Corsi** joined the Robert H. Smith School of Business in 1976 as a Professor of Logistics and Transportation. He served as Chairperson of the Logistics and Transportation Group from 1986 through 1994. He is an associate editor of the *Logistics and Transportation Review* and serves on the editorial review board of the *Transportation Journal*. He has authored more than 100 articles on logistics and transportation. He has consulted for such organizations as the Interstate Commerce Commission, the Maryland State Department of Transportation, the National Science Foundation, the United States Department of Transportation, the National Truck Stop Operators, United Parcel Service, the United States Department of Energy, and the U.S. Army Logistics Agency. He has authored three books entitled: *The Economic Effects of Surface Freight Deregulation*, published in 1990 by the Brookings Institution in Washington, D.C., *Logistics and the Extended Enterprise (Benchmarks and Best Practices for the Manufacturing Professional)*, published in 1999 by John Wiley & Sons in New York City and *In Real Time: Managing the New Supply Chain*, published in 2004 by Praeger in Westport, CT.

Dr. Leslie S. Hough is Director of Research at the W.J. Usery Center for the Workplace at Georgia State University in Atlanta. Prior to his current position he was Director of the Walter P. Reuther Library of Labor and Urban Affairs. Dr. Hough served as editor of the Usery Center series of publications on the express package industry, including *The Economic Significance of the Express Package Industry*, and *Labor Law and the Express Package Industry: An Unlevel Playing Field*, 2000.

Dr. Lee Husting is a Scientific Program Administrator in the Office of Extramural Programs of the National Institute for Occupational Safety and Health (NIOSH) in Atlanta. He is a member of the Committee on Truck and Bus Safety of the Transportation Research Board (TRB) of the National Academies, the TRB Task Force on Trucking Industry Research, the ANSI Z-15 Standard Committee on Fleet Safety, the NIOSH Motor Vehicle Steering Committee, and planning committees for the Future of Truck and Bus Safety Research conference and the International Truck and Bus Safety Symposium in 2005.

Dr. **Jennifer N. Karlin** is an Assistant Professor of Industrial Engineering at the South Dakota School of Mines and Technology. While earning her Ph.D at the University of Michigan, her work was partially funded by the Trucking Industry Program. Her research focuses on transformational systems at all levels, including product production, organizational systems, and whole value chains. She is particularly interested in the decision making points that occur through the transformational process.

Francine Lafontaine is Professor of Business Economics and Public Policy, Stephen M. Ross School of Business and Professor of Economics, Department of Economics, University of Michigan, Ann Arbor, USA. Professor Lafontaine joined the University of Michigan in 1991, after 3 years at Carnegie Mellon University. Most of her research has been concerned with forms of contracting, with special emphasis on franchising and on the role of owner operators in the trucking industry.

Dr. **C. John Langley, Jr.** is Professor of Supply Chain Management and Director of Supply Chain Executive Programs at the Georgia Institute of Technology in Atlanta, Georgia, USA. Dr. Langley is a former President of the Council of Logistics Management, and a recipient of the Council's Distinguished Service Award. Dr. Langley has co-authored several books, including *The Management of Business Logistics*, a 7th edition textbook published in 2003. He also serves on the Boards of Directors of UTi Worldwide, Inc., Averitt Express, Inc., and Forward Air Corporation. He is also lead author of the annual study on the 3PL industry, the most recent of which is titled *2004 Ninth Annual Study of 3PL Service Providers: Views from the Customers.*

Dr. **Jeffrey K. Liker** is Professor of Industrial and Operations Engineering at the University of Michigan. He is the Director of the Japan Technology Management Program (JTMP). Dr. Liker has authored or co-authored over 65 articles and book chapters and five books. His is author of the best-selling *The Toyota Way: 14 Management Principles from the World's Greatest Manufacturer*, McGraw Hill, 2004 which speaks to the underlying philosophy and principles that drive Toyota's quality and efficiency-obsessed culture. The book and articles in Harvard Business Review and Sloan Management Review address issues of developing a lean logistics process, including partnering with third party logistics providers.

B. Starr McMullen is Professor and Chair of the Department of Economics at Oregon State University where she specializes in transportation economics. She has published articles and books on transportation issues including regulation/deregulation, pricing, costs, efficiency, productivity, and competition. A past president of TPUG (the Transportation and Public Utilities Group of the American Economic Association), she is on several editorial boards and has served as managing editor of *Research in Transportation Economics.*

Will Mitchell is the J. Rex Fuqua Professor of International Management at the Fuqua School of Business of Duke University in Durham, North Carolina. Will's research focuses on business dynamics, studying how firms change in the face of constraints to change. Several of his studies focus on firms in the trucking industry, particularly how they use information technology to expand within their existing markets and to help them enter new markets.

Kristen A. Monaco is Professor of Economics at California State University Long Beach. She earned her PhD in Economics from the University of Wisconsin-Milwaukee. Her research centers on the relationship between industry structure and labor market outcomes, with a focus on the trucking industry.

Dr. **Anuradha Nagarajan** is a faculty member in the Corporate Strategy and International Business department at the Stephen M. Ross School of Business Administration at the University of Michigan. Her research interests include the study of emerging industries, technology strategy, and the competitive implications of inter-organizational arrangements in highly uncertain, networked environments. Her recent research on the use of technology and the internet in the trucking industry include chapters in: *US Industry in 2000 – Studies in Competitive Performance* published by the National Academy Press in 2000, *Tracking a Transformation – e-commerce and the terms of competition in industries* published by the Brookings Institution Press in 2001, and *The Economic Payoff from the Internet Revolution* published by the Brookings Institution Press in 2001. She received her Ph.D. in Corporate Strategy from the University of Michigan School of Business Administration in 1996.

Maciek Nowak is an Assistant Professor of Logistics in the College of Business Administration at Georgia Southern University. He is actively involved in vehicle routing research, collaborating with several package express service providers. His primary area of interest is in the reduction of excess capacity found in the trucking industry.

James Peoples is professor of economics at the University of Wisconsin-Milwaukee. His areas of specialty are labor issues in transportation and telecommunications industries. Current research explores managerial earnings trends in deregulated transportation industries. He has also co-edited books that cover labor issues in transportation industries such as *Transportation Labor Issues and Regulatory Reform* with Wayne Talley and *Product Market Structure and Labor Market Treatment*, with John Heywood.

Peter F. Swan is an Assistant Professor of Supply Chain Management at the Smeal College of Business at The Pennsylvania State University. His lifelong interest in transportation has led to a brief career in the railroad industry and to many years associated with the Trucking Industry Program (then at the University of Michigan). Dr. Swan chairs the Committee for Freight Transportation Economics and Regulation at the Transportation Research Board and researches issues related to transportation markets, productivity, and operations.

Chelsea C. White III is the Schneider National Chair of Transportation and Logistics at Georgia Institute of Technology, the director of the Trucking Industry Program, which is part of the Sloan Industry Study Center Network, and the executive director of The Logistics Institute (TLI). He is a director of ITS America and of CNF, Inc. His most recent research interests include analyzing the role of real-time information and enabling information technology for improved logistics and, more generally, supply chain productivity and risk, with special focus on the U.S. trucking industry.

Preface

Dale L. Belman, Elyce A. Biddle, Lee Hustings and Chelsea C. White III

Dominant technologies often provide an intuitive reference to an era. The imagery of the "Age of Sail," the "Age of Steam" and the "Age of Iron" are a part of the vocabulary of economic history. Similarly, the latter part of the 19th century is frequently referenced as the "Age of Steel," the early part of the 20th century as the "Age of Electricity," while the middle years of the 20th century are increasingly referred to as the "Age of the Automobile." Although we do not yet understand the full impact of information technology, we do know that it is increasingly profound and that it may be appropriate to reference the closing decades of the 20th century and the opening decades of the 21st century as "The Age of Information". Information technologies (IT) and improvements in wired and wireless technologies have changed how businesses and economies are organized and how they interacted with one another. These changes appear to be sufficiently profound that they support an ongoing debate over the emergence of a "new economy."

The nature of the "Age of Information" differs by industry and sector. For many industries, the initial applications of IT were internal to the firm and the production process. The exploitation of IT and virtually instantaneous communications between locations and between firms followed both because of the greater complexity of external systems and because the external systems linked the internal systems. In other industries, including trucking, demands and capabilities external to the industry have compelled it to adapt new technologies and ways of business. What is increasingly true for all industries is that IT has underlain profound changes in the way business are run, how they are organized and in their inter-operations. It is through such changes that the "Age of Information" is increasingly viewed as altering and possibly even transforming economic processes.

Trucks, tractor-trailers, straight trucks, flatbeds, vehicle haulers, refrigerated vehicles, and specialized trucking vehicles – have been integral to the nation's transportation system for almost a century. What began in the 1920s as small local cartage operations has grown into the core freight moving industry. Despite its central role in the U.S. economy, trucking has not been a leading or innovative sector. Rather, for most of its history, trucking has been characterized by simple organizational structures and the relatively unsophisticated use of technology.

This situation is changing in the face of the demands of firms for faster, more efficient and more encompassing transportation and logistics providers. Although small parts of the industry have yet to be deeply affected by the changes brought about by the "Age of Information," much of the industry is undergoing extensive change. Although recognizably similar to the earliest trucks, current tractors are much larger, more streamlined, and more powerful than those of even ten and twenty years ago. The internal systems and components, including the advanced electronics, fuel, braking and gearing systems of today's vehicles, have changed dramatically, transforming trucks from straightforward internal combustion driven vehicles with simple mechanical systems and chassis parts, to sophisticated integrated systems with electro-mechanical, fuel, suspension, and transmission components dependent on advanced technologies such as integrated circuits.

Within the past two decades optimization software, sophisticated database tools, and advances in telecommunications have made trucking fleets integrated components of advanced transportation and delivery systems. Companies specializing in delivery have revolutionized the trucking industry with their shipment tracking, reporting, and management algorithms and software. Incorporating advanced concepts, real-time information, and specialized applications, transportation managers have the ability to control shipping in ways unthinkable in the past.

Within the commercial trucking industry, advances in vehicle technology, systems integration, electronic communications, control technologies and scientific knowledge of human physiology have brought about profound changes. These changes affect the way that commercial motor vehicles are operated, dispatched, tracked and managed. In practical terms, the "Age of Information" means that commercial trucks are dispatched based on advanced routing procedures; that trucks incorporate sensor-based technology that continuously monitors fuel flow, temperature, and other operating conditions; and that drivers are in contact with dispatchers and fleet managers throughout the course of the day. Managers passively monitor vehicle locations through Global Positioning System-based reporting systems; on-board data recorders maintain records of vehicle speed and other data; and state and federal highway administrators maintain traffic management systems, traveler information systems and incident management systems. Further, it means that driver work/rest cycles are increasingly mandated by scientific data on human performance and fatigue and that sophisticated databases are used to collect and analyze data on the operation of all the components of the commercial trucking and transportation systems.

As might be expected, these technologies, and their applications in freight transportation, continue to evolve. The efforts to establish intelligent vehicles and transportation systems, highway and communications infrastructures, vehicle-based data recording, and automatic management/reporting systems will be implemented in the not-too-distant future. Advanced technologies are being developed that will link to data created on vehicles, uplink through established and enabled communications protocols, and interface with environmental control technologies, such as embedded roadway sensors. In many cases it will be a simple-enough matter to "plug in" new technologies. Although the primary focus of much of the development and implementation of this "intelligent" technology is maximizing productivity and profitability for the individual firm, much will focus on improving safety and health for the worker and others who share the road, a benefit to the American society.

The drivers of change are not just the availability of technologies. Rather, the fundamental force has been the needs of business for more extensive, faster, reliable, and flexible transportation services. Lean manufacturing systems with Just-in-Time inventory require more sophisticated transportation systems than do systems with large in-plant inventories. The distribution systems of the big box retail stores, with time sensitive deliveries to cross docks, has made the transportation link between producers and retailers more complex and placed new demands on the transportation companies. Tracking cargo, and having that information available to not only the trucking firm but the shipper and consignee, have required trucking firms to install cargo tracking systems and make the data available over the Internet. Global commerce makes further demands on truck transportation as the once leisurely international shipping industry becomes more tightly integrated into the economy with consequent needs to move goods from ports to warehousing to consignee on a predictable schedule. The needs of firms to efficiently utilize a full range of ever more diverse transportation services such as fixed route and irregular route Truck Load, Less-the-Truckload, Package Express and Expedited Services as well as a variety of international transportation services has underlain the development of a logistics industry that links shippers to transportation providers.

Although there are many sources of information on the freight transportation industry, no recent source provides a comprehensive overview of contemporary trucking and freight transportation. This volume has the dual purpose of providing both an introduction to the trucking industry for those who are not familiar with the current industry and in depth information for those interested and knowledgeable on specific topics. We are fortunate to count among the authors both recognized authorities in the field of trucking research and younger scholars who are establishing their presence in the respective fields. Many of the authors are associated with the Sloan Foundation Trucking Industry Program (TIP). TIP was established in 1995 as a venture by the Sloan Foundation Industry Program and the University of Michigan to promote interdisciplinary studies of the trucking industry. The program later moved to The Georgia Institute of Technology to a home in The Logistic Institute. The members of TIP have been actively engaged in research on trucking and increasingly on global logistics; some of this research appears in chapters in this volume. However, the authors are not limited to members of TIP. We have reached out to authorities in areas such as the history of the industry, the truckload segment, and safety and health to assure that each chapter represents the current state of knowledge about the industry.

The eleven chapters in this volume are organized into two sections. The first five chapters – those covering the history of the industry and the truckload, less-than-truckload, and package express segments of the industry and logistics function – provide a comprehensive overview of the trucking industry. The balance of the chapters address specific topics including the evolution of technology, the regulatory environment, labor markets, safety and health, the role of trucking in the lean enterprise, and the situation of the driver in the evolving industry. Although the novice may wish to read the entire book to become familiar with the industry, each chapter also stands on its own as a current reference.

In closing, the editors would like to express their gratitude to the Sloan Foundation for supporting the Trucking Industry Program. Interdisciplinary research can be uniquely rich and productive as it brings many perspectives to bear on an issue. Such research is time consuming and follows a less direct path than disciplinary research if for no other reason than the participants have to reconcile disciplinary approaches and develop a shared vocabulary. The patience of the Foundation in seeing the fruits of its investments has been critical to the success of TIP and has provided the members of TIP with unique opportunities. In closing, we also wish to acknowledge the outstanding work of Russell Ormiston, Mary Hoffman and Kaumudi Misra, doctoral students at Michigan State University, who played important roles in bringing this volume to press.

Chapter 1

The Evolution of the U.S. Motor Carrier Industry

B. Starr McMullen

Introduction

Motor carriage is the dominant mode of freight transportation in the United States today. Trucking firms accounted for over 62 percent of the shipment value and over 59 percent of tonnage shipped in the U.S. in 1997 (USDOT, Bureau of Transportation Statistics, 2002). This contrasts drastically with the situation a century ago when the motor carrier industry was non-existent and railroads were the primary mode of both freight and passenger transportation. The purpose of this chapter is to examine the emergence and continued growth of the motor carrier industry as the core of the U.S. freight transportation system.

The development of the U.S. motor carrier industry during the twentieth century resulted from a combination of historical circumstance as well as timing of technological innovations, government intervention, and economic development that led to changes in freight markets and the demand for trucking services. Of all of these influences, government intervention, especially economic regulation, played a pivotal role.

Accordingly, we can identify three distinct periods of industry development corresponding to different regimes of Federal government regulation. The period before 1935 can be thought of as the "infancy" stage when there was no Federal regulation and the industry was first coming into existence as a viable mode of freight transportation. The Motor Carrier Act of 1935 (MCA) placed the trucking industry under the regulatory auspices of the Interstate Commerce Commission (ICC) and began the "regulated" era. Although significant easing of regulatory restrictions began in the late 1970s, it was the Motor Carrier Act of 1980 that heralded the beginning of the "deregulated" regulatory environment that prevails in the industry today.

This chapter will be organized as follows. First, a review of the structure of the motor carrier industry is presented to provide enough background and terminology necessary to understand its evolution over time. The subsequent sections consider key factors influencing industry development in each era as well as policy issues that have emerged as both the motor carrier industry and the overall economy have changed.

Background: The U.S. Motor Carrier Industry

The diversity of the motor carrier industry makes it difficult to implement a single classification system to encompass the many distinct types of carriers and operations. The taxonomy employed here follows Talley (1983) and first divides the industry into private and for-hire carriers.

Private carriage refers to the use of trucks owned and operated by a manufacturing or retail company whose primary business is not the production of transportation services. Private carriers usually do not transport freight for other firms although the Motor Carrier Act of 1980 made it easier for firms to do so. Except for basic safety requirements, the private trucking sector has not been subject to federal or state agency oversight. In the absence of regulatory reporting requirements, it has been difficult to obtain reliable financial and operating statistics for this sector of the trucking industry.

In an effort to gain perspective on the importance of private trucking, historical data on the number of trucks registered in the U.S. is provided in Table 1.1. A breakdown of registrations into private and for-hire trucks was only available for 1960, 1970 and 1980. In those years private trucks (including pickups and light trucks) constituted about 95 percent of all registered trucks. The National Private Truck Council estimates that in 2002 private fleets operated about 82 percent of all U.S. registered medium and heavy duty trucks (those typically dedicated to commercial freight transport) and accounted for around 53 percent of the truck miles and 56 percent of the tonnage shipped by these trucks. However, private trucking fleets only account for about 47 percent of the revenues generated by the commercial trucking sector (Corridore, 2003).

Table 1.1   U.S. Truck Registrations

Year	Number Private Trucks (%)	Number For-Hire Truck (%)	Total Trucks
1904	---	---	700
1910	---	---	10123
1920	---	---	1107639
1930	---	---	3578747
1940	---	---	4590386
1950	---	---	8272153
1960	10559300 (93%)	940700 (8%)	11352618
1970	17016800 (96%)	783200 (4%)	17754468
1980	30692700 (95%)	1404700 (5%)	32238223
1988	---	---	*42529000

* this figure is rounded off.
--- indicates that the data were not available.
Note: Comparable data for subsequent years were not available.
Source: American Trucking Trends (various issues).

Given the lack of available data and the dominance of for-hire trucking in commercial freight revenues, research on the U.S. trucking industry has focused on the for-hire portion of the industry. Indeed, it is the for-hire part of the industry where the serious policy problems arise especially in regard to economic regulation and industry competitiveness.

In the regulated trucking industry, for-hire firms were categorized as either common or contract carriers. A common carrier was defined as one that provides services to the general public and stands ready to serve all shippers in a market. A contract carrier provides services under contract to a specific shipper or group of shippers. Under Federal regulation by the Interstate Commerce Commission (ICC), there was little crossover between the two types of carriers, but since deregulation the distinction between common and contract carriers has blurred. Indeed, many carriers now provide both types of service.

Another distinction is whether carriers are classified as general freight or specialized commodity carriers. General freight firms are common carriers that carry a wide variety of different commodity types, often in the same vehicle. This distinguishes them from carriers that serve shippers in markets where specialized equipment or services are required. Examples of specialized commodity carriers include those involved in the transportation of hazardous waste, liquid petroleum products, refrigerated goods, household goods, forest products, heavy machinery, automobile transporters, and mine ores.

One of the most important distinctions to make in any discussion of the industry is the difference between truckload (TL) and less-than-truckload (LTL) trucking operations. Truckload operations usually involve the transportation of a large single shipment from origin to destination, typically without making intermediate stops. These carriers may not operate regular routes but instead go to where they are needed to handle a shipment. TL operations dominate the trucking industry, with private trucking being predominantly of a TL nature. In the for-hire sector, 81 per cent of for-hire trucking revenues derive from TL shipments. In the TL part of the for-hire industry there are ten large, publicly traded firms and literally tens of thousands of small companies (Standard and Poor's, 2003). The TL sector of the industry has relatively low entry barriers since all that is required to enter the industry is a truck. As a result, economists argue that this portion of the industry is extremely competitive.

Accordingly to the definition originally implemented by the ICC in to report operating statistics, a TL shipment is defined as one exceeding 10,000 pounds whereas a LTL shipment weighs less than 10,000 pounds. This led to confusion in the literature, as well as the industry, regarding how to define a carrier as TL or LTL. TL carriers may transport LTL shipments, especially on the backhaul where it pays to fill up the truck with something rather than nothing. Similarly, a LTL carrier may transport TL shipments. McMullen and Tanaka (1995) provide a discussion of some of the pitfalls in trying to classify a carrier as TL or LTL using ICC reporting categories.

What truly distinguishes a LTL carrier from a TL carrier is the fact that a LTL carrier requires terminal facilities to consolidate LTL shipments, often from several shippers originating in different physical locations. LTL carrier operations require pick-up and delivery vehicles to collect shipments and bring them to the terminal where individual LTL shipments are consolidated into a single truck for the line haul (long distance) part of the journey. At the destination terminal individual LTL shipments must be handled again as they are offloaded to local delivery vehicles to transport to the final destination.

From an economic perspective, a LTL carrier with terminal facilities requires considerably more capital and has higher fixed costs than a TL carrier. In addition to truck drivers and office personnel, LTL operations require terminal employees to consolidate and disperse shipments. These carriers, especially the large national LTL firms, usually have higher labor costs than TL carriers due to the heavy unionization of this sector by the Teamsters.

LTL carriers are able to reduce per unit costs by increasing the size of their network system to increase the density of traffic on the line haul portions of their shipments. Thus, they have the incentive to increase the size and complexity of their network system and their customer base to take advantage of network economies. Network economies are a kind of "economies of scope" that refer to the situation in which a single firm can produce multiple outputs more efficiently (at a lower cost) than if separate firms were to produce the outputs independently.

Finally, for-hire motor carriers can be classified by size. A motor carrier firm, whether for-hire or private, may consist of one truck owned and driven by an owner-operator, or a fleet of hundreds of trucks. A large motor carrier usually owns a fleet of trucks and employs company drivers, supplementing its fleet when necessary by hiring the services of owner-operators. A single truck owner-operator is the smallest possible trucking firm when size is measured by the number of trucks owned and operated.

The conventional measure of motor carrier size used by the ICC was based on annual revenues and this method of size classification continues to the present day. Carriers are defined as Class I, II or III, with Class I being those with the greatest annual revenues. The exact dollar amounts used to define these classes have been revised upwards over time as the economy has grown. Table 1.2 provides a snapshot summary of the number of ICC regulated, for-hire carriers by revenue class between 1945 and 1990.

Between 1935 and the mid-1970s the number of ICC certified carriers declined from almost 26,000 to about 15,000. Easing of entry restrictions that occurred in the late 1970s, followed by the Motor Carrier Act of 1980, resulted in an increase in the number of ICC certified carriers to over 40,000 by 1990 with most entry coming from the smaller, Class III firms. Further, most of these smaller industry entrants were truckload operations because it takes such a small capital investment (basically the purchase/rental of a truck) to enter.

At the same time that there was an increase in the number of small, TL carriers, there was a decrease in the number of large LTL firms following deregulation. There has been little, if any entry into the LTL trucking industry but many incumbents either became bankrupt or merged with other trucking firms. The September 2002 bankruptcy filing by Consolidated Freightways and the December 2003 merger of Roadway and Yellow Freight are recent examples. Increases in the concentration of LTL industry revenues among a few large firms has raised the concern that these carriers may be able to use their dominant position to exercise market power, raise rates, and earn monopoly profits It is for this reason that the LTL portion of the industry commands so much attention from both academic researchers and policymakers.

Table 1.2   Number of ICC Certified Carriers by Size Class[a]

Year	Class I	Class II	Class III	Total
	$100,000 or more	$25,000 to $100,000	Under $25,000	
1945[b]		2,001	18,871	20,872
	$200,000 or more	$50,000 to $200,000	Under $50,000	
1950[b]	2,053	17,544		19,597
1955[b]	1,834	15,298		18,141
	$1,000,000 or more	$200,000 to $1,000,000	Under $200,000	
1960	1,053	2,276	12,947	16,276
1965	1,250	2,615	11,700	15,565
	$1,000,000 or more	$300,000 to $1,000,000	Under $300,000	
1970	1,571	2,061	11,468	15,100
	$3,000,000 or more	$500,000 to $3,000,000	Under $500,000	
1975	885	2,670	12,450	16,005
1980[c]	3,104		14,941	18,045
	$5,000,000 or more	$1,000,000 to $5,000,000	Under $1,000,000	
1990[c]	2,418		43,373	45,791

a) Separate figures on Class II and Class III carriers not available prior to 1957.
b) One figure is given for the combined total of Class II and Class III carriers for this year.
c) One figure is given for the combined total of Class I and II carriers for this year.
Source: American Trucking Associations, American Trucking Trends, various years.

A couple of caveats need to be made regarding the availability and quality of motor carrier industry data on which most empirical studies have been based. First, individual states have regulated and collected data from trucking firms, but this data has been collected in an inconsistent manner from state to state and has not been easily available to researchers. Accordingly, most industry studies have used data collected at the Federal level. Federal data on motor carrier operating and financial statistics during the regulated years, 1935-1980, was comprehensive, reliable and comparable on a year-to-year basis, especially for the larger firms in the industry. However, the quality of Federal data deteriorated following the Motor Carrier Act of 1980 as efforts were made to simplify reporting requirements for motor carriers. By the mid-1990s, significant changes in the ICC reporting instrument, Form M, and in data reporting requirements resulted in Federal data being more aggregate and less detailed than in the past. These changes have rendered it increasingly difficult to evaluate and compare industry performance over time (Burks, Guy, and Maxwell, 2004).

The Infant Industry: Prior to 1935

At the beginning of the twentieth century, the U.S. economy was largely agrarian. Most freight transportation, especially inland movement, was provided by railroads that were well suited to carry bulk agricultural commodities. The U.S. rail system was highly developed and railroads did not have much competition in the provision of freight services. Indeed, it was the monopoly position of railroads in many markets, combined with anti-competitive behavior that led to the passage Interstate Commerce Act of 1887 and the creation of the Interstate Commerce Commission (ICC) as a regulatory authority.

The trucking industry was not technologically feasible as a mode of freight transportation until the introduction of the internal combustion engine around the turn of the twentieth century. In 1904 there were only 700 trucks registered in the entire U.S. (see Table 1.1). Richter (1995) argues that the advantages of freight transportation by truck did not become apparent until during World War I when there was a shortage of trains to transport military trucks to coastal ports for shipment to Europe. Because of the lack of available rail service, military trucks were driven from inland locations directly to export ports. The War Department took advantage of the opportunity to load the trucks with supplies and the flexible, door-to-door freight transportation made possible by motor carriage, became recognized.

After World War I, several events contributed to the emergence of the motor carrier industry as a viable mode of freight transportation. First, there was a surplus of unemployed military truck drivers available to domestic fleets. Second, the 1920s brought many new consumer goods to market. Many of the new products were manufactured goods that weighed less and were less bulky than the products usually transported by rail. These new products typically comprised shipment sizes that could not fill a railcar but which were ideal for filling a truck or tractor-trailer. Since motor carrier trailers were smaller than rail cars, they could easily accommodate the smaller shipment sizes with TL shipments whereas partially filled rail cars were not cost effective for railroads since they had higher unit costs than full cars. The shift in freight demand to smaller shipment sizes thus gave trucks a cost advantage over rail for these commodities. As discussed later, this trend towards smaller shipment size started in the 1920s but persisted throughout the rest of the century, continually eroding the competitive position of railroads.

Third, the growth in truck traffic during World War I led to rapid deterioration of roads that had been designed for lighter automobile and bicycle traffic, resulting in increased public pressure for internal road improvements. The U.S. government had been involved in road construction early in the 1800s when it started construction of the National Pike. This project came to a halt in the Jackson era when it was deemed inappropriate for the Federal government to be involved in internal improvements and road construction was left to state and local governments that did not have money earmarked to finance either road maintenance or construction. Eventually the Federal Aid Act of 1916 and the Highway Act of 1921 created programs where Federal funds were made available to match state funds for highway development. This cooperative Federal and state support of highway construction marked the beginning of Federal involvement in highway infrastructure that persists to this day. Most state highway department were formed at this time in order to participate in the Federal roads program (Talley, 1983), increasing the involvement of state government in highway construction and finance.

Technological developments in road construction, tire technology, and diesel engines during the 1920s, also stimulated the growth of the motor carrier industry. Advances in the road building process and a movement towards standardization of highway design resulted in an increase in the number and quality of roadways, helping make motor carriage a more accessible and faster freight transport option. Progress in pneumatic tire technology during this decade resulted in less wear and tear on trucks, a more comfortable ride, and allowed trucks to operate at higher speeds – all important factors in popularizing motor carriage as a viable mode of freight transportation. The introduction of diesel engines on trucks in the early 1930s provided fuel cost savings to truckers at a time when the price of diesel was approximately one-third that of gasoline, providing further impetus to the competitiveness of truck transport (Zeitner and Sons, 2004).

Finally, the great Depression of the 1930s brought significant Federal government intervention to the transportation sector that, despite no stated governmental intention, ultimately spurred growth in motor carriage at the expense of the railroads. The massive public works projects of the 1930s accelerated improvements in the highway system giving motor carriers an increasingly larger network over which to operate. Meanwhile the miles of track in the railroad system peaked in 1930 and then began a decline that continues to this day. The fact that railroad track is privately owned and must be built and maintained by railroads results in deferred rail maintenance, deterioration of the infrastructure, and slower travel times for railroads when they hit poor financial times and are unable to replace and maintain capital. On the other hand, highways are provided by the government and trucks pay highway user fees which are a variable cost to motor carrier firms. The deterioration and decrease in the miles of track in the rail network system over time resulted in lower service quality (in terms of speed, safety, availability, and reliability) at the same time that service quality was growing in importance amongst shippers as manufacturing grew as a percentage of economic activity.

Many individual states had a variety of motor carrier regulations in place prior to 1935, especially those regarding user fees and size and weight limits. For instance, in 1919 Oregon became the first state to impose a fuel tax to raise money to finance road maintenance and construction and other states quickly followed suit. However, the motor carrier industry was not subject to regulation at the Federal level prior to 1935 when the economy was still suffering from the aftermath of the Great Depression and various government regulatory authorities were created in an effort to provide a "safety net" of protection for various industries and interest groups.

The Regulated Trucking Industry: 1935-1980

The Motor Carrier Act of 1935 (MCA of 1935) brought the motor carrier industry under the regulatory authority of the ICC, the same agency responsible for railroad industry regulation. In addition to imposing stricter size and weight requirements on the industry, the MCA of 1935 imposed economic regulations on motor carriers that paralleled those applied to the railroad industry. As explained below, this regulation ultimately led to various economic distortions that hastened the decline of the railroad industry and gave further advantage to motor carriage.

Ironically, the railroad industry was a major advocate for motor carrier regulation as trucks competed with railroads for freight traffic and railroads operated under the mistaken belief that the ICC would protect them from intermodal competition (Keeler, 1983). Railroads also supported water carriers being brought under the regulatory auspices of the ICC in 1938 using the same reasoning – that the ICC would protect railroads from intermodal competition on routes where they directly faced other ICC regulated carriers.

Although economic regulation refers to control over pricing and entry that is imposed to replace competitive market forces, it was never argued that the unregulated motor carrier industry would exhibit any of the natural monopoly characteristics that had led to railroad regulation. Unlike rail, which was generally acknowledged to exhibit the characteristics of a natural monopoly, the trucking industry of the 1930s seemed to suffer from excessive competition. It was claimed that "destructive competition" resulted in a large number of firm bankruptcies and regulation was seen as a means to stabilize an industry that could not survive if left to function on its own. Indeed, the trucking industry itself seemed more concerned about intramodal competition from other motor carrier firms, than intermodal competition from railroads (Felton, 1989).

Finally, the "infant industry" argument was suggested as a rationale for economic regulation of trucking carriage until the industry was mature enough to survive on its own. Of course, both rail and trucking suffered during the Great

Depression since freight transportation demand is derived from overall aggregate demand. Thus it is difficult to sort out whether the trucking industry was having trouble in the 1930s because it was subject to "destructive competition," because it was an infant industry, or simply because of general economic conditions.

In any case, the MCA of 1935 imposed entry regulations that required firms to obtain ICC certificates of convenience and necessity to operate in any interstate markets. Firms already in operation when the MCA of 1935 was implemented, were "grandfathered" into the industry, but new entrants were required to engage in an expensive and often lengthy, application process to operate in ICC regulated markets. The result was that few new firms entered the industry in the ICC regulated period. Indeed, between 1935 and 1973, the number of Class I, II, and III ICC certified carriers dropped from about 26,000 to about 15,000 (McMullen, 1987).

ICC operating authorities included detailed information on specific geographic markets, commodities, and individual routes that a carrier could serve. It has been argued that the ICC specified circuitous routes that often resulted in empty backhauls and higher per unit costs. This was done in an effort to sustain service to small communities, although there is some debate as to the extent this was a problem (Boyer, 1993).

In order to enter a new route or area, or transport a different sort of commodity, a carrier had to obtain a "certificate of public convenience" from the ICC. The ICC was reluctant to issue new certificates and had to be convinced that there was a public need for the proposed service. Further, the ICC also required a new entrant to show that firms with existing authority in the market, would not be harmed. This effectively protected existing carriers from competition and discouraged new entrants. In fact, since the certification process was long, costly, and usually unsuccessful, many mergers resulted between existing firms who found it easier to expand their authorities through acquisition rather than obtaining new ICC approved certificates. This phenomena was referred to by Friedlaender and Spady (1981) as ICC induced "regulatory" economies of scale.

In the post WWII period, economic activity in the U.S. shifted towards higher valued manufactured goods and shippers became increasingly concerned with the service quality aspects of freight transportation such as time in transit, reliability, and door-to-door service. The trend towards product differentiation also resulted in a greater variety of products being shipped in smaller loads, where trucks had a clear advantage over rail. The result was the emergence of LTL trucking firms that specialized in providing such service. However, restrictive operating authorities made it difficult for motor carriers to form efficient network systems and achieve economies by consolidating LTL shipments. The inflexibility of entry and routing thus constrained the growth and viability of LTL network systems under ICC regulation. LTL carriers had fragmented route authorities that were not conducive to the achievement of network economies. The only way that LTL carriers were able to thrive in this regulated environment was because of a regulatory rate structure that allowed LTL carriers to earn excess profits while entry barriers kept out competition.

ICC regulation of motor carrier and intermodal freight rate structures were a factor that spurred motor carrier growth at the expense of the railroads. Since the ICC had regulatory authority over railroads and inland water carriers as well as motor carriers, it was responsible for intermodal rate structures when modes competed as well as the rate structure for each individual mode. For railroads to remain competitive with motor carriers for the high valued manufactured commodities called for a rail/truck rate structure in which the differential between rail and truck rates was sufficient to compensate shippers for the difference in service quality between modes. However, the ICC would not allow railroads to lower rates on these commodities enough to keep them competitive with trucks.

As a result, railroads lost business from shippers of high value commodities to trucks and were left with low value bulk commodities that also commanded low rates. This was a vestige of the "value of service" pricing structure that was successful for the railroad industry prior to the emergence of truck competition. Essentially railroads had been able to charge high rates for high valued commodities and lower rates for low valued bulk commodities and cover costs through cross subsidization of low valued commodities by the higher valued ones. Once trucks bid away the higher valued commodities, railroads were left with revenues insufficient to cover costs, resulting in deferral of maintenance and eventual numerous rail bankruptcies.

In addition to ICC rate regulation effectively eliminating railroad competition for high value commodities, it also served to limit intramodal competition between carriers and did not provide incentives to increase overall efficiency. Examples are when the ICC refused to allow railroads to set rates that passed along cost savings from new technologies as the "Big John Hopper" cars in the 1970s or piggyback technologies such as trailer on freight car (TOFC) or container on freight car (COFC), thus discouraging innovation. Both TOFC and COFC technologies were used more extensively in Canada than in the U.S. during the regulatory period because Canadian regulators allowed carriers to pass on cost savings to customers through rate reductions (Friedlaender and Harrington, 1979).

Under ICC regulation there were literally hundreds of published motor carrier "tariffs" or rates that were established for individual commodities and routes. All carriers were obligated to provide service at the published rates approved by the ICC. Further, these tariffs were set in rate conference meetings where carriers discussed and voted on rates or "tariffs". While such obviously collusive behavior would normally violate antitrust laws, the Reed-Bulwinkle Act of 1948 exempted these activities for ICC regulated industries.

In this rate setting it was relatively easy for motor carriers to pass along cost increases to shippers in the form of higher rates – which did not encourage economic efficiency. The motor carrier industry enjoyed large profits from a combination of the entry restrictions imposed by the ICC along with its rate policies. Moore (1978) argues that the clear beneficiaries of regulation were the trucking firms, especially the LTL firms that earned supranormal profits, and unionized (largely Teamster) labor. From an economic perspective this would be expected in an environment where excess profits are earned and cannot be dissipated by new firms entering or from existing firms engaging in rate competition. Economic regulation by the ICC essentially allowed the industry to operate as a government protected cartel.

The growth in the importance of the trucking industry vis-à-vis the railroads is illustrated by observing the percentage of U.S. freight revenue accounted for by the different freight modes. As seen in Table 1.3, in 1948 railroads still dominated with 71.14 per cent of total freight revenues going to rail and only 23.21 per cent to trucks. By the time regulatory reform was getting started (around 1978), the rail share was down to 12.80 per cent and the truck share of freight revenue had grown to 74.10 percent.

Table 1.3   Percent of Total U.S. Freight Revenue by Mode (%)

Year	Truck	Rail	Pipeline	Water	Air	Other
1948	23.21	71.14	3.24	1.64	0.77	0.00
1958	38.77	53.19	4.56	2.06	1.43	0.00
1968	50.91	41.22	4.11	1.29	2.47	0.00
1978	74.10	12.80	3.00	7.10	1.30	1.70
1988	76.90	9.60	2.50	6.50	3.30	1.10
1998	80.70	11.00	2.90	2.60	3.30	N/A

Sources: Percentages for 1948-1988 derived from freight revenue figures in American Trucking Associations, American Trucking Trends, various years. The 1998 figure is from McCarthy (2001), Table 1.7 and his figures are derived from a slightly different data source.

Although most research on trucking regulation has focused on economic regulation, it is interesting to note that the stricter size and weight limits contained in the MCA of 1935 had an important feedback on technology. In particular, these provisions spurred development of lighter weight aluminum trailers that enabled firms to carry larger payloads for a given gross weight, although there was a slowdown in the adoption of new technology during WWII when resources were diverted to the war effort. After the war aluminum trailers and more powerful tractors were adopted, allowing motor carriers to achieve cost savings. Another significant development was the adoption of sleeper compartments in tractors to accommodate overnight trips and allow teams of drivers to work on long distance hauls. With increased haul length, tractor-trailer sizes increased – although the patchwork of state size and weight limits placed constraints on the efficiencies that could be gained from the use of longer combination vehicles (LCVs) in interstate commerce. These interstate differences in size and weight limits persist to this day, preventing motor carriers from attaining maximum efficiency.

A final important factor that contributed to the increasing service advantage of truck over rail during the 1935-1980 period, was the continued development of the highway system. Of particular significance was the Federal Aid

Highway Act of 1956, which established the Federal Highway Trust fund for financing the interstate highway system as well as a variety of other Federal highway aid programs. The interstate highway system provided trucks a limited access, high quality road that further increased the speed and ease of trucking services. As Talley (1983) notes, the interstate highway system is significant for being the largest peacetime public works project in U.S. history.

At the same time that there was an expansion and increase in the quality of highway infrastructure, losses made by the railroads began to affect their rail maintenance programs and the resulting deterioration in rail infrastructure slowed train speeds and further increased the service quality gap between railroads and trucks. A particularly controversial recurring issue is whether the user fees that trucks pay for using the government provided highways, are sufficient to pay for providing and maintaining highway infrastructure. It is often argued that railroads are at a cost disadvantage because they are responsible for building and maintaining their own right of way whereas motor carriers have infrastructure provided by the government and only pay user fees, which are thus a variable cost for truckers. If the railroad infrastructure had been provided in a manner similar to roads, the track might not have been allowed to deteriorate as much and the resultant decline in rail service quality due to ever decreasing speeds might not have been as great.

Although many important economic principles were developed in the early part of the twentieth century as economists grappled with the natural monopoly problems of the railroads, economists did not pay much attention to the transportation sector again until the 1950s when the railroad problems became apparent. This led to renewed interest in government intervention in the transportation sector, especially economic regulation.

In the 1970s academic economists became interested in the impact of economic regulation on the transportation industries, especially railroads and motor carriage. This led to a reevaluation of the rationale for motor carrier regulation. Using newly developed econometric tools, economists found that the industry did not exhibit a natural monopoly type of market structure; rather there were repeated findings of constant returns to scale for the overall industry They further argued that regulation itself had led to various economic inefficiencies that resulted in higher costs of providing truck services (Friedlaender and Spady, 1981). Deregulation of the trucking industry was predicted to increase competition, lower costs and thus rates, benefiting shippers.

As the deregulatory movement in transportation gained steam in the 1970s, the ICC loosened its regulatory grip on the motor carrier industry. It made the entry process easier and firms began to enter the industry and industry numbers started to grow again by 1978 (see Table 1.2). Further, the ICC began to relax rate regulation in various ways so that carriers began to use price competition as a marketing tool. The Motor Carrier Act of 1980 (MCA of 1980) was implemented along with other acts of regulatory reform for the transportation industries in the early 1980s.

The Deregulated Motor Carrier Industry: 1980-present

The MCA 1980 did not specifically contain the word "deregulation", largely due to objections from labor and trucking groups that had hoped that the Act would be interpreted in a conservative manner so that regulations would be relaxed, but not eliminated. The ICC chose, however, to implement the Act's provisions in a way that resulted in virtual deregulation by the mid-1980s.

The easing of entry requirements contained in the MCA of 1980 resulted in an influx of carriers both to the industry and to individual routes. Most new industry entrants were small firms that did not have operating certificates prior to 1980 due to the costly process required to obtain an ICC certificate. These were typically owner-operators that, prior to deregulation could only operate in interstate markets by selling their services to an existing certified carrier and operating under that carrier's ICC certificate. After 1980, these firms were able to obtain their own certificates and provide services in interstate markets as independent firms (McMullen, 1987). Thus, many of the "new" carriers in the industry were not really new, they just acquired the designation of being an ICC certified firm. As mentioned previously, most of these new firms were small, Class III TL carriers.

The other kind of entry following 1980 came from existing ICC certified carriers obtaining new geographic route authorities (Boyer, 1993). Ease of entry into new geographic regions made it possible for firms to specialize more in LTL services by allowing them to expand, consolidate, and coordinate networks so as to take advantage of network economies in a way not possible with the fragmented network structures that had existed under the ICC regulatory regime.

The post-MCA expansion in LTL networks led to an increase in the size of existing LTL firms, resulting in a greater proportion of industry revenues going to a few large LTL firms (Kling, 1990). Glaskowsky (1986) reports an increase in the four firm LTL industry concentration ratio from 20 percent in 1978 to about 35 per cent in 1985. The concern is that such increases in concentration could lead to oligopolistic pricing behavior and eventually require the re-imposition of governmental economic regulation (Rakowski, 1988).

The observed increases in LTL concentration in the 1980s raised questions regarding whether deregulation was the right policy to pursue for the motor carrier industry. Boyer (1998) expresses concern over what he sees as a tightening oligopoly, but stops short of arguing for re-regulation. He correctly recognizes that it is not the industry structure that dictates an economic rationale for regulation, but rather the ability of carriers to extract monopoly (or oligopoly) rents from shippers. As long as there are viable options available to shippers who face high-priced carriers, trucking firms are not in the same position as monopoly railroads with captive shippers that have no alternative mode of transport.

Recent data on LTL concentration ratios suggests that there has been a reversal of the upward trend in industry concentration observed immediately following deregulation. Table 1.4 shows concentration ratios for the top 100 LTL firms from 1993-2002 where CR3 refers to the share of industry revenues going to the largest three revenue firms, CR4 the share going to the largest four firms, and so forth. Indeed, the three firm concentration ratio (CR3) fell to 12.7 in 2002 from

30.9 percent in 1985 and 21.3 percent in 1979. The ten firm concentration ration (CR10) was 44.5 percent in 2002 as compared to 53 percent in 1985 and 41 percent in 1979. Indeed, it appears that the downward trend in concentration ratios during the 1990s shown in Table 1.4 has resulted in LTL industry concentration similar to that of the regulated era. It remains to be seen whether these ratios will change significantly in the future, but it is clear that this portion of the trucking industry is more concentrated than the TL portion and this is one of the reasons that LTL carrier interests dominate policy debate despite the fact that the competitive TL sector is much larger.

Table 1.4   Concentration Ratios for Class I LTL Carriers, 1993-2002 (as percentage of top 100 firm revenue)

	CR3	CR4	CR5	CR10	CR20
1993	0.25649	0.29315	0.32950	0.46462	0.60015
1994	0.21931	0.25723	0.29403	0.42985	0.58190
1995	0.22412	0.26463	0.30021	0.43819	0.56904
1996	0.22869	0.27238	0.31226	0.47399	0.64073
1997	0.22954	0.27244	0.31507	0.47357	0.64253
1998	0.20509	0.25805	0.30385	0.46022	0.65046
1999	0.19939	0.25366	0.30123	0.46328	0.65953
2000	0.18238	0.23259	0.27867	0.43354	0.61894
2001	0.17381	0.22329	0.26841	0.42978	0.60924
2002	0.12728	0.17901	0.22664	0.44489	0.62885

Sources: Computations from USDOT, Bureau of Transportation Statistics, Motor Carrier Financial and Operating Statistics, Annual Report of Earning for the Top 100 Class I Motor Carriers of Property, various years.

While industry cost studies following deregulation continued to show evidence of the constant returns to scale cost structure consistent with a competitive industry (McMullen, 1987; McMullen and Stanley, 1987; Grimm, Corsi, and Jarrell, 1989; McMullen and Lee, 1993; Winston, Corsi, Grimm, and Evans, 1993), economists in the 1980s struggled with explaining the observed increases in concentration. In particular, why did existing firms expand in size when there were no technological scale economies?

Several interesting economic concepts, including "contestability", "economies of scope", and "networking economies" were introduced into the empirical literature in the 1980s, with important implications for the proper interpretation of what was happening in the trucking industry. The notion of contestability recognized the fact that mere monopoly presence in a market was not sufficient for a firm to charge "monopoly" prices; for this to take place, barriers to entry had to be high enough to prevent entrants from coming in and competing away profits. Once ICC entry restrictions were loosened, the regulatory barriers to entry were virtually eliminated. As far as capital requirements creating a barrier to entry, this was not seen as a great issue in trucking markets except possibly in LTL markets where a considerable investment in terminal infrastructure was required. However, the capital costs involved in shifting trucks from one route to another are minimal so capital was mobile between routes. This meant that a monopoly position on a route would still not allow a carrier to earn excess profits because there were many potential entrants who would enter an individual route if excessively high prices were charged.

The idea of economies of scope was introduced along with contestability. This was the idea that an industry may be technically a constant returns to scale industry, but there may be economies associated with producing more than one product that allows one firm to produce multiple outputs more efficiently than if separate firms were to produce these outputs independently. In the case of transportation, this is often referred to as "network" economies that are associated with expansions in the overall network system. In the 1980s LTL firms expanded their network systems in a way that previous ICC regulation had not allowed and took advantage of route density economies that persisted until at least the late 1980s. McMullen and Lee (1993), McMullen and Stanley (1987), and Grimm, Corsi, and Jarrell (1989) all find evidence that Class I and II ICC certified carriers could lower costs by increasing average loads and, to some extent, average lengths of haul. Thus an important reason for the continued increases in motor carrier firm size following deregulation was due to firm's capturing these "network" economies so they could lower costs and be competitive.

The problem economists have traditionally had with large firms is when a monopoly position allows firms to exert market power, usually evidenced by earning excess profits. Thus the "natural monopoly" rationale for economic regulation was originally applied to the railroad industry where there were high capital barriers to entry and virtually no intermodal competition for freight shippers. In this situation railroad firms were able to charge prices well above marginal costs and earn consistent monopoly profits. Thus, from a public policy point of view, the important question is not whether a firm has market dominance, but whether it can exert market power in pricing and earn monopoly (or excess) profits. This is usually the rationale for advocating government intervention, especially economic regulation of entry and exit and rate regulation.

While there is evidence that LTL motor carrier firms earned excess or monopoly profit under ICC regulation (Moore, 1978), trucking firms in the post-1980 period have struggled to earn a normal return on investment. In a study using new empirical industrial organization techniques for assessment, Nebesky, McMullen, and Lee (1995) find no evidence of market power being exerted in the post-1980 industry – although they do find evidence of market power prior to 1980 when LTL carriers were subject to strict ICC regulation. The operating ratio for the LTL group of motor carriers in 2002 was only 95.6 per cent (Corridore, 2003), certainly not indicative of monopoly type pricing. Thus, the current profit situation in the industry does not suggest that monopoly power is being exerted.

Evidence of increasing concentration immediately following deregulation is consistent with LTL firms expanding in size to take advantage of network economies that ICC regulation had prevented them from exploiting. While some firms were successful, others failed. An early study (McMullen and Miklius, 1987) found that the increase in firm's bankruptcies reflected an increased number of firms in the industry and that bankruptcy rates in trucking did not seem to be any more volatile than the average U.S. industry. Indeed, in a competitive industry failures are expected as unsuccessful firms are forced out of business and efficient firms survive.

While motor carrier deregulation has produced clear economic benefits for some groups, namely shippers and their customers, it has largely been through increases in service quality rather than just lower rates anticipated by deregulators (Winston, Corsi, Grimm, and Evans, 1990). Increases in service quality in such dimensions as service frequency have been experienced even in service to small communities – service that had been predicted to deteriorate without ICC imposed regulations.

There are some groups that have not benefited from deregulation such as trucking labor and the motor carrier firms themselves. Motor carrier firms have faced increased competition and must be very efficient if they are to remain in business in the long run. Indeed, the calls for re-regulation come less from those who are afraid of monopoly power from large trucking firms and more from those who rekindle the old argument that the industry is engaging in destructive competition and carriers need to be protected to ensure the long run viability of the industry.

The "destructive competition" arguments for industry regulation were first heard in the 1930s but also surfaced in the 1970s during the deregulation debate. Those opposed to deregulation argued that entry by small trucking firms would fail because without set prices and the information systems that large carriers maintained, small entrepreneurs would be faced with "chaos" and be unable to function. This chaos was quickly eliminated after 1980 by the large scale (and unpredicted) entry of third party brokers and other intermediaries that effectively disseminated required information (McMullen, 1987; Crum, 1985). The development of the internet in the 1990s made it possible for almost anyone to access enough information to function effectively.

Carriers have changed marketing strategies to meet the increasingly diverse demands of shippers. Some carriers still compete on price, but increasingly carriers have become more focused on selling service quality. Important aspects of service quality include fast service, reliable service guarantees, availability of equipment (especially critical for specialized carriers), and the use of various information technologies such as electronic data interchange (EDI) that have been adopted largely to meet shipper demands (Crumm, Johnson, and Allen, 1998).

Evidence from the 1980s shows that motor carrier efficiency increased and that the more efficient firms were the ones that survived (McMullen and Okuyama, 2000; McMullen and Lee, 1999). It appears that that firms exploited most of the economies associated with increased size by the 1990s. McMullen (2004) finds that large efficiency and productivity gains did not continue into the

1990s, even with the new technologies and information systems that were adopted. The exception is that adoption of EDI appears to contribute significantly to economic efficiency for trucking firms in the 1990s. However, the large overall efficiency gains observed in the 1980s appear to have been a result of the industry's adjustment from a regulated industry to a competitive industry in which it was important to do business as efficiently as possible. In the future firms may have to accept a lower rate of productivity growth that may be more in line with what is sustainable in the long run.

The deregulated period has seen continued movement towards even smaller shipment size, continuing a trend that originally started in the 1920s. The rapid development of computers and technology since 1980 has facilitated the use of just-in-time inventory (JIT) strategies by firms that makes timely and available service even more critical to shipper and continues to result in smaller shipment size. The advent of the internet in the 1990s has resulted in a change in the way many business sell at the retail level. The increase in direct sales to consumers has resulted in even smaller shipment size and stimulated the small package delivery part of the freight transportation business, much of which is carried by truck. Deregulation was the original impetus to this trend by creating a more flexible transportation system where carriers can engage in both common and contract service and pursue variable routes. All of these factors have contributed to placing motor carriage in the dominant position it holds today in freight transportation markets.

Deregulation has introduced more competition into the freight transport industries and combined with other factors such as deteriorating roads, increasing environmental concerns, and fossil fuel supplies, it is reasonable to believe that there is a limit to the continued growth of motor carriage vis-à-vis other freight modes. For instance, deregulation resulted in the adoption of cost saving intermodal technologies that were discouraged in the regulatory environment. The increased use of piggyback (TOFC and COFC) has been spurred by the pricing flexibility allowed to all modes of freight transport in the deregulated market setting. Railroads, which under previous ICC regulation had not been allowed to pass along cost savings to consumers, have increasingly adopted new technologies such as double stack containers in an effort to be competitive – especially with the newly emerging advanced TL motor carriers such as H.B. Hunt. Growth in the global economy has also been an impetus to such intermodal technology that often involves freight movement by truck, ship, and rail. Thus, the deregulated trucking industry faces competition not only from other motor carriers, but more competition from rail than existed in the pre-1980 regulatory setting.

Deterioration in highways and bridges is a serious problem that will face the motor carrier industry in the next few years. Existing highway user fees are no longer adequate to maintain roads and bridges that were not engineered for today's heavy truck traffic flows. Adoption of more efficient highway user fees and road charges in the future may place financial pressure on motor carriers that are already operating with small profit margins. As increased trucking costs are passed along to shippers in rate increases, some of the intermodal advantage enjoyed by trucks in the past century may be erased. However, the trucking rates would have to increase enormously to outweigh the huge service quality advantages trucks now have over alternative freight modes, particularly rail.

In summary, the motor carrier industry has been strongly influenced by government activity, including infrastructure development and various sorts of regulation. It further appears that most of the large structural changes initiated by the Motor Carrier Act of 1980 and others that followed, have now had a chance to work through the industry. It is likely that future changes in industry structure may be the result of long run trends in technology and the response of the overall transportation systems to factors such as congestion and the global economy – factors that may ultimately alter the current advantage that truck has had over rail and other modes since the 1930s.

Although the issues faced by the industry in the future may be quite different than they were in the past century, one thing is for sure – motor carriage is an integral part of freight transportation today and it promises to be the dominant freight transportation mode for the next 25 years. The other chapters in this book will examine some of the issues that will be crucial to determining the future path of the industry.

References

Boyer, Kenneth D. (1998) *Principles of Transportation Economics*, Addison-Wesley.

Boyer, Kenneth D. (1993) 'Deregulation of the Trucking sector: Specialization, Concentration, Entry, and Financial Distress,' *Southern Economic Journal*, Vol. 59, No.3, January: 481-495.

Burks, Stephen V., Frederick Guy, and Benjamin Maxwell (2004) 'Shifting Gears in the Corner Office: Deregulation and the Earnings of Trucking Executives,' *Research in Transportation Economics*, Vol. 10, Elsevier, Amsterdam, pp. 137-164.

Corridore, Jim (2003) 'Trucking: Driver Shortages Return,' in *Industry Profile: Industry Trends*, Standard and Poors, NetAdvantage.com, December 25, 2003.

Crum, Michael R. (1985) 'The Expanded Role of Motor Freight Brokers in the Wake of Regulatory Reform,' *Transportation Journal*, Summer: 5-15.

Crum, M.R., Johnson, and B. Allen (1998) 'A Longitudinal Assessment of EDI Use in the U.S. Motor Carrier Industry,' *Transportation Journal*, Vol. 38, No.1: 15-29.

Felton, John R. (1989) 'Background of the Motor Carrier Act of 1935,' in Felton, John Felton and Dale G. Anderson (editors) *Regulation and Deregulation of the Motor Carrier Industry*, Iowa State University Press, Ames, IA: 3-13.

Friedlaender, A.F. and I. Harrington (1979) 'Intermodalism and Integrated Transport Companies in the United States and Canada,' *Journal of Transport Economics and Policy*, September: 247-267.

Friedlaender, Anne and Richard Spady (1981) *Freight Transportation Regulation: Equity, Efficiency, and Competition*, MIT Press, Cambridge, MA.

Glaskowsky, Nichohlas A. (1986) *Effects of Deregulation on Motor Carriers*, Eno Foundation for Transportation, Inc. Westport, CT.

Grimm, C., T. Corsi, and J. Jarrell (1989) 'U.S. Motor Carrier Cost Structure Under Deregulation,' *Logistics and Transportation Review*, Vol. 25, No.3: pp. 231-249.

Keeler, Theodore E. (1983) *Railroads, Freight, and Public Policy*, the Brookings Institution, Washington, D.C.

Kling, Robert W. (1990) 'Deregulation and Structural Change in the LTL Motor Freight Industry,' *Transportation Journal*, Vol. 29, No.3, Spring: 47-53.

McMullen, B.S. (1987) 'A Preliminary Examination of the Impact of Regulatory Reform on U.S. Motor Carrier Costs,' *Journal of Transportation Economics and Policy*, September: 307-319.

McMullen, B.S. and Walter Miklius (1987) 'Measuring the Impact of Regulatory Reform on Firm Bankruptcies: The U.S. Motor Carrier Industry,' *The International Journal of Transport Economics*, Vol. 10, No.1-2, April-August: 182-188.

McMullen, B.S. and L.R. Stanley (1987) 'The Impact of Deregulation on the Production Structure of the Motor Carrier Industry,' *Economic Inquiry*, Vol. 26: pp. 299-316.

McMullen, B.S. and Man-Keung Lee (1993) 'Assessing the Impact of Regulatory Reform on Motor Carrier Cost,' *Journal of the Transportation Research Forum*, Vol. 33, No.2: 1-9.

McMullen, B.S. and H. Tanaka (1995) 'An Econometric Analysis of Differences Between Motor Carriers: Implications for Market Structure,' *Quarterly Journal of Business and Economics*, Vol. 34, No.4, Autumn: 16-28.

McMullen, B.S. and Man-Keung Lee (1999) 'Cost Efficiency in the U.S. Motor Carrier Industry Before and After Deregulation: A Stochastic Frontier Approach,' *Journal of Transport Economics and Policy*, Vol. 33, No.3: 303-317.

McMullen, B.S. and K. Okuyama (2000) 'Productivity Changes in the U.S. Motor Carrier Industry Following Deregulation: A Malmquist Approach,' *International Journal of Transport Economics*, Vol. 27: 335-354.

McMullen, B.S. (2004) 'The Impact of Information Technology and Marketing Strategy on U.S. Motor Carrier Productivity,' *Journal of the Transportation Research Forum*, Vol. 42, No.2, Fall: 7-23.

Moore, Thomas Gale (1978) 'The Beneficiaries of Trucking Deregulation,' *Journal of Law and Economics*, Vol. 21, No.2, October: 327-343.

Nebesky, William E., B. Starr McMullen, and Man-Keung Lee (1995) 'Testing for Market Power in the U.S. Motor Carrier Industry,' *Review of Industrial Organization*, Vol. 10: 559-576.

Rakowski, James P. (1988) 'Marketing Economics and the Results of Trucking Deregulation in the Less-Than-Truckload Sector,' *Transportation Journal*, Vol. 27, No.3, Spring: 11-22.

Richter, William L. (1995) *Transportation in America*, ABC-CLIO Inc., Santa Barbara, California.

Talley, Wayne Kenneth (1983) *Introduction to Transportation*, South-Western Publishing Co., Cincinnati, Ohio.

U.S. Department of Transportation, Bureau of Transportation Statistics (2002) *Pocket Guide to Transportation*, Table 15.

Winston, Clifford, Thomas M. Corsi, Curtis M. Grimm, and Carol A. Evans (1990) *The Economic Effects of Surface Freight Deregulation*, the Brookings Institution, Washington, D.C.

Zeitner and Sons, Inc. (2004) 'History of the Truck and the Industry' at: http:www.zettinerandsons.com/truckhistory.htm.

Chapter 2

The Truckload Carrier Industry Segment

Thomas M. Corsi

Introduction

The objective of this section is to profile the truckload carrier segment of the industry. In order to accomplish this objective, it is useful to define the size and importance of truckload carriers among all freight carriers. Second, it is important to understand the size and structure of each of the components of the truckload segment.

As will be shown, truckload carriers have experienced tremendous changes in the time since Congress removed the regulatory chokehold on the trucking industry in 1980. This section traces the productivity and operational dynamics of the truckload carriers with a particular emphasis on the 1987-2001 time period.

While the industry made vast productivity and operational improvements in the studied time period, its profitability position remained, on average, quite weak. Furthermore, truckload carriers as a whole face a series of tremendous challenges, which have the potential to adversely impact the operations of the truckload carriers. Each of these challenges and their potential impact on the truckload carriers will be discussed.

The final part of this section moves the clock forward to 2010 to offer a prognosis about how the truckload industry segment will look at that time. There is a breakdown of how truckload firms will adopt their operations, their technologies, and their business plans to meet the very real challenges that they currently face. There is an optimistic opinion expressed that there will emerge very successful truckload carriers who will match operational/productivity gains with profitability improvements. Yet, even this optimistic viewpoint must be tempered with a range of uncertainties and issues over which neither truckload carriers or anyone, for that matter, has complete control.

Size and Importance Among Freight Carriers

For-hire truckload carriers constituted the single largest commercial freight carrier segment in terms of total revenue for 2001. Table 2.1 provides a distribution of commercial freight revenues across each of the modal segments.[1] It shows that the total transportation freight bill in 2001 equaled $713.6 billion. Of that total, the trucking industry was responsible for 85.5 percent or $610.2 billion. The largest individual portion belonged to truckload for-hire carriers with $273.9 billion in revenues or 38.4 percent of the total. Many firms handle freight for their own supply chains, with limited or no for-hire operations. In 2001, private trucking accounted for 38.3 percent of the total commercial transportation dollar or $273.6 billion. It should be noted that in contrast to for-hire commercial trucking operations, the private carriers do not receive direct payments for their services. Many firms account for these transportation services through internal charge-back accounting entries. A third important component of the trucking total is a result of less-than-truckload for-hire transportation. Carriers in this segment generated $62.7 billion in revenue in 2001 or 8.8 percent of the total.

Table 2.1   Commercial Freight Distribution-2001 (in billions of dollars)

Transportation Mode	Billions $	% of Total
Trucking, total	610.2	85.5
◆ Private Trucking	273.6	38.3
◆ Truckload	273.9	38.4
◆ Less-than-Truckload	62.7	8.8
Railroad	35.4	5.0
Rail Intermodal	6.7	0.9
Pipeline (oil and gas)	27.2	3.8
Airfreight, package domestic	20.0	2.8
Airfreight, heavy domestic	6.0	0.8
Water (Great Lakes/rivers)	8.1	1.1
Transportation Total	**713.6**	**100.0**

Source: Jim Corridore, "Standard and Poor's Industry Surveys", Transportation Commercial, June 19, 2003, p. 8. Sources cited by Standard and Poor's: Cass Information Systems and Standard and Poor's own estimates.

Size and Importance of Major Segments

Table 2.2 focuses on the subset of the largest for-hire carriers (i.e., less-than-truckload, package courier operators, and truckload carriers). It is specifically based on the 2,363 carriers who filed financial reports (Form M) with the U.S. Department of Transportation. All interstate for-hire carriers generating $3 million or more in annual revenues (i.e., Class I and Class II carriers) are required to file the financial reports. Class III carriers with less than $3 million in annual revenues are exempt from filing annual reports with the DOT. While there are clearly some issues of non-reporting, the database summarizing the activities of these 2,363 carriers is an important one and will be used extensively to demonstrate the dynamics of the for-hire truckload carriers.

Table 2.2 distributes the total revenue and the number of Class I and II for-hire firms across each of the major industry segments. As shown, the 2,363 firms accounted for in Table 2.2 generated $94 billion in total revenues in 2001.[2] Some comments are in order to explain the difference between the total revenues for trucking industry shown in Tables 2.1 and 2.2. First, Table 2.1 includes all trucking carriers, while Table 2.2 is limited to the carriers involved in interstate commerce. Thus, all intrastate and local trucking operations are excluded from the revenues reported in Table 2.2. Second, as noted, Table 2.2 summarizes data from Class I and II carriers who complied with DOT reporting requirements. Some Class I and II carriers do not file their Annual Report forms and, as a result, do not have their revenues represented in Table 2.2. Third, the Class I and II carriers, as a group, represent only a small portion of the total for-hire carrier base. There are several hundred thousand Class III carriers operating in the United States whose revenues are not accounted for in Table 2.2.

Table 2.2   Distribution of Revenues and Firms Across Major Segments of the Trucking Industry, 2001

Industry Segment	2001 Revenues in Billions $	Percent of Total Revenues	Number of Firms	% of Total
Building Materials	2.0	2.13	60	2.54
Bulk	2.2	2.34	98	4.15
General Freight TL	50.0	53.19	1,199	50.74
Less-than-Truckload	21.0	22.34	181	7.66
Household Goods	4.5	4.79	88	3.72
Heavy Machinery	3.1	3.30	84	3.55
Motor Vehicles	7.5	0.80	27	1.14
Other Specialized	4.8	5.11	355	15.02
Package Courier	1.9	0.20	11	0.47
Refrigerated	3.2	3.40	136	5.76
Tank	2.2	2.34	124	5.25
Total	**94.0**	**100.0**	**2,363**	**100.0**

Source: Author's calculations from Motor Carrier Annual Report, 2001, American Trucking Associations, Alexandria, Virginia. Author compiled results from CD of Annual Report data for Calendar Year 2001.

Table 2.2 does show, however, the general freight truckload carriers generate that 53.2 percent of the total revenues of the reporting Class I and II carriers. These carriers represent over half of the total number of Class I and II carriers. The second largest revenue-generating industry segment is the less-than-truckload segment. Although this segment represents only 7.7 percent of the total number of carriers, they are responsible for 22.34 percent of the total revenues from the Class I and II carriers. Household goods carriers had 4.8 percent of the total revenues, while other specialized carriers generated 5.1 percent.

Obviously, the less-than-truckload carriers generate substantially higher average revenues than do carriers in the other segments. The LTL carriers represent only 7.7 percent of the total carrier base, but account for 22.34 percent of the revenues. In contrast, carriers in the other specialized commodity segment are substantially smaller. They represent 15 percent of the total number of carriers, but generate only 5.11 percent of the total revenues.

The remainder of this chapter focuses on the following individual segments within the truckload portion of the industry: building materials, bulk, general freight, household goods, heavy machinery, motor vehicles, other specialized, refrigerated, and tank. The discussion will initially compare these segments on a set of basic operating and financial performance indicators to develop an understanding of inter-segment differences. The performance of each segment will be compared with a 1987 database to highlight the dynamics of each segment over this 14 year time period.

The focus of the chapter will then shift to a discussion of a series of challenges that all truckload carriers are currently experiencing. These challenges include: adjusting to disintermediation and the Internet economy; responding to the adoption by U.S. firms of real-time supply chain management practices; and improving the industry's safety performance. Each of these challenges has the potential to have a significant adverse impact on the truckload segment.

The final section of the chapter represents a look into the future, specifically a look ahead to the year 2010. It will be argued that truckload carriers in 2010 will have fundamental differences from typical truckload carriers operating in 2003. Although the typical truckload carrier operating in 2003 had significant productivity advantages over the typical truckload carrier operating in 1987, the new-look truckload carriers will have adopted to the Internet economy with its emphasis on real-time supply chains. The new-look 2010 carriers will achieve this level of integration by employing the best technology and management practices to improve their efficiency in order to achieve full-synchronization with their customers' supply chain activities. The new-look 2010 truckload carriers will have completely re-focused their driver management skills and safety practices to insure significantly safer operations with fewer crashes.

Operating Performance Dynamics: 1987-2001

In a comprehensive review of the trucking industry dynamics covering the 1977 to 1987 time period, i.e., the early experience under deregulation, it was noted that a sub-class of carriers of highly-efficient advanced truckload firms (ATLFs) emerged in the post-1980 time period. These ATLFs or high-service carriers operated primarily in the TL general freight segment, but were also present in several other truckload segments as well. Some characteristics of these carriers involve the use of driver teams and relays to keep their tractors operating more hours per day, with a significant increase in annual tractor mileage. Furthermore, these ATLF carriers leveraged their rapid growth to purchase tractors and trailers in large quantities at sizable discounts. These ATLF carriers also demonstrated sophisticated load matching capabilities, focused on securing freight in long-distance medium- to high-density corridors with balanced trade flows. In combination, these factors allowed the ATLFs to achieve lower empty mileage rates than typically achieved by more traditional TL firms.[3]

Tables 2.3, 2.4, and 2.5 present comparative data on productivity measures for the various truckload carrier industry segments in 1987 and 2001. The productivity measures involve annual miles per truck, average load, and average length of haul. The most interesting aspects of Tables 2.3, 2.4, and 2.5 are that the productivity gains achieved by the ATLF carriers as early as 1987 represent the mean performance for each of the industry segments in 2001. In other words, while the ATLFs figured out some of the key requirements of a successful transition from a regulated to a deregulated environment by 1987, the mean performance for each industry segment lagged significantly behind in their productivity performance. However, by 2001, the mean truckload carrier in each of the truckload industry segments had essentially duplicated the success of the ATLFs through significant productivity improvements.

Table 2.3   Annual Miles Per Truck Across Major Truckload Segments, 2001 vs. 1987

Industry Segment	Calendar Year 2001	Calendar Year 1987
Building Materials	98,272	68,400
Bulk Commodities	86,971	76,500
General Freight	105.859	73,400
Household Goods	52,119	n/a
Heavy Machinery	76,252	50,000
Motor Vehicles	94,876	61,400
Other Specialized Commodities	85,199	67,000
Refrigerated Commodities	125,626	90,900
Tank	83,516	64,100
All Carriers Combined	96,344	65,700
Advanced Truckload (ATLFs)	n/a	104,400

Sources: 1987 data cited in Thomas M. Corsi and Joseph R. Stowers, "Effects of a Deregulated Environment on Motor Carriers: A Systematic, Multi-Segment Analysis", Transportation Journal, Vol. 30, No. 3, Spring 1991, p. 20. Data from 2001 based on Author's calculations from Motor Carrier Annual Report, 2001, American Trucking Associations, Alexandria, Virginia.

Table 2.3 focuses on the key productivity measure of annual miles per truck. By operating trucks additional miles on an annual basis, the fixed vehicle costs associated with the equipment can be spread out over more operating miles to lower the average cost per mile. In 1987, while the ATLF carriers averaged over 100,000 miles annually per truck, all carriers together averaged only 65,700 on an annual basis. However, between 1987 and 2001, the average annual miles per truck across the entire set of carriers increased from 65,700 to 96,344, an increase of nearly 47 percent. In fact, increases occurred in every segment of the truckload industry. Among the general freight truckload carriers, the average annual miles per truck increased from 73,400 in 1987 to 105,859 in 2001. Among the refrigerated truckload carriers, the average miles per truck went from 90,900 in 1987 to 125,626 in 2001.

Table 2.4 provides detailed information on the average load for carriers in each segment of the truckload industry in 1987 and 2001. As shown, the ATLF carriers had an average load in 1987 of 16.3 tons, which was significantly higher than the average load of 13.1 tons for all truckload carriers combined. However, between 1987 and 2001, all truckload carriers combined increased their average load from 13.1 to 17.2 tons – slightly higher than the average achieved by the ATLF carriers in 1987. The average load increased for carriers in each individual industry segment between 1987 and 2001. The general freight truckload carriers increased their average load from 13.2 tons in 1987 to 16.7 tons in 2001. The comparable figures for bulk carriers are 13.7 and 20.5 tons.

Table 2.4   Average Load (in tons) Across Major Truckload Segments, 2001 vs. 1987

Industry Segment	Calendar Year 2001	Calendar Year 1987
Building Materials	18.5	15.4
Bulk Commodities	20.5	13.7
General Freight	16.7	13.2
Household Goods	4.3	n/a
Heavy Machinery	19.8	12.4
Motor Vehicles	15.2	8.1
Other Specialized Commodities	18.7	13.6
Refrigerated Commodities	17.5	14.5
Tank	21.6	15.4
All Carriers Combined	17.2	13.1
Advanced Truckload (ATLFs)	n/a	16.3

Sources: 1987 data cited in Thomas M. Corsi and Joseph R. Stowers, "Effects of a Deregulated Environment on Motor Carriers: A Systematic, Multi-Segment Analysis", Transportation Journal, Vol. 30, No. 3, Spring 1991, p. 20. Data from 2001 based on Author's calculations from Motor Carrier Annual Report, 2001, American Trucking Associations, Alexandria, Virginia.

These increases in average loads are quite remarkable indeed. Clearly, significant changes occurred in truck size and weight legislation in the 1977-1987 time periods (e.g., the Surface Transportation Assistance Act of 1982). While there were some changes in truck sizes and weights in the 1987-2001, these legislative changes do not provide sufficient explanation for the observed productivity improvements. Instead, it is clear that basic and fundamental improvements in load matching and vehicle routing led to the observed increases in average load. By 2001, the average truckload carriers reached average load totals equal to those achieved by the ATLF carriers in 1987.

Table 2.5 focuses on average length of haul as a productivity measure. As noted, the ATLF carrier strategy often involved a concentration on high- to medium-density corridors with balanced freight flows. These corridors tended to be longer than average and, as a result, the ATLF carriers achieved an average length of haul of over 1,000 miles. Table 2.5 demonstrates that carriers in all but one truckload segment (other specialized commodities) increased average length of haul between 1987 and 2001. For all carriers combined the average length of haul increased from 380 miles in 1987 to 516 miles in 2001, an increase of 36 percent. Among the truckload general freight carriers, the average length of haul increased from 313 to 564 miles between 1987 and 2001. Among the refrigerated carriers, the average length of haul increased from 727 to 907 miles. While these increases in average lengths of haul are substantial, the averages across the various segments are still below the level reached by the ATLF carriers in 1987.

Table 2.5　Average Haul Length (in miles) Across Major Truckload Segments, 2001 vs. 1987

Industry Segment	Calendar Year 2001	Calendar Year 1987
Building Materials	560	312
Bulk Commodities	350	272
General Freight	564	313
Household Goods	619	n/a
Heavy Machinery	499	411
Motor Vehicles	638	294
Other Specialized Commodities	381	393
Refrigerated Commodities	907	727
Tank	145	143
All Carriers Combined	516	380
Advanced Truckload (ATLFs)	n/a	1,232

Sources: 1987 data cited in Thomas M. Corsi and Joseph R. Stowers, "Effects of a Deregulated Environment on Motor Carriers: A Systematic, Multi-Segment Analysis", Transportation Journal, Vol. 30, No. 3, Spring 1991, p. 20. Data from 2001 based on Author's calculations from Motor Carrier Annual Report, 2001, American Trucking Associations, Alexandria, Virginia.

There are various explanations for the observed increases in average lengths of haul. Perhaps the best is one that combines the increases in average loads with the increases in average lengths of haul. Indeed, there is a greater frequency for truckload carriers in 2001 to combine multiple loads in a single truckload movement with multiple drop points to achieve operating efficiencies and to reduce the frequency of empty dead trips. The multiple-load trip reduces transaction costs as well as wait times between trips.

In a 2001 article, two executives from J.B. Hunt, a truckload carrier with $2 billion in annual revenues, outlined the following three components of their strategy to achieve efficiency gains: load consolidation, route optimization, and dedicated fleets. The Hunt executives reported that they have worked with large retail customers to consolidate LTL shipments into more efficient, multi-stop truckload networks. The executives report that this shift enabled the retailer to 'achieve significant gains through increased on-time deliveries and significant reductions in freight damages.'[4] A second widely used efficiency strategy by Hunt involves route optimization. According to the Hunt executives, they have worked with other large retailers to develop 'customized optimization applications that route daily outbound cross dock shipments. Daily store order detail and pallet counts are captured and loaded via wireless technology with a routing application in which loads with similar destinations are routed in multi-stop fashion ... Backhaul loads are also factored in to minimize total transportation costs.'[5] Finally, the Hunt executives speak about their practice of dedicating equipment to customers with a high volume, regular pattern flow of cargo in major corridors. The service improvements from dedicating equipment in these situations are matched by significant efficiency gains to Hunt itself. Clearly, the situation is a 'win-win' for customers and carriers. J.B. Hunt is, indeed, a leader in designing services and implementing technology to enhance the delivery of trucking services.

As a result of these productivity gains in the 1987-2001 periods, as exemplified by the Hunt strategy, truckload carriers were able to control their operating expenses per mile. Table 2.6 presents a comparison in operating expenses per mile for each segment of the industry between 1987 and 2001. The operating expenses per mile figures in Table 2.6 are in actual dollars with no inflation adjustment. The productivity gains enabled all carriers to have average operating expenses per mile in 2001 of $1.93 in comparison to average expenses of $1.99 in 1987. Thus, in actual dollars, the average expense per mile for the truckload carriers taken together decreased between 1987 and 2001 – a remarkable testament to the efficiency gains in this industry segment. It should be noted, however, that only two segments within the sector, general freight and heavy machinery, led the way in decreasing operating expenses per mile in actual dollars between 1987 and 2001: The other segments experienced increases in actual average operating expenses per mile. However, these expense increases were small and do not, in any way, diminish the point that truckload carriers made significant productivity gains during the 1987-2001 time period.

The model of an efficient truckload carrier that emerged in the immediate post-deregulation time period disseminated throughout the industry in the 1990s and beyond. This process of innovation diffusion was so widespread that by 2001 in most segments the average carriers achieved efficiency gains that were comparable to the gains experienced by the ATLF carriers by the mid-1980s. The next section focuses on the transfer of these productivity and cost gains into changes in the financial viability of the industry segments.

Financial Performance Dynamics: 1987-2001

The previous section demonstrated that the truckload carriers in each of the various segments made significant productivity gains during the 1987-2001 time periods. From the perspective of the individual companies, however, the critical issue is translating these productivity gains into a solid financial performance. Tables 2.7 and 2.8 address the financial performance of the various segments of the truckload industry during the 1987-2001 time periods by examining two dimensions of financial performance, operating ratio and net profit margin, respectively.

Table 2.6   Operating Expenses Per Mile (in $) Across Major Truckload Segments, 2001 vs. 1987

Industry Segment	Calendar Year 2001	Calendar Year 1987
Building Materials	1.72	1.50
Bulk Commodities	1.95	1.29
General Freight	1.67	1.80
Household Goods	3.83	n/a
Heavy Machinery	2.50	2.52
Motor Vehicles	2.55	2.20
Other Specialized Commodities	2.02	1.73
Refrigerated Commodities	1.57	1.39
Tank	2.23	1.80
All Carriers Combined	1.93	1.99

Sources: 1987 data cited in Thomas M. Corsi and Joseph R. Stowers, "Effects of a Deregulated Environment on Motor Carriers: A Systematic, Multi-Segment Analysis", Transportation Journal, Vol. 30, No. 3, Spring 1991, p. 13. Data from 2001 based on Author's calculations from Motor Carrier Annual Report, 2001, American Trucking Associations, Alexandria, Virginia. Data in Table 2.6 are actual dollars.

As shown in Table 2.7, among all carriers, the average operating ratio, i.e., operating expenses divided by operating ratio, increased from 97.7 to 98.4 between 1987 and 2001. The operating ratio is the most frequently used measure of financial performance in the trucking industry, especially the truckload segment, with limited capital investments beyond the equipment used for the actual transportation of freight. Average operating ratios increased during this time in the following industry segments: building materials, bulk commodities, general freight, other specialized commodities, refrigerated, and tank operations. The only improvements in operating ratio occurred in the following industry segments: heavy machinery, and motor vehicles. Although the changes in average operating ratio between 1987 and 2001 are frequently small, no more than one or two percentage points, they are indicative of an industry whose total operating revenues are, on average, less than 2 percentage points below total operating expenses. With the previously documented gains in productivity, the only explanation for the failure of operating ratios to improve is that the carriers were under extreme pressure to lower freight rates.

Table 2.7   Operating Ratio Across Major Truckload Segments, 2001 vs. 1987

Industry Segment	Calendar Year 2001	Calendar Year 1987
Building Materials	97.2	96.7
Bulk Commodities	98.1	96.5
General Freight	98.7	96.6
Household Goods	101.4	n/a
Heavy Machinery	96.6	100.0
Motor Vehicles	95.2	97.0
Other Specialized Commodities	98.5	97.9
Refrigerated Commodities	97.4	97.0
Tank	97.2	97.0
All Carriers Combined	98.4	97.7

Sources: 1987 data cited in Thomas M. Corsi and Joseph R. Stowers, "Effects of a Deregulated Environment on Motor Carriers: A Systematic, Multi-Segment Analysis", Transportation Journal, Vol. 30, No. 3, Spring 1991, p. 24. Data from 2001 based on Author's calculations from Motor Carrier Annual Report, 2001, American Trucking Associations, Alexandria, Virginia.

Table 2.8 addresses the dynamics of net profit margin. Again, there is a worsening of the situation for the carriers between 1987 and 2001. Among all carriers, the net profit margin decreased from an average of 1.6 percent in 1987 to an average of 1.2 percent in 2001. Carriers in a number of sectors experienced declines in net profit margin. On average the profit margin for bulk carriers decreased from 2.1 percent in 1987 to 0.6 percent in 2001. Similarly, for general freight carriers the average net profit margin decreased from 2.3 percent in 1987 to 0.6 percent in 2001. The largest increase in net profit margin was among the tank carriers who experienced an increase from 2.0 percent in 1987 to 4.1 percent in 2001. On average, there was a net profit margin improvement among the heavy machinery and motor vehicle carriers.

Table 2.8   Net Profit Margin (in percent) Across Major Truckload Segments, 2001 vs. 1987

Industry Segment	Calendar Year 2001	Calendar Year 1987
Building Materials	2.4	2.4
Bulk Commodities	0.6	2.1
General Freight	0.6	2.3
Household Goods	1.9	n/a
Heavy Machinery	1.7	0.3
Motor Vehicles	2.1	1.5
Other Specialized Commodities	1.6	1.7
Refrigerated Commodities	1.2	1.3
Tank	4.1	2.0
All Carriers Combined	1.2	1.6

Sources: 1987 data cited in Thomas M. Corsi and Joseph R. Stowers, "Effects of a Deregulated Environment on Motor Carriers: A Systematic, Multi-Segment Analysis", Transportation Journal, Vol. 30, No. 3, Spring 1991, p. 24. Data from 2001 based on Author's calculations from Motor Carrier Annual Report, 2001, American Trucking Associations, Alexandria, Virginia.

It is important not to underestimate the significance of the findings of the productivity and profitability dynamics. The truckload carriers have experienced rapid productivity improvements. Clearly, the ATLF carrier who emerged in the early post-deregulation years, set a standard that, by 2001 the average carrier across each of the individual segments was able to emulate in many critical respects. Yet, despite these very significant improvements in operations and efficiency, the average financial performance of carriers did not improve. In fact, on the dimensions of operating ratio and net profit margin, the average performance of the carriers decreased. The only explanation is that the improvements initiated by carriers constituted survival strategies in a highly competitive marketplace whose customers demanded lower freight rates. In fact, the entire 1987-2001 time period, witnessed fundamental changes in the economic climate that required American firms to put tremendous pressures on all suppliers to reduce costs in order for the firms to survive in a rapidly changing, globally competitive, and technologically sophisticated economic climate. The following section will specifically address some of the challenges that the truckload carriers face in this environment. The final section of the chapter will address the truckload carrier of the future and how it will adapt to these very ominous threats.

Major Challenges Facing the Truckload Carriers

Disintermediation and the Internet Economy

Fundamental changes have occurred in the economy that has had a direct impact on truckload carriers over the past decade, in particular. Many of these changes have been somewhat unfavorable to traditional business practices of the truckload carriers and have required them to make fundamental adjustments in order to keep pace with rapidly changing events.

Over the past decade, there has been a fundamental re-structuring of traditional supply chains. The technology of the Internet and the ability of companies to reach directly to their customers have resulted in a physical re-structuring of supply chains that have relied on warehouses and retail distribution outlets. Indeed, the disintermediation of traditional links in the supply chain has resulted in an increasing reliance on direct small-sized shipments from manufacturers to customers.

The growth of business-to-customer Internet sales, with its associated disintermediation of retailers, has particularly affected the supply chains for certain types of goods. Indeed, computer hardware accounted in 2001 for 15 percent of total online sales. It was followed by apparel and accessories (10 percent), office equipment (8 percent), consumer electronics (6 percent), and books (4 percent).[6]

This fundamental shift in traditional supply chains has significant adverse impacts for truckload general freight carriers. The traditional supply chain relied heavily on truckload shipments both from manufacturers to distribution centers and, often times, from distribution centers to large retail outlets. In contrast, the Internet sales often involve direct small-sized shipments from manufacturers to customers. Indeed, it is reported that United Parcel Service and the U.S. Postal Service are the predominant modes used in the delivery of business to customer packages. According to Zona Research, UPS was the default shipper on 15,000 web sites, with a 55 percent share of all e-commerce transactions. The United States Postal Service was number two with a 32 percent share.[7]

Clearly this fundamental shift is a cause for alarm among the general freight truckload carriers, in particular. Yet, this restructuring of the supply chain and its disintermediation of retailers has only begun to emerge. Indeed, it is estimated that the Internet accounted for only 1.6 percent of retail sales in the fourth quarter of 2002. Many manufacturers do not want to abandon their traditional retail outlets so they have kept their traditional supply chain in place and only view the Internet chain as an alternate.[8] The next section of the chapter examines how truckload carriers need to adapt in order to meet this challenge.

Move to Real-Time Supply Chains

Increasingly, U.S. firms are fundamentally changing and re-structuring their business practices as they shift to real-time supply chains. It is important, however, to detail what is involved in a shift by a company to a real-time supply chain.[9]

During the past decade a number of firms have moved their business transaction data from legacy systems to enterprise resource planning or ERP systems. These ERP systems provide the organization with a central database that feeds all of its major business functions: i.e., order entry, manufacturing, procurement, order tracking, accounting and finance, human resource, and order fulfillment and customer service. The common ERP database allows information to be shared across functional groups within an organization and provides data visibility in real-time across each unit in the organization. With this core ERP system in place, organizations can integrate in real-time all major functions in a way that achieves maximum efficiency while meeting major corporate objectives (i.e., a combination of on-time delivery targets, inventory optimization, and profit maximization).

The integration tool that sits on top of an ERP system is the Advanced Supply Chain Planning functionality. An Advanced Supply Chain Planner provides control over manufacturing and procurement in a way that dynamically optimizes corporate objectives. The Advanced Supply Chain Planner releases orders to the manufacturing plant and procures supplies in a timely fashion that minimizes inventory but maximizes ability to meet customer orders given material and labor constraints. The beauty of the Advanced Supply Chain Planner is that the optimization algorithm can be run in real-time and results can be dynamically updated. The Advanced Supply Chain Planning functionality facilitates the shift from push-based processes to one that is predominately pull-based. In the pull-based process, inventories of supplies are minimized as well as are inventories of products.

This trend toward firms adopting the real-time supply chain has adverse impacts on truckload carriers. The movement of supplies and the production of products are tied closely with customer demands. The focus is on minimum quantities delivered expediently. This type of transportation service does not play to the strengths of the traditional TL leaders. In fact, such a shift is bound to have a stimulating impact on the LTL carriers and the small package delivery firms. Indeed, by October of 2002, FedEx had finished rolling out its ground delivery service that covers 100 percent of the United States.[10]

Once again, while serious, there are significant limits to the adoption of the real-time supply chain by U.S. firms. Indeed, there are very few that are in the position to do so at the present time. Industry leaders like Dell and Cisco have set standards that will take others a long time to copy. Clearly, however, the real-time supply chain model will present a real threat to the traditional TL Carriers. How the TL carriers can respond to this challenge is the focus of the next section of the chapter.

Improving Safety

At the federal level, the Motor Carrier Safety Administration remains committed to achieving a substantial reduction in the number of truck crashes and the resulting injuries, fatalities, and property damage. Tables 2.9 and 2.10 present information on the safety performance records of the various segments of the truckload industry. Table 2.9 shows the crash record of the various segments in terms of a fatal crash rate per power unit as well as a total crash rate per power unit. These crash rates are compiled in the SafeStat database compiled by the Volpe Center on behalf of the Motor Carrier Safety Administration. The SafeStat database includes safety performance information based on vehicle inspections, driver inspections, enforcement action, carrier reviews, and crashes and aggregates this information at a carrier level. While the overall average fatal crash rate per power unit for all truckload segments combined is .0160, the fatal crash rate varies from a low of .0118 for tank operators to a high of .0203 for bulk carriers and .0174 for refrigerated carriers. All carriers taken together had a total crash rate per power unit of .3209, with the tank carriers having the lowest average at .2272 crashes per power unit and the bulk carriers with the highest average of .3786. Thus, the overall crash rate for the bulk carriers is about 66 percent higher than is the overall crash rate for the tank operators. Clearly, these differences constitute significant safety concerns that need to be addressed through public policy initiatives.

Table 2.9   Crash Rates Across Major Truckload Segments, 2002

Industry Segment	Fatal Crashes/ Power Units	Total Crashes/ Power Unit
Building Materials	.0156	.3174
Bulk Commodities	.0203	.3786
General Freight	.0158	.3460
Heavy Machinery	.0140	.3027
Refrigerated Commodities	.0174	.3455
Tank	.0118	.2272
All Carriers Combined	.0160	.3209

Source: Based on author's calculations from the Motor Carrier Safety Administration's SafeStat database, for September 2002, compiled by Volpe Transportation Systems Center, Cambridge, MA., 2003.

The safety performance indicators in Table 2.10 are also based on SafeStat. Table 2.10 focuses on two general measures of vehicle and driver performance. The Vehicle Safety Evaluation Area (VHSEA) focuses on measures of a carrier's performance with respect to operation and maintenance of vehicles. It includes information about how frequently a carrier's vehicles are taken out-of-service during inspections as a result of vehicle maintenance problems. It also reflects how well a carrier performs in the vehicle maintenance area based on the results of onsite inspections. The Driver Safety Evaluation Area (DRSEA) concentrates on measures of a carrier's performance with respect to drivers. It includes information about how frequently a carrier's drivers are taken out-of-service during inspections as a result of driver problems. It also reflects how well a carrier performs in the driver management area based on the results of onsite inspections. Both the VHSEA and the DRSEA are percentile scores with a maximum of 100. As a carrier's VHSEA and DRSEA increases, it is indicative of poorer performance. While all carriers taken together have an average VHSEA of 45.08, there are several segments with higher rates. For example, the heavy machinery carriers have an average VHSEA of 50.45 and the building materials carriers have an average VHSEA of 48.62. With respect to the DRSEA score, the overall average across all segments is 38.24. However, the average among the refrigerated carriers is 48.49 and it is 45.34 among the household goods carriers. Clearly, these differences are significant and indicative of variations among carriers in each of the segments in the safety management practices in place to insure safe operations.

Table 2.10 Vehicle and Driver Safety Evaluation Area Scores Across Major Truckload Segments, 2002

Industry Segment	VHSEA	DRSEA
Building Materials	48.62	38.90
Bulk Commodities	45.44	36.55
General Freight	46.45	42.14
Heavy Machinery	50.45	38.23
Refrigerated Commodities	44.10	48.49
Tank	43.93	36.60
All Carriers Combined	45.08	38.24

Source: Based on author's calculations from the Motor Carrier Safety Administration's SafeStat database for September 2002, compiled by Volpe Transportation Systems Center, Cambridge, MA., 2003.

One factor that seems to contribute to problems with managing drivers is the high annual driver turnover rates among carriers in the TL segment. Indeed, many truckload carriers have driver annual turnover rates that approach 100 percent. (Standard and Poor's Industry Survey) These exceedingly high turnover rates have very negative impacts on the carrier's cost structure. The requirement to hire so many new drivers on an annual basis drives costs up and leaves carriers with a base of drivers who are young, inexperienced, and not familiar with company practices.[11] Indeed, "for drivers who average three or more jobs with different carriers per year, the odds of being involved in an at-fault crash were found to be more than twice as high as for those with lower job change rates."[12]

The high turnover rates provide direct indication of driver dissatisfaction with pay and working conditions. Indeed, low pay is often a motivation for drivers, in particular, the owner-operators, to drive beyond the legal hour-of-service limits on work hours. Since the owner-operators are often only paid by the load and not by the hour, they have a strong incentive to carry additional loads and to drive additional hours.

Truckload carriers are caught in a severe bind over this issue. They face huge pressures to keep their rates low and their costs down. This makes it difficult for them to increase driver pay. During the economic expansion of the 1990s, many truckload carriers experienced driver shortages. During the period of the expansion, there was a little room for the carriers to improve the conditions of the drivers. Carriers improved pay and conditions of work (fewer nights on the road) as a way to attract drivers. According to Standard and Poor's Industry Survey, "In March 2002, J.B. Hunt, one of the industry's largest carriers, cut its starting pay to between 32 and 34 cents per mile, a sharp decrease from its prior starting salary of as high as 41 cents per mile. USA Truck, Inc and Swift Transportation Co., Inc. are also cited by SignPost as carriers that have cut starting salaries."[13] However, cutting salaries for drivers would seem to encourage driver behavior that is inconsistent with best safety management practices. Indeed, the practice of cutting wages for drivers during a period of recession contrasts with employment policies in much of the rest of the economy in which wages do not decline during recessions. Indeed, the tendency of some major truckload carriers to cut wages could be taken as further evidence of extremity of the competitive pressure faced by firms in the truckload segment. However, there are very recent signs that as the nation moves into an economic recovery mode, trucking companies are reversing the recent trend and increasing driver pay as there is renewed talk of driver shortages. Clearly, this is a positive direction and is consistent with achieving safety performance enhancements.

The TL carriers are caught in a competitive squeeze that makes it very difficult to secure a steady driver work force. This contrast markedly with less-than-truckload carriers, whose drivers accumulate on average a much lower number of annual miles and whose pay is significantly higher on average than is the pay of the typical TL driver.

The next section focuses on how TL carriers might address this very difficult situation of driver pay, driver stability, and safe operating practices. Clearly, some segments of the TL carriers have dealt poorly with managing these challenges to date.

Truckload Carriers in 2010

The truckload carrier segment has been anything but static in the 1987-2001 time periods as evidenced by the significant productivity gains cited in an earlier section of the chapter. In fact, while a certain small group of truckload carriers, conveniently labeled the ATLF carriers, led a wave of productivity improvements and operational changes in the immediate years after deregulation, by 2001, their achievements became the industry norm or average, overall as well as in each of the truckload segments. Yet, despite the noted productivity improvements and cost control measures that became widespread in the 1987-2001 time period, the profitability of the truckload carriers remained weak at best in 2001. In fact, the average profitability performance for truckload carriers overall and in most of the major segments decreased.

Added to this assault on the profitability of the truckload carriers, is the series of previously discussed challenges each of which has the potential for serious economic consequences for the truckload carriers. The focus of this section, however, is a somewhat brighter. It takes the point of view that there is a path forward for the truckload carriers. Indeed, this section will attempt to outline how the truckload carrier segment will look in 2010. In essence, the section will focus on how the truckload carriers will emerge after addressing the serious challenges they must confront.

Enhanced Technology to Achieve Integration with Real-time Supply Chain

By 2010, firms will have increasingly shifted to a real-time supply chain model. Embedded within this concept is a totally integrated, netcentric supply chain database that circulated information in real-time across the entire supply chain and provides visibility of that data not only within the separate functional departments within a firm but across the extended enterprise partners (e.g., suppliers and customers). Each department and partner is given visibility and can execute actions according to a set of pre-arranged business rules. Each department and partner's authorized actions and decisions is communicated across the supply chain in real time. This shift to a real-time environment radically improves communication, reduces uncertainties, and improves supply chain efficiency.

The truckload carriers have a vital function to play in this real-time supply chain world. Carriers are responsible for the physical movement of components and products. The successful truckload carriers must be fully integrated as a supply chain partner with their customers. Full integration is necessary so that components and products can move precisely according to schedules and commitments without variations or slippages. Truckload carriers must have total 24/7 satellite communication with vehicle drivers and must be able to track individual shipments in real time. However, tracking and tracing capabilities for carriers are not sufficient to achieve full supply chain integration. Such integration requires the carriers to merge their real-time tracking and tracing data into the ERP and Advanced Planning systems of their customers. It is only at this level that the carriers will have achieved full real-time supply chain integration with their customers.

Clearly, there are some industry leaders who are well on their way to achieving this level of integration. Schneider National, for example, has two-way, real-time satellite communication with its drivers/equipment that gives it immediate shipment visibility through the Internet.[14] There is no question, however, that the technology investment required to achieve full real-time integration is significant and favors the growth of large truckload firms. The conclusion is that increasingly truckload firms will have to make significant large technology investments that will enable them to integrate with their customers' supply chains. Indeed, companies like Schneider National and J.B. Hunt are leading the way in this regard.

Enhanced Technology to Achieve Safer Operations

By 2010 truckload carriers will fully implement new technologies for monitoring driver and vehicle performance as well as "smart" devices that will provide sufficient advance warnings to drivers in order to prevent collisions. These technologies and "smart" devices will significantly enhance the safety of truckload carrier operations and result in significantly fewer truck crashes and the resulting injuries and fatalities. Many of these technologies exist today in one form or another, but they have not been adopted on wide-scale. During the next seven years, however, these technologies will diffuse across the truckload carriers with resulting benefits to the public in terms of improved public safety.

There exists a range of recording and monitoring devices that can be mounted inside a truck to capture information about driver performance/alertness as well as to produce audible signals to the driver to warn of impending risk. According to a recent Transportation Research Board Report: "One concept is to employ on-board monitoring and recording devices to obtain (driver) behavioral and performance observations. Many behavioral correlates of safe or unsafe driving can be directly measured and recorded, including driving speed, acceleration, brake use, and driving times. Newly marketed sensors can continuously measure forward headway, rollover risk on curves, lane tracking, lateral encroachment sensing, and even driver alertness. Such technologies may provide safety performance feedback, both to drivers and their managers, in addition to providing collision warnings."[15] Indeed, the adoption of these on-board monitoring devices and sensors will become widespread in the next decade and will become standard equipment for the truckload carriers.

The on-board sensors discussed in the above paragraph have great potential both to provide forward collision warnings and also to provide diagnostic monitoring of safety-critical mechanical components. Indeed, in the recent Transportation Research Board report on truck safety, there is a summary statement about the potential benefits of on board vehicle sensors: "In the past decade, various advanced technology collision avoidance systems have been designed, developed, tested and marketed. Perhaps the best known and widely deployed of these are forward collision warning systems. One vendor advertises crash reductions of 35% or more for its users. Other advanced technologies under development, and in some cases marketed, include adaptive cruise control systems (often in combination with forward collision warning), side collision warning systems (to prevent encroachment onto adjacent vehicles during lane changes), roll stability advisors and controllers, and lane tracking systems that advise of overall lane tracking quality (a measure of driver alertness and overall performance) and provide lane departure warnings. Advanced on-board sensor systems can provide diagnostic monitoring of safety-critical components such as brakes and tires."[16]

These new technologies and sensors represent a significant enhancement over current procedures that will result in public safety gains. Truckload carriers will have incentives to implement these devices as a result of growing public impatience with "unsafe" motor carrier operations. Clearly, the trends toward the real-time supply chain model with its requirements for precise transportation shipments and deliveries will provide overwhelming momentum to the implementation of these new technologies and sensors by the truckload carriers.

Enhanced Operational Flexibility

In 2010, successful truckload firms will have an expanded range of services that will allow them to respond to a wide range of shipper needs and requirements. With few exceptions, most truckload firms today tend to focus on a limited number of activities/specialties. For example, there is still a division among the truckload firms on the basis of their specialty – e.g. tank operations, flatbed services, refrigerated vans, etc. However, as of late, some of the established industry leaders in the truckload segment – e.g. J.B. Hunt and Schneider National, have expanded significantly the range of services they provide.

For example, Schneider National, the largest truckload carrier in North America with annual revenues in excess of $1.2 billion has the following set of trademarked services: One-way Van Truckload, Dedicated, TruckRail/InterModal, Brokerage, and Expedited.[17] While some of these services are self-explanatory, it should be noted that Dedicated Services assign equipment and drivers exclusively to specific customers as a supplement to or replacement for private carriers. The InterModal services are integrated with rail operations to facilitate intermodal shipments. The Expedited Services division of Schneider National provides time definite deliveries by team or solo drivers, depending upon the distances involved.

The main theme emerging from this review of the breadth of services provided today by Schneider National is that the truckload carrier in 2010 will need to pattern its services in a similar fashion to Schneider's in order to meet the needs of a very sophisticated shipper community with widespread implementation of real-time supply chain technology and systems in place by 2010. As the shipping community transitions to this new environment, carriers will need to fully integrate their technology and information systems with those of their customers as well as to provide the broad array of services that will meet the requirements of a globally competitive, high-technology marketplace with agile, highly-reconfigurable supply chains.

The Competitive Landscape

In 2010, the truckload carrier industry segment will look markedly different from its current makeup. Nevertheless, just as the Advanced Truckload Firms (ATLFs) in 1987 set the standards for the truckload carriers through their innovations in the years immediately after de-regulation, J.B. Hunt and Schneider National are leading the way for significant changes that will be commonplace among truckload carriers by 2010.

Indeed, by 2010, the truckload carrier industry segment will see continuing growth and development for the mega-carriers like Hunt and Schneider. The mega-truckload carriers will mix flexibility in service offerings with a range of technological sophistication that will enable them to more efficiently manage their operations, improve public safety, and fully integrate with a complex, highly sophisticated set of requirements from the shipping community.

There is a fundamental difference between the mega-truckload carrier of 2010 with the typical truckload carrier of 2003. This chapter has documented that between 1987 and 2001, the truckload carriers made significant productivity gains and introduced remarkable cost control measures. Yet, because of extreme competitive pressures, the profitability picture remains quite bleak. In contrast, the technologically sophisticated, highly flexible truckload carrier in 2010 will be in a better position to reap the financial rewards of its industry position.

The major difference allowing for this profitability improvement is that the truckload carrier that will meet the competitive standards of the 2010 economy will have significant market power. There will be fewer carriers who are capable of providing the technological sophistication or operational flexibility. Those carriers who are successful in meeting these requirements will be able to charge revenues that allow them to meet reasonable profitability targets and goals. Indeed, J.B. Hunt, the largest of the truckload carriers with over $2 billion in annual revenues has consistently improved its operating ratio over the past several years from 96.6 percent in 2001 to 95.5 percent in 2002, to 90.7 percent through the third quarter of 2003. These operating ratios are significantly better than the operating ratios of the truckload carriers grouped together (98.4 percent in 2001).

Plethora of Uncertainties

The discussion in the previous section does not mean to imply that there are not significant issues on the horizon that the truckload carriers must come to grips with. There are huge questions and uncertainties as a result of the War on Terrorism and the requirements of Homeland Security in the area of cargo inspection and driver integrity. New requirements for inspections of the contents of trailers/containers would create significant delays/add huge costs with very significant adverse consequences to both the carrier and the shipper. While the driver shortage situation temporarily abated during the early years of the current decade, Homeland Security requirements will lead to greater scrutiny of driver backgrounds and may significantly reduce the pool of available drivers by significant numbers for years to come.

In addition to the War on Terrorism and the demands of Homeland Security, there are other important issues that the truckload carriers will face in 2010. There are real concerns about the integrity of the U.S. highway infrastructure in view of budget cuts and deferred maintenance. Highway traffic continues to grow at a pace significantly faster than the growth in capacity. There is a continuing deterioration in infrastructure quality with direct implications for the quality of truckload service as well as its ability to meet the time-sensitive requirements of shippers who have migrated to real-time supply chains.

Clearly both infrastructure concerns and Homeland Security requirements will drive up the cost of truckload operations. A final issue with the potential to disrupt the industry is the cost of fuel. The Iraq War has, if nothing else, re-emphasized the vulnerabilities of the U.S. economy to fluctuations in oil prices. The trucking industry remains particularly vulnerable.

The overall expectation, however, is that the truckload carrier segment will be dominated by strong, large carriers with advanced technology and providing a wide array of services designed to meet the uncertainties and provide high quality services to their increasingly sophisticated customers.

Notes

1. Jim Corridore, Standard and Poor's Industry Surveys, *Transportation: Commercial*, Vol. 171, No. 25, Section 2, June 19, 2003, p. 8.
2. Author's calculations from Motor Carrier Annual Report, 2001, American Trucking Associations, Alexandria, Virginia. Author compiled results from CD of Annual Report data for Calendar Year 2001.
3. Thomas M. Corsi and Joseph R. Stowers, "Effects of a Deregulated Environment on Motor Carriers: A Systematic, Multi-Segment Analysis," *Transportation Journal*, Vol. 30, No. 3, Spring 1991, p. 11.
4. Gary Whicker and Grant DuCote, "Turn Data into Dollars," *Transportation and Distribution*, September 2001, Cover Story, Penton Media, Inc, Cleveland, Ohio.
5. Gary Whicker and Grant DuCote, "Turn Data into Dollars," *Transportation and Distribution*, September 2001, Cover Story, Penton Media, Inc, Cleveland, Ohio.
6. Jim Corridore, Standard and Poor's Industry Surveys, *Transportation: Commercial*, Vol. 171, No. 25, Section 2, June 19, 2003, p. 11.
7. Jim Corridore, Standard and Poor's Industry Surveys, *Transportation: Commercial*, Vol. 171, No. 25, Section 2, June 19, 2003, p. 11.
8. Jim Corridore, Standard and Poor's Industry Surveys, *Transportation: Commercial*, Vol. 171, No. 25, Section 2, June 19, 2003, p. 11.
9. Thomas M. Corsi, Sandor Boyson, Lisa Harrington, *In Real Time: Managing the New Supply Chain*, Praeger Books, Westport, Connecticut, 2004.
10. Jim Corridore, Standard and Poor's Industry Surveys, *Transportation: Commercial*, Vol. 171, No. 25, Section 2, June 19, 2003, p. 11.
11. Jim Corridore, Standard and Poor's Industry Surveys, *Transportation: Commercial*, Vol. 171, No. 25, Section 2, June 19, 2003, p. 13.
12. Ronald Knipling, Jeffrey Hickman, Gene Bergoffen, *Effective Commercial Truck and Bus Safety Management Techniques*, Transportation Research Board, Washington, D.C., 2003, p. 19.
13. Jim Corridore, Standard and Poor's Industry Surveys, *Transportation: Commercial*, Vol. 171, No. 25, Section 2, June 19, 2003, p. 13.
14. http://www.schneider.com/index.html.
15. Ronald Knipling Jeffrey Hickman, Gene Bergoffen, *Effective Commercial Truck and Bus Safety Management Techniques*, Transportation Research Board, Washington, D.C., 2003, p. 29.
16. Ronald Knipling Jeffrey Hickman, Gene Bergoffen, *Effective Commercial Truck and Bus Safety Management Techniques*, Transportation Research Board, Washington, D.C., 2003, p. 34.
17. http://www.schneider.com.

References

American Trucking Associations. *Motor Carrier Annual Reports 2001*. Transport Topics Press, Alexandria, Virginia, 2002.

Corridore, Jim. "Transportation Commercial". *Standard and Poor's Industry Surveys*, Vol. 171, No. 25, June 19, 2003.

Corsi, Thomas M. and Barnard, Richard E. "Best Highway Safety Practices: A Survey Among the Safest Motor Carriers," Supply Chain Management Center, Robert H. Smith School of Business, University of Maryland, College Park, MD, prepared for Analysis Division, Office of Information Management, Federal Motor Carrier Safety Administration, November 2002.

Corsi, Thomas M.; Mejza, Michael, and Keane, Thomas, "Driver Management Practices of Motor Carriers with High Compliance and Safety Performance," *Transportation Journal*, Summer 2003, Vol. 42, No. 3, pp. 16-29.

Corsi, Thomas M. and Stowers, Joseph R. "Effects of a Deregulated Environment on Motor Carriers: A Systematic, Multi-Segment Analysis," *Transportation Journal*, Vol. 30, No. 3, Spring 1991, pp. 11-22.

Corsi, Thomas; Boyson, Sandor; and Harrington, Lisa. *In Real Time: Managing the New Supply Chain*, Praeger Books, Westport, Connecticut, 2004.

Knipling, Ronald; Hickman, Jeffrey, and Bergeoffen, Gene. "Effective Commercial Truck and Bus Safety," *Management Inquiries*, Transportation Research Board, Washington, D.C., 2003.

Mejza, Michael C. and Corsi, Thomas M. "Assessing Motor Carrier Potential for Improving Safety Processes," *Transportation Journal*, Vol. 38, No. 4, Summer 1999, pp. 36-50.

Ostria, Sergio. "Evaluation of U.S. Commercial Motor Carrier Industry Challenges and Opportunities," *ICF Consulting*, Fairfax, Virginia, March 31, 2003.

Whicker, Gary and DuCote, Grant. "Turn Data into Dollars," *Transportation and Distribution*, September 2001, Penton, Media, Inc., Cleveland, Ohio, p. 1.

Chapter 3

Less-Than-Truckload Motor Carriers: A Story of Diversity and Change

Peter F. Swan and Stephen V. Burks

Introduction

Beginning in 1998, the University of Michigan Trucking Industry Program (UMTIP) undertook a series of case studies of less-than-truckload (LTL) motor carriers. We expected to find those policies and skills that would lead to success for LTL motor carriers. Instead we found incredible diversity in strategy, operations, network structures, markets, labor-management relations, and technology. In the long-run, some strategies may prove more viable than others, but it is not obvious which strategies those will be. One reason is that LTL motor carriers are facing continuing changes in business conditions and in the competitive landscape. However, while the UMTIP Case Study of LTL motor carriers did not find the 'magic bullet' that leads to superior performance for all firms using it, we did find some of the causes of the diversity and did identify some of the different strategies LTL firms use to survive in particular niches in an extremely competitive marketplace.

In this chapter we sketch a picture of the LTL industry at the dawn of the twenty-first century. We place the specific insights gained from in-depth interviews in a wider industry context using data from annual reports of the financial and operating statistics of LTL carriers (ATA 1985-2002) submitted to initially the Interstate Commerce Commission (ICC) and later to the Bureau of Transportation Statistics (BTS), and supplemented with geographic coverage and terminal counts obtained from the American Motor Carrier Directory (AMCD 1990-1997). We also draw on the larger scale information provided by the Economic Census in establishing the larger economic and competitive context. We use data from 1997 (and some from 1998)[1] because these data provide greater breadth of measurements and greater depth in firms than later years.[2]

The story of how the end of economic regulation forced poor competitors to drop out and permitted efficient competitors to prosper and grow is by this time old. A newer twist to the old story is how technology has played a role in who wins and who loses. Not just new technology, but the right technology. As part of the UMTIP LTL Case Study we found not only remarkable examples of new technology providing competitive advantage, but also examples of old technology being used effectively and cheaply to provide competitive advantage.

What is a Less-Than-Truckload Motor Carrier?

Less-than-truckload motor carriers specialize in hauling 'middle-sized' shipments, as opposed to very small shipments (the domain of parcel carriers), or very large ones (the domain of truckload carriers). Firms that specialize primarily in each of these three shipment sizes have distinct production processes. They organize their operational routines differently and utilize somewhat distinct types of trucks and other equipment. It is easiest to understand the specific case of LTL firms by first considering the two shipment-size extremes, parcel service, and full-truckload service.

Parcel service moves small shipments, composed of parcels or packages that have an average weight of less than 50 pounds and may weigh up to 150 pounds. The shipments are picked up using small vans and brought back to local terminals. There, shipments are aggregated into full loads for inter-terminal movements in tractor-trailers on fixed routes. Because of the large volume of small shipments handled (on the order of one billion in 1997),[3] package carriers utilize many local terminals, specialized small vans and specialized material handling equipment at each terminal. Package carriers also frequently use high-cubic-volume, drop-frame trailers for inter-terminal movements to improve productivity.

In contrast to package carriers, truckload (TL) carriers move shipments directly from origin to destination without the use of terminals. For TL shipments, a TL carrier sends a driver with a tractor-trailer to a shipper's dock to fill up the trailer with a load typically weighing from 10,000 to 48,000 pounds. The driver takes the loaded trailer wherever shipment is destined (within North America), and unloads it at the consignee's dock. The driver is then dispatched empty, possibly after waiting for a while, to the next location where a full load is available for pickup. TL shipments are much less numerous than parcel shipments, on the order of 150 million versus one billion for parcel service in 1997,[4] but each shipment represents the movement of a whole truck.[5] Because freight is handled only at customer shipping and receiving docks, little or no material handling equipment is needed by TL carriers. Truckload carriers may use specialized equipment for special commodities, but most use general purpose equipment to maximize the chance of backhauls.

In between the two shipment-size extremes of parcel service and TL service lies the LTL segment. This segment is like parcel service in that it uses local drivers to collect shipments which are later aggregated at local terminals into full trailer loads for inter-terminal movement. Shipments handled by LTL carriers can run the gamut from 50 pounds to 48,000 pounds, with a typical average in the range of 1,000 pounds.[6] Because LTL carriers handle 'middle-sized' shipments, their freight-handling equipment, which will be described in detail later, is less specialized than package carrier equipment and their trucks are somewhat more specialized than TL carrier equipment.

Although LTL is not the largest segment of the trucking industry, it is still very large (over twenty billion dollars of revenue in 1997) and fills an important niche in the U.S. transportation system. Unlike the prior system of industrial classification, the North American Industry Classification System (NAICS) categories distinguish TL from LTL. The 1997 Economic Census does not allow the parcel segment to be broken out separately, but the North American Industry Classification System (NAICS) categories do nicely distinguish TL from LTL (see Table 3.1). In 1997, within the general freight portion of (non-parcel) for-hire trucking, the LTL segment had 38.8% of the total employment, and 31.4% of the total revenue (see Table 3.1).

Table 3.1 TL versus LTL Trucking in the 1997 Economic Census (firms that operated at least 10 months of the year)

NAICS Segment Code		NAICS Segment Name	Number of Firms	Number of Establish-ments	Number of Employees	Annual Revenue (billions)
48412		Freight Trucking, **Long Distance**	17,037	23,901	669,465	$74.60
	484121	**TL** segment of 48412	15,278	18,270	411,805	$49.70
	484122	**LTL** segment of 48412	1,835	5,625	257,649	$24.80
48411		Freight Trucking, **Local**	10,805	11,542	123,537	$11.21
	4841101, 4841103	**TL** segments of 48411, with & w/o storage	7,920	8,197	77,494	$8.01
	4841102, 4841104	**LTL** segments of 48411, with & w/o storage,	2,885	3,345	46,043	$3.20
LTL versus **TL** Segments Comparison		Share of LTL in All General Freight	17.0%	25.3%	38.3%	28.5%

Source: US Census (2001).

However, while Table 3.1 shows the relative position of the entire LTL segment in for-hire trucking, it includes a large number of LTL firms that we will not be focusing on in this chapter. We are primarily interested in the LTL firms that are engaged in inter-city freight movement and are above a modest size threshold. These can be identified in Table 3.2 as the firms with five or more total business establishments.[7] In 1997, there were about 90 such firms in the U.S., with total revenue of a bit more than $20 billion, and about 215,000 total employees.

Table 3.2   Long Distance LTL Firms in the 1997 Economic Census

(NAICS 484122; including firms operating less than 10 months of the year)					
Single unit/Multi-unit Firms	Total number of firms	Number of locations	Revenue ($1,000)	Annual payroll ($1,000)	Number of employees
All firms	2,413	6,210	$25,010,091	$9,509,916	258,972
Single unit firms	2,107	2,107	$2,449,836	$746,297	25,263
Multiunit firms	306	4,103	$22,560,255	$8,763,619	233,709
Firms with 1 loc.	119	119	$1,155,410	$345,571	9,801
Firms with 2 locs.	51	102	$335,836	$103,890	3,321
Firms with 3 or 4 locs.	47	158	$629,708	$179,702	5,713
Firms with 5 to 9 locs.	29	201	$746,944	$236,645	6,812
Firms with 10+ locs.	60	3,523	$19,692,357	$7,897,811	208,062

Source: US Census (2001).

To understand the diversity of LTL carriers, it is necessary to first understand how the industry segment formed. The difference between LTL and TL segments was not as sharp when trucking was under economic regulation, from 1935 to 1980. While firms combining both TL and LTL operations existed in 1935 and were granted grandfathered rights the by the ICC, firms with LTL operations were more numerous. Supported by ICC regulatory decisions which made it more difficult for TL operations to expand with the changes in economic geography, LTL operations came to dominate the industry (Rothenberg 1994). By the end of economic regulation a large proportion of full truckload freight was hauled by carriers that used the LTL approach to production, with freight-handling local terminals and fixed routes.

Another side effect of regulation was that the wages of trucking labor were substantially above the level of other blue collar jobs requiring similar human capital, due to the Teamsters Union's National Master Freight Contract, which was anchored on conditions set in the regulatory-era predecessors of LTL firms (Belzer 1995, Rose 1987). Because prices to shippers were set collectively, through the institution of rate bureaus, trucking firms were for the most part able to pass these costs to customers (Rose 1985; US Senate 1980).

Deregulation brought about a dramatic restructuring of the trucking industry (Belzer 2000; Burks 1999; Glaskowski 1990; Perry 1986). Incumbent TL-type firms expanded, and thousands of new, small TL firms entered the industry. Without the overhead costs of a terminal system, and paying much less than Teamster wages, entering TL firms sharply cut the cost of TL transportation. This new and vibrant TL segment took most of the truckload freight that firms using LTL type production had been hauling, and in addition began taking market share from both railroads and private carriage (Campbell 1987). LTL firms scrambled to adjust and expand route structures,[8] while coping with the loss of the majority of their TL freight. The result was the specialization of individual carriers into TL and

LTL types which is reflected in today's NAICS categories. This specialization was fully in place by 1992.

Structure of the LTL Segment

The basis of LTL operations, the combining of many medium-sized shipments from multiple customers into larger loads for long-haul movement, creates modest barrier to entry in this trucking industry segment. A new LTL firm offering service beyond a single area must establish dense enough shipment flows over a network of local terminals to be cost-competitive with incumbent firms serving the same points. Generating this much demand requires earning the confidence of shippers in its service area, which does not happen immediately. As a result, there are sunk costs of entry whenever an LTL firm serves a new point, until enough new customers have been acquired in the new area. Keaton (1996) showed that while LTL carriers can efficiently enter new, high-density long-haul lanes, it is much more difficult to build enough traffic density to in-between points on such lanes to attain 'economies of density' sufficient to profitably compete with incumbents.

By contrast, barriers to entry in TL are nominal, and a one-truck firm can compete with most of the services offered by an industry leader on a load-by-load basis. Indeed, pure TL general commodity trucking is arguably one of the few large business areas in the U.S. economy, outside of some parts of agriculture, which meets the microeconomist's theoretical definition of a perfectly competitive industry. According to the 1997 *Economic Census* there were 15,278 firms in the long-distance TL segment, but only 63 of these firms were large enough to operate ten or more separate business establishments. The group operating ten or more establishments earned only 20.0% of the total TL revenue in 1997, and the four largest firms by revenue earned only 11.4% of the total revenue of all firms in the segment (U.S. Census Bureau 2001).

In contrast, the evolution of the LTL segment since deregulation has created a modest degree of concentration. There were many fewer firms – only 1,835 – in long-distance LTL in 1997, and 60 of these (about the same as in TL) had sufficient geographic scope to have ten or more separate establishments. That group of 60 firms earned 85.5% of the total revenues of the entire segment, and the top four firms by revenue earned 39.3% of the segment total (U.S. Census Bureau 2001).

Table 3.3 shows how general freight carriers have grown between 1984 and 2000. LTL carriers have continued to grow larger, while the number of firms has declined and the total revenue for the industry segment has remained relatively stagnant. As a result of mergers and failures, one quarter of the fifteen major LTL carriers listed on Table 3.3 have failed, and the LTL segment has shrunk from over 350 major carriers in 1984 to under 100 major carriers in 2000 (ATA 1985, 2001). Even with this consolidation, LTL competition remains intense with no evidence of pricing power within the LTL segment (Nebesky, et al. 1995).

Table 3.3   Growth of General Freight Carriers

General Freight Carrier Firms 1984-2000	1984 Rev ($000,000)	1994 Rev ($000,000)	2000 Rev ($000,000)
United Parcel Service	6,196	14,697[b]	29,795[b]
Federal Express (now FedEx)	NA	NA	19,629[b]
Con-Way Transportation	New	1,983[b]	5,572[b]
Yellow Freight System Inc. (now Yellow Trans.)	1,344	2,197	3,588
Schneider National Carriers	193	1,325[a]	3,100
Roadway Express Inc.	1,401	2,137	3,040
USF Freightways Corp.	453	800	2,539[b]
Consolidated Freightways Corp. of De	1,284	1,847	2,352
ANR Freight System	174	1,513	Closed
J.B. Hunt Transport, Inc.	98	1,069	2,160
P*I*E Nationwide Inc	891	Closed	Closed
McLean Trucking	488	Closed	Closed
ABF Freight Systems Inc.	386	903	1,840
Landstar Ranger, Inc.	4	383	1,418
Swift Transportation Co., Inc.	NA	360	1,259
Werner Enterprises, Inc.	53	516	1,215
Overnite Transportation Co.	414	1,037	1,114
Watkins Motor Lines Inc.	115	488	944
Carolina Freight Carriers Corp.	373	624	Purchased
American Freightways Inc.	NA	466	NA
Preston Trucking Company Inc.	285	419	Closed
Total for LTL Carriers Reporting to BTS	**1984**	**1994**	**2000**
Total Revenue ($000,000)	15,347	15,452	19,691
Average Revenue per Carrier ($000,000)	43	231	246
Number of Carriers	353	67	80
Total for TL Gen. Frt. Carriers reporting to BTS	**1984**	**1994**	**2000**
Total Revenue ($000,000)	14,998	28,294	61,795
Average Revenue per Carrier ($000,000)	19	103	31
Number of Carriers	803	276	2026

Source: ATA (1985,1994,1995,2001) and a = CCJ (1995) b = substantial non-trucking revenue [ ] *= LTL Carriers.*

Geographic Scope

National LTL Carriers LTL motor carries can be divided into four general categories based on geographic coverage: national, interregional, regional, and local. National LTL carriers provide coverage to most or all forty-eight contiguous states and sometimes to other countries as well as to Hawaii and Alaska. National LTL carriers have historically specialized in long-haul LTL traffic. The average length of haul for national LTL carriers is over one thousand miles. The largest LTL carriers had revenues in excess of three billion dollars in 2000: Yellow Freight System (now Yellow Transportation) and Roadway Express.[9] National carriers usually make heavy use of intermediate terminals (described later) and typically have much lower revenue per ton-mile[10] than other types of carriers.

Local LTL Carriers   In contrast to the broad geographic scope of national carriers, 'Local' carriers perform only pickup and delivery services. A local carrier operates in a very limited area, such as a metropolitan area. These carriers have historically faced little economic regulation because they are engaged in intra-city transportation, which is exempt from most economic regulation. Local service is often characterized by delivery of large items that are bought by consumers but are too large to be taken home after purchase (for example beds, refrigerators, and ovens). Local LTL carriers perform pickup and delivery operations, but they seldom have their own over-the-road or linehaul operations. Local LTL carriers are often contracted by other types of LTL carriers (or sometimes by freight forwarders) for shipment consolidation, and/or delivery and pickup of shipments, as a market extension for the contracting carrier. Many regional LTL carriers have historically also functioned as local carriers by delivering freight as agents of other firms.[11] Some of the newer regional LTL carriers are local carriers that expanded into regional carriers.

Regional LTL Carriers 'Regional' LTL carriers are LTL carriers that serve a few states in one or two regions[12] of the country. Because the geographic range of regional LTL carriers is limited, they specialize in shipments that travel shorter distances (usually less than 300 miles.) They often provide intrastate service, but also provide single-line (versus interline)[13] interstate service throughout their regions. The smaller size of regional LTL carriers (in comparison with national LTL carriers) enables them to offer more flexible service to their customers (Quinn 1989; Feldman 1986). Regional LTL carriers (like local LTL carriers) have also historically served as agents for other carriers who wish to serve larger regions without hiring new employees or buying new terminals. Regional LTL carriers receive greater revenue per ton-mile than national LTL carriers, but also have much higher costs per ton-mile.

Interregional LTL Carriers Several regional carriers have grown through expansion beyond traditional boundaries or coordinated service to evolve into 'interregional' LTL carriers, a new form of LTL carrier (Hoffman 1995). Con-Way Transportation Services has merged two of its subsidiaries together (Con-Way

South and Con-Way Southwest) and is offering coordinated service between all of the remaining subsidiaries. American Freightways (purchased by FedEx) and Spartan (now closed) grew from regional firms into interregional firms. Others, such as Clipper Express and NationsWay (now closed), offered interregional service on a limited basis, by concentrating on heavy-traffic lanes only. Because interregional carriers operate with both longer and shorter hauls, they have characteristics of both national and regional carriers.

LTL Operations

Like all transportation firms, operations at LTL firms can be divided into three generic activities: pickup and delivery (P&D), over-the-road intercity movements (linehaul or OTR), and consolidation/-terminal/sort operations (dock in LTL). Most LTL motor carriers perform all three activities. Because these activities are interlinked, the allocation of labor and capital to each, and the degree of efficiency achieved in each, are also connected. Improvement in one activity's performance will often come at the expense of performance levels in another activity. Individual firms organize these activities and the tradeoffs between them in different ways based on their market segment, geographic scope, and/or service strategy.

These differences can be seen in Tables 3.4 and 3.5 which compile firm level annual data for 1997.[14] Each activity has different performance indicators. Although each activity can be performed using different methods and technologies, terminal and freight consolidation activities provide the most notable firm differences. The way these three activities fit together is determined jointly with the firm's terminal network design.

Pickup and Delivery

To handle customer shipments, freight must first be picked up and moved to a terminal serving a local area. Such terminals are usually referred to as end-of-line (EOL) terminals.[15] Usually freight is picked up in the afternoon and delivered in the morning. To accomplish this, the daily pickups and deliveries to and from each terminal must be allocated to drivers. Drivers are frequently assigned to specific areas and/or customers. Such an allocation is made within the broader area served by the terminal, based on an estimate of the normal pattern of stops to be made. The remaining local drivers are then used to fill in gaps and handle temporary increases in freight. In some situations, sophisticated allocation algorithms are used to maximize driver (and truck) utilization and to fully meet customer requirements for pickup and delivery times. The route that the driver follows can also be optimized to further improve pickup and delivery of freight. However, the tradeoffs here illustrate the interconnections between the different functions performed by each firm.

Table 3.4   1997 LTL Firm Statistics by Carrier Type

Nationals	Avg. Length of Haul	Tons per Truck	Terms	Ships. per Term	Miles[2] per Term	Rev. per Emp. (000)	Rev. per Power Unit (000)	Rev. per Ton-Mile	EBIT per Tot Assets
ABF	1,185	13.8	307	64	9,649	$95	$266	$0.26	16%
CFMF	1,269	14.9	314	128	9,433	$94	$296	$0.25	6%
Roadway	1,307	15	382	105	7,754	$96	$272	$0.25	7%
Watkins	1,551	11.8	116	213	20,814	$61	$311	$0.23	33%
Yellow	1,257	14.4	387	99	7,654	$105	$286	$0.23	8%
Composite	1,283	14.4	301	97	9,471	$94	$283	$0.24	9%
Interregionals									
AAA Cooper	389	8.3	74	682	12,407	$77	$193	$0.47	14%
American FW	587	9.9	203	195	7,370	$82	$169	$0.32	8%
Averitt	NA	NA	74	640	12,697	$77	$174	NA	19%
Con-Way	497	9.5	397 (est)	70	7,466	$86	NA	$0.45	21%
Estes	334	9.6	63	883	11,249	$73	$164	$0.45	22%
Jevic	649	12.4	9	8,461	58,592	$107	$181	$0.17	14%
Motor Cargo	630	11.8	38	565	25,901	$85	$168	$0.35	15%
Old Dominion	869	16.2	80	407	24,043	$73	$170	$0.18	10%
Overnite	610	10.7	245	126	11,694	$78	$194	$0.32	2%
Preston	479	12.1	69	783	11,237	$58	$208	$0.39	0%
Saia	301	6.6	72	613	10,524	$76	$168	$0.48	11%
Southeastern	300	6.5	48	1,858	12,480	$79	$204	$0.45	20%
Southwestern	637	8.4	39	344	29,039	$115	$147	$0.23	4%
Bestway	395	8.9	33	1,127	28,343	$81	$212	$0.45	27%
Holland	381	9.6	48	2,726	18,963	$98	$206	$0.40	24%
Composite	485	10	84	333	14,953	$78	$185	$0.35	9%
Regionals									
Alvan	143	5.6	19	1,643	13,530	$99	$175	$0.88	7%
New Penn	215	7.9	23	3,652	9,318	$114	$280	$0.87	31%
Oak Harbor	206	18.7	23	1,399	22,231	NA	$222	$0.69	12%
Parker	167	4.6	16	1,035	17,729	$99	$156	$0.67	0%
Silver Eagle	NA	NA	19	1,234	21,128	$78	$176	NA	9%
Ward	228	5.2	13	4,142	15,496	$95	$199	$0.47	11%
Composite	201	6.9	19	2,296	15,615	$106	$225	$0.73	22%

Source: ATA (1998) and AMCD (1997).

Table 3.5   1997 (1998) LTL Firm Statistics by Carrier Type

Nationals	Op. Ratio	Pct. Tons from LTL	Avg. Ship. Wgt. (tons)	Ships. per Non-Op Emp. (000)	1998 Ships. per P&D Hr.	1998 Tons per P&D Hr.	Mile per PU (000)	Ships per Mile^2	OO Mile per HW Mile	Rev per Non-Op Emp. (000)
ABF	95%	80%	0.62	1.6	0.88	0.44	64	2	NA	$307
CFMF	98%	83%	0.55	2.0	1.12	0.51	57	3.3	0%	$348
Roadway	98%	82%	0.52	1.6	1.18	0.53	51	5.2	0%	$264
Watkins	93%	83%	0.63	1.0	1.77	0.94	81	1.2	27%	$235
Yellow	97%	82%	0.58	1.8	1.17	0.58	63	5	0%	$310
Composite	97%	82%	0.56	1.7	1.14	0.54	59	3.6	3%	$296
Interregionals										
AAA Cooper	91%	84%	0.51	2.5	1.12	0.49	49	3.1	NA	$226
American FW	95%	88%	0.58	1.7	0.75	0.39	51	5.4	5%	$183
Averitt	92%	50%	0.98	3.1	NA	NA	90	3.7	NA	$332
Con-Way	89%	87%	0.55	2.9	NA	NA	NA	3.7	4%	$353
Estes	87%	70%	0.77	2.6	0.85	0.46	38	3.9	NA	$298
Jevic	92%	40%	2.55	0.9	NA	NA	87	1.3	NA	$262
Motor Cargo	91%	76%	0.57	2.1	NA	NA	15	0.8	64%	$261
Old Dominion	94%	65%	0.79	1.7	0.89	0.47	52	1.4	8%	$214
Overnite	97%	71%	0.64	2.0	0.97	0.45	51	2.6	NA	$244
Preston	100%	79%	0.65	1.6	NA	NA	41	3.8	NA	$194
Saia	94%	75%	0.68	2.5	1.04	0.56	51	3.2	4%	$244
Southeastern	90%	78%	0.60	3.2	1.17	0.7	64	7.1	10%	$257
Southwestern	98%	40%	1.21	1.1	1.15	0.6	8	0.5	89%	$186
Bestway	87%	83%	0.62	2.9	NA	NA	54	1.3	NA	$314
Holland	91%	82%	0.74	4.6	0.7	0.6	54	6.9	NA	$525
Composite	94%	77%	0.65	2.2	0.88	0.47	48	3.2	7%	$244
Regionals										
Alvan	98%	63%	0.78	3.3	0.99	0.51	35	2.3	0%	$324
New Penn	79%	86%	0.56	3.1	1.3	0.62	41	9	0%	$330
Oak Harbor	96%	74%	0.61	NA	NA	NA	17	1.4	0%	
Parker	100%	58%	0.94	2.4	0.72	0.71	50	0.9	0%	$249
Silver Eagle	98%	58%	0.70	2.7	1.08	NA	24	1.1	0%	$231
Ward	94%	50%	0.94	2.7	1.03	0.53	73	3.5	9%	$268
Composite	88%	70%	0.69	3.0	1.12	0.59	43	2.8	3%	$307

Source: ATA (1998, 1999) and AMCD (1997).

The basic problem is that optimizing the delivery portion of a local driver's run is costly in terms of freight re-handling and space utilization on the dock. Because LTL shipments come in all shapes, sizes and weights (barrels, bins, cartons, large and small skids, bundles of steel, with an average shipment weight of around 1,000 pounds), the driver generally has to make deliveries in the reverse of the order that shipments were initially loaded, because re-ordering freight once it is on the local trailer is feasible for only a minority of shipments. To precisely order the shipments on a given city trailer requires knowing which inbound shipments will be allocated to that trailer, generating an ordering based on local knowledge of not only consignee locations but also any special features that constrain delivery times, and then implementing that loading order.

However, the freight for an individual city run generally comes from multiple inbound road trailers, which arrive and are worked at different times. So implementing the desired ordering requires 'staging,' or temporarily storing on the dock, shipments that belong at the rear of the delivery trailer. This requires extra dock space, and means that the shipment must be re-handled (increasing the risk of damage). It also may imply having a large number of employees on hand together early in each morning, when all the local delivery loads with staged freight need to be completed. The delivery drivers can perform some of this work, but this, of course, trades off against the amount of time they have to spend on the street.

Most of the firms we visited managed the tradeoff between dock efficiency and delivery efficiency by only approximating the best shipment order and by also only approximately loading in the order they selected. A typical plan was to use the knowledge of local dispatchers to allocate each shipment to a delivery run, and within that run, to a given quarter (for long trailers) or a given third (for short trailers) of the trailer's floor space, based on the usual pattern of driver travel through the different parts of the delivery area. Dock workers would then load shipments approximately in the correct floor section, trying to keep very large shipments assigned to the rear of the trailer staged on the dock until everything else is loaded. This procedure produced an acceptable level of city delivery productivity (typically around 2 stops per hour) at an acceptable level of dock cost and shipment damage.

The use of appointments by customers for pickups and deliveries presents a serious challenge to LTL firms, as appointments impede the efficiency of P&D routes. Making efficient P&D routes that meet all appointment requirements is problematic, because the temporal order of stops rarely matches the geographic order of stops. Worse, multiple stops with matching appointment times can make efficient runs virtually impossible. Many carriers have responded with higher charges for appointment or guaranteed delivery and pickup times. The situation is exacerbated where shipment density is low. Because pickups may not be known until after drivers have left to deliver freight, scheduling pickups before drivers leave the terminal is difficult or impossible. As a result, drivers must communicate with dispatchers throughout the day. Radio, cellular phone, beeper, or periodic stops by drivers to use public phones (or customer phones in some cases) are used to accomplish such communications.

The productivity of P&D operations is affected by several factors that related to driver productivity. Because P&D drivers are paid by the hour, productivity is often measured in activity per hour. Such measures include stops per hour, tons per hour, and shipments per hour.[16] These measures are affected not only by driver skill, but also by shipment demographics and customer characteristics. Productivity increases with the number of shipments (or tons)[17] picked up or delivered at each customer stop. Shipment characteristics can also affect P&D productivity. Shipments that must be unloaded by hand (or fingerprinted) take longer to unload and thus lower productivity. Second, shorter distances between customers leads to increased productivity, because less time is spent driving between customers. This can be measured with driver stops per hour. These two factors make up what Keaton (1996) refers to as 'shipment density.' Third, the distance between the terminal and customers determines how much time a driver may spend actually delivering freight. The time spent driving between a terminal and the first (or last) customer is called 'stem time.' Greater amounts of stem-time increase the likelihood that traffic conditions will cause problems with meeting appointments at customers. However, terminal networks with larger coverage areas (and greater stem-time) will have a decreased number of travel lanes and an increased amount of traffic moving between each pair of terminals, thus improving the efficiency of linehaul operations. Finally, the type of customer affects driver productivity. Locating customers for home delivery and delivering to locations without docks slows operations. Many firms therefore have surcharges for special services that add significant cost to P&D operations.

Over-The-Road Movement of Freight

Once freight has been picked up and carried to freight terminals, it must be transferred between freight terminals before final delivery. This process is called over-the-road or linehaul movement of freight. Over-the-road movement of freight is very similar for LTL and TL firms. The planning and scheduling of over-the-road operations, on the other hand, are very different between LTL and TL firms. Truckload firms assign drivers to loads based primarily on minimizing empty miles (Powell 1995). In TL, customers are widely dispersed and the trucks become available at different times depending on when and where they delivered their previous load. In contrast, LTL firms generally dispatch over-the-road drivers from central points (terminals) at fixed times (when the freight becomes available). In addition to minimizing empty miles, LTL carriers attempt to minimize cost (miles, trucks, and handling) for a given amount of freight. Loaded mile efficiency is also important for LTL carriers, so they usually measure the average amount of freight carried in over-the-road trucks.[18] Finally, the truck and driver productivity can be measured using performance indicators such as accidents per million miles and miles per gallon.

Long-distance over-the-road operations can vary significantly among LTL carriers, although all carriers are affected by hours of service regulations and driver fatigue that effectively limit the range of drivers to 400 to 600 miles per shift. Freight that travels for long distances may move in three different ways:[19] relay drivers, sleeper teams, or intermodal. Relay drivers move trucks between points strategically placed in long-distance routes. Because the 'hand-off' of the truck between drivers takes up to four hours, as much as a day can be lost when relay drivers are used for transcontinental shipments. To avoid this loss of time and to improve service, many long-haul LTL carriers are now using sleeper teams. Sleeper teams use a tractor with a bed in it and a team of two drivers. This permits one driver to sleep while the other drives, thus avoiding stops and significant delay (Gooley 1995). Sleeper teams are also more flexible than relay drivers, because they do not require freight to move on a fixed route (Trunick 1995). Lastly, intermodal movement of trailers involves dropping off a trailer at a rail yard for over-the-road movement by the railroad. The trailer is then picked up at a destination rail yard for movement to a terminal or customer. Intermodal movements are limited by the points between which railroad service exists and by the quality of service provided by the railroads. The shortage of drivers, [20] reduced intermodal cost and improvements in service (Bowman 1995; Gooley 1995) have encouraged increased use of intermodal, but this has temporarily peaked because of congestion in the rail system (TM 1993; JOC 2005). In some traffic lanes, virtually all truck trailers move in intermodal trains (Frailey 1996).

Consolidation/Terminal/Sort Operations

Consolidation of freight moving from a similar origin or moving to a similar destination is a function that differentiates LTL carriers. While all LTL carriers consolidate freight in some manner, the actual method by which freight is consolidated varies greatly among firms. Additionally, several strategic factors affect the difficulty and relative importance associated with consolidating freight. These factors include terminal placement, terminal size, number of terminals, size of cities served, service quality, length of haul for shipments, average shipment size, and cost of dock workers.

LTL carriers follow two general consolidation strategies with some variations: direct movement of freight between end-of-line terminals (*point-to-point* network) and movement of freight through intermediate (consolidation) terminals. For carriers using intermediate terminals for most shipments, there are two network strategies: *hub-and-spoke* and *pulse-point*.

Hub-and-Spoke Networks

For carriers moving shipments in lanes that require multiple days and for carriers with greater geographic scope, efficiency of linehaul operations is of greater importance. For these carriers, shipments often travel through three or more terminals on the way to their destination in order to build lane density and improve the efficiency of linehaul operations. The third terminal in addition to the origin and the destination terminals is an intermediate terminal.

Historically, national LTL carriers have employed a hub-and-spoke network with end-of-line (EOL) terminals feeding and being fed by regional intermediate terminals.[21] A network using intermediate terminals is shown in

Figure 3.1. Traffic usually flows from end-of-line terminals, represented by letters
a-m in Figure 3.1, to an intermediate terminal to which the end-of-line terminal is
assigned (BB1 or BB2 in Figure 3.1). It is a distinctive feature of hub-and-spoke
networks (in comparison to pulse-point networks[22]) that each EOL normally
connects to exactly one hub, and never to more than two. From the first
intermediate terminal, traffic usually flows to a subsequent intermediate terminal
and eventually to another end-of-line terminal.[23] For example, traffic from EOL *f*
moving to EOL *g* will move via BB1 and BB2 in turn. For a carrier specializing in
long-haul LTL traffic, this system permits most movements to be in full trailers,
because large amounts of traffic can be consolidated. However, this system is
inefficient for shorter movements. The use of intermediate terminals often results
in freight moving in the wrong direction. An example of this would be freight
moving between EOL *f* and EOL *g* in Figure 3.1.

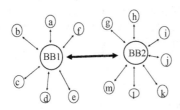   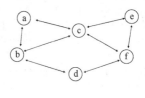

Figure 3.1   **Figure 3.2**
Hub and Spoke Network   **Point-to-Point Network**

The hub-and-spoke terminal networks used by national LTL carriers have
shipments with longer average lengths of haul than regional carriers and average
more than 1,000 miles per shipment (see Table 3.4). National LTL carriers also
have more terminals in their networks, both because of their larger geographic
scope and their smaller geographic coverage per terminal (about 9,500 square
miles per terminal versus 15,600 for regional LTL carriers). The hub-and-spoke
network permits consolidation of shipments for long-distance movements to occur
at a nearby hub terminal rather than at end-of-line terminals. Thus, end-of-line
terminals can cover a smaller area without sacrificing linehaul efficiency, even
though lane density in 1997 was 97 shipments for national LTL carriers versus
2,296 shipments for regional carriers.[24] By consolidating many shipments at a
limited number of regional hub terminals, national LTL carriers achieved higher
loading for linehaul vehicles in 1997 (14.4 tons per truck versus 6.9 tons per truck
for regional carriers). The very low lane density number for national carriers along
with the very high tons carried per truck in linehaul service is evidence of the
efficiency of the hub-and-spoke network.

Point-to-Point Networks

In contrast to national LTL carriers, many regional LTL carriers are able to consolidate freight without the use of intermediate terminals. They have historically used a point-to-point network (see Figure 3.2). Direct movement between end-of-line terminals has two advantages. First, direct movements are faster because freight doesn't have to be handled at intermediate terminals. Second, the lack of intermediate handling saves money on expenses for dock operations. Because regional carriers compete in the market for short-haul LTL freight, overnight delivery is a requirement of service and revenue per ton-mile is higher ($0.73 versus $0.24 for national LTL carriers, shown in Table 3.4). These carriers can build density for linehaul operations by having larger terminals covering larger geographic areas.

This strategy helps in two ways. First, a network with larger terminals is a network with fewer terminals. With fewer terminals in the network, each origin terminal has fewer destinations to ship to. Second, terminals covering larger areas have more shipments available for linehaul operations. The result of these two factors is increased freight density for linehaul lanes. However, illustrating again the nature of the tradeoffs between efficiency in one part of LTL operations versus another; larger local service areas generally reduce pickup and delivery efficiency by increasing stem-time. Thus, using larger local service areas lowers linehaul costs while increasing P&D costs. Additionally, point-to-point networks generally have less efficient linehaul operations than hub-and-spoke networks, because such networks provide less opportunity to consolidate shipments, even with larger terminal areas. Even so, in 1997, the average regional carrier and the average interregional carrier both had operating ratios lower the average national carrier (88%, 94%, and 97% respectively), even though linehaul operations were substantially more efficient for national carriers.

A point-to-point network has several other advantages. First, traffic will travel out of route less often, because it does not have to go through an assigned intermediate terminal that may or may not be in its route. Second, the lack of intermediate terminals permits more flexible adjustment of over-the-road operations (including pickup cutoff times)[25] to respond to changes in demand or customer needs. Finally, the lack of extra handling (no intermediate terminals) permits longer overnight service lanes. A disadvantage of point-to-point operation is the difficulty in obtaining full loads to move over-the-road. To some extent, this problem is balanced out by lower total terminal costs, although costs per terminal may be higher.

The use of direct shipments between terminals does not preclude the consolidation of freight from multiple terminals. Even when dedicated intermediate terminals are not used, traffic can also be consolidated by picking up and setting off freight at multiple locations while traveling from one end of the system to the other.

As regional LTL carriers have expanded into interregional and national LTL traffic, they have added dedicated break-bulk facilities to their terminal networks. Barks (1986) described how regional trucking companies are extending their hauls through 'hand-offs' between regional LTL carriers. Traffic interchanged between regional LTL carriers will typically move through a break-bulk facility at the point of interchange. For example, USF Holland did this with freight from other United States Freightways' companies at Kalamazoo, Michigan in the mid-nineties.

Pulse-Point Networks

A pulse-point system is a hybrid that combines the efficiency of hub-and-spoke with the flexibility of point-to-point. In contrast with the hub and spoke system, the end-of-line terminals do not have a single dedicated hub terminal through which they route freight. Instead, each end-of-line terminal may have several terminals which it uses as intermediate terminals, or accumulation points, when transferring freight. In addition, pulse-point linehaul operations are timed so that all drivers arrive at the accumulation point terminals almost simultaneously. The drivers then become dock workers temporarily, to transfer the freight between trailers, after which they return to their home terminals.

The name pulse-point refers to the timing of freight in and out of intermediate terminals which acts like the pulse of linehaul operations. Pulse-point provides advantage in its flexibility (freight can be routed through different terminals), its scalability (no dedicated dock workers are needed), and its simplicity (trucks and drivers used in linehaul operations always stay in balance, because they return to their home terminal at the end of each run). The challenge of pulse-point comes from its time constraints. For pulse-point to work, all freight must arrive within a narrow time window at intermediate terminals. This necessitates hard cut-off times for picking up freight in the afternoon (sometimes relatively early). It also makes long-distance lanes harder to handle reliably. Some carriers using pulse-point have used meet-and-turn to create high speed links over longer distances between very distant pulse-point accumulation points.

Other Network Factors

LTL carriers can also build density for linehaul moves in other ways. Some LTL carriers avoid the use of break-bulk terminals in longer-haul shipments by participating only in high density traffic lanes[26] or by handling larger shipments. Although such strategies can be useful in geographic expansion, the market available for such operations is limited and these carriers would have problems trying to serve lower density traffic lanes (Keaton 1996).

LTL firms may also obtain efficiencies though the flexible use of labor. Many companies, both union and non-union, use P&D drivers to sort freight at end-of-line terminals. Some firms also use drivers to sort freight at intermediate terminals.[27] At end-of-line terminals, it is common for drivers to load their own freight because drivers often plan their own route. This may be less desirable where P&D routes have longer stem times, due to problems with hours of service. Some regional LTL carriers use existing end-of-line terminals as intermediate terminals in the evening and cross-dock[28] freight between trailers from different end-of-line terminals (Swan 1995). Such terminals are operated primarily as break-bulks in evening hours due to the shorter distances involved with regional LTL traffic. Such facilities can use drivers, or part-time cargo handlers to unload, sort, and reload freight. Using drivers to move freight can be effective for shorter-haul movements because drivers have time to drive from an end-of-line terminal to the intermediate terminal, unload the freight, load freight for the end-of-line terminal, and drive back. For longer-haul moves, over-the-road drivers are restricted by hours-of-service laws. National carriers with their longer distances may not be able to time arrivals to coincide as effectively and mostly use full-time dock workers at intermediate terminals.

Technology and Productivity

While many of the technologies that have been used to improve the productivity of TL carriers are also used by LTL carriers, they are used to answer fundamentally different question. While TL carriers use information technology (IT) to answer the question '*where is my truck*,' the question for LTL firms is '*what is on my truck*.' LTL over-the-road drivers follow generally fixed routes and leave at scheduled times. Arrival times only vary in the case of accident or unexpected travel delay and IT equipment, such as global positioning systems, provides less value to LTL firms than to TL carriers. LTL carriers have however invested heavily in systems that can track shipments as they move through the network. Most systems use bar-codes on shipments, freight docks, trailers, and employees to track shipments and to enhance the productivity of operations. This information can be used in all phases of LTL operation: P&D, Linehaul, and Terminal/Sort.

P&D Technology and Productivity

Pickup and delivery operations can be better planned if end-or-line terminals know exactly what is coming to them for morning delivery and which truck each shipment is on. Planning operations for the upcoming day cannot begin until this information is received. Knowledge of the make-up of inbound traffic can be used for two major purposes. First, it can be used to design P&D runs for the upcoming day. This promises to eventually ease the terms of the trade-off between dock work and delivery work. As IT applications permit greater visibility of inbound shipments, it will become more cost-effective to provide increasingly intelligent computer assistance for the assignment and ordering of delivery stops. This will allow managers to move beyond the assignment of shipments to quarters or thirds of a delivery trailer and will improve load planning. Many firms studied in the UMTIP LTL Case Study were experimenting with algorithms to allocate shipments to routes and/or to design daily routes to make P&D drivers more productive. Although such algorithms hold great promise, they do not currently incorporate driver knowledge about customers and road conditions. They also do not account for the value that customers place on having the same driver show up at the same time every morning. However, the increased customer insistence on appointments for pickups and deliveries and the expanding product line for LTL carriers is placing great pressure on LTL firms to develop more sophisticated IT systems which avoid requiring drivers to be two places at once or require multiple drivers to serve the same area.

One firm in the UMTIP LTL Case Study accomplished this task by using straight trucks to deliver freight close to its terminals. By using smaller trucks, drivers can make two or more delivery runs in one morning. When such operations are anticipated, freight inbound to the end-of-line terminal can be loaded with later deliveries in the nose of the trailer so that less dock space is needed to process inbound freight, because not all inbound freight needs to be unloaded at one time. A possible disadvantage is that multiple deliveries runs are not feasible where long stem-times exist.

The second use for timely data on the make-up of inbound traffic for end-of-line terminals is the positioning of trailers at the dock to minimize the distance that freight moves when it is transferred from inbound trailers to outbound P&D trailers (and vice versa).

Information technology is also critical in capturing actual driver time to move from customer to customer and driver time unload each shipment. LTL carriers use shared production. Effectively allocating the cost of P&D drivers and trucks to each shipment can only be accomplished with sophisticated systems that track both driver activity and shipment status in real-time. The importance of getting this right in a competitive marketplace cannot be overemphasized.[29] When pickups and deliveries are matched with time (and miles) between customers, as well as time at customers, accurate cost information can be developed at a shipment level.

P&D drivers often use PDA (personal digital assistant) like devices, similar in many ways to the devices employed by UPS and FedEx drivers, to capture information on time spent, proof of delivery, and other data associated with shipments. Complete and timely data on pickups is critical to the efficiency of outbound linehaul operations. One firm, Viking Freight, now part of FedEx Freight, announced in 1999 it was moving towards full package – as opposed to shipment – tracking, using their handheld digital devices as part of the process of following freight through their system (Schulz, 1999).[30] For competitive reasons IT of this sort is becoming more critical to the efficiency of P&D operations.

Productivity of P&D operations is often measured in stops per hour, tons per hour, and shipments per hour. While no public data is available on stops per hour, LTL tons per hour and LTL shipments per hour can be calculated from existing data for many years. Many firms in the UMTIP LTL Case Study used a composite productivity measure for P&D employees. Such measures estimated the time necessary for the work done by the P&D driver (including dock work) and the number of hours necessary to perform the work.[31] These estimates could be then compared to actual time taken. Performance is typically measured on the terminal level. Table 3.6 shows average LTL shipments per P&D hour for several years between 1984 and 2001 for which data is available. Maximum productivity is attained in 1992 (1.20 shipments per P&D hour). By 1998 productivity has fallen to 1.00 shipments per P&D hour. LTL tons handled per P&D hour (shown in Table 3.9) also declined between 1992 and 1998 (from 0.58 to 0.51). Even with the decline, the measure is still above what it was shortly after deregulation 0.45 tons per hour. There are several possible explanations of this decline. First, the deregulation of intrastate trucking may have resulted in more carriers serving each local market, with each carrier getting a smaller piece of the pie. The resulting reduction in shipment density (shipments per square mile of service area) would reduce productivity. Second, increased use of appointment deliveries and time-definite deliveries may also have reduced productivity substantially during this period. Finally, the expansion of the interregional market segment by the growth of regional carriers may have come at the expense of P&D efficiency.

Table 3.6   Annual Industry Performance

YEAR	Ships per P&D Hr.	Tons per P&D Hr.	Tons per LH Mile	HW Mile per Pwr Unit	Ships per Office Emp.
1984	1.16	0.45	12.5	50,613	NA
1985	1.13	0.46	12.3	47,924	NA
1986	1.11	0.47	12.5	49,584	NA
1987	1.16	0.49	12.5	50,213	NA
1988	1.16	0.51	13	45,492	2,185
1989	1.18	0.53	12.7	45,140	2,191
1990	1.18	0.54	12.9	46,254	2,279
1991	1.20	0.56	13.1	47,578	2,226
1992	1.20	0.58	13.1	48,432	2,346
1993	NA	NA	13	48,896	2,427
1994	NA	NA	13.2	49,315	2,333
1995	NA	NA	12.4	50,554	2,437
1996	NA	NA	12.3	52,762	2,589
1997	NA	NA	12.3	53,732	2,495
1998	1.00	0.51	11.7	52,077	2,625
1999	0.99	0.49	12.3	50,916	2,901
2000	1.08	0.55	11.9	50,812	2,956
2001	1.02	0.51	11.3	49,273	2,959

Source: ATA (1985-2002).

Linehaul Information Technology

Optimization of over-the-road operations can usually be accomplished in the short-term by minimizing miles driven and trucks used. This is true for point-to-point networks, pulse-point networks, and for hub-and-spoke networks. However, the task of scheduling and coordinating linehaul operations is made more difficult by several factors. There exists significant daily, weekly, and monthly variation in shipment volume, shipment origins, and shipment destinations. The position of drivers (and trucks) at the beginning of the evening, changes day-to-day (except with pulse-point). All movements of freight to EOL terminals, need to be completed in time for AM deliveries. Linehaul drivers and equipment need to finish their shift positioned for the next evening's operations (except with pulse-point). Finally, most drivers need to return to domiciles at the end of specific time periods, usually weekly.

Point-to-point networks are the most difficult to dispatch. This is because choices are numerous, both in terms of how freight will move, but also in terms of which driver will move which shipments. Pulse-point networks are easier to dispatch because the choice of intermediate terminals through which any shipment may move through is limited to very few terminals. The fact that drivers meet and turn complicates dispatching somewhat as does the possibility of moving freight directly between two terminals (as opposed to moving via an intermediate terminal).

Hub-and-spoke networks have even more limited choices and are the easiest to operate on a nightly basis. However, intermediate terminals are often bypassed when sufficient freight exists for direct moves, making the job of balancing equipment and drivers more difficult. Whichever type of network an LTL carrier operates, its information system must perform two tasks to optimize linehaul operations. First, the information system must rapidly collect and process shipment information to be used in dispatching linehaul operations. Second, the information system must estimate the volume, origins, and destinations of the remaining freight that is not yet entered into the carrier's system. This ability permits carriers to make multiple cuts[32] at the evening's operating plan. The multiple cuts are useful for helping end-of-line terminal managers plan and begin the loading of outbound trailers before the evening's plan is finalized.[33] Additionally, preliminary plans are useful in assuring that adequate resources are available moving projected freight.

During the UMTIP LTL Case Study, we found carriers with pulse-point networks and point-to-point networks were developing automated systems for dispatching drivers. While current dispatchers proved to be good at their jobs, many firms worried about the risk associated with the increasing age of hard-to-replace linehaul dispatchers or thought that optimizations systems could provide lower cost and/or quicker solutions. Carriers using hub-and-spoke systems had already developed simulation models to determine the best way to move freight that bypassed normal routing through intermediate terminals (Braklow, et al. 1992).

In addition to dispatch software, most firms in the UMTIP LTL Case Study used software for linehaul routing. However, most firms still used dispatchers for planning linehaul operations. Software was predominantly used for determining mileage and the shortest route.

Efficiency of linehaul operations can be measured in several ways: tons carried per truck, empty highway miles as a percentage of total highway miles,

miles per power unit, and revenue per power unit. As previously described, these metrics will be different for firms using a hub-and-spoke network versus a point-to-point network. Linehaul loading efficiency for the industry reached a peak 1994 of thirteen tons per truck (see Table 3.6). Since 1994, the measures have fallen to just over eleven tons per truck in 2001.

Profitability has not, however, followed the same trend. There are at least two potential reasons. One is that, as with the trade-off between dock and delivery efficiency, there is also a trade-of between local terminal and linehaul efficiency. Some firms may be choosing a different location on this frontier, accepting lower linehaul efficiency in return for gains in local terminal operations. More likely, however, is that the overall traffic mix is shifting towards more short distance higher-speed shipments, as regional and interregional carriers appear to be mostly responsible for this decline in the aggregate figure.

In terms of miles per power unit, efficiency has varied quite a bit over the years, but has remained near 50,000 miles per year for each power unit owned (shown in Table 3.6).[34] The peak of 53,732 miles per power unit was reached in 1997 and has since dropped to under 50,000 in 2001.[35] Carriers have used a wide variety of policies to attain this improvement seen before 1997. The early policy of using one fleet for P&D and one fleet for linehaul has been largely replaced with a policy of dual-use tractors.[36] The use of team drivers has permitted tractors to stay on motion for longer periods on long-distance moves. Economic leasing deals have permitted carriers to adjust fleet sizes dynamically to reflect business cycles or to enable easy expansion. On the other side, the increased use of owner operators and intermodal has increased the proportion of power units that are used primarily for P&D, thus decreasing the linehaul miles traveled per power unit.

Dock Information Technology and Productivity

Intermediate terminals can also increase their efficiency by planning their operations in advance to equalize workload for dockworkers and to minimize work. This can be done by effective planning of the order of work and by positioning inbound trailers close to the outbound trailers into which the inbound freight will be loaded. Additionally, just like in P&D, dock productivity and cost can be more accurately measured when freight movements are accurately tracked. Generally this is done by registering the starting location, ending location, shipment, and worker involved with each movement of freight on a dock. Currently, this is usually done by scanning bar-codes for shipments, employee IDs, and equipment, but radio frequency ID tags may replace bar-codes in the near future. Given some time standards for unloading trailers, loading trailers, and moving freight, estimated time for allocated work can be generated and compared to actual time. While individual employee productivity can be measured in this way, such measures are more meaningful on a terminal level, due to the volatility of individual measures. Public metrics for dock productivity are unavailable because firms using combination dock/P&D driver employees typically do not report hours spent in each activity accurately. Also, while the number of tons and shipments handled by a firm is reported, the number of times that the shipment is handled is not. Another measure of dock productivity tracked by firms is the percentage of shipments that are over, short, or damaged (OS&D ratio). Terminal handling is known to increase damage and greater handling should be associated with greater damage. Some firms do not use linehaul drivers for handling freight because they think this would increase their OS&D ratio, while other firms regularly used linehaul drivers for sorting freight at intermediate terminals to enhance productivity.

Back Office Productivity

Although drivers and dock workers make up the bulk of LTL employees, there are significant numbers of office workers as well. Table 3.6 shows how office worker productivity (measured as shipments per office worker) has changed between 1988 and 2001.[37] The measure has moved generally upward, increasing approximately twenty percent in the ten years between 1988 and 1998. In 1999 however, the measure jumps from 2,626 shipments per office employee to 2,905 shipments per office employee, or a jump of over ten percent in one year. Nor does this change appear to be a fluke. Shipments per office employee remained relatively steady for 2000 and 2001. While the reason for this dramatic jump in office worker productivity is now known, possibly firms dramatically improved office productivity when they replaced legacy information systems to avoid possible problems associated with the year 2000 (Y2K).

Firm Productivity

Because different LTL operations represent cost trade-offs for firms and because carriers serve different markets, measuring productivity is difficult and can be risky. However, both comparing partial productivity measures between similar carriers and comparing total productivity measures on a firm level have validity. Two firm level measures of total productivity used by many researchers are operating ratio and earnings before interest and taxes divided by total assets (EBIT/TA). Of the two measures, EBIT/TA is a better measure of firm performance because it provides some measure of return on assets. Using data reported to the Bureau of Transportation Statistics between 1990 and 2001, we found EBIT/TA (higher numbers were related to higher return on assets) positively and significantly associated with:[38] Average length of haul ($p < .001$), revenue per power unit[39] ($p < .001$), linehaul miles per power unit ($p < .01$), percent of tons coming from LTL shipments ($p < .05$), average shipment weight ($p < .01$), revenue per employee ($p < .001$), shipments per non-operating employee ($p < .01$), revenue per non-operating employee ($p < .001$) and tons per P&D hour worked ($p < .05$). EBIT/TA was not significantly associated with the number of LTL shipments handled per P&D hour.

The UMTIP LTL Case Study also compared unionized firms to non-union firms. Union firms appeared to more productive in the UMTIP LTL Case Study with revenue per employee being significantly higher than non-union firms. Firm measures such as EBIT/TA and operating ratio were better for non-union firms, but the difference was not significant due to the limited sample size of the UMTIP LTL Case Study. The only significant difference[40] between the two groups for wage rates and benefits was the ratio of benefits to wages (higher for union firms). New (non-union) firms often use defined contribution pension plans and cheaper health plans, thus gaining a competitive edge over union firms.

Equipment

LTL companies that re-handle the majority of their shipments at intermediate terminals often move freight over-the-road in 28-foot trailers (short trailers) rather than 48 or 53-foot trailers.[41] The use of short trailers is advantageous for many reasons. Twenty eight-foot trailers are easy to maneuver in urban areas for pickup and delivery service. Multiple short-trailer semi-trucks often can carry more freight than a single long trailer. In some states semi-trucks can be operated with three 28-foot trailers (triples), further increasing the amount of cargo that can be hauled. Most importantly, use of short trailers reduces cargo handling at intermediate terminals when an entire trailer is loaded with freight to a single destination. Short trailers also have disadvantages. First, they cannot handle large TL shipments in a single trailer. Second, the process of hooking trailers together (using a dolly) is much more difficult than hooking a tractor to a trailer.

Freight handling provided interesting comparisons between firms studied in the UMTIP LTL Case Study. Some firms desired loose freight because is permitted them to load trailers 'high and tight.'[42] Other firms eschewed loose freight for palletized freight to improve freight handling. One carrier had a rather sophisticated method of seeking out freight that was easy to handle and paid more per ton-mile. Many firms had a variety of material handling equipment on freight docks, due to the diversity of freight that moves via LTL carriers including: fork lifts, pallet jacks, four-wheel carts, Johnson bars, rollers, two-wheel hand carts, drum dollies, and other similar equipment. Many carriers also used decking in trailers to increase productivity of all operations. Some carriers still used draglines[43] at major intermediate terminals, although most did not. It appears that each carrier adapts it equipment and procedures to the market in which it serves.

Competitive Environment

The post-deregulation environment for LTL motor carriers can be characterized as one of continual change. The relaxing of regulations in the late 1970s and early 1980s led to a dramatic reorganization of the industry (Kling 1990; Burks 1999). The majority of the incumbent LTL firms failed, and survivors grew to larger geographic scope, as both national and regional incumbent firms filled in gaps in their terminal networks and expanded their geographic coverage. Entry in LTL also became possible with deregulation, but almost entirely at a small geographic scope.[44] However, firms that entered early after deregulation and consistently invested in expanding their territory have grown over time to larger scope. They have done so while building networks that are optimized for high speed short-haul shipments, a service which has seen significant growth due to the logistics revolution.

Other firms have tried to expand by moving into new markets. Several regional carriers have attempted to become national carriers, but the complications with reconciling regional carriers' need for speed of movement with national carriers' emphasis on minimizing the cost of movement have caused such carriers to serve one or both of these markets poorly (Isidore 1997). The operations of combined regional/national carriers are also impeded by problems of integrating the network structure needed for regional traffic (usually point-to-point) with the hub-and-spoke network needed for long-haul traffic. Wang Chiang and Friedlaender (1985) showed that firms that handled both short-haul and long-haul LTL freight were not as efficient as firms that exclusively hauled either short-haul traffic or long-haul traffic. Swan (1997) showed that market expansion was associated with greater risk of firm failure for short-haul LTL firms.

Two more recent developments may provide a way to successfully serve both long-haul and short-haul markets. First, the pulse point network structure appears to provide a way to effectively merge short-haul lanes with long-haul lanes, although the requirement that trucks arrive at transfer points simultaneously adds considerable complexity. The other development is the merger of Yellow Transportation with Roadway Express. While it is not entirely clear how this merger will work, it could be that each firm will devote its network to different markets: long-haul versus short-haul, loose versus palletized freight, and/or expedited versus standard delivery.

More recently, the LTL environment has been undergoing further changes: shippers have changed their shipping patterns and shipment demographics; there has been increased competition from other types of carriers has increased; and shippers have favored LTL carriers that serve more origins and destinations.

Shipment Demographics

Deregulation of the trucking industry dramatically lowered the cost of shipping goods relative to GNP and other logistics costs (Delaney 1995; Boyer and Burks 2004). This has made it possible for shippers to replace inventory with more transportation in the form of, smaller, more frequent shipments, shipments over greater distances, and more use of premium transportation.

Increased use of just-in-time (JIT) manufacturing has also changed the nature of shipping. JIT programs often decrease shipment size and increase shipment frequency, thus increasing transportation cost per unit and encouraging suppliers to locate production nearer the point of demand (Gupta and Bagchi 1987). This situation has reduced the average length of haul for LTL shipments (USDOC 1994), but not for LTL carriers.[45]

Increased Competition

Although the number of shipments under 10,000 pounds has surely increased over the last twenty years, LTL carriers have failed to participate in much of this growth. Real dollar revenue for large, for-hire LTL firms declined between 1984 and 1993 while ton-miles increased slightly during the same period (ATA 1985, 1994). In contrast, large TL firms saw their revenue (in real dollars) and ton-miles more than double during the same period (ATA 1985, 1994).

The LTL carriers that emerged as the largest players at the national level in LTL after deregulation (ABF, Consolidated Freightways, PIE Nationwide, Roadway Express, and Yellow Freight System), focused initially on competing with each other, and not with the regionals. An 'arms race' in terminal counts left the three largest LTL carriers (Consolidated, Roadway, and Yellow) with 600-terminal networks that were structured to provide low-cost long-haul LTL movements, with comprehensive geographic coverage. However, as the competitive environment changed, these firms either failed (PIE in 1991, Consolidated in 2002), or restructured to meet growing regional (and national) competition, first by cutting their terminal counts to 400 or fewer to cut transit times (and cost) in the 1990s, and then restructuring their inter-terminal line-hauls to do the same thing again on even shorter lanes in the new century.

Competition between LTL truckers, TL truckers, package carriers, air express companies, railroads, freight brokers, and third-party logistics providers has impeded revenue growth for LTL carriers. Small shipments have been captured by package carriers and air express companies, while larger shipments have been targeted by TL carriers and consolidators who pool larger LTL shipments into a single TL shipment. As a result of this increasing competition, the market for LTL carriers has shrunk to shipments that range from 300 to 2,800 pounds (Schulz 1991a).[46]

Truckload carriers have attracted freight that has traditionally been hauled by LTL carriers. This competition centers on shipments greater than 3,000 pounds (Schulz 1991a). Truckload carriers and consolidators are often able to consolidate a few such shipments going in the same direction into a truckload, without the use of terminals. Many software packages for reducing logistics costs can actively identify LTL shipments that can be efficiently pooled to be handled by TL carriers. Occasionally, TL carriers that need a backhaul to avoid moving equipment empty will accept a single small shipment at marginal cost.

Competition has also increased in long-haul and short-haul LTL markets. Long-haul shipments are attractive to consolidators because they offer opportunities to use lower-cost TL carriers. Freight brokers often perform this service on a local basis in major metropolitan areas. Larger companies are using third parties to consolidate both inbound and outbound long-haul transportation through distribution and consolidation centers. Some regional LTL carriers participate in long-haul LTL freight by making truckloads of LTL freight going to major metropolitan areas, to be delivered by local cartage companies.[47] The competitive situation for long-haul LTL carriers appears to be improving in 2004 as new hours-of-service regulations have caused TL carriers to begin charging for the detention of trucks by customers. The pooling of multiple shipments is becoming less economical and some of the traffic is moving back to national LTL carriers (Schulz 2004), but the future is uncertain (Schulz and Cassidy 2004).

Competition for short-haul LTL freight has also increased. Many TL carriers and third-party logistics providers are collecting LTL freight for automobile companies, previously carried by for-hire LTL firms, in regular TL 'milk runs.'[48] Third-party logistics providers have been able to turn these LTL moves into regular traffic that can be handled efficiently by trucks moving on a fixed route and schedule. The regular nature of these moves, the presence of a single consignee, and the lower labor costs of third party logistics providers make it feasible and cost effective to move these shipments without a terminal network.[49]

Although there is some evidence the short-haul, regional LTL market has experienced growth in traffic (Barks 1986; Feldman 1986; Harrington 1987; Schulz 1991b), the growth of regional LTL carriers is better explained as a result of geographic expansion and the continual reduction in the number of regional LTL carriers.[50] These two processes have taken several of the interregional LTL carriers to the verge of becoming national LTL carriers. For example, CF, Inc., spun-off its national LTL carrier (which later closed) and retained three regional LTL carriers (Con-Way Central, West, and South). These three regional LTL carriers offer regional service over almost all of the U.S. and coordinated service east of the Mississippi. They have moved aggressively into the long-haul market and, as a result, their average length of haul was around 500 miles in 1997.

One-Stop Shipping

The final environmental change in LTL trucking is the movement of shippers toward smaller numbers of larger vendors. Several trade publications have cited the desire of shippers to reduce the number of carriers they use (PUR 1993; Gentry 1993; Foster 1992; S&P 1994). The higher fixed transaction costs of closer relationships between customers and suppliers make reduction of the number of suppliers a necessity (Helper and Levine 1992). A carrier with broader geographic coverage permits shippers to reduce the number of carriers that they have to deal with, thus making that carrier more attractive to shippers (Kling 1990). This trend toward fewer transportation providers is influencing national LTL carriers to serve shorter-haul shippers and regional LTL carriers to become quasi-national LTL carriers and serve at least selected long-haul markets (Hoffman 1995).

The Future

Where is the LTL industry going? While predicting the future is risky, past trends may provide guidance. The economies of density present for LTL motor carriers provide a strong incentive for continued concentration. This was realized with the formation of the big 3 carriers: Yellow, Roadway and Consolidated Freightways. Increased concentration was initiated by inter-state deregulation and continued by intra-state deregulation. More recently, Consolidated Freightways closed and

Yellow merged with Roadway. The number of LTL carriers reporting to the BTS has declined from under three hundred in 1984 to about eighty in 2001.

More recently, other factors have favored increasing concentration. These include closer relationships between carriers and shippers, increasing use of information technology, and broader services provided from LTL carriers. Closer relationships between shippers and carriers are leading shippers to limit the number of carriers that they use. Closer relationships can lower transaction costs through greater use of electronic data interchange and/or web-based transactions, but the fixed IT costs of coordinating information systems, making contracts, and merging operations each relationship militates against shippers using more than a few LTL firms. The relationship between carrier and shipper has also gotten closer in order for carriers to provide customized services, for lower cost, often using dedicated equipment. Carriers now routinely offer value-added services such as warehousing, packaging, assembly, and labeling along with their transportation services.

Initially, shippers desired to use different types of LTL carriers depending on shipment distance to decide which to use. More recently however, there are signs that shippers are moving towards single carriers to handle all of their LTL shipments. Historically, local carriers have been best for overnight service; interregional carriers were best for movements more than overnight and national carriers provide efficient long-haul service. More recently, interregional carriers have begun to provide national service and national carriers may be targeting shorter-haul shipments. FedEx recently purchased Viking and American Freightways to provide national LTL to supplement their air freight, ground, and package delivery services. Can UPS be far behind in acquiring an LTL carrier? Could the recent Yellow/Roadway merger have been a defensive move as a response to a possible merger with UPS that would have left one of the two carriers out in the cold?[51] Merging LTL networks is tricky business as Viking, Spartan, Central, and Coles found out when their merger failed dramatically. Possibly Yellow and Roadway plan to develop separate networks for providing different services as previously mentioned. It is interesting that FedEx is putting together a multi-modal transportation company at this time. CSX tried to do this previously when it owned an airline, a barge company, and an ocean shipping company. Synergy never developed. Perhaps the systems necessary for handling air freight, packages, home deliveries, and LTL shipments are similar enough to provide significant economies of scale for information technology to make mergers attractive among these types of carriers.

And what will happen to the regional LTL carriers? Can they survive indefinitely serving smaller markets? Will they have to expand into national carriers? Will they associate themselves with national carriers like Roadway has done with New Penn or can they survive indefinitely as niche players in an ever shrinking world? Expect to see some hybrid networks in the future that have both terminals specialized for particular types of shipments and networks specialized for particular types of service. While it is clear that a single network cannot provide all services to all customers, there is no reason why an EOL terminal can be associated with more than one network. If and when this happens, it will be information technology that will make it possible.

Notes

1. Data on hours worked by dock workers and pickup and delivery drivers is unavailable for 1997, but is available for 1998.
2. The use of relatively older data was made necessary by changes in the scope of terminal information reported in the AMCD after 1997. Annual financial and operating statistics data collected by the BTS has improved in recent years. The continued availability of BTS data is critical to any future comprehensive study of the trucking industry.
3. This is an approximate calculation by the authors from the national summary report of the Commodity Flow Survey (CFS) for 1997 (US Census Bureau 1998) The CFS does not report shipment counts, but aggregate weights by weight category are reported, and a crude estimate can be computed by using the midpoint of each category as the average weight of shipments in that category.
4. US Census Bureau 1998 using same method described in footnote 2.
5. Some TL trucks carry a few smaller shipments that are traveling between the same general origin and destination. In this case, the truck may make multiple stops (stop-offs) to pickup or deliver freight. As with other TL moves, no terminal is involved.
6. The standard dividing line between LTL and TL shipment is drawn at 10,000 lbs. Though this represented about half the maximum load that could be carried at the time the definition was established by the ICC in the 1930s, and is less than a quarter of the maximum load now. It remains a useful distinction as long as it continues to be the case that the average shipment size of an LTL firm is below this threshold. Both TL and LTL firms haul some shipments in the size range that the other type of firm specializes in. As explained above, the distinction is in how production is organized: LTL firms haul enough smaller shipments that they require a network of terminals to aggregate and disaggregate small shipments into fuller loads for long-haul movement, whereas TL firms do very little freight handling except at customer docks.
7. Since LTL firms use networks of terminals, a firm with fewer than five establishments has at most 4 terminals, and this confines it to local service in a relatively small geographic area. Such a firm may be correctly classified in the long distance category if at least one of its terminals is in a different metropolitan area from the others, or if its primary business is providing the local pickup and delivery function to other firms that provide intercity movements for LTL freight loads.
8. Many smaller LTL firms were unable to adjust to the new environment and failed within a few years after 1980. The subsequent ending of all economic regulation of intrastate truck traffic at the end of 1994 led to another wave of expansion and failures of LTL firms.
9. Yellow Freight acquired Roadway Express in 2003, and at the time of writing is combining back office functions but operating the two terminal networks independently.
10. A ton-mile is the primary measure of freight transportation output. Ton-miles are significant because they are comparable across industry segments and modes of transportation. Unfortunately, such comparisons often ignore important differences in shipment characteristics and in service. One hundred ton-miles can represent one hundred tons hauled for one mile, ten tons hauled for ten miles, or any other combination of tons and miles whose product is one hundred.
11. As carriers have expanded coverage through expansion and partnering, the need for agents to provide local delivery has decreased. This have been the downfall of many firms which profited by delivering freight for other firms in remote areas or congested

metropolitan areas. One LTL firm visited as an UMTIP LTL Case Study made a conscious strategy of keeping a remote terminal open to deliver freight for other firms. Unfortunately for this carrier (now closed) and others like it, contracting firms have increasingly replaced agents with their own terminals and drivers. This is true, even though terminal networks often require pickup and delivery drivers to travel one hundred miles or more to make pickups and deliveries (Swan 1996).

12. These regions have been historically defined by the rate bureaus that served specific regions. These bureaus are similar to those generally given to various areas of the U.S., including Northeast, Mid-Atlantic, Southern, Central, Middlewest, Rocky Mountain, Western, and Pacific.

13. Interline service is a term which has its roots in regulation. Because operations for LTL carriers were limited by regulation, many shipments had an origin and destination which were not both served by a single motor carrier. Regulated carriers developed a practice of interchanging freight at designated cities (called gateways). Such traffic often traveled under a single rate (although individual carrier tariffs often affected the rate) using two or more carriers to move the shipment to destination. Deregulation reduced the need for interlining by permitting motor carriers to expand easily. Customers have reduced the use of interlining by demanding single carriers service. To some extent, interlining still exists where several carriers have banded together to provide quasi-single line service over large areas. Examples of carriers offering joint service include USF carriers, Con-Way carriers, Alvan and Putman (before Alvan bought Putman, and R&L Transfer (with Greenwood Motor Lines and Gator Freightways).

14. All data are from 1997, except measures on P&D productivity (using P&D hours). P&D hourly productivity data are from 1998, due to a lack of data for P&D hours from 1993 to 1997.

15. The term end-of-line terminal comes from the hub-and-spoke network description. However, the name fits any terminal that serves as a home base for local P&D operations.

16. The ATA data from 1984 to 1992 (and after 1998) shows an average of one shipment handled (inbound or outbound or two handling) per driver hour. Because a forklift can load and unload shipments in 1-10 minutes, considerable time must be spent preparing to deliver or receive shipments. This time is spent driving from shipper (or consignee) to shipper, handling paperwork for pickups, and waiting for a forklift (or loading dock space) to load or unload the truck. Increasing the number of shipments handled at one location or increasing the number of shipments handled in a small area will increase the productivity of pickup and delivery drivers.

17. Both shipments per hour and tons per hour are often tracked as performance indicators. This is because freight charges (and costs) are based on both the number of shipments and shipment weights. Ideally a driver with be able to deliver several pallets of freight at a single customer, with each pallet being a separate shipment.

18. This measure is an indication of more than just linehaul planning. It also is affected by the efficiency of the network structure employed by the firm, as well as the service provided. An old policy followed by many long-haul firms was to hold freight at terminals to generate full loads. This policy has been losing favor due to customer requirements for quick and dependable service.

19. The effective range of drivers is limited to between 400 and 600 miles.

20. However, since LTL firms pay higher wages on average than do TL ones, they have much lower turnover and relatively less difficulty in recruiting drivers compared to the typical TL firm. Partly this is due to the fact that union LTL drivers still command a large wage premium compared to TL employees. But many non-union LTL drivers

enjoy a modestly higher wage than is available in TL, and most have the opportunity to get home more often than long-haul TL employees.

21. These intermediate terminals are also called break-bulks, break-bulk terminals, and freight accumulation centers.

22. In pulse-point networks, EOL terminals are assigned to multiple intermediate terminals. Between any two EOL terminals, there is usually more than one intermediate terminal through which freight can be routed.

23. Where traffic levels are great enough or where quicker service times are needed, shipments may go directly from end-of-line terminal to end-of-line terminal or direct to a distant intermediate terminal (e.g. from EOL f to BB2. In other cases, shipments move through only one intermediate terminal (see Braklow, et al. 1992). In recent years, national carriers have reduced the number of end-of-line terminals and intermediate terminals in order to increase the percentage of shipments which move without use of an intermediate terminal and to decrease the number of intermediate terminals used for each shipment (Schulz 1994, 1995).

24. Lane density is the average number of shipments handled at each pair of terminals (shipments divided by number of terminals squared). Greater lane density permits carriers to run more full trucks directly between origin and destination more often.

25. This was an important strategic advantage for one interregional LTL carrier, who could pick up shipments much later in the afternoon or evening than competitors.

26. These carriers locate terminals in major metropolitan areas and specialize in traffic moving only between their own terminals. The available traffic base permits full trucks to be run between terminals and lowers costs for these carriers. The downside is that other carriers can also run full trucks without moving freight through intermediate terminals between major metropolitan areas as well, and can often match rates. As a result, this traffic is low-cost and low-revenue.

27. The job classifications built into the Teamster's National Master Freight Contract were often cited as a reason that few union carriers used this practice, which is a mainstay of regional firms that have pulse-point terminals. However, the most recent NMFA (2002) has a clause that permits flexibility in this regard for "premium" service, and both Yellow and ABF have announced in 2004 that they are exploring using this flexibility to enter overnight short-haul markets.

28. The term cross-docking refers to the practice of unloading freight from a truck and immediately loading it into another truck such as with the pulse-point system.

29. In a competitive marketplace, overpriced shipments will be taken by competitors while under-priced shipments will be captured from competitors. The result is losing profitable traffic and gaining unprofitable traffic.

30. The potential importance for pricing and planning of detailed stop-level data generated by PDA-type devices carried by drivers is hard to overemphasize. Using proprietary data from Burks found that shipment information explained less than half the variance in driver time.

31. The index created by Transportation Productivity Consultants (TPC) was used by several firms.

32. As information is updated and becomes more complete, the previous plan is revised as necessary.

33. Freight for points beyond the local hub terminal can be loaded in the nose of a trailer or can fill an entire 28-foot trailer to avoid the need to handle the freight at subsequent terminals.

34. This metric is (total motor miles – owner operator miles) / total power units owned or leased.

35. The metric declined significantly in 2001. However, this may have been a result of inefficiencies resulting form the terrorist attacks on September 11, 2001 or may be due to speculative buying new trucks prior to the new emissions controls that became mandatory in late 2002.

36. Some dedicated P&D units still exist for operating in restricted areas or for urban delivery. This isn't a problem because more power units are needed for P&D than are required for linehaul. Also, carriers operating point-to-point networks cannot plan on where all of the equipment will end up night-to-night.

37. Data from 1984-1987 appears to use a different definition for the employee fields and is excluded.

38. Not all fields are available for all years and obviously erroneous data points were excluded

39. A power unit is either a tractor or a straight truck.

40. Significant is measured as the p value at or below .05. Union annual wages were greater than non-union annual wages, but due to the sample, the difference was not significant.

41. Package carriers also use 28-foot trailers, but use mostly drop-frame 28-foot trailers due to the lack of palletized freight handled by package carriers.

42. The practice of fully loading trailers, high to the ceiling and tightly packing freight, in order to utilize all the available volume within the trailer.

43. Draglines are used to move carts containing loose shipments from one dock door to another. Carts are attached to a cable running in a loop around the freight dock (under the floor). We saw evidence of deactivated draglines at many LTL terminals in the UMTIP LTL Case Study.

44. The most prominent firm that ever tried large scale entry, Leaseway Corporation, failed in two and a half years.

45. Average length of haul for LTL carriers appears to be increasing rather than decreasing (ATA 1985-1992). It appears that many shipments for JIT programs have been captured by third party logistics providers and TL firms. The regular nature of these shipments permits these firms to handle them without using terminals. The lower wage scale of TL carriers makes LTL companies less competitive for this business.

46. Data from earlier years is not available. However, in the ATA (1985-1993) data for LTL carriers, the average size of LTL shipments grew (788 to 968 pounds) and the average size of TL shipments shrank (25,922 to 20,290 pounds) between 1984 and 1992. This does indicate a narrower range of shipments are being handled over time.

47. This practice was described by Cullen (1995) as "precision bombing."

48. Swan (1995) learned of one instance of this, both from the LTL carrier that lost the business and from the third-party logistics provider that took over the business.

49. In some cases, a destination terminal is provided where multiple customer locations (auto plants) are served. In these cases, the customer plants are closely located and the single terminal is still more efficient than a network of terminals used by most LTL companies (Swan 1995).

50. Although some national LTL carriers such as PIE Nationwide, Bowman Transportation, and Transcon have closed their doors, more than 100 of the LTL carriers that have failed since deregulation were smaller, regional LTL carriers.

51. A merger between one of these carriers with UPS seemed inevitable prior to the Yellow-Roadway merger. Unfortunately for these carriers, the weaker of the two would probably have been the most attractive target, so being second best might have been a viable strategy. Now UPS must merge with the combined company, take in ABF, or develop an LTL firm from scratch. Either way, a combined Yellow-Roadway is probably better positioned to compete than either firm was on its own.

References

AMCD (1984-1997). *American Motor Carrier Directory*. Atlanta, GA.

ATA (1985-2002). *Financial and Operating Statistics Data on Disk from ICC Form M1 reports*. Compiled by American Trucking Associations. Alexandria, VA.

Barks, J. V. (1986). 'Regional Trucking Checks In.' *Distribution*, 85(6): 28-36.

Belzer, M. H. (1995). 'Collective Bargaining After Deregulation: Do the Teamsters Still Count?' *Industrial and Labor Relations Review*, 48(4): 636-655.

Belzer, M. H. (2000). *Sweatshops on Wheels: Winners and Losers in Trucking Deregulation*. New York, New York, Oxford University Press, Inc.

Bowman, R. J. (1995). 'Moving Out of the Intermodal Void.' *Distribution*, 94 (April): 40-42.

Boyer, K. and S. V. Burks (2004). 'Which One was Driving? Productivity and Cost Trends in US Trucking, 1977-1977,' Michigan State University. Working Paper.

Braklow, J. W., W. W. Graham, S. M. Hassler, K. E. Peck, and W. B. Powell (1992). 'Interactive Optimization Improves Service and Performance for Yellow Freight System.' *Interfaces*, 22(1): 147-172.

Burks, S. V. (1999). *The Origins of Parallel Segmented Labor and Product Markets: A Reciprocity-Based Agency Model with an Application to Motor Freight*. Ph.D. Dissertation, University of Massachusetts at Amherst.

Campbell, B. G. (1987). 'Deregulation and the Motor Carrier Industry.' *Data Resources U.S. Review* (March): 24-29.

Cullen, D. (1995). 'Taking On The Sights.' *Fleet Owner*, 1995 (January): 43-51.

Delaney, R. V. (1995). 'The State of Logistics and Transportation – Fast Forward to the Year 2000.' *CLM Eastern Michigan Roundtable*. Detroit, Michigan.

Feldman, J. M. (1986). 'LTL Looks To Regionals.' *Handling and Shipping Management*, 27(3): 56-59.

Foster, T. A. (1992). 'The Multiple Benefit of Single Sourcing LTL.' *Distribution*, 91(11): 38-46.

Frailey, F. W. (1996, 11). 'Twenty-four Hours at Supai Summit.' *Trains*, 56(11): 38-51.

Gentry, J. J. (1993). 'Strategic Alliances in Purchasing: Transportation is the Vital Link.' *International Journal of Purchasing and Materials*, 29(3): 11-17.

Glaskowski, N. A. (1990). *Effects of Deregulation on Motor Carriers*. Westport, Connecticut, Eno Foundation for Transportation.

Gooley, T. B. (1995). 'LTL Truckers Add Intermodal to Menu.' *Traffic Management* (April): 43, 45.

Gupta, Y. P. and P. K. Bagchi (1987). 'Inbound Freight Consolidation Under Just-In-Time Procurement: Application of Clearing Models.' *Journal of Business Logistics*, 8(2): 74-94.

Harrington, L. H. (1987). 'Regional Trucking: Expanding the Horizons.' *Traffic Management*, 26: 58-63.

Helper, S., and D. I. Levine (1992). 'Long-term Supplier Relations and Product-Market Structure.' *Journal of Law, Economics and Organization*, 8(3): 561-581.

Hoffman, K. (1995). 'Two sides of the equation.' *Distribution*, 94 (July): 18-25.

Isidore, Chris (1997). 'Do Long-Haul, Regional Truckers have a Future Together.' *Journal of Commerce*, 10 April, 1997, Transportation, 1B.

Journal of Commerce (JOC) (2005). 'Union Pacific Cancels UPS Transcon Pact.' *Journal of Commerce*, 6 May, 2005, Logistics Section, WP.

Keaton, M. H. (1996). 'Economies of Density and the Less-Than-Truckload Motor Carrier Industry Since Deregulation.' *Journal of the Transportation Research Forum*, 26-40.

Kling, R. W. (1990). 'Deregulation and Structural Change in the LTL Motor Freight Industry.' *Transportation Journal*, 29 (Spring), 47-53.

Nebesky, William, B. S. McMullen, and M. K. Lee (1995). 'Testing for Market Power in the U.S. Motor Carrier Industry.' *Review of Industrial Organization*, 10(5): 559-576.

Perry, C. R. (1986). *Deregulation and the Decline of the Unionized Trucking Industry*. Philadelphia, PA: Industrial Research Unit. The Wharton School, University of Pennsylvania.

Powell, W. B. (1995). 'Finding the Yellow Brick Road.' Report (SOR-96-02). Princeton University.

PUR (1993). 'Truckers Face a Hard Road.' *Purchasing*, 115 (December 16): 39+.

Quinn, F. J. (1989). 'The Regionals: Carving Out a niche.' *Traffic Management*, 28 (July): 57-60.

Rose, N. L. (1985). 'The incidence of regulatory rents in the motor carrier industry.' *Rand Journal of Economics*, 16(3): 299-318.

Rose, N. (1987). 'Labor Rent Sharing and Regulation: Evidence from the Trucking Industry.' *Journal of Political Economy*, 95(6): 1146-1178.

Rothenberg, L. S. (1994). *Regulation, Organizations, and Politics: Motor Freight Policy at the Interstate Commerce Commission*. Ann Arbor, Michigan, University of Michigan Press.

S&P (1994). *Industry Surveys*. Standard and Poors.

Schulz, J. D. (1991a). 'Continued Change and Innovation Only Transport Certainty in 1990s.' *Traffic World*, 228 (November 18): 21,23.

Schulz, J. D. (1991b). 'Yield-Management Rate Strategies May Boost Truckers' Ailing Fortunes.' *Traffic World*, 228 (October 7): 33-34.

Schulz, J. D. (1994). 'Preston Starts SuperRegion; CF Cuts Service Times.' *Traffic World*, 240 (October 3): 44.

Schulz, J. D. (1995). 'Absolute shipper service demands driving growth in regional markets.' *Traffic World*, 243 (July 31): 36-42.

Schulz, J. D. (1999). 'Going High-tech.' *Traffic World*, 247 (November 29): 25.

Schulz, J. D. (2004). 'Hours of Leverage?' *Traffic World*, 252 (April 26): 21.

Schulz, J. D. and W. B. Cassidy (2004). 'Time Out!' *Traffic World*, 252 (July 26): 10.

Swan, P. F. (1995). Case Study Notes from Interviews with LTL executives from several firms.

Swan, P. F. (1996). Case Study Notes from Interviews with LTL executives from several firms.

Swan, P. F. (1997). *The Effect of Changes in Operations on Less-Than-Truckload Motor Carrier Productivity and Survival*. Ph.D. Dissertation, University of Michigan School of Business at Ann Arbor.

TM (1993). 'Third Party Success Stories: Doing What You Do Best.' *Traffic Management*, 31(7): 38-39.

Trunick, P. A. (1995). 'A Constant State of Change.' *Transportation and Distribution*, January, 47-50.

U.S. Census Bureau (1998). *1997 Commodity Flow Survey*. Washington DC, U.S. Dept of Commerce.

U.S. Census Bureau (2001). *Econ97 Report Series: Economic Census*. CD-EC97-1, Disc1E.

United States Senate (1980). Federal Restraints on Competition in the Trucking Industry: Antitrust Immunity and Economic Regulation. Washington, DC, Judiciary Committee, U.S. Senate: 1-351.

USDOC (1994). U.S. Industrial Outlook 1994, U.S. Department of Commerce.

Wang Chiang, J. S. and A. F. Friedlaender (1985). 'Truck Technology and Efficient Market Structure.' *Review of Economics and Statistics*, 67 (May): 250-258.

Chapter 4

The Package Express Industry:
A Historical and Current Perspective

Leslie S. Hough and Maciek Nowak

Introduction

The package express industry in the United States has evolved from its origins on bicycles on the streets of Seattle to its current position as a central player in today's internet driven supply chain. It is a central and dynamic element of the world economy, playing a critical role in the rapid movement of freight within an increasingly globalized economy. It "is a huge multi-billion dollar market that appears to be doubling in size every five years or so."[1]

It may also be revolutionizing the freight transportation industry. Our understanding of transportation has been based on a modal analysis in which firms specialize in a particular mode such as rail or trucking with considerable firm specialization even within modes. The largest package express firms have successfully combined air and truck transportation of small packages over the last twenty years. They are increasingly moving towards becoming integrated providers of a variety of trucking and air services as well as logistics services. The traditional organization of transportation may then be outdated.[2] Hopefully this chapter will help scholars and policy makers to consider the express package industry in a new way, and to see that the industry is having a transformative effect on freight transportation as a whole.

The package express (PE) industry is comprised of three segments: small parcels, overnight letters and courier services. The former two segments account for the majority of packages and revenue and are the focus of this study.[3] Although the term package express has been unchanged for many years, the weight of packages handled by PE firms has increased considerably over the last decade. For many years the maximum package size was about seventy-five pounds. In 1994 UPS moved into the lower end of the LTL freight segment by offering to take packages of up to 150 pounds. UPS has moved further into larger package sizes with its Less than Pallet Load hundred weight service, while Fedex's movement toward integrating package express and LTL services has also increased the size of the package which the firm is able to handle.

Many firms offer services in the small package and overnight letter segments of the industry, nevertheless, a few established companies dominate each segment. In 2000, FedEx accounted for 58.2% of the revenue from overnight letters generated in the United States, UPS earned 15.6% of revenue in this segment, while the United States Postal Service accounted for 12.2% of revenue. Airborne and DHL merged in 2002, in 2000 their combined total was 13.3%. The balance of the industry accounted for 0.6% of revenue. Again considering the United States, United Parcel Service (UPS) was the dominant firm in ground parcels weighing between two and seventy-five pounds, accounting for 63.9% of revenue. The only other significant competitors were FedEx with 18.8% of revenue and the USPS with 9.2% of revenue. The most competitive segment is small parcels, or those weighing less than two pounds. FedEx accounted for slightly more than one third of the revenue, UPS and the USPS each account for an additional 17.8% and DHL airborne accounted for 10.6% of revenue (see Table 4.1).

Table 4.1   Revenue Market Share in Package Express by Shape and Speed

Sub-market	Carrier						
	Airborne*	DHL*	Emery	FedEx	United Parcel Express	USPS	All Others
Overnight Letters	10.9%	2.4%	0.1%	58.2%	15.6%	12.2%	0.5%
Packages Under 2 lbs	9.7%	0.9%	0.1%	33.8%	17.8%	17.8%	3.6%
Packages 2 to 75 lbs	4.0%	0.9%	0.2%	18.8%	63.9%	9.2%	3.1%

*Since merged.
Source: From A. Robinson, Competition within the United States Parcel Delivery Market, distributed by the Association for Postal Commerce, Arlington, VA, February 5, 2003.

With close to $44 billion in total global revenues, the biggest player in the small package delivery business remains Deutsche Post World Net (DPWN). DHL, now under ownership of DPWN, generated $18.6 billion of total global revenue for the industry in 2003, with over 90% earned internationally, and an approximate 40% market share in international express, more than UPS and FedEx combined. UPS is second with $33.5 billion in global revenues, but with only $5.6 billion earned from international package delivery. FedEx comes in at third with $24.7 billion total revenues, $4.6 billion generated outside the U.S.

Despite ranking second in international delivery, UPS and FedEx dominate the world's largest domestic market, the $50 billion-a-year plus U.S. parcel delivery sector. With an estimated 70% of the market, they form a duopoly that has a strong grip on the industry. Although both firms have evolved effective means of delivering services, they are very different businesses.

UPS has a long-standing history in the parcel delivery business. Their reputation is built on years of experience, long known for being the "tightest ship in the shipping business." A company based on traditions, recognized the world over by their big brown Pullman trucks, UPS has many managers and planners who have started as warehouse employees or drivers, most notably former CEO Jim Kelly. This has led to a company culture that, while resistant to drastic change, fosters faithfulness among employees and customers alike. Although the drivers' strike in 1997 damaged the company, UPS has been able to use its strong reputation to slowly rebound and regain many lost customers.

FedEx is a newer entrant into the package delivery industry. The company was built on a set of innovative ideas for express delivery and this foundation has carried through to today. Over the last 40 years they have become the standard when a package has to "absolutely, positively" be there as quickly as possible. They are so synonymous with their service that the company name is used as a verb (as in to "FedEx" a package). A key to success at FedEx has been rapid adaptation to the needs of current and potential customers. They were the first company dedicated to overnight delivery, the first to offer Saturday delivery, the first to offer next day delivery by 10:30 AM, and the first to start Internet package status tracking services in 1994. But just as UPS has faced challenges, Fedex faces stagnation and decline in its core business, overnight letter delivery, as electronic transmission reduces the need to send copies of many documents.

In the following three sections, We present a detailed review of UPS and Fedex's history and report selected economic indicators of firm performance for the last decade. Additionally, UPS and FedEx are compared to the newest competitor in the U.S. market, DHL, and the United States Postal Service.

I. United Parcel Service

In 1907 two Seattle teenagers, Jim Casey and Claude Ryan, started the American Messenger Company. The company's messengers ran errands, delivered packages, and carried notes, baggage, and food from restaurants. They made most deliveries on foot and used bicycles for longer trips. The American Messenger Company was soon delivering small parcels for local retail stores and changed its name to Merchants Parcel Delivery. As trucks became more an integral part of the delivery process, the company expanded outside Seattle in 1919 with the acquisition of Oakland based Motor Parcel Delivery and changed its name to United Parcel Service.

In the early 1950s, UPS began the process of expanding its services by acquiring "common carrier" rights for the entire country over the objections of both the Post Office and other transportation providers.[4] When this process began, each state had separate authorization procedures to allow movement of packages within its borders and this resulted in multiple transfers between several carriers along a delivery route. Over three decades (1950s-1970s), UPS expanded its coverage, systematically obtaining authorization to ship between states. In 1975, UPS became the first package delivery company to serve every address in the 48 contiguous United States.

With growing demand for faster service, UPS entered the overnight air delivery business, and by 1985, UPS Next Day Air service was available in all 48 states and Puerto Rico. That same year, UPS entered a new era with international air package and document service, linking the U.S. and six European nations. In 1988, UPS received authorization from the Federal Aviation Administration (FAA) to operate its own aircraft, thereby officially becoming an airline, UPS Airlines. UPS Airlines was the fastest-growing airline in FAA history, formed in little more than one year with all the necessary technology and support systems. UPS Airlines is currently one of the 10 largest airlines in the United States.

In the early 90s, UPSnet, a global electronic data communications network, was developed to provide an information-processing pipeline for international package processing and delivery, which tracked 821,000 packages daily. In 1994, UPS.com went live, and consumer demand for information about packages in transit soared. The following year, UPS upgraded its website to allow customers to track packages in transport.

UPS has also significantly expanded the range of services offered over the last 10 years. Although the core of the business remained the distribution of goods and the information that accompanies them, by the early 90s UPS had begun to branch out and focus on new services (Figure 4.1). As UPS management saw it, the company's expertise in shipping and tracking positioned it to become an enabler of global commerce, and a facilitator of the three flows that make up commerce: goods, information, and capital.

In 1995 UPS Logistics Group was formed to provide global supply chain management solutions and consulting services based on customers' individual needs. UPS also acquired a company called SonicAir, making them the first company to offer same-day, "next flight-out" service. In 1998 UPS Capital was founded with a mission to provide a comprehensive menu of integrated financial products and services that enable companies to grow their business.

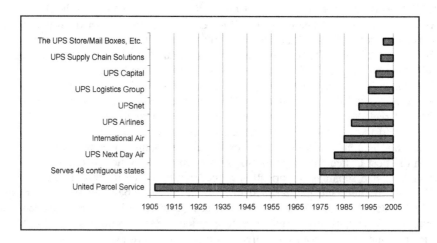

Figure 4.1 UPS Expansion

Until November 10, 1999, UPS had been employee owned and, as a consequence, had always been able to keep decision making within the tight knit organization. Rapid expansion and increasingly competitive conditions created a need for additional funds, and UPS acquired $5.47 billion in what was, at the time, the largest initial public offering in United States history. Although going public exposes the company to additional external influences and oversight from federal agencies such as the S.E.C., the cash acquired from the sales left the firm cash-rich and able to pursue strategic acquisitions and mergers.

UPS Supply Chain Solutions was formed in response to UPS customers increasing requests to utilize the expertise of the company in transportation and logistics. Supply Chain Solutions provides logistics, global freight, financial services, mail services, and consulting to enhance customers' business performance and improve their global supply chains. UPS Capital, UPS Logistics Group, UPS Freight Services, UPS Mail Innovations and UPS Consulting are all a part of UPS Supply Chain Solutions.

In 2001, UPS acquired Mail Boxes Etc, the world's largest franchiser of retail shipping, postal, and business supplies. Franchises located in the U.S. were renamed The UPS Store in 2003. With its 3,400 stores, UPS hopes to gain ground in the retail sector, but more importantly, to bring in corporate customers who do not have a regular contract with UPS and would like to make semi-regular shipments. Almost 80% of UPS and FedEx packages are discounted for high-volume shippers, infrequent shippers who do not receive these discounts produce significantly more revenue per package. UPS expects The UPS Store to grow to 5,000 outlets by 2007.

UPS's ground operations involve the pickup, sorting, line haul and delivery. The familiar brown Pullman trucks generally pick up packages in the afternoon, but tractor trailers may be used for pick-ups for larger customers. UPS has dozens of distribution hubs, which are the primary site for sorting. Packages may move through multiple hubs on their way to their final destination. Line haul operations between distribution centers are provided by tractor-trailers or, for long distances, trailers are moved by rail. Parcels are delivered in the morning by the same trucks used for afternoon pickups.[5] In contrast with the decentralization of its ground system, UPS's air freight system is centralized. UPS's primary airhub, the UPS WorldPort in Louisville Kentucky has 23,000 employees and can handle 300,000 packages hourly. There are six additional regional air hubs. The UPS airfreight system is integrated with its ground delivery system, and the same trucks that deliver ground freight deliver air parcels. The ground and air operations are supported by extensive technology operations. UPS has about 5,000 information technology employees and several hundreds of thousands of computers ranging from mainframes to workstations and PCs. In addition, the firm has 70,000 devices to provide real time information on deliveries and pick-ups.[6]

One of the more traumatic events in the recent history of the company was the fifteen-day work stoppage in 1997. The work stoppage was a consequence of long standing authoritarian labor relations practices at UPS, the political dynamics of the election campaign for the president of the Teamsters, miscalculations about the UPS's ability to operate during a strike, the system of labor law which applies to UPS, the reluctance of the federal government to intervene and careful planning and public relations efforts by the Teamsters. In all, it was largely favorable to the employees of UPS. The length of the work stoppage resulted in long-term loss of market share, which the company has only gradually recovered. A more in depth discussion of employment relations in package express is provided toward the end of this chapter.

Economic Indicators

Today, UPS operates an international small package and document network in more than 200 countries and territories, spanning both the Atlantic and Pacific oceans. Approximately 357,000 employees (317,000 U.S. and 40,000 International), 88,000 motor vehicles and more than 575 jets satisfy their transportation needs.[7] With its international service, UPS can reach over four billion people, twice the number of people who can be reached by any telephone network. Over 13 million packages and documents are transported per day, serving over 7.9 million customers per day.

The events of 9/11 and the concurrent economic downturn had an impact on net profit in 2001 (Table 4.2). Although revenues continue to grow, the profit margin has decreased considerably. Similarly, the strike in 1997 had a severe effect on the company's bottom line. Although the strike lasted less than a month, the repercussions are still felt today because some long time customers made a permanent switch to competitors and others moved from single to multiple sourcing their package express providers. The large drop in net income in 1999 was the result of a $2 billion payment of back taxes because of an unfavorable ruling. Much of this loss was recouped in 2002 when a court overturned part of the ruling, resulting in a spike in net income.

Another important indicator is the rapid growth in non-package revenue. This is revenue generated by the Logistics Group, UPS Freight Services, Supply Chain Solutions, and other service oriented divisions. UPS and FedEx have both gone beyond just delivering packages. They now aid in company decision-making regarding timing of deliveries, optimal routing and general supply chain alignment. For UPS more so than FedEx, non-package services are becoming an important, revenue generating division within the company.

The effects of the 1997 strike and of 9/11 are also apparent in UPS's annual shipments (Table 4.3) and Domestic Revenue (Table 4.2). The strike primarily involved drivers, resulting in a drop in the number of UPS Ground shipments and revenues in 1997. Ground shipments took three years to return to 1996 levels. The events of 9/11 and consequent legislation governing air travel resulted in increased costs related to air shipments. Most of the resulting losses were incurred in overnight and deferred shipments in 2001, although ground operations were also affected due to the overall economic downturn.

Table 4.2   Economic Indicators for United Parcel Service ($ millions)

	2003	2002	2001	2000	1999	1998	1997	1996	1995
Revenue:									
Domestic Package	25,022	23,924	23,997	24,002	22,313	20,650	18,868	18,881	17,773
International Package	5,561	4,680	4,245	4,078	3,718	3,399	3,067	3,074	2,958
Non-Package	2,902	2,668	2,079	1,418	841	739	523	413	314
Total Revenue	33,485	31,272	30,321	29,498	26,872	24,788	22,458	22,368	21,045
Operating Expenses	29,040	27,176	26,359	24,986	22,967	21,698	20,760	20,339	19,251
Operating Profits	4,445	4,096	3,962	4,512	3,905	3,090	1,698	2,029	1,794
Net Income	2,898	3,182	2,399	2,934	883	1,741	909	1,146	1,043

Source: United Parcel Service Form 10-K, 1999-2003.

Although the number of overnight shipments did not fall substantially, the stagnation in volume from 2001 to 2003 broke their prior steady ascent. The decline in domestic revenues from overnight service also reflects the large impact of 9/11 and the recession of the early 2001-2002. However, there was an increase in international shipments in 2000, after UPS had gone public and invested heavily in international capacity.

Table 4.3   United Parcel Service Annual Shipments (millions)

	Overnight	Deferred	UPS Ground	Total Domestic	International	Total
1994	148.1	158.2	2,506.5	2,812.8	N/A	N/A
1995	169.0	181.1	2,517.1	2,867.2	N/A	N/A
1996	193.0	193.8	2,543.8	2,930.7	N/A	N/A
1997	208.0	195.1	2,408.8	2,811.8	226.4	3,038.2
1998	238.3	198.9	2,449.8	2,887.0	250.4	3,137.4
1999	262.3	208.3	2,519.0	2,989.6	254.5	3,244.1
2000	283.3	230.2	2,624.1	3,137.6	290.8	3,428.4
2001	281.2	225.5	2,599.8	3,106.5	299.6	3,406.1
2002	280.0	225.5	2,548.2	3,053.7	305.7	3,359.4
2003	298.6	231.3	2,587.5	3,117.4	307.9	3,425.3

Source: United Parcel Service Form 10-K, 1999-2003.

II. Federal Express

Federal Express (FedEx) is a dramatic example of the dynamics of the express package industry; it is the second largest express package carrier in the world after UPS. In 1965, Yale University undergraduate Frederick W. Smith wrote a term paper about inadequacies of the passenger route systems used by most airfreight shippers. Smith wrote of the need for shippers to have a system designed specifically for airfreight that could accommodate time-sensitive shipments such as medicines, computer parts and electronics.

In 1973, Smith put his analysis to the test. He bought controlling interest in Arkansas Aviation Sales, moved the company headquarters to Memphis, Tennessee, and opened operations as Federal Express in 1973. FedEx then introduced an air transportation model with a hub concept that transformed the express package industry over three decades. The hub model involved collecting packages from across a wide geographical area, flying them to Memphis where a large, sophisticated and very fast sorting operation would direct them to the proper plane flying later in the night to a point near each package's intended destination. FedEx quickly became the dominant air carrier in the industry, and UPS responded by starting its own air service and hub system based in Louisville, Kentucky.

In the mid-1970s, Federal Express took a leading role in lobbying for air cargo deregulation that finally came in 1977. These changes allowed FedEx to use larger aircraft and spurred the company's rapid growth. Today FedEx Express has the world's largest all-cargo air fleet. The company entered its maturing phase in the first half of the 1980s. With an annual growth rate of about 40 percent, FedEx reported $1 billion in revenues in 1983, making American business history as the first company to reach that financial hallmark inside ten years of start-up without mergers or acquisitions. Following the first of several international acquisitions, FedEx began intercontinental operations in 1984 with service to Europe and Asia.

FedEx's focus on air transportation and rapid delivery has placed it at a cost disadvantage relative to UPS in its ground operations. UPS had a very dense ground delivery system prior to offering overnight and expedited delivery. Airfreight could be loaded into existing trucks for delivery without placing too great a burden on UPS's delivery system. Although the logistics of using the existing package delivery system for expedited services was complex, airfreight has been close to a pure value added service for UPS's ground operations. In contrast, FedEx had to maintain an extensive fleet of package cars and drivers dedicated to rapid delivery and pick up of packages. Maintaining such a system is expensive as, until recently, there has been no way to spread those expenses over other types of shipments.

In 1989, FedEx acquired Tiger International, Inc. The acquisition included routes to 21 countries, a fleet of Boeing 747 and 727 aircraft, facilities throughout the world and Tigers' expertise in international airfreight. China has clearly become the most dynamic economic power in the world over the last decade and more. FedEx obtained authority to serve China through its acquisition from Evergreen International Airlines in 1995 at a very fortuitous time given world economic growth trends.

The first evolution of the company's corporate identity came in 1994 when Federal Express officially adopted "FedEx" as its primary brand, taking a cue from its customers, who had long-referred to the company by the shortened name. The second evolution came in 2000 when the company was renamed FedEx Express to reflect its position in the overall FedEx Corporation portfolio of services. This also signified the expanding breadth of the FedEx Express-specific service offerings, as well as a FedEx that was no longer just overnight delivery. Today, FedEx Express is the largest operating company in the FedEx family, handling about 3.3 million packages and documents every business day.[8]

As indicated above, FedEx is led by FedEx Corporation, which provides strategic direction and consolidated financial reporting for six independent operating companies that compete collectively under the FedEx name worldwide: FedEx Express, FedEx Ground, FedEx Freight, FedEx Custom Critical, FedEx Trade Networks and FedEx Services. The majority of these divisions were established through acquisitions of other companies. Figure 4.2 displays the growth of FedEx through these acquisitions and the establishment of new operating companies.

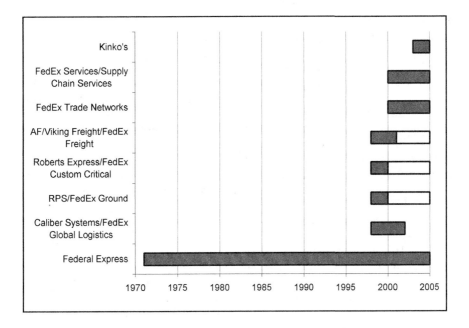

Figure 4.2 Federal Express Expansion

In 1998, FedEx acquired Caliber System, Inc., a leading provider of value-added transportation, logistics and related information services. Its operating companies included Roadway Package Systems, Inc. (RPS), a business-to-business non-express package carrier; Viking Freight, Inc., a supplier of regional freight service in the West; Caliber Logistics, Inc., a contract logistics provider; Roberts Express, Inc., a critical-shipment carrier; and Caliber Technology, Inc., a producer of system-wide information services. The acquisition of RPS almost immediately made FedEx a major player in the ground express package industry, which had been UPS' strength since its founding. RPS introduced bar codes to the business of delivering packages quickly, and began to introduce automatic sorting of packages. RPS was re-named FedEx Ground in 2000, and delivered over two million packages every business day in 2004.

FedEx took another step into the broader world of transporting goods with Viking Freight. Viking was a regional, less-than-truckload (LTL) freight carrier, focusing on service in the western United States. Shortly after the acquisition of Caliber, FedEx moved further into the LTL arena with its acquisition of American Freightways (AF) in 2001. Following this expansion of services, FedEx re-named Viking, "FedEx Freight West" and AF, "FedEx Freight East", to reflect their greatest geographical strengths. By acquiring and integrating these two existing freight companies, FedEx Freight became the largest U.S. provider of regional LTL freight services.

The acquisition of Roberts Express as part of Caliber System allowed FedEx to move toward a global and highly integrated presence in the express package industry. Roberts specialized in custom surface shipment, providing exclusive-use, non-stop service matching vehicle size to the customer's shipment in order to move goods faster and at a lower cost than airfreight. Roberts Express became FedEx Custom Critical in 2000.

The final piece of the Caliber System acquisition was the combination of Caliber Logistics and Caliber Technology to create FedEx Global Logistics. In 2001, this group was realigned under FedEx Supply Chain Services, which is a part of the broader FedEx Services. FedEx Supply Chain Services provides transportation and logistics management, consulting services and other customized supply chain solutions so customers can maximize potential and minimize costs. FedEx Services is responsible for the data management and networking expertise behind the package tracking capabilities used by FedEx Express and FedEx Ground, as well as the e-commerce services that today's global marketplace demands.

The next step in FedEx's drive to cover a very broad range of the goods shipping business worldwide was its acquisition in 2000 of Tower Group International, which had focused on international trade logistics and the information technology required to serve that sector in a state of the art manner. Information technology has become a priority for FedEx and its major competitors, as reflected by heavy financial investment.[9] FedEx created a new operating company based on this initiative, combining Tower Group with another acquisition, WorldTariff, into FedEx Trade Networks. This subsidiary of FedEx is now one of the largest customs entry filers in North America.[10]

In late August 2001, under strong protest from the Teamsters Union and UPS, FedEx entered into an agreement with the USPS. Under this alliance, the Postal Service buys space on FedEx airplanes to transport Express Mail, Priority

Mail and First-Class Mail, with FedEx also placing overnight service collection boxes at post offices nationwide. Building on this already profitable relationship, FedEx extended the contract with USPS in mid-2004, taking on responsibility for the USPS' Global Express Guaranteed international delivery service, displacing competitor DHL Worldwide Express in the process. Under the new agreement, all packages and shipping labels will be co-branded with both USPS and FedEx logos. This was after the partners added a fourth addendum to the original agreement in early 2004 that allows FedEx to continue carrying incremental pounds of mail at higher volumes than spelled out in the original agreement.

Seemingly in response to UPS' acquisition of Mail Boxes Etc., FedEx's most recent move has been the purchase of Kinko's, the copying and office services company, for $2.4 billion. This acquisition is meant to drive consumers of express package and related services to a particular provider. As Fedex paid far more for Kinko's 1,256 locations than the $191 million paid by UPS for its 3,400 Mail Boxes Etc outlets, FedEx has less room for error. However, Kinko's stores produce significantly more revenue on average than a UPS Store. FedEx plans on spending an additional $20 million to re-name their stores FedEx Kinko's in 2004.

Economic Indicators

FedEx services over 5.5 million packages daily throughout the U.S. and approximately 210 other countries. With more than 245,000 employees, FedEx operates over 640 aircraft and approximately 71,000 motorized vehicles and trailers. FedEx Express, the world's largest express transportation company, ships over 3.1 million packages daily; FedEx Ground, second to UPS in small-package ground delivery service, ships over 2.3 million packages daily; and FedEx Freight, the largest U.S. provider of regional LTL freight services, makes over 60,000 shipments daily.

Table 4.4 provides economic indicators for FedEx, Table 4.5 annual worldwide shipments and Table 4.6 provides annual revenues by source. As indicated in the discussion of UPS, one of the most significant events in the package express industry was the UPS strike in 1997. The largest jump in both revenue and shipments for FedEx was in this year. UPS customers were forced to go elsewhere for their shipping needs and many never returned to UPS after the strike. During the 12 operating days of the strike, FedEx delivered an additional 800,000 U.S. domestic express packages per day, and RPS (FedEx Ground) delivered another 300,000 packages per day.

Similarly, the events of 9/11 and the concurrent downturn in the economy had far reaching effects on the entire industry, but this time FedEx was on the losing end. FedEx saw marked drops in overnight and deferred shipments in 2001, as well as a drop in revenues from these shipments. As the economy remained stagnant, more people opted to ship via ground rather than express, which is reflected in the significant increase in FedEx Ground shipments matched by a leveling off of FedEx Express shipments.

Table 4.4 Economic Indicators for FedEx Corporation ($ millions)[1]

	2003	2002	2001	2000	1999	1998	1997
Revenue:							
FedEx Express[2]	16,761	15,924	15,413	15,340	14,614	13,677	12,532
FedEx Ground[3]	3,641	3,121	2,514	2,152	1,968	1,808	1,559
FedEx Freight[4]	2,385	2,053	1,491	N/A	N/A	N/A	N/A
Non-Package	326	606	782	1,078	1,056	912	1,100
Total Revenue	23,112	21,704	20,200	19,057	17,639	16,398	15,192
Operating Expenses:							
FedEx Express	16,260	15,128	14,587	14,471	13,726	12,821	11,753
FedEx Ground	3,152	2,691	2,244	1,956	1,740	1,602	1,402
FedEx Freight	2,184	1,880	1,370	N/A	N/A	N/A	N/A
Total Operating Expense	21,912	20,295	18,983	17,923	16,441	15,298	14,390
Operating Income:							
FedEx Express	500	796	826	869	888	857	780
FedEx Ground	489	429	270	196	228	206	157
FedEx Freight	202	174	121	N/A	N/A	N/A	N/A
Total Operating Income	1,200	1,409	1,217	1,134	1,197	1,099	800
Net Income	677	780	658	627	664	578	375

1 Original data is defined for the fiscal year ending May 31. Data in the table has been adjusted for the calendar year ending Dec. 31 by adding 5/12 of the value for the current fiscal year and 7/12 of the value for the next fiscal year.
2 FedEx Express includes overnight, deferred, and freight.
3 FedEx Ground was RPS from 1998-2000.
4 FedEx Freight was Viking Freight from 1998-2001.
Source: Federal Express Form 10-K.

However, the operational changes FedEx had made prior to 9/11 allowed for continued success. The relationship with the USPS detailed above began to pay off in 2003 and the majority of the benefit accrued to FedEx Express as reflected in 2003 revenue figures. The acquisition of Viking Freight and American Freightways, while risky because of the weakness of Viking, continued to pay off as the increased operating income of FedEx Freight offset declining operating margins at FedEx Express. FedEx Ground provided even more of a boost.

Table 4.5   Federal Express Annual Shipments (millions)*

	Overnight	Deferred	FedEx Ground	Total Domestic	International Priority
1993	327.1	110.5	N/A	437.6	N/A
1994	368.5	132.7	N/A	501.2	N/A
1995	411.5	144.4	N/A	555.9	N/A
1996	446.6	160.6	N/A	607.2	N/A
1997	470.8	200.6	271.0	942.4	0.06
1998	491.9	225.7	336.8	1,054.4	0.07
1999	511.6	232.7	359.7	1,104.0	0.07
2000	516.9	231.8	377.8	1,126.5	0.08
2001	492.7	224.6	421.9	1,139.2	0.09
2002	473.2	225.8	505.8	1,204.8	0.09
2003	467.9	233.0	582.8	1,283.7	0.10

* Original data is defined for the fiscal year ending May 31. Data in the table has been adjusted for the calendar year ending Dec. 31 by adding 5/12 of the value for the current fiscal year and 7/12 of the value for the next fiscal year.
Source: Edward K. Morlok, et al., "The Parcel Service Industry in the U.S.: Its Size and Role in Commerce," University of Pennsylvania, 2000, p. 42, Federal Express Form 10-K.

The significant drop in income and FedEx Express operating income in 2003 is attributed to $429 million in business realignment costs. This was somewhat offset by an increase in International Priority (IP) volume growth. IP growth rates were 21% and 11% in the Asian and European markets, respectively. IP continues to be one of the most profitable ventures for FedEx, with increasing return per package shipped, along with rapidly increasing volumes.

The greatest single challenge faced by FedEx is the steady rise in electronic commerce and transmission of documents. The core of FedEx's business has been overnight delivery of documents. Electronic transmission greatly reduces the need for business to use overnight services except for the final drafts of legal documents. The continued stagnation of FedEx's overnight shipments and revenue several years after the end of the recession reflects a decline in this part of FedEx's business. It may be that FedEx's rapid move into ground transportation was inspired as much by concerns over growing problems in their domestic overnight business as by a desire to exploit potential synergies in the coordination of transportation and logistics.

Table 4.6   Federal Express Revenues By Source ($ millions)*

	Overnight	Deferred	FedEx Ground	Total Domestic	International Priority
1988	3,109	565	654	4,329	N/A
1989	3,634	620	730	4,984	N/A
1990	4,025	682	806	5,513	N/A
1991	4,156	760	883	5,799	N/A
1992	4,358	902	957	6,218	N/A
1993	4,735	1,058	1,039	6,832	N/A
1994	5,130	1,212	1,135	7,477	N/A
1995	5,577	1,332	1,265	8,174	N/A
1996	6,053	1,515	1,326	8,895	N/A
1997	6,574	1,947	1,559	10,080	2,509
1998	7,029	2,233	1,808	11,070	2,851
1999	7,391	2,363	1,968	11,722	3,241
2000	7,633	2,465	2,152	12,250	3,714
2001	7,346	2,428	2,514	12,288	3,896
2002	7,125	2,457	3,121	12,703	4,056
2003	7,114	2,538	3,640	13,292	4,685

* Original data is defined for the fiscal year ending May 31. Data in the table has been adjusted for the calendar year ending Dec. 31 by adding 5/12 of the value for the current fiscal year and 7/12 of the value for the next fiscal year.
Source: Edward K. Morlok, et al., "The Parcel Service Industry in the U.S.: Its Size and Role in Commerce," University of Pennsylvania, 2000, p. 42, Federal Express Form 10-K.

III. DHL

The broader world competitive landscape of the express package industry took another leap recently when DHL and Deutsche Post joined forces in 2002. DHL has long been a major force in worldwide express package deliveries, arguably "the best network in the world for express mail, documents, and parcels."[11] With the resources that Deutsche Post can provide, DHL promises to play an important role in the future of the industry, in the U.S. and around the world.[12]

In 1969, Adrian Dalsey, Larry Hillblom and Robert Lynn (D, H, and L) founded DHL as a service shuttling bills of lading between San Francisco and Honolulu. The success of the company was founded in its innovative idea of sending out documentation in advance of cargo arriving, thereby speeding up the process of importing goods. The company grew rapidly and in a few years initiated service to Asia and Australia, creating an entirely new industry of international door-to-door express service in the Pacific Basin. Steady expansion continued in the 1970s as DHL initiated service to Europe (1974), Latin America (1977), the Middle East (1978) and Africa (1978). The international delivery company was the first to bring air express to the Eastern Bloc countries in 1983 and to the People's Republic of China in 1986. Today, DHL is the world's largest international air express network with service to 120,000 destinations in more than 220 countries and territories.[13]

More than 5,000 offices support DHL's extensive worldwide coverage. Of that total, over two-thirds are owned and operated by DHL, far greater than any other company in the air express industry. As a result, DHL has a significant advantage over other carriers who often use third party agents in the foreign countries they serve. DHL is also a licensed customs broker in more than 140 countries. These advantages afford DLH faster transit times, streamlined customs clearance, effective tracking of shipments and simplified billing.

As mentioned previously, Deutsche Post purchased DHL, beginning with a major investment in the company in 1998 and a full takeover in 2002. This acquisition is especially interesting because Deutsche Post had earlier been a major European Government postal agency until it was partially privatized in the 1990s and then went on to takeover DLH, a major global private sector express package company.[14]

Privatization of Deutsche Post began in 1990, progressing over the course of that decade until the company went public with an IPO in 2000, officially becoming Deutsche Post World Net (DPWN). It still maintains a strong connection with the German government; a majority of the company is still state-owned and employees are considered to be government employees, which is widely controversial since DPWN continues to acquire private companies around the world. The immediate success of a privatized DPWN has led many other state-owned mail services to begin some form of privatization. It has also placed a great deal of pressure on the USPS, which remains firmly within the sphere of control of the federal government.

DPWN made its initial move into the global package business by buying 25% of DHL in 1998, and then completed the move with a 100% takeover in 2002. Very little is known about DHL's financial holdings because prior to the takeover it was a private company, and it is now difficult to distinguish DHL from the rest of DPWN's holdings. Starting in 2003, DPWN combined domestic and international parcels and express business as well as its logistics activities all under DHL.

Also in 2003, DHL purchased the ground operations of Airborne Express, Inc., at the time the number three company in the U.S. air express market. Airborne Express was the first to introduce same day, nationwide delivery service with their Sky Courier service. The merger was a good move for DHL and it advanced their efforts to gain market share in the parcel delivery sector relative to FedEx and UPS. Dr. Klaus Zumwinkel, Chairman of DPWN's Management Board, said: "We are going to combine the importance of the world's market leader DHL with the strength of Airborne in the U.S. That's how we create a strong No. 3 in the large and profitable U.S. market. Our clients will benefit from a unique presence in the U.S., in Europe and in Asia."[15]

However, since a non-U.S. company owns DHL, it has had to spin off Airborne's flight operations into a separate company, ABX Air. This company will be owned by Airborne's current shareholders, to avoid falling foul of U.S. law banning foreigners owning more than 25% of a U.S. airline. The same law has applied to DHL's own air unit, now called Astar after a recent management buyout, and has had no affect on the running of the business.

None of these moves has sat well with UPS or FedEx. Both companies have fought the intrusion of a foreign competitor in the U.S. market at every step. The Astar deal has brought DHL into court as a result of a Congressional decision following lobbying by UPS and FedEx. They say that because DHL gives Astar most of its business and guarantees it a minimum 7% return, DPWN effectively controls the airline. UPS also accuses DPWN of selling below cost and financing its acquisitions by charging some of the highest prices in the world for regular mail, 60 cents for each letter, which is almost twice the price in the U.S. Most recently, UPS has charged DPWN with financing many of their acquisitions with funding from the German government.

DHL continues its expansion unabated, with the support of DPWN. In June 2004, the express courier unit announced that it will spend $1.2 billion to bolster its business in the United States and launch a $150 million U.S. marketing program. The money will be invested in sorting centers and information over the next three years.

IV. United States Postal Service

The United States Postal Service (USPS) is a significant competitor in the package express and overnight delivery market. In 2003, USPS delivered 1.1 billion packages, about 42% of the packages delivered by UPS and twice Fedex's volume, and earned $2.2 billion in revenue from this service. USPS plays a much smaller role in the overnight market, delivering only 56 million express mail letters in 2003 compared to 528 million overnight deliveries by Fedex and 299 million by UPS.

A full discussion of the structure of the USPS and issues facing the organization, an independent entity of the Federal government, is beyond the scope of this essay. Here we do no more than broadly sketch some issues about its structure and finances to briefly outline its role in the package express industry. The USPS was formed from the United States Post Office in 1971 in response to a national strike by postal employees in 1970. The Post Office was a cabinet-level organization and its employees were civil servants. Most were classified as low-level clerical employees. The strike, a response to low wages and poor working conditions, created a crisis for the Nixon administration as federal employees were not allowed to bargain over wages and working conditions and were subject to penalties up to, and including, termination. The strike was resolved by a significant wage increase and the promise of further legislated reforms. This promise was realized in the Postal Reorganization Act of 1970 that established the USPS as an independent agency with financial autonomy. The PRA required the USPS to restructure its operations, take on a corporate structure, provide universal service at uniform rates and eventually cover all costs with postage revenues as taxpayer subsidies to the Postal Service were phased out. The USPS was permitted to bargain with its employees under rules similar to those applied to the private sector except that impasses in bargaining were to be resolved by interest arbitration rather than strikes. The budgetary and administrative control granted the USPS was also intended to allow the Service to undertake the investments and other actions required to modernize.

Its status as a public organization has been both an advantage and a burden for the USPS. The Postal Service has a limited legal monopoly on the delivery of addressed letters and no other organization is permitted to place such letters in the nation's mailboxes. The price of privately delivered overnight letters is also set relative to the price of USPS postage rates, making USPS the low price provider of overnight service.[16]

At its creation, the USPS received the assets and liabilities of the United States Post Office. The most important asset was the extensive delivery network that had been developed over the prior one hundred and ninety-five years. The USPS has maintained the densest delivery and pick-up network of any of the package express carriers, reaching 140 million homes and businesses in America every day (typically six days a week). The range of products delivered by the USPS also creates the potential for economies of scope as well as cross subsidization from monopoly services (first class mail) to competitive services (package express and overnight delivery).[17]

Table 4.7   United States Postal Service: Volume and Revenue from Package, Express and Priority Mail

	Parcel		Express		Priority	
	pieces	revenue	pieces	revenue	pieces	revenue
2003	1128.5	$2,215.7	55.8	$888.1	859.6	$4,494.3
2002	1075.1	$2,080.1	61.3	$910.5	998.2	$4,722.5
2001	1093	$1,993.9	69.4	$995.7	1117.8	$4,916.4
2000	1128.4	$1,912.3	70.9	$996.1	1222.5	$4,837.1
1999	1043.1	$1,823.5	68.7	$942.0	1189.5	$4,533.3
1998	971.4	$1,626.6	66.2	$854.5	1163.8	$4,149.6
1997	988.4	$1,627.6	63.6	$824.7	1068.2	$3,856.9
1996	948.9	$1,524.1	57.6	$736.8	937.3	$3,321.5
1995	936.2	$1,524.7	56.7	$710.9	869	$3,074.7
1994	871.5	$1,352.7	56.2	$671.4	769.6	$2,653.4
1993	743.8	$1,183.3	52.4	$627.1	664.4	$2,299.7
1992	764.5	$1,186.4	53.2	$639.0	584.4	$2,070.8
1991	695.4	$1,000.9	58	$668.0	530.4	$1,764.6
1990	663	$919.5	58.6	$680.7	527.9	$1,554.7

Pieces and revenues in thousands.

The competitiveness of the USPS in the parcel express industry is limited by legislated limitations on its competitive products. Prices for postal services are regulated by the Postal Rate Commission (PRC) under rules established by Congress. Unlike private firms, the USPS is not allowed to cross subsidize services or grant volume discounts to its best customers. In recent years, the PRC has permitted the USPS to provide discounts to large-volume mailers when it can be shown that there is a cost basis for discounts. However, these so-called Negotiated Service Agreements have not been applied to competitive products and typically take months of hearings to establish. Indeed, the process of establishing new rates for any postal product through the Commission is slow and public, giving notice to competitors of proposed changes in rates. Although the USPS has been able to somewhat reduce the costs of prime shippers by engaging in joint advertising campaigns or other ploys, both Fedex and UPS have regularly taken large accounts from the USPS through modestly under pricing the USPS rates.[18]

Unlike its competitors, USPS is not permitted to lobby Congress about its regulatory framework. While its package express competitors maintain a powerful lobbying presence in Washington, the USPS is dependent on other groups, such as the postal unions and mailers, to represent its interests in legislation. UPS has been particularly active in crafting legislation in ways that protect UPS from competition from the Postal Service and postal reform efforts have required quid pro quos to the private package express carriers.

Although the USPS is holding its own in parcel deliveries, its overnight and priority services have declined since 2000 (Table 4.7). Parcel deliveries grew slowly but steadily between 1993 and 2000, declined modestly in 2001 and 2002 and then began to increase again in 2003. Parcel revenue rose steadily between 1993 and 2003. In contrast, the express segment peaked in 1998-2000 and has seen substantial decline in the volume of letters and in revenue in recent years. Priority mail volume and revenues show a similar pattern of growth from 1993 leading to a peak in 1999-2001 and a substantial decline in both volume and revenue after that.

Although the USPS has considerable potential to become a powerful competitor in the package express industry, this potential is unlikely to be realized in the near term. It is more likely to remain as it has been, a capable and convenient reserve carrier.

The Significance of Package Express

The importance of the express package industry to the contemporary economy is understated in purely statistical descriptions of its size and scale. The industry has made it possible for other innovators to pursue their ventures, including Michael Dell of Dell Computers and Jeff Bezos of Amazon.com, who have in turn transformed the world of computers and commerce.[19] The express package industry has become an essential part of the modern economy, carrying by one estimate between 8.6% and 14.3% of the nation's Gross Domestic Product.[20]

A recent study on the package delivery industry at the University of Pennsylvania concluded that there are two reasons why the package delivery industry has become so important in recent years:

> One consists of changes in the way goods and services are produced and distributed in our economy – globalization, customized mass production, lean inventory management, rapid customer response, and growth in e-commerce, among others. The other is parcel service itself, which is at the vanguard of transportation service modernization with such features as differentiated time-definite service options, intermodal service, in-transit visibility, and data integration with the management systems of customers. Thus parcel service is a major element of the transportation infrastructure of the nation. It is essential for modern commerce.[21]

Revolutions in information technology have also contributed to the dramatic transformation of the industry. Advances in package tracking that allow customers to track their packages from sender to receiver and at every point along the way are truly amazing. Moreover, complex supply chain information systems allow companies to track both inputs and outputs of all kinds, whatever the nature of the enterprise. These information systems are of great value not only to retailing, wholesaling and warehousing of goods, but to manufacturing as well. In fact, the supply chain systems provided by the express package industry have been key to the just-in-time, lean inventory, and lean manufacturing approaches of the most competitive companies in the early twenty-first century.

The dramatic changes and expansion in the express package industry over the last several decades have not occurred without complications. The evolving regulatory environment in which the industry operates has been a constant challenge. After the demise of Railway Express in the early 1970s, when movement of large quantities of packages by air was still in its relative infancy, most express packages moved by ground. The trucking of packages over long distances had been going on for decades, but freight rates had been tightly controlled by the Interstate Commerce Commission. Deregulation of the trucking industry at the federal level occurred in 1980 with the passage of the Motor Carrier Act as a part of a larger program of deregulation of commerce during the Carter Presidency. Deregulation at the state level occurred on a piecemeal basis thereafter. Under pressure from UPS and FedEx in 1994, state regulation of truck freight was removed by congressional act.[22] That legislative change altered the structure of the trucking industry as described elsewhere in this volume. It also changed the competitive landscape in which the express package industry operated.

One of the most persistent themes in the neoconservative political agenda is postal reform. Think tanks in Washington like the American Enterprise Institute and the Cato Institute, have devoted significant attention to regulatory changes in the U.S. Postal Service,[23] which would greatly impact the express package industry.

Employment Relations in Package Express

Unlike most industries, the dominant firms in the package express industry operate under different labor relations statutes and have dissimilar relations between managers and employees. Because of UPS's origins as a trucking company, labor relations at UPS are governed by the National Labor Relations Act and regulated by the National Labor Relations Board. Under the NLRA collective bargaining units are organized establishment by establishment. Once organized, employers are required to bargain with employees in good faith. If impasse is reached the parties are permitted to strike or lock out on the expiration of the existing contract. The NLRA was structured to encourage the parties to engage in negotiations and problem solving. The NLRB in turn enforces rules that prevent the parties from using tactics that are destructive to the bargaining relationship and strongly encourages the parties to craft an agreement that fits their circumstances. The parties can, but are not required, to use the services of the Federal Mediation and Conciliation Service, to aid in negotiations. Despite the ability to strike and lock out under the NLRA, work stoppages are fairly rare. Less than 1% of organized workers were involved in work stoppages in 2003 and the duration of the stoppages that did occur accounted for only 0.2% of the working hours of organized workers.

Labor relations at FedEx Express are governed by the Railway Labor Act (RLA) because FedEx began as an air carrier. The RLA, which covers railroad and airline employees, differs from the NLRA in both the rules for organizing and bargaining. While the NLRA allows for a firm to be organized establishment by establishment, the RLA requires company wide organizing by trade. This makes organizing more difficult and has proved a barrier to organization of FedEx's Express's package car drivers. FedEx pilots are organized.

Bargaining under the RLA is administered by the National Mediation Board (NMB). The NMB combines the policing functions of the NLRB with the mediation functions of FMCS. However unlike the FMCS, the NMB may intervene absent a request from the parties. Parties are not allowed to strike or lockout when their contract expires; strikes are only allowed when the NMB has certified that further mediation would not be fruitful. In event of a work stoppage, the NMB can request a presidential emergency board. If established, there is a mandatory sixty-day cooling-off period during which the parties are not allowed to strike. The presidential board uses the cooling-off period to investigate the issues between the parties and make recommendations. At the end of the period the parties may strike. A similar process for an emergency board and cooling-off period is provided under the Taft-Hartley amendments to the NLRA, but the standard for invoking the board is more stringent.

The situation at FedEx has become more complex with the addition of its ground delivery system. FedEx's attempt to have its FedEx Freight covered under the RLA was denied by the NLRB in 2001 and, in theory, the ground operations could be organized establishment by establishment. Although this is unlikely in the current employment environment, FedEx has avoided integrating its air and ground operations in a fashion similar to UPS, trading off operating efficiencies to maintain the protections against further organization of its air operations.

The USPS operates under a variant of the NLRA statutory system. Postal labor relations are covered by the NLRA. However, because of the importance of the postal system to the U.S. economy and its historic tie to the federal government bargaining impasses are resolved by tri-partite interest arbitration rather than a strike. If the parties are unable to negotiate a settlement, they present their issues, supporting arguments and facts to a panel comprised of a postal representative, a union representative and a neutral. After the presentations the panel meets in private to continue negotiations. Matters that cannot be settled by negotiations between the postal and union representatives are decided by the neutral.

Each framework brings with it distinct advantages and disadvantages. The NLRA framework emphasizes the parties' fashioning of their own relationship and allows the parties to utilize every legal means, including economic leverage, in fashioning that relationship. The major restraint on the use of economic leverage, aside from legal limitations on tactics, is that the parties have an interest to continue working together and advancing their mutual interest in the firm. The RLA operates more slowly than the NLRA, negotiations take longer, there is more governmental intervention and process delays. Although the RLA delays strikes, change in employment systems is glacial, which leads to frustration among workers and line management and ongoing problems in day-to-day employment relations. Arguably, the postal framework combines the fleetness of the NLRA with the impediments to strikes of the RLA, but the USPS often argues that arbitration results in overly generous settlements and excessive inertia in modernizing the postal employment system. Employee ability to pursue grievances through the civil service and the grievance/arbitration system provided in the collective bargaining agreement also burdens the Postal Service.

UPS has sought coverage under the RLA. It requested reclassification in the mid 1990s but the request was rejected by the NLRB in 1996. UPS's concern over differences in the legal framework of labor relations became more intent during and after the 1997 work stoppage. Negotiations between UPS and the Teamsters, who represent the drivers and other blue collar workers at UPS, were conducted during a bitter campaign for the presidency of the Teamsters between Ron Carey, a former UPS driver, and James Hoffa Junior, son and namesake of the legendary president of the union. UPS's use of temporary workers and their effect on bargaining unit work was a central issue in negotiations. The fifteen-day strike was a victory for the Teamsters because of their lengthy preparation and depth of organization at UPS. UPS's inability to run their system during the strike caused customers to defect to other package express companies, which placed considerable pressure on UPS to settle. Although UPS requested a Taft-Hartley back to work order, the Clinton administration limited itself to serving as an honest broker between the parties. The administrations' refusal to act reflected both its friendly relations with organized labor and the modest economic impact of the strike on the national economy. Although the strike was threatening to UPS, it did not rise to the level of a national emergency required to invoke presidential powers.

The strike also reflected the conflicted relationship between UPS and its employees. Although UPS commands the loyalty of its employees, its employment relations are unilateral and authoritarian. The company places great emphasis on enforcing work rules and using discipline to obtain the desired performance from employees. UPS also has a history of making unilateral changes in company policies without bargaining with the Teamsters. For example, UPS unilaterally increased the weight limit on packages from 50 to 150 pounds shortly after completing the 1993 negotiations. This change, which increased work-load and stress for package car drivers and sorters caused a national wildcat strike in February of 1994. UPS's current effort to achieve changes in its pension system through legislation, after having failed to accomplish it through negotiation, is another example of opportunistic behavior, which reflects the general pattern of conflict in labor relations at UPS.

UPS's labor relations strategy contrasts with that of FedEx. While UPS has marketed itself as a high wage employer for whom it is worth working despite the job, FedEx has developed more cooperative relations with their package car drivers. FedEx's success in this respect was reflected in the United Auto Workers approach to organizing it's East Coast drivers. Rather than portray FedEx as a bad employer to rally support for the union, the UAW campaign emphasized the role of the union in making a good job better and more secure. FedEx faces a challenge in maintaining the positive qualities of its employment system as it adds employees and businesses and becomes more involved in lower margin ground transportation.

Should the package express industry be placed under a single statutory scheme? UPS believes that the current situation places it on an uneven playing field and the company would prefer to operate under the RLA. Because work stoppages are more difficult to accomplish under the Railway Labor Act, it could be argued that it is in the interest of the public to avoid disruptions of service and thus it would be appropriate to make the RLA the standard for private sector competitors in the industry. One of the authors of this study has suggested that all private sector competitors in the express package industry be brought under the Railway Labor Act "To eliminate competitive imbalance, offset the post office's statutory protection from strike, and protect the consumer from undue disruption in the distribution chain."[24] This view may not be shared by those familiar with Package Express who believe the strike had its origins in UPS's approach to its employees and do not agree that the disruption accompanying the strike burdened the public beyond the shareholders of UPS.[25]

Conclusion

This chapter has outlined the increasing importance and international development of the express package industry. The rapid growth of international commerce in general sets the stage for American companies to rapidly develop their international networks. Both UPS and FedEx are seeking to aggressively capture a higher market share of international shipments. The U.S. companies see the international market as the key to high growth levels in sales and profits, given the highly competitive and relatively slow growing American market for express delivery services. At the same time, companies based outside the United States are also seeking to develop their own capabilities both in North America, Asia and Europe, and between the world's major economically developed regions.

To a significant degree, international commerce is dependent on enabling enterprises in order to move critical materials quickly and efficiently anywhere in the world. Thus, the dynamic and highly competitive express package industry plays an integral role in the global economy.

Notes

1. Robert M. Cambell, *The Politics of Postal Transformation: Modernizing Postal Systems in the Electronic and Global World*, 2002, p. 11.
2. Edward K. Morlok, Bradley F. Nitzberg, Karthik Balasubramaniam, with the assistance of Mark L. Sand, "The Parcel Service Industry in the U.S.: Its Size and Role in Commerce," University of Pennsylvania, 2000, p. 39.
3. Robert M. Campbell, *The Politics of Postal Transformation: Modernizing Postal Systems in the Electronic and Global World*, 2002, p. 96.
4. "*Company History,*" United Parcel Service website, 2004.
5. A. Robinson, *Competition Within the United States Parcel Delivery Market*, Postcom. pp. 52-53.
6. A. Robinson, *Competition Within the United States Parcel Delivery Market*, Postcom. p. 53.
7. http://www.hoovers.com/ups/--ID__40483--/free-co-factsheet.xhtml.
8. FedEx History, FedEx company website, 2004.
9. Tetsuo Wada and Jack A Nickerson, "Proprietary Information Networks and the Scope of the Firm: The Case of International Courier and Small Package Service in Japan," Michael A. Crew and Paul R. Kleindorfer, *Emerging Competition in Postal and Delivery Services*, 1999.
10. "FedEx Corporate History," FedEx website, 2004.
11. Robert M. Campbell, *The Politics of Postal Transformation: Modernizing Postal Systems in the Electronic and Global World*, 2002, p. 433.
12. "DHL Company Portrait," Deutsche Post website, 2004.
13. DHL Timeline, DHL website, 2004.
14. "The History of Deutsche Post World Net," Deutsche Post World Net Website, 2004.
15. Recent news, Deutsche Post website, 2003.
16. By regulation, private companies must charge at least $3.00 or double postage, whichever is greater, to qualify for the "urgent letter" exception to the Private Express Statutes, the laws that delineate the Postal Service's monopoly.
17. Although the assets received by USPS were advantageous to the Service, the capital other firms had to pay for was provided at no cost, the USPS also inherited substantial liabilities. The capital stock of the USPS was out of date and deteriorated and the Service had to undertake an extensive program of modernization and investment. Also, the USPS was made responsible for a seriously under funded pension liability which has required billions of dollars in funding. In contrast, Deutsche Post was not required to fund its under funded pension system when it was privatized, instead the German government took on the liability.

18. The Package Express firms have increasingly ceded the return of small packages to USPS because of the costs of household pickups are very high for private package car drivers but low letters carriers who visit households on a regular basis.

19. "A Brief History of the Package Delivery Industry, May 4, 2003," President's Commission on the United States Postal Service, pp. 7, 8.

20. *The Economic Significance of the Express Package Industry*, the W.J. Usery, Jr. Center for the Workplace at Georgia State University, June 2000.

21. *The Parcel Service Industry in the U.S.: Its Size and Role in Commerce*, Center for Human Resources, the Wharton School, University of Pennsylvania, September 2000, at p. i.

22. Paul Teske, Samuel Best and Michael Mintrom, *Deregulating Freight Transportation: Delivering the Goods*, AEI Press, 1995.

23. J. Gregory Sidak and Daniel F. Spulber, *Protecting Competition from the Postal Monopoly*, AEI Press, 1996; Edward L. Hudgins, ed., *Mail @ the Millennium: Will the Postal Service Go Private?*, Cato Institute, 2000; Rick Geddes, *Saving the Mail: How to Solve the Problems of the U.S. Postal Service*, AEI Press, 2003.

24. *Labor Law and the Express Package Industry: An Unlevel Playing Field*, the W.J. Usery, Jr. Center for the Workplace at Georgia State University, June, 2000.

25. A careful analysis of the advantages and disadvantages of the various labor law frameworks may be found in "Who Has the Advantage: Evaluating the Playing Field Facing Parcel Competitors in the United States." Alan Robinson and Krisshawn Stanley, Direct Communications Group, January 2003.

Chapter 5

Logistics Service Providers

C. John Langley, Jr.

Introduction

As indicated throughout this book, many firms have directed significant attention toward working more closely with supply chain partners, including not only customers and product suppliers, but also with various suppliers of logistics services. Considering that one of the fundamental objectives of effective supply chain management is to achieve coordination and integration among participating organizations, the development of more meaningful "relationships" through the supply chain has become a high priority.

This chapter will cover two types of information relating to logistics service providers. The first is an overview of the outsourced logistics services industry, more commonly referred to as "third party logistics (3PL)." This coverage will include definitions of interest, types of 3PL providers, and current metrics of industry business activity. The second portion of the chapter provides significant detail concerning how the 3PL industry serves the needs of its customers. The content of this portion is derived from the current results of a major yearly study of 3PL customers and their perceptions and evaluations about the services they have purchased. The study covers a broad range of industries and includes findings from customers in North America, Western Europe, and Asia Pacific. Generally speaking the 3PL industry has exhibited significant growth over recent years, and so there is a sense of urgency about understanding as much as possible in relation to this important area of logistics and supply chain management.

As suggested by the late Robert V. Delaney in his *11th Annual State of Logistics Report,*[1] relationships are what will carry the logistics industry into the future. In commenting on the current rise of interest in e-Commerce and the development of electronic markets and exchanges, he states, "We recognize and appreciate the power of the new technology and the power it will deliver, but, in the frantic search for space, it is still about relationships." This message not only captures the importance of developing logistics relationships, but suggests that the ability to form relationships is a prerequisite to future success. Also, the essence of this priority is captured in a quote from noted management guru, Rosabeth Moss Kanter,[2] who stated that "being a good partner has become a key corporate asset; in the global economy, a well-developed ability to create and sustain fruitful collaborations gives companies a significant leg up."

Third Party Logistics – Industry Overview

As indicated throughout this book, firms have directed considerable attention toward working more closely with other supply chain participants, including customers, product suppliers, and various types of logistics suppliers. In essence, this has resulted in the development of more meaningful relationships among the companies involved in overall supply chain activity. As a result, many companies have been in the process of "extending" their logistics organizations into those of other supply chain participants and facilitators.

One way of extending the logistics organization beyond the boundaries of the company is through the use of a supplier of third party or contract logistics services.[3] While the emergence and growth of the 3PL industry was recognized as a major phenomenon in the 1990s, thoughts differ as to how to best define this type of logistics provider, and what services might be included.

Definition of Third Party Logistics

A third party logistics firm may be defined as an external supplier that performs all or part of a company's logistics functions. This definition is purposely broad, and is intended to encompass suppliers of services such as transportation, warehousing, distribution, financial services, etc. As will be discussed later, there are other desirable characteristics of a "true" 3PL. Among these are: multiple logistics activities are included; those that are included are "integrated" or managed together; and they provide "solutions" to logistics/supply chain problems.

Recently, there have been significant increases in the number of firms offering such services, and this trend is expected to continue. While many of these firms are small, niche players, the industry has a number of large firms as well. Examples of the latter include Ryder, FedEx, UPS Worldwide Logistics, Exel, Menlo Logistics, Schneider Logistics, UTi Worldwide, and Caterpillar Logistics Services.

Depending on the firm and its positioning in the industry, the terms "contract logistics" and "outsourcing" are sometimes used in place of "third party logistics." While some industry executives take care to distinguish among terms such as these, the terms refer to the use of external suppliers of logistics services. Except for the suggestion that the term "contract logistics" generally includes some form of contract, or formal agreement, this text will not suggest any unique definitional differences between these terms.

Beyond the concept of a third party logistics provider, the next evolution may be thought of as a 4PL, or a provider of "fourth party logistics[TM],"[4] services. Essentially a supply chain integrator, a 4PL is thought of as a firm that "assembles and manages the resources, capabilities, and technology of its own organization with those of complementary service providers to deliver a comprehensive supply chain solution."[5]

As suggested by Figure 5.1, a 4PL leverages the capabilities of 3PL's and suppliers of technology services through a centralized point of contact. In one sense, an important role of the 4PL is to manage and direct the activities of multiple 3PL's. In another, more strategic role, the 4PL serves as the integrator that brings together the needs of the client and the resources available through the 3PL providers, the IT providers, and the elements of business process management. Among the key competencies of a 4PL are the management of information, knowledge, relationships, and integration.

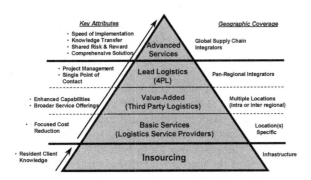

Figure 5.1 Next Generation of Logistics Outsourcing Models?

Source: 2003 3PL Study, C. John Langley Jr., Ph.D., Georgia Institute of Technology, Capgemini U.S. LLC, and FedEx Supply Chain Services.

To provide an understanding of the framework suggested by Figure 5.1, consider the example of a manufacturer of electronics products. In the case that this company chooses to conduct all of its logistics activities on an internal, proprietary basis, this would be referred to as *insourcing*. If this same company elects to use individual providers of logistics services such as trucking, warehousing, shipping, etc., it may be said that these are *basic services* that are available from logistics service providers. Some of the larger providers of basic services are Yellow Transportation, UPS and the Union Pacific Railroad. Next, if the company contracts with a third party provider of multiple logistics services (3PL), this arrangement may refer to the *value-added* services that are available. Leading value added service providers include FedEx Supply Chain Services, UPS Supply Chain Solutions, Exel Logistics, UTi Worldwide, Menlo Logistics, Averitt Logistics, and DSC Logistics and UTi/Standard Corporation. In the case that the customer contracts with a logistics provider for project management skills, and/or the management of multiple relationships with individual 3PL's, this model may be referred to as a *lead logistics* or 4PL arrangement. Prominent providers include Vector (4PL joint venture between Menlo Logistics and General Motors Corporation to serve General Motors Corporation); Kuehne & Nagel (4PL services to Nortel). Last, many providers of logistics services are continually searching for and developing *advanced services* that may create additional value for their customers.

Types of 3PL Providers

Although most 3PL firms promote themselves as providers of a comprehensive range of logistics services, it is useful to categorize them in one of several ways. Included are transportation-based, warehouse/distribution-based, forwarder-based, shipper/management-based, financial based, and information-based. Each of these is discussed briefly below.

Transportation-Based Included among the transportation-based suppliers are firms such as Ryder, Menlo Logistics, Schneider Logistics, FedEx Logistics, and UPS Logistics, most of which are subsidiaries or major divisions of large transportation firms. Some of the services provided by these firms are "leveraged" in that they utilize the assets of other companies, and some are "non-leveraged," where the principal emphasis is on utilizing the transportation-based assets of the parent organization. In all instances, these firms extend beyond the transportation activity to provide a more comprehensive set of logistics offerings.

In early 2000, Transplace was formed through the merger of the logistics business units of several of the largest publicly-held truckload carriers in the U.S. While this new company is transportation-based in that major elements of its corporate heritage do involve the commercial transportation industry, its approaches to operations, management, and planning significant utilize and leverage information technologies. For this reason, a more comprehensive description of this company will be found later in this section under the topic of "Information-Based" providers.

Warehouse/Distribution-Based Traditionally, most warehouse/distribution-based logistics suppliers have been in the public or contract warehousing business and have expanded into a broader range of logistics services. Examples of such firms include DSC Logistics, USCO, and Exel. The latter firm, Exel, has a much broader range of expertise, considering the 2000 merger of the former Exel Logistics (predominantly a warehousing/distribution-based firm), and MSAS (having strength in the forwarding and ocean shipping areas).

Based on their traditional orientation, these firms have already been involved in logistics activities such as inventory management, warehousing, distribution, etc. Experienced has indicated that these "facility-based" operators have found the transition to integrated logistics services to be less complex than have the transportation providers.

Also this category should include a number of 3PL firms that have emerged from larger corporate logistics organizations. Prominent among these are Caterpillar Logistics Services (Caterpillar, Inc.), Intral Corporation (Gillette), and Odyssey Logistics (Union Carbide Corporation and Rely Software). These providers have had significant experience in managing the logistics operations of the parent firm, and as a result, prove to be very capable providers of such services to external customers.

Forwarder-Based This category includes companies such as UTi Worldwide, Inc., Expeditors, Kuehne & Nagle, Fritz (now part of UPS), Circle, C.H. Robinson, and Hub Group, which have extended their middleman roles as forwarders and/or brokers into the broader range of 3PL services. Essentially, these firms are non-asset owners, are very independent, and deal with a wide range of suppliers of logistics services. They have proven quite capable at putting together packages of logistics services that meet customers' needs.

Financial-Based This category of 3PL provider includes firms such as Cass Information Systems (a division of Cass Commercial Corporation), CTC (Commercial Traffic Corporation), GE Information Services (General Electric), and FleetBoston Financial Corporation. These firms provide services such as freight payment and auditing, cost accounting and control, and logistics management tools for monitoring, booking, tracking, tracing, and inventory management.

Information-Based At the time of the writing of this chapter, there existed significant growth and development of internet-based, business-to-business, electronic markets for transportation and logistics services. Since these resources effectively represent alternative source for those in need of purchasing transportation and logistics services, they may be thought of as a newer, innovative type of third party provider.

Transplace is an Internet-based company that represents the merger of the 3PL business units from six of the largest publicly-held truckload carriers in the U.S. The founding carriers are Covenant Transport, Inc., J.B. Hunt Transport Services, Inc., M.S. Carriers, Inc. (since merged with Swift Transportation Co., Inc.), Swift Transportation Co., Inc., U.S. Xpress Enterprises, Inc., and Werner Enterprises, Inc. Transplace offers a web-enabled platform to bring together shippers and carriers worldwide to collaborate on their transportation logistics planning and execution in the most efficient and effective manner. Nistevo is a leading provider of in Internet-based, Collaborative Logistics Network. Nistevo's collaborative network is an Internet service that allows shippers and carriers to collaborate to improve profitability and performance. Both shippers and carriers using Nistevo's capabilities have gained through improved operating performance through online, real-time network visibility; management of the entire procurement, service, and delivery cycle from a single application; and improved contract and relationship management.

Industry Business Metrics

Table 5.1 provides a profile of 3PL industry revenues in the United States for 2002. As indicated, the total industry revenues were estimated at $65 billions, with significant revenues attributed to dedicated contract carriage; domestic transportation management; value-added warehouse/distribution; international transportation management; and 3Pl software. Although growth rates for these individual services tend to differ, the overall industry growth rate was estimated to be 6.9% for 2002.[6]

Table 5.1   Third Party Revenues Estimated at $65.0B in 2002

Third Party Service Providers	*2002 Turnover ($ Billions)*	*Current Growth Rate (%)*
Dedicated Contract Carriage	9.0%	8.4%
Domestic Transportation Management	19.5	11.4
Value-Added Warehouse/Distribution	16.9	10.5
International Transportation Management	6.6	5.7
3PL Software	3.0	- 25.0
Total Third Party Logistics Market	*$65.0B*	*6.9%*

Source: Armstrong's Guide to Third Party Logistics Service Providers.

Third Party Logistics Research Study

One significant research study, "Third Party Logistics Study: Views from the Customers," is conducted on an annual basis by the author in conjunction with Capgemini U.S. LLC and FedEx Supply Chain Services.[7] This study identifies and tracks key trends and views of the third-party logistics (3PL) industry from the perspectives of customers who purchase and use 3PL services. Over the years, this study has grown in terms of the regional areas and industries examined. Each study has attempted to address key issues that emerge from time to time relevant to the logistics and 3PL industries. The objectives of the study include: first, the measurement of the development and growth of the 3PL industry across major industry segments and diverse global regions; second, the identification of customer needs and 3PL providers response to those needs; third, understanding how customers select and manage 3PL providers; fourth, assessment of why customers outsource; fifth, summarizing the current use of 3PL services; sixth, investigation of leading topics, including 3PL service offerings and capabilities, how to structure and manage effective 3PL relationships, and how to properly measure 3PL performance and assess the benefits and value from 3PL relationships; and seventh, providing a strategic assessment of the future of the 3PL industry.

Data was collected by sending e-mails to logistics and supply chain executives across North America, Western Europe, Asia-Pacific, and South Africa, asking for their participation in the study. (In this study, an "executive" holds the title of manager, director, or vice-president of logistics or supply chain management.) In the e-mail, executives were asked to "click on" a web address that would access the 2003 3PL survey. Once the survey was completed, a final click on "end survey" entered the responses into the overall study database.

Industries Studied

The key industries represented by the intended recipients were: aerospace; automotive; chemical; computers and peripherals; consumer products; electronics;

government; industrial manufacturing; life sciences; medical; retail; and telecommunications. These industries were selected because they view logistics as strategically important and because they are purposefully moving toward integrated supply chain management.

Survey recipients were asked to think of a "3PL or third-party logistics provider" as one that provides multiple logistics services for its clients and customers. Following several examples of firms that would be typical of such a definition, recipients were asked to think of a "4PL or fourth-party provider" of logistics services as one that may include more project program management of sub-contractor 3PL operations.

Although a broad range of company types were targeted for inclusion in this study,[8] the manufacturing sector comprised 65% of respondents in North America, 85% in Western Europe, and 72% in Asia-Pacific. Raw materials suppliers comprised 12% of respondents in Asia-Pacific, while the North American and Western European sectors yielded very few such firms. One quarter of respondents in North America were wholesale/distribution/retail firms, while these comprised 14% of the sample for Western Europe, and 16% in Asia-Pacific.

The 3PL users indicated their logistics operations were regional rather than global, but included large areas and involved significant responsibilities. For example, 98% of the respondents in North America, 100% in Western Europe, and 90% in Asia-Pacific indicated the scope of their logistics responsibilities at least included their own immediate region. In general, the responding executives had responsibilities for logistics operations in other major areas of the world. For example, among North American respondents, 47% indicated responsibilities that included Europe, Asia-Pacific (47%), the Middle East (21%), South America (32%), and Africa (13%). North American 3PL users tend to have broader geographic responsibility than non-users of 3PL services; non-users more often have strictly local responsibility.[9]

Respondent firms have a relatively broad range of anticipated sales revenues for 2003.[10] Of the North American respondents, about half of the firms have revenues between US$1 billion and US$25 billion; another 10% project revenues over US$25 billion. This is similar to Western Europe where more than half of the firms project revenues greater than US$1 billion, while less than 5% of the Asia-Pacific firms anticipate total sales greater than US$1 billion.

North American respondents expect that logistics expenditures will represent approximately 11% of their organizations' total sales for 2003. Western European respondents indicated that logistics comprised 6% of expenditures, those in Asia-Pacific 8%. One factor influencing these results is the relatively greater percentage of intra-European and intra-Asia-Pacific business by companies in those regions. The greater involvement of respondents from North America in the consumer products and retail industries may partially explain the higher percentage by logistics expenditures to total sales.

Respondents reported that the dominant pressures faced by their industry included pressures to reduce cost, enhance customer service, and improve supply chain management. Lesser issues included globalization, consolidation and mergers, implementation of new information technologies and rapidly accelerating new product introductions. Security issues have also increased among North American respondents, as well as for respondents from Western Europe and Asia-Pacific. The 3PL users also attach great importance to logistics processes and supply chain issues. For example, 95% of the North American respondents, 100% of the Western European respondents, and 68% of those from Asia-Pacific agree "logistics represents a strategic, competitive advantage for our company." In addition, 90% in North America, 100% in Western Europe, and 81% in Asia-Pacific agreed that "our customers are placing greater emphasis on logistics customer service." Slightly more than half of the North American and Western European respondents agree with "our customers are more interested in price than service," while less than half of those in Asia-Pacific agree with that statement. Overall, 73% in North America and in Western Europe, and 58% in Asia-Pacific agreed that "using 3PLs is a key to satisfying their company's customers."

In addition to the formal survey, a day-long 3PL user session was held at Cap Gemini Ernst & Young's Accelerated Solutions Environment (ASE) in Atlanta, Georgia. Approximately 30 logistics executives participated in this session that helped to provide a better understanding of the perspectives of 3PL users. In addition to reviewing and evaluating the results of the 2003 study, the executives offered their opinions on matters of strategic and operational relevance to the provision and use of 3PL services.

Logistics Outsourcing Practices in Profile

Overall Trends

3PL use is significant in the regions of the world included in this study. Table 5.2 provides an 8-year view of the firms using 3PL services. From 1996 through 2001, the percentage of 3PL users remained relatively constant among North American respondents, generally between 68% to 73%; however, this percentage increased to 78% in 2002 and remained at 78% in 2003. Looking at the two years of usage data available for Western Europe, 3PL use appears significant, between 79% and 90%. The decrease in usage from 2002 to 2003 in Western Europe may be more from sampling methodology than from substantive differences in usage. The single year of results for Asia-Pacific suggests that fewer respondents (53%) outsource 3PL services than respondents in the other regions studied. Because the Asia-Pacific responses were predominantly from China, the results are obviously reflecting the current state of 3PL use in that country, in contrast to the broader Asia-Pacific area.[11]

Although the number of companies using 3PL providers is generally stable from year to year, the survey confirms that 3PL use does vary by industry. For example, two industries that tend to have greater use of 3PL services are computers and peripherals, and consumer products. Among those industries that tend to use fewer 3PL services are automotive, chemical, and retail. Future studies will more closely examine 3PL use in various industries.

Table 5.2   Overall Use of Third-Party Logistics Service Providers, 1996-2003

Year	North America	Western Europe	China/Asia-Pacific
1996	71 %	N/A	N/A
1997	73 %	N/A	N/A
1998	71 %	N/A	N/A
1999	68 %	N/A	N/A
2000	73 %	N/A	N/A
2001	71 %	N/A	N/A
2002	78 %	94 %	N/A
2003	78 %	79 %	58 %

Note: Figures indicate percent of respondents who were "users" of 3PL services.
Source: 2003 3PL Study, C. John Langley Jr., Ph.D., Georgia Institute of Technology, Capgemini U.S. LLC, and FedEx Supply Chain Services.

Again in this year's study, respondents were asked what percent of total logistics expenditures, defined as transportation, distribution, or value-added services, are directed to outsourcing. Table 5.3 shows the current (2003) versus projected (2006-2008) percentages directed to outsourcing for North American, Western European, and Asia-Pacific 3PL users. Western European respondents currently spend a greater percentage of their logistics dollar or Euro (65%) on outsourcing than do those in North America (49%) and Asia-Pacific (50%). Of significance is that respondents from all three regions expect these percentages (i.e., the use of 3PL services) to increase over the next three to five years. As shown in Table 5.3, respondents in Western Europe project a greater relative increase in their future spending (from 65% to 81%) than do those in North America (49% to 56%) and Asia-Pacific (50% to 60%).

**Table 5.3   Current vs. Projected Percentages of Logistics Expenditures
                    Directed to Outsourcing**

Region	Current 2003	Projected 2006-2008
North America	49 %	56 %
Western Europe	65 %	81 %
Asia-Pacific	50 %	60 %

Source: 2003 3PL Study, C. John Langley Jr., Ph.D., Georgia Institute of Technology, Capgemini U.S. LLC, and FedEx Supply Chain Services.

When asked for details concerning total logistics expenditures, North American 3PL users responded that, on average, 58% of their expenditures were related to transportation, 32% to distribution, and 10% to value-added services. Although Western European and Asia-Pacific respondents tend to spend a smaller percentage of their logistics budgets on transportation (45% and 44%, respectively) than North American respondents, they spend a larger proportion on distribution and value-added services.[12] Conversely, 3PL customers in Asia-Pacific tend to spend the greatest percentage of their logistics budget on value-added services (23%) than 3PL customers from North America (10%) or Western Europe (18%).

Outsourcing of Logistics Activities

Table 5.4 summarizes the specific logistics services outsourced by 3PL customers in 2003. Generally, the percentages shown in Table 5.4 for 2003 tend to be greater than comparable figures for 2002.

Table 5.4   Outsourced Logistics Services

Logistics Activity	North America	Western Europe	Asia-Pacific
Warehousing	73 %	91 %	46 %
Outbound Transportation	71 %	95 %	87 %
Customs Brokerage	66 %	57 %	--
Inbound Transportation	62 %	71 %	62 %
Customs Clearance	62 %	67 %	33 %
Freight Forwarding	57 %	67 %	41 %
Freight Bill Auditing/Payment	54 %	24 %	8 %
Cross-Docking	37 %	43 %	33 %
Shipment Consolidation/Distribution	37 %	62 %	16 %
Consulting Services	29 %	14 %	10 %
Return/Reverse Logistics	28 %	38 %	--
Carrier Selection	24 %	24 %	19 %
Order Fulfillment	23 %	24 %	19 %
Procurement of Logistics	23 %	29 %	--
Selected Manufacturing Activities	23 %	19 %	--
Product Marking/Labeling	20 %	33 %	17 %
Rate Negotiation	19 %	10 %	6 %
Inventory Management	19 %	14 %	24 %
Product Returns and Repair	16 %	43 %	5 %
Information Technology	16 %	24 %	13 %
Fleet Management	12 %	38 %	21 %
Order Entry/Processing	10 %	10 %	6 %
Product Assembly/Installation	9 %	14 %	8 %
Distribution Control	9 %	5 %	11 %
Customer Service	9 %	14 %	14 %
4PL Services	7 %	10 %	--
Inventory Ownership	6 %	0 %	--
Factoring (Trade Financing)	2 %	5 %	5 %
Supply Chain Manager/Integrator	--	--	6 %

Source: 2003 3PL Study, C. John Langley Jr., Ph.D., Georgia Institute of Technology, Capgemini U.S. LLC, and FedEx Supply Chain Services.

According to the 2003 study, the activities most frequently outsourced to 3PL providers are: warehousing (73%, 91%, but only 46% in Asia-Pacific), outbound transportation (71% in North America, 95% in Western Europe, and 87% in Asia-Pacific), customs brokerage (66%, 57%, figures not available for Asia-Pacific), and inbound transportation (62%, 71%, and 62%). The figures in Table 5.3 suggest that other frequently outsourced activities in North America are customs clearance (62%), freight forwarding (57%), and freight bill auditing/payment (54%). These figures are comparable with those of Western Europe, with the exception of the lesser use of freight bill auditing/payment services (24%) by 3PL users in Western Europe. Overall usage of these services in Asia-Pacific is somewhat less than in the two other regions.

Also of note from Table 5.4 is that Western Europe appears to use outsourcing more for activities such as outbound and inbound transportation, warehousing, shipment consolidation/distribution, and fleet management. As explained in the 2002 report, Western European business firms may have always been more involved historically in the use of outsourced logistics services than their counterparts in North America. Interestingly, the finding that Western European 3PL customers exhibit significantly less use of freight bill auditing/payment services suggests again this year that the use of financially related logistics services is less well developed in Western Europe than in North America.

In contrast, a number of activities appear to be outsourced less frequently in North America, Western Europe, and Asia-Pacific. These activities include those directly related to customers (e.g., order fulfillment, customer service, and order entry/order processing), IT, and strategic services (e.g., consulting, procurement of logistics, and 4PL services). A modest use of certain operationally focused activities seems to exist, such as cross-docking and carrier selection.

To what extent are 3PL services "integrated" or "tied together" by the 3PL service providers? This is a critical to the industry as integrating logistics services is considered by many to be a defining requirement of a 3PL service. A common example of integration would be when a 3PL manages transportation and warehousing/distribution services jointly, or in a collaborative manner, as opposed to separately. The concept of integration can apply to any number or combination of 3PL services. The 2003 finding for 3PL users in North America is that 64% suggest that their 3PL services are "integrated" or "tied together" to some extent by the providers of such services. This is consistent with the results of previous years' studies that found 60% to 70% of such services in North America met this description. Interestingly, when 3PL customers in Western Europe and Asia-Pacific were asked this same question, the positive responses represented 94% and 82%, respectively. The apparent conclusion is that 3PL services in Western Europe and Asia-Pacific tend to be more integrated than those in North America. On a more positive note, 84% of North American 3PL users say the integration of these services is desirable. (Users in the other regions also have expectations of further integration.)

Another strategic issue is how customers feel 3PL providers should position themselves in terms of the depth and breadth of their service. When asked whether "third-party suppliers should provide a broad, comprehensive set of service offerings," most of the 3PL users in the various regions strongly agreed (93% in North America, 88% in Western Europe, and 90% in Asia-Pacific). Of interest is that these users generally agree that "our company is moving to rationalize or reduce the number of third parties we use." This suggests that 3PL users are thinking about how to improve and streamline their procurement practices in relation to the need for externally provided, integrated logistics services.

Views of Non-Users

The 2003 study asked a number of questions to help better understand why some respondents were not using 3PL provider services (see Table 5.5). Their primary reasons: logistics are too important to outsource, logistics is a core competency, costs would not be reduced, control would diminish, and they have more logistics expertise than the 3PL providers. Interestingly, sometimes the same reasons certain organizations offer to explain their decision *not* to outsource are considered by others as reasons *to support* outsourcing. For example, while some non-users suggest that a consequence of using a 3PL provider would be to lose control, others indicate that using a 3PL provider actually helps gain or improve control over certain outsourced activities.

Table 5.5   Non-User Respondents: Rationale for Not Using 3PL Services

Statement	North America	Asia-Pacific
Logistics a Core Competency at Our Firm	45 %	40 %
Logistics Too Important to Outsource	40 %	39 %
Costs Would Not Be Reduced	34 %	26 %
Control Would Diminish	34 %	25 %
We Have More Expertise	21 %	36 %
Service Levels Would Not Be Realized	18 %	26 %
Customer Complaints Would Increase	8 %	24 %

Note: Figures indicate percent of non-users of 3PL services indicating agreement with various rationale for not using 3PL services. Western European response was insufficient for meaningful analysis of this question.
Source: 2003 3PL Study, C. John Langley Jr., Ph.D., Georgia Institute of Technology, Capgemini U.S. LLC, and FedEx Supply Chain Services.

Regarding issues relating to expertise and results, it would not make sense for a firm to outsource an activity when doing so may likely produce an inferior result. In cases such as this, the choice of not using a 3PL is understandable. What is important to consider in the decision to outsource, however, is whether internalizing certain logistics activities strategically fits the firm's core competencies, and whether the internal alternative will produce an acceptable financial return. Regardless of these explanations, good logistics management suggests that non-users should investigate the 3PL alternative.

3PL Service Offerings and Capabilities

Overall, survey respondents are satisfied with their 3PL providers (90% checked "extremely successful" or "somewhat successful"). However, the responses were mixed when asked about the individual capabilities of the 3PL providers. The 3PL users expect the 3PL providers to have core competency in traditional 3PL capabilities, such as transportation, warehousing, and shipment track/trace. The 3PL users also expect 3PL providers to enhance offerings by bundling these service offerings and by expanding their capabilities further up the supply chain.

ASE participants said that managing the expectations around capabilities needs improvement Among the "areas for improvement" they identified were the following: "must have" core offerings; "nice to have" value-added services and offerings; industry focus; geographic coverage; and established business infrastructure.

Another topic, technology, continually came up when discussing 3PL providers' infrastructure. ASE participants expect their 3PL providers to have the right technology – and that technology should easily integrate into the 3PL user's business/IT operations.

Information Technology-Based Services

As in previous years, the 2003 3PL survey identified what IT-based services were available through 3PL providers, what services the respondents use, and what services those respondents will require in the future. The survey also attempted to quantify the respondents' satisfaction with these technologies and tried to identify the leading 3PL-specific information technologies. Not surprisingly, the findings support the contention that IT-based services continue to be among the key expectations of 3PL users.

The top five 3PL-centric information technologies that North American respondents in 2003 are using are (see Table 5.6): warehouse/distribution center management (70%), shipment tracking/tracing/event management (66%), export/import/freight forwarding/customs clearance (66%), web-enabled communications (60%), and transportation management (52%).

For Western Europe respondents, the top five information technologies in 2003 are warehouse/distribution center management (75%), export/import/freight forwarding/customs clearance (71%), transportation management (68%), shipment tracking/tracing/event management (60%), and web-enabled communications (55%). The leading responses from Asia-Pacific are transportation management (71%) and export/import/freight forwarding/customs clearance (47%). Almost a third of the respondents also indicated that warehouse/distribution center management and shipment tracking/tracing/event management are available.

Table 5.6   Current Availability of IT-Based Services

IT-Based Services	North America	Western Europe	Asia-Pacific
Warehouse/DC Management	70 %	75 %	33 %
Shipment Tracking/Tracing	66 %	60 %	32 %
Export/Import/ Customs	66 %	71 %	47 %
Web-Enabled Communications	60 %	55 %	21 %
Transportation Management	52 %	68 %	71 %
Customer Order Management	21 %	21 %	15 %
Transp/Log Electronic Markets	19 %	18 %	8 %
Product Vertical Electronic Markets	17 %	11 %	8 %
Supplier/Mgt Systems	15 %	20 %	15 %
Supply Chain Planning	9 %	16 %	7 %

Note: Figures indicate percent of users who indicated availability of the indicated services from their 3PL's.
Source: 2003 3PL Study, C. John Langley Jr., Ph.D., Georgia Institute of Technology, Capgemini U.S. LLC, and FedEx Supply Chain Services.

Future Customer IT Needs

Table 5.7 compares the future requirements of IT-based 3PL services in North America, Western Europe, and Asia-Pacific. Respondents from North America and Western Europe identified the same top five IT-based services as future requirements. In the first and second spots, supplier management systems (44%) ranks as the number one future requirement for North America, while product vertical markets (44%) is the top future need for Western Europe. The North American responses suggest the need for 3PL providers to continue to be an enabler of the expanding requirement for collaboration in the marketplace. The other three IT-based services in the top five are: supply chain planning systems, transportation/logistics electronic markets, and web-enabled communications.

On the other hand, Asia-Pacific participants may be looking to expand the use of Internet capabilities in the future through transportation/logistics electronic markets (31%) and web-enabled communications (27%). These participants seem to be searching for basic, broad, management systems as well; also in the Asia-Pacific "top five" are supply chain planning systems (28%), transportation management (27%), and warehouse/distribution center management (27%).

Table 5.7 Future Requirements of IT-Based Services

Future Requirements	North America	Western Europe	Asia-Pacific
Supplier Management Systems	44%	35%	18%
Product Vertical Electronic Markets	37%	44%	23%
Supply Chain Planning Systems	36%	37%	28%
Transportation/Logistics Electronic Markets	35%	41%	31%
Web-Enabled Communications	22%	35%	27%
Customer Order Management	22%	21%	18%
Transportation Management	16%	26%	27%
Shipment Tracking/Tracing/Event Management	16%	25%	21%
Warehouse/Distribution Center Management	13%	15%	27%
Export/Import/Freight Forwarding/Customs Clearance	11%	10%	20%

Source: 2003 3PL Study, C. John Langley Jr., Ph.D., Georgia Institute of Technology, Capgemini U.S. LLC, and FedEx Supply Chain Services.

Perceptions of 3PL Technology Capabilities

As in 2002, the majority of respondents in North America (97%) and Western Europe (94%), as well as those surveyed this year in Asia-Pacific (74%), agree that IT capabilities are a necessity for 3PL providers. However, as seen in Table 5.8, only a third to a half of the respondents from any of the regions rely on 3PL providers for IT leadership.

On a positive note, around 93% of respondents in North America and 81% in Western Europe indicate that "having the right software" would give a 3PL provider a competitive advantage in the marketplace. This suggests an opportunity for 3PL providers: to become IT leaders for their clients in the future.

Table 5.8 Customers Speak Out About 3PL IT Capabilities

	North America	Western Europe	Asia-Pacific
IT Capabilities Necessary for 3PLs	85 %	88 %	74 %
Rely on 3PL for IT Leadership	24 %	19 %	28 %
Satisfied with 3PL IT Capabilities	38 %	19 %	27 %
Having the "Right" Software is Critical	72 %	69 %	52 %

Note: Figures indicate percentage of users agreeing with statements about 3PL IT capabilities.
Source: 2003 3PL Study, C. John Langley Jr., Ph.D., Georgia Institute of Technology, Capgemini U.S. LLC, and FedEx Supply Chain Services.

Management and Relationship Issues

Since the inception of the annual *Third Party Logistics Study*, the level of customer satisfaction based on the degree of success with 3PL user-provider relationships has been measured. In 2003, 89% of those surveyed viewed their relationship as successful (55% "somewhat successful" and 34% "extremely successful"). The 2003 results also showed a slight increase of 6% for "extremely successful." This is a positive trend and indicates that 3PL providers are improving their relationships with existing clients. The real challenge now is for 3PL providers to continually enhance their relationships while expanding their service offerings.

      As suggested in Table 5.9, 70%-80% of 3PL users tend to think of their 3PL as a "resource provider," rather than as a more strategic business partner. Less than one-half of users think of their 3PL in more strategic terms such as "resource manager," "problem solver," etc. As the quality and sophistication of customer-3PL relationships increases, it may be that a greater number of relationships will be viewed as "strategic" in terms of how they address issues relating to transportation, distribution, and supply chain management. Longer-term, a worthy objective is to see more relationships characterized best as that of an "orchestrator" where the 3PL provides a broad range of strategic services and orchestrates the best set of resources to meet the client's business objectives.

Table 5.9   3PL Provider Roles

Role	North America	Western Europe
Resource Provider	82 %	71%
Resource Manager	43 %	24 %
Problem Solver	39 %	38 %
Transportation Strategist	32 %	33 %
Distribution Strategist	24 %	19 %
Supply Chain Strategist	13 %	19 %
Orchestrator	9 %	14 %

Note: Figures indicate percent of users agreeing with role played by their 3PL's.
Source: 2003 3PL Study, C. John Langley Jr., Ph.D., Georgia Institute of Technology, Capgemini U.S. LLC, and FedEx Supply Chain Services.

      As 3PL providers continue to expand their capabilities to match client expectations, users should be prepared to pay a premium for advanced services. These advanced relationship models must incorporate risk-and-reward pricing mechanisms to offset the higher cost of satisfying service level expectations.

Relationship Processes

In a number of areas, the 2003 study provided insight into the relationships between 3PL providers and their customers. When asked whether "using 3PLs is a key to satisfying our company's customers," 73% of the respondents responded "yes" or "somewhat." This is a slight decrease over the last two years (down from 80%). Also, 78% responded similarly to the question of whether they feel they have a "collaborative" relationship with their 3PL providers. This response equals last year's response. There is an exception: the Western European response was lower (69%). These two findings suggest customers are concerned about developing – and benefiting from – improved relationships with their 3PL providers.

Figure 5.2 provides a perspective on a broader range of alternative "deal structures" that may be part of a 3PL relationship. The survey results show that the risk/reward sharing and cost sharing clearly are the preferred approaches to customer-3PL revenue and cost management objectives.

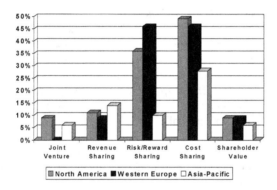

Figure 5.2 Types of Deal Structures

Source: 2003 3PL Study, C. John Langley Jr., Ph.D., Georgia Institute of Technology, Capgemini U.S. LLC, and FedEx Supply Chain Services.

As discussed in previous years, 3PL providers are evolving their business models to accommodate increasing customer expectations and to implement alternative deal structures. Essentially, many buyers and sellers of logistics services are currently searching for the type of financial arrangement that is satisfactory to both parties, and which provides continuing incentives for operational improvement. Also, these models are based on both a broadening of enhanced service offerings across the supply chain and an expansion of geographic coverage. The evolution includes a shift from Logistics Service Providers to 3PL providers, to Lead Logistics Providers (LLP), and finally to 4PL providers. The earlier-discussed Figure 5.1 depicts the changes in key attributes as the 3PL relationship models evolve.

Impacts of Globalization

The globalization of traditional businesses is a major factor affecting logistics and supply chain management. In particular, globalization involves these considerations: market expansion, new sources of supply, advanced security processes, continuous improvement initiatives, and redesigning logistics and supply chains for greater efficiency and effectiveness.

For a broader world view of 3PL services, the scope of this year's study was expanded across Western Europe and within China. Approximately 86% of the 3PL study respondents worldwide feel that 3PL providers would be able to keep up with the challenges of global supply chain integration. This suggests that 3PL providers would be up to this challenge, and that 3PL providers have been addressing the demand for global supply-chain solutions.

Customer Value Framework

This section focuses on the perceived value that 3PL users get from the availability of 3PL services. As indicated in Table 5.10, North American 3PL users continue to have successful outsourcing experiences – 89% reported their 2003 logistics outsourcing experience as either "extremely successful" or "very successful." Western European respondents' outsourcing success decreased slightly from 81% in 2002 to 77% in 2003. The respondents from Asia-Pacific indicated a 79% success factor. This is somewhat lower than last year (89%); however, last year's Asia-Pacific sample was much smaller.

Table 5.10 Customer Evaluation of Outsourcing (Percent Successful – Yearly Comparisons)

Year	North America	Western Europe	Asia-Pacific
1996	90 %	N/A	N/A
1997	83 %	N/A	N/A
1998	86 %	N/A	N/A
1999	88 %	N/A	N/A
2000	82 %	N/A	N/A
2001	85 %	N/A	N/A
2002	89 %	81 %	89 %
2003	90 %	76 %	79 %

Source: 2003 3PL Study, C. John Langley Jr., Ph.D., Georgia Institute of Technology, Capgemini U.S. LLC, and FedEx Supply Chain Services.

3PL Supply Chain Accomplishments

Respondents were asked if they felt that 3PL providers were accomplishing a number of specific supply chain challenges. On a positive note, 68% of the North American respondents indicated that 3PL providers were "facilitating supply chain improvement" and 58% thought that 3PL providers were "providing international supply chain solutions" (see Figure 5.3). Less than half of the Western European respondents felt the same about these accomplishments ("supply chain improvement" at 47% and "international supply chain solutions" at 41%).

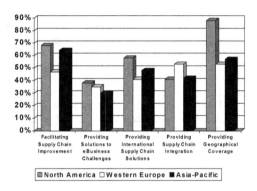

Figure 5.3 3PL Provider Accomplishments

Source: 2003 3PL Study, C. John Langley Jr., Ph.D., Georgia Institute of Technology, Capgemini U.S. LLC, and FedEx Supply Chain Services.

Measuring Success

As in previous years, the survey asked participants to quantify the improvements in their supply chains by using 3PL providers. Table 5.11 summarizes the various performance metrics the North American and Western European respondents reported (not enough Asia-Pacific responses were available to include statistics). Overall, 3PL users appear to be receiving quantifiable financial benefits from using 3PL providers. The benefits received are not only those activities directly controlled by the 3PL (logistics cost reduction), but could also be attributable to the internal changes made by users in contracting 3PL services.

Areas for Improvement

After identifying measures of success, participants were asked to respond to a list of "areas for improvement" for 3PL usage (Table 5.12). The greatest concern for both North American and European respondents was over meeting "service level commitments", while "lack of strategic management skills" was identified by the

Asia-Pacific respondents as the biggest opportunity for improvement. "Lack of continuous, on-going improvements and achievements in offerings" was also highlighted by North American and Western European users as a key area for improvement. Western European respondents felt that the time and effort spent on logistics has not been reduced, which could explain why the same group indicated that cost reductions are not being realized as anticipated.

Table 5.11 Average North America Customer Results from Use of Third-Party Logistics Provider

Type of Result	Average for Users of 3PL Services
Logistics Cost Reduction	9 %
Logistics Asset Reduction	16 %
Order Cycle Length Change	From 9.8 to 7.9 Days
Overall Inventory Reduction	8 %
Cash-To-Cash Cycle	From 25.6 to 18.3 Days

Source: 2003 3PL Study, C. John Langley Jr., Ph.D., Georgia Institute of Technology, Capgemini U.S. LLC, and FedEx Supply Chain Services.

More than half of the North American respondents indicated that cost creep after relationship with a 3PL provider has begun was important to them. Western European and Asia-Pacific users also believe that 3PL providers lack global capabilities. Finally, some users within North America and Western Europe perceive problems with a 3PL provider's lack of strategic management skills. This may partly explain the Western European concern with the unsatisfactory transition to a 3PL provider during implementation.

Strategic Assessment

The 3PL industry continues to go through an evolutionary change. Not only are 3PL providers and their capabilities changing, but the expectations that user firms have of their 3PL providers and their services are also changing. In fact, the 3PL industry is finding itself moving forward and beginning to show signs of progress toward maturity.

Table 5.12 Key 3PL "Concerns" Reported by Study Respondents (North America Results)

Concerns	Percent of Users Agreeing
Service Level Commitments Not Realized	66 %
Lack of Strategic Management Skills	53 %
Lack of Continuous, Ongoing Improvements	53 %
Cost "Creep" and Price Increases Once Relationship Begins	51 %
Time and Effort Spent on Logistics Not Decreased	43 %
Cost Reductions Not Realized	43 %
Unsatisfactory Transition During Implementation Stage	30 %
Lack of Consultative, Knowledge-Based Skills	30 %
Inability to Form Meaningful, Trusting Relationships	30 %
Not Keeping Up With IT Advances	26 %
Technology Skills Available, But Not Delivered to Client	23 %
Lack of Global Capabilities	22 %

Source: 2003 3PL Study, C. John Langley Jr., Ph.D., Georgia Institute of Technology, Capgemini U.S. LLC, and FedEx Supply Chain Services.

The 2003 3PL study found disappointment with some key 3PL core competencies. Although many 3PL users rate their relationships as either "extremely" or "somewhat" successful, numerous instances exist where these users identified "areas for improvement." Principal among these were concerns such as: "service level commitments not realized," "lack of continuous, ongoing improvements," "lack of strategic management skills," and "cost 'creep' and price increases once the relationship has commenced." 3PL users and providers appear to have increasing problems with the service level agreements being negotiated before the commencement of 3PL service. This is significant because it suggests that 3PL users have genuine concerns and that they may be looking for alternatives to the current arrangements with their 3PL providers. The study results suggest that users have high levels of expectations about their 3PL providers that may precipitate a movement back to "insourcing" 3PL services as an alternative to commercially available services.

There is also ambiguity with regard to on greater process integration and broader-based solutions in 3PL relationships. Although 3PL users want to further integrate 3PL provider processes with their own organizations, they also want "severability" of those same processes. This suggests that customers place a high priority on process integration and they continue to look for broad, comprehensive service offerings from the 3PL provider industry. However, they still want to separate processes and partner responsibilities when and if needed.

The evolution of logistics has increased the value of information. Successful supply chain integration causes the value of information (baseline and real-time user and provider information, real-time supply chain logistical information, and more) to increase in relation to the value of functional execution. Although the need for successful functional execution is great, a strategic shift has occurred: The need for capable data and process management, coupled with the availability of low-cost standard information, is now a high priority for both 3PL users and providers.

Supply chain integration is viewed as being increasingly important. The stated need for additional supply chain integration and for organizations that may serve as "integrators" has validated the 4PL model. Specifically, providers that can bring multiple service capabilities relating to the use of logistics information, operational knowledge, user-provider relationships, and supply chain integration are of critical importance. Realistically, however, the use of 4PLs may be limited – and financially justifiable – to supply chains that are complex, large, and rapidly changing, as well as limited to user organizations that are themselves large, complex, and global.

Respondents to the survey also saw the need for 3PL providers and customers to re-invent themselves. Clearly, customers expect more from the 3PL sector than they say they receive. While this may be partially explained by increases in expectations over time, it also may signal a need for 3PL providers and customers to "re-invent" themselves to be more capable business partners of one another. Recent study results point to a trend in which customers selectively use services from 3PL providers, and for "value-added" services that become core or "expected" services. While this 2003 3PL study has identified a number of 3PL priorities, the success of future 3PL relationships will depend on the ability of both parties to take their individual and collective capabilities "to a new level"; they will have to effectively "re-invent" themselves to be more responsive to changing logistics and supply chain environments. The short-term response by some 3PL customers may be a reversion to insourcing; the intermediate and longer-term response will be the tailoring of 3PL capabilities to meet the changing and increasing needs and requirements of the buyers of those 3PL services.

A principal strategic issue is the need for 3PL providers that offer globally capable services; that is, providers that can integrate processes and information across vast geographical boundaries. Although many 3PL providers market their "global" abilities, 3PL users indicate significant improvement is needed before most of these claims are realistic. One way to accomplish this objective is for existing 3PL providers to sufficiently modify their abilities so that the goal of being globally capable is within reach. The other is to suggest that the truly global business model is not only an extension of the capabilities of existing providers, but an area of core competency for the 3PL provider organization as a whole. Achieving this goal may be more realistic as a result of "re-invention" rather than "marginal improvement."

Respondents also indicated a set of factors that are critical to the success of any client-3PL relationship (Figure 5.4). Although no single respondent identified all of these factors, each was mentioned by a large number of respondents. What all respondents indicated was the urgent need for 3PLs and clients to address issues such as these during the formative stages of relationships. Any resources spent on the front-end to assure success in these areas will be of advantage during the term of the relationship.

■ Well-understood goals and objectives of relationship	■ Understanding of business needs of both client and 3PL organizations
■ Trust and commitment	
■ Communications	■ Multi-level organizational alignment between client firm and 3PL provider
■ Willingness to share risks and rewards	
■ Corporate compatibility	■ Ability to reach consensus on matters of strategic and operational importance
■ Management capability and philosophy	
■ Useful measurements and measurement strategies	■ Clear exit strategy

Figure 5.4 Key Critical 3PL Success Factors

Source: C. John Langley Jr., Ph.D.

UTi Ireland: A Case Study in Customer Responsiveness

The Sales Director of UTi Ireland was pleased ... in six weeks, a company by the name of Ergo developed a solution around the requirements of UTi Ireland, when the typical experience is that this would take much longer to accomplish. UTi Ireland Ltd., just two years in Ireland and part of UTi Worldwide, is a broadly based, information focused supply chain management business that provides freight forwarding, customs brokerage, order management and postponement warehousing services to customers around the globe. As a provider of these services, UTi Ireland is accurately thought of as a provider of third party logistics services.

The Problem

UTi's technology called eMpower is one of the best track and trace systems in the logistics industry, allowing visibility at the individual item level whether the product is at 'rest' or in 'motion', anywhere in the supply chain at any time. Realizing that local software/network support was a must in order to customize solutions in line with specific customer requirements, the module built by Ergo provided a valuable link with the existing UTi system that would enable clients in Ireland to communicate with UTi as an extension of the seamless supply chain worldwide.

The Solution

Ergo was called in and within four weeks the solution had been designed and was operating in pilot form. In effect the solution allowed full visibility from the time the goods left the U.K. customers back door right through to delivery to the end user. By way of example where 3,000 cartons arrive in Dublin port and 600 deliveries need to be made within the next 24 hours. The process as created by Ergo allows the bar codes on the cartons to be scanned and verified, to ensure all 3,000 cartons have arrived. The information is automatically sent back to UTi, where the main system is updated, thus producing the manifest for the 600 deliveries. When the customer signs for the delivery, the signature is scanned and held on the main system. With this automated system the paper trail is minimized, goods are delivered faster, the delivery paperwork is produced faster and there is instant information on all deliveries. UTi customers can just go on to the UTi web site to feed in an order number and see exactly were their goods are.

The Result

The UTi road freight business between the UK and Ireland is significant and continuing to grow. With this technology UTi Ireland can confidentially go to a potential customer and win their business. Plans are to continue using Ergo to support the system but also to help meet additional customer specific requirements. In addition to a very capable global information infrastructure, the relationship with Ergo will help UTi Ireland grow its business and develop supply chain solutions for its customers.

Source: http://www.smartbusiness.ie/casestudies/systemsintegration/.

Notes

1.   Robert V. Delaney, *11th Annual State of Logistics Report©* (St. Louis, MO: Cass Information Systems, June 5, 2000): 25.
2.   Rosabeth Moss Kanter, *Harvard Business Review* (July-August, 1994).
3.   For further information, see Robert C. Lieb and Arnold Maltz, "What's the Future for Third Party Logistics," *Supply Chain Management Review* (Fall 1999): 85-95; Leslie Hansen Harps, "Managing 3PL Relationships: Partnering for Performance," *Inbound Logistics* (July, 1998): 26-40; Armstrong & Associates, Inc., *Armstrong's Guide to Third Party Logistics Services Providers*, 8th edition, 2000; Donald J. Bowersox, "The Strategic Benefits of Logistics Alliances," *Harvard Business Review*, 90, 4 (July-August 1990): 36-45; Harry L. Sink, C. John Langley Jr., and Brian J. Gibson, "Buyer Observations of the U.S. Third Party Logistics Market," *International Journal of Physical Distribution and Logistics Management*, 26, 3 (1996): 38-46; Harry L. Sink and C. John Langley Jr., "A Managerial Framework for the Acquisition of Third Party Logistics Services," *Journal of Business Logistics*, 18, 2 (1997): 163-190; and C. John Langley Jr., Brian F. Newton, and Gene R. Tyndall, "Third Party Logistics: Has the Future Already Arrived?," *Supply Chain Management Review*, III, 3 (Fall 1999): 85-94.
4.   Trademark, Accenture, Inc.
5.   Accenture, Inc., by permission.
6.   Although 3PL software represents a small portion of overall turnover, the estimated negative growth rate was due to the very difficult market for software in the early 2000s.

7. C. John Langley Jr., Ph.D., Georgia Institute of Technology, Capgemini U.S. LLC, and FedEx Supply Chain Services, *Third Party Logistics Study: Results and Findings of the 2003 Eighth Annual Study*, September, 2003. Available for download at www.tli.gatech.edu.
8. Respondents were asked to classify their firms in one of the following categories: raw materials supplier, manufacturer (components/ingredients, contract manufacturer), manufacturer (finished product), wholesale/distribution, and retail.
9. For comparison, the percentages of North American users versus non-users indicating responsibilities in other areas of the world were as follow: Europe (47% vs. 32%), Asia-Pacific (47% vs. 32%), Middle East (21% vs. 15%), South America (32% vs. 18%), and Africa (13% vs. 6%).
10. Respondents from areas surveyed were given the option of responding to financial questions in customary monetary units (e.g., US$, euro, and RMB). Results were then converted to US$.
11. Although the 2002 study results indicated an "Asia-Pacific" 3PL usage rate of 92%, this figure was based on a small sample and may have been less reliable than the results from North America and Western Europe.
12. Data relating to Asia-Pacific logistics expenditures is based solely on results from non-China respondents, as the version of the study used in China was slightly modified from the one in more general use.

Chapter 6

Industry Performance Following Reformation of Economic and Social Regulation in the Trucking Industry

James Peoples

Introduction

Transportation plays a central role in the economic development of nations and thus has been supported and regulated by government. Beginning with support for a national pike from the Eastern Seaboard to the Ohio River, federal and state governments have been deeply involved in the development of the transportation infrastructure of the United States. This support has typically been accompanied by economic and social regulation intended to ameliorate the consequences of perceived monopoly power and industry instability and also to address public safety concerns.

Although the trucking industry has always benefited from extensive federal and state investment in road networks, it has evolved through three distinct regulatory regimes. From the beginning of the 20th century to 1935 the trucking industry was virtually unregulated. In contrast to railroads and shipping, which were subject to both economic and safety regulations, the small size and newness of the trucking industry effectively exempted it from government oversight until the Motor Carrier Act of 1935. The Motor Carrier Act gave the Interstate Commerce Commission the power to regulate entry into the industry, rates charged for trucking services, and the routing of goods. Following precedents established in the railroad industry, the Act also gave the Interstate Commerce Commission power to limit drivers' driving and working time.

Economic regulation was fundamental to the structure of the industry from the time the Act was passed until the deregulation of the late 1970s and early 1980s. As described in the first chapter of this volume, deregulation brought about fundamental change during the late 1970s and early 1980s, splitting companies into TL and LTL, causing large numbers of bankruptcies and providing opportunities for leading firms to develop and profit from new modes of operation. However, regulation of trucking did not end in the early 1980s. Many states continued to regulate intrastate trucking into the 1990s; remnants of the federal regulation system remained in place until 1995.

Building on the momentum of partial deregulation in the late 1970s to early 1980s, federal and state governments completed the economic deregulation of inter and intrastate trucking in the mid 1990s. Although the federal and state governments withdrew from regulation of trucking rates and entry, the federal government has continued to intervene to standardize state rules regulating the trucking industry, improve safety conditions and address homeland security issues. These policy changes have impacted drivers' hours of service, the requirements for commercial driver licenses and the weight, width and size restrictions on trucks.

This chapter investigates the evolution of the regulatory environment in the trucking industry since the early 1980s and seeks to explain the economic consequences of continued economic deregulation and increased safety regulation on the economic performance of the industry. Following the introduction (Section I), Section II presents a detailed overview of the evolution of economic regulation of trucking; Section III presents a similar overview of safety regulation. Section IV uses microeconomic theory to develop hypotheses on the expected industry performance effects of economic deregulation and safety regulation and provides some empirical measures of industry performance since deregulation. Concluding remarks are provided in section V.

Current Regulatory Environment

The first chapter in this volume relates the history and effects of deregulation on the motor carrier industry. As the first chapter in this volume explains, although the passage of the Motor Carrier Act (MCA) of 1980 did a great deal to economically deregulate the industry, remnants of economic regulation remain and the consequences of economic deregulation have spurred more extensive regulation of safety.

Economic Deregulation

The 1980 MCA intensified competition in the industry. As a result, many carriers negotiated rates with shippers that were below the tariffs filed with the interstate commerce commission (ICC). Although shippers directly benefited from the low freight rates, the trustees of bankrupt carriers that engaged in so-called 'undercharging' often sued shippers for the difference between the filed rate and the lower negotiated rate. In response, Congress passed the Negotiated Rate Act of 1993. The act limited suits brought by the trustees of bankrupt carriers occurring prior to 1990 and capped the value of claims for future undercharging lawsuits. The act also established that filed tariffs apply only to rate transactions and not reported discounts on verbal or written promise (Moore, 1995). Together, these policies constituted a key step toward assuring shippers that negotiated competitive prices would not be impeded by court action.

Continued governmental intervention in rate setting limited the role of the market. In keeping with the general policy shift toward less federal government participation in the economics of transportation, the 1994 Trucking Industry

Regulatory Reform Act (TIRRA) eliminated the filing of motor carrier tariffs as well as the statutory convenience and necessity standard. The new application for trucking firms focused only on the carrier's legal and financial fitness.

The abolition of the ICC on December 31, 1995 further reduced Federal involvement in the motor carrier industry. Most of the economic functions of the ICC were permitted to lapse, others including licensing were transferred to the Federal Highway Administration. As a consequence of this reform individuals who wish to provide interstate motor carrier service are now only required to file an application with the Federal Motor Carrier Safety Administration (FMCSA), file evidence of the proper insurance, designate an agent for the services of legal process and comply with FMCSA's safety regulation (Moore, 1995).

The End of Economic Regulation by States

While regulatory reform following the 1980 MCA resulted in almost complete federal deregulation of interstate trucking by 1994, some states continued economic regulation into the early 1990s. Prior to the 1980 MCA only New Jersey and Delaware were deregulated. Florida deregulated intrastate trucking operations in 1980, the same year that the MCA was enacted. Arizona and Maine followed in 1981 and 1982, respectively. By 1992 Wisconsin, Alaska, Vermont and Maryland had also deregulated intrastate trucking operations. Many of the remaining 41 states continued to require proof of need and financial fitness to secure common carrier authority. Others required only proof of fitness. Several states protected existing carriers from competition both through limiting the entry of new carriers and the expansion of authority of existing carriers (Taylor, 1994). The majority of these states retained strict entry restrictions into the mid 1990s (column 3, Table 6.1) and many imposed pricing controls designed to assure that rates covered relevant costs (column 2, Table 6.1) but often these controls were not strictly enforced. Despite an absence of strict enforcement, price controls may allow the pass through of costs to shippers. Work by Taylor suggests that freight rates in Texas, with its highly regulated intrastate market, were 40 percent higher than comparable interstate rates. Seventy-five percent of shippers in Michigan believed that intrastate rates were higher than equivalent deregulated interstate rates, while 55 percent of shippers in Florida reported a rate decline after state deregulation.[1]

Table 6.1   Intrastate Economic Regulatory Environment

State Deregulation	Pre-AIA Regulatory Environment		Year of State
	Rate Regulation (severity of rate regulation just prior to intra-state deregulation)	Entry Regulation (severity of entry regulation just prior to intra-state deregulation)	
	(1)	(2)	(3)
Alabama	strict	strict	1995 AIA
Alaska	none	none	1984
Arizona	none	none	1982
Arkansas	limited	moderately liberal	1995 AIA
California	strict	strict	1995 AIA
Colorado	limited	strict	1995 AIA
Connecticut	limited	strict	1995 AIA
Delaware	none	none	never regulated
Florida	none	none	1980
Georgia	strict	strict	1995 AIA
Hawaii	strict	strict	1995 AIA
Idaho	limited	partly deregulated	1995 AIA
Illinois	strict	strict	1995 AIA
Indiana	little control	strict	1995 AIA
Iowa	limited	moderately liberal	1995 AIA
Kansas	limited	liberal	1995 AIA
Kentucky	limited	strict	1995 AIA
Louisiana	strict	strict	1995 AIA
Maine	none	none	1982
Maryland	little control	partly deregulated	1995 AIA
Massachusetts	little control	strict	1995 AIA
Michigan	strict	strict	1995 AIA
Minnesota	little control	strict	1995 AIA
Mississippi	strict	strict	1995 AIA
Missouri	strict	strict	1995 AIA
Montana	strict	strict	1995 AIA
Nebraska	strict	strict	1995 AIA
Nevada	strict	strict	1995 AIA
New Hampshire	little control	strict	1995 AIA
New Jersey	none	none	never regulated
New Mexico	strict	strict	1995 AIA
North Carolina	limited	strict	1995 AIA
North Dakota	little control	moderately liberal	1995 AIA
Ohio	little control	strict	1995 AIA

Table 6.1   continued

State Deregulation	Pre-AIA Regulatory Environment		Year of State
	Rate Regulation (severity of rate regulation just prior to intra-state deregulation)	Entry Regulation (severity of entry regulation just prior to intra-state deregulation)	
	(1)	(2)	(3)
Oklahoma	strict	strict	1995 AIA
Oregon	strict	strict	1995 AIA
Pennsylvania	strict	strict	1995 AIA
Rhode Island	strict	strict	1995 AIA
South Carolina	strict	strict	1995 AIA
South Dakota	little control	strict	1995 AIA
Tennessee	little control	strict	1995 AIA
Texas	strict	strict	1995 AIA
Utah	little control	partly deregulated	1995 AIA
Vermont	none	partly deregulated	1986
Virginia	little control	strict	1995 AIA
Washington	strict	strict	1995 AIA
West Virginia	strict	partly deregulated	1995 AIA
Wisconsin	none	partly deregulated	1982
Wyoming	strict	strict	1995 AIA

Sources: Daniel Baker "State Regulatory Activity and Federal Pre-emption." 21st Transportation Law Institute, pp. 83-95 and "The Impact of State Economic Regulation of Motor Carriage on Intrastate and Interstate Commerce," US Department of Transportation.

Federal legislation was enacted in 1994 to pre-empt remaining state economic regulation over intrastate trucking routes. Effective January 1, 1995 Section 601 of the 1995 Airport Improvement Act (AIA) prohibited state and local authorities from regulation of rates, routes or services within the transportation industry. This act, which remains in effect today, permits state governments to exercise regulatory authority over safety, financial fitness, insurance, vehicle size and weight and highway route controls for hazardous materials. The elimination of intrastate regulation of rates and entry in the industry today should promote the growth of new trucking establishments. Regulatory reform supports a more competitive business environment and makes it riskier for carriers to charge increased rates absent cost justification. Information on the effect of the AIA on competition and shipping prices is presented in Table 6.2. Column (1) presents the number of trucking establishment for the pre and post AIA period. These findings indicate that the motor carrier industry added 9,826 establishments in the six years following passage of the AIA. Such growth easily surpasses the growth during the period from 1970 to 1980 before the 1980 MCA. It compares less favorably with the growth between 1980 and 1994. Although the number of additional trucking firms is similar in the pre and post AIA period, about 2750 firms every year, the annual average rate of growth from 1980 to 1994 was 4 percent against 2.5 percent in the post AIA period.

Table 6.2   Market Trends in the Motor Carrier Sector*

Year	(1) No. of Trucking And Courier Establishments	(2) Real Avg. Freight Revenue Per Ton-Mile** (1982 cents)	(3) Nominal Avg. Freight Revenue Per Ton-Mile	(4) Price Index for Motor Fuel*** (1982-84=100)
1970	64,756	21.79	8.5	27.9
1980	69,796	20.45	11.6	97.4
1990	90,709	20.05	18.0	101.2
1994	108,971	19.84	24.4	98.5
1995	112,887	19.60	25.0	100
1996	116,861	19.84	25.1	106.3
1997	121,111	19.77	26.0	106.2
1998	119,572	20.00	26.2	92.2
1999	120,687	19.69	26.2	100.7
2000	122,713	19.56	27.0	129.3

* *Source: Bureau of Transportation Statistics.*
** *Freight revenue is deflated using the producer price index.*
*** *Source: 2004 Economic Report for the President.*

The elimination of intrastate regulation has been associated with small declines in real average revenue per ton-mile relative to 1980-1994 (Table 6.2, column 2). Real rates declined from 19.84 to 19.56 cents per mile between 1994 and 2000, but the year to year fluctuations suggest that the low rate reported in 2000 may only be temporary. The increases in the nominal trucking rate post AIA reflect general inflationary patterns in the overall economy, with only a modest increase of 2 cents per ton mile following intrastate deregulation. Even this increase in rates might be cost justified, since nominal trucking rate increases generally follow the upward trend in fuel prices (column (4)). Although the modest observed impact of deregulation of intrastate trucking in 1995 may be due to the conflating effects of other factors, at first blush intrastate deregulation appears to be the tail on the dog of economic deregulation.

Table 6.3   Vehicle Weight and Length Limits by State (1994)

State	Gross Vehicle Weight (1,000 lbs)		Max. Semitrailer Length	
	Interstate	Other Highways	National Network	Other Highways
Alabama	80	84	57'	53'
Alaska	---	90	48'	45'
Arizona	80	80	57' 6"	53'
Arkansas	80	80	53' 6"	53' 6"
California	80	80	53'	53'
Colorado	80	85	57' 4"	57' 4"
Connecticut	80	80	53'	48'
Delaware	80	80	53'	53'
D.C.	80	80	48'	48'
Florida	80	80	53'	53'
Georgia	80	80	53'	53'
Hawaii	80.8	88	No limit	45'
Idaho	80	105.5	53'	53'
Illinois	80	80	53'	53'
Indiana	80	80	53'	53'
Iowa	80	80	53'	53'
Kansas	80	85.5	59' 6"	59' 6"
Kentucky	80	80	53'	No limit
Louisiana	80	80	59' 6"	No limit
Maine	80	80	53'	53'
Maryland	80	80	53'	53'
Massachusetts	80	80	53'	53'
Michigan	80	80	53'	50'
Minnesota	80	80	53'	53'
Mississippi	80	80	53'	53'
Missouri	80	80	53'	No limit
Montana	80	80	53'	53'
Nebraska	80	95	53'	53'
Nevada	80	129	53'	53'
New Hampshire	80	80	53'	53'
New Jersey	80	80	53'	53'
New Mexico	86.4	86.4	57' 6"	No limit
New York	80	80	53'	48'
North Carolina	80	80	53'	No limit
North Dakota	80	105.5	53'	53'
Ohio	80	80	53'	53'
Oklahoma	80	80	59' 6"	50' 6"
Oregon	80	80	53'	Varies
Pennsylvania	80	80	53'	No limit

Table 6.3   continued

State	Gross Vehicle Weight (1,000 lbs)		Max. Semitrailer Length	
	Interstate	Other Highways	National Network	Other Highways
Rhode Island	80	80	48' 6"	48' 6"
South Carolina	80	80	53'	48'
South Dakota	80	129	53'	53'
Tennessee	80	80	53'	53'
Texas	80	80	59'	59'
Utah	80	80	53'	53'
Vermont	80	80	53'	48'
Virginia	80	80	53'	No limit
Washington	80	105.5	53'	53'
West Virginia	80	80	53'	No limit
Wisconsin	80	80	53'	No limit
Wyoming	117	117	60'	60'

Standardizing Limits on Weight and Length

The standards governing road systems can have an effect on operations of interstate trucking networks. In the past, standards were established by the states with limited federal oversight and consequently there have been substantial differences in state standards, particularly with respect to the maximum weight and length of trucks and the number of trailers that may be pulled by a tractor. Although some of these differences reflect differences between states in the construction of roads and traffic conditions, other result from the idiosyncrasies of state politics.

Lack of uniformity has been a problem for motor carriers because differences in state standards can force firms to purchase additional equipment and may require reloading freight or altering routes. Federally imposed limits on state regulation of the dimension and weight of commercial trucks have resulted in relative uniformity in weight, width and size regulations across states. Federal law prohibits states from imposing weight limits below 80,000. Federal law also requires states to allow width of up to 102 inches on the national network for large trucks. In addition, federal law requires that states allow single trailers to be at least 48 feet long and prescribe a maximum length of 53 feet (57 feet in some states). The length limit for tractors pulling two trailers is 28 feet per trailer on the national network. As a result of these federal mandates, the states' maximum gross vehicle weight limits are generally set at 80,000 pounds and semi-trailer lengths are generally set at 53 feet. Only Hawaii and New Mexico permit weight limits above the 80,000 pounds on interstate roads, and only 12 states set maximum length requirements that differ from 53 feet. Recently, the Transportation Research Board (2002) has recommended increasing the maximum weight from the current level of 80,000 to 90,000 pounds, as well as lengthening double-trailer configurations to 33 feet per trailer from the current length of 28 feet. According to the TRB, highways are now able to handle large and more economically efficient trucks due to increased funding for state highway programs during the period from 1990 to 2000.

Safety Regulation

Creating and maintaining safer roads have been ongoing objectives for trucking regulators, particularly because of the large number of motor vehicle injuries occurring on interstate routes and their arteries. Thus far, much of the safety effort has focused on improved highway design and on the equipage of trucks (this topic is addressed in the chapter on safety), but federal efforts to improve safety have also entailed standardizing and tightening requirements for truck driver licensure, regulating working hours and funding state safety programs.

Standardizing Licensing through Federal Regulation

Licensure provides assurance that drivers have the minimum level of the knowledge and skills required for safe operation of trucks. Licensing has historically been the responsibility of state governments and, as a consequence, standards have varied considerably. Before 1986, some states permitted anyone licensed to drive an automobile to drive a tractor-trailer. Even among those states that had a classified licensing system, not all required that skills be tested in a representative vehicle. Because state driver licenses are accepted throughout the United States, this system allowed significant numbers of drivers with modest knowledge of trucks and safety regulations to be employed in an increasingly national truck transportation system.

Awareness of the need to revise safety rules and regulations grew following the passage of the 1980 MCA. Roads became increasingly congested and dangerous, in part due to greater competition in the motor carrier sector.[2] Congress responded with the 1986 Commercial Motor Vehicle Safety Act (CMVSA) of 1986 which overhauled driver's license requirements and classification for commercial motor vehicles. The CMVSA established the National Commercial Drivers License program charged with the task of improving highway safety by ensuring that drivers of large trucks are qualified and removing unsafe drivers from highways. The act maintained states' rights to issue drivers' licenses but established CDL classifications, and minimum standards, which states must meet when licensing commercial motor vehicle drivers.

The CMVSA classifies CDL's into three groups according to size and vehicle combination.[3] This act also prohibits operators from holding more than one license and requires states to adopt testing licensing standards for truck drivers that test an applicant's ability to operate the type of vehicle he/she plans to drive. State license examinations are required to be at least as stringent as the federal standards, and comprise both a general knowledge and a driving skills component. The general knowledge test must contain at least 30 questions, and the applicant must correctly answer at least 80 percent of those questions to pass the knowledge test. Applicants must successfully perform all the required skills listed in 49CFR 383.113 to pass the driving skills test.[4]

Applicants must also be physically qualified to attain a CDL. For instance, vision requirements listed in 49CFR591.41 (b) 10 require applicants to have a distance visual acuity of at least 20/40 (Snellen) in each eye, with or without corrective lenses, and a field vision of at least 70 degrees in the horizontal meridian in each eye. Applicants must also be able to recognize the colors of traffic signals and devices showing standard red, green, and amber.

The implementation of the CDL has had a large impact on drivers. By some estimates 30 percent of individuals who were driving trucks before the CDL were later disqualified from such work due to lack of knowledge or ability to handle trucks or because of physical limitations. The effectiveness of these regulations is also reflected in regular re-evaluation of motor vehicle department employees who issue CDLs.

Regulation of Hours of Work

Section 204(a) of the Motor Carrier Act of 1935 gave the ICC responsibility for establishing safety regulations in trucking including qualifications for becoming a truck driver and limitations on working time. Following hearings in 1936 and 1937, the Hours of Service (HOS) regulations, which limited drivers to 15 hours on-duty in a 24-hour period, were enacted. On-duty hours were divided into 12 hours for driving and non-driving work time, such as loading, unloading and completing paperwork, and 3 hours for rest breaks and meals (Federal Register, 2000, p. 25547). The nine hours off-duty implicit in these regulations were believed to be sufficient to provide the opportunity for eight hours of sleep. Drivers were also limited to 60 hours of work in a seven-day period or 70 hours in an eight-day period.

Labor groups, who favored the standard eight hour work day typical in other industries, challenged the proposed regulations. The ICC held that "The evidence before us clearly does not suffice to enable us to conclude that a duty period as low as eight hours in 24 is required in the interest of safety." (Federal Register, 2000, p. 25547). The ICC modified the rules to restrict drivers to 10 hours of driving time but also reduced off-duty time from nine hours to eight. Under the modified rules drivers could, work 16 hours of on-duty time, allocate one hour of off duty time during that period, before being required to take eight hours off duty. Other limitations on working time were not modified and the ICC noted, "The fact that we hereinafter prescribe 60 hours on duty as the weekly maximum should not interfere with the negotiations by organized labor of contracts providing for shorter hours." (Federal Register, 2000, p. 25548.) Drivers were also exempted from the overtime provisions of the Fair Labor Standards Act because of the ICC's jurisdiction over working time.

The original regulations were structured around a 24-hour work cycle, but this practice was abandoned in the 1962 revision. Prior to 1962, drivers were limited to 10 hours of driving time in a maximum of 15 hours of on-duty time and they were required to take a minimum of eight hours off-duty in a 24-hour period. The 1962 amendments allowed drivers to begin driving after a period of eight consecutive hours off-duty. This permitted the start of work to be moved up each working day. For example, if a driver began at 8am on a Monday morning, he could conceivably drive 10 hours (until 6pm) take eight hours off-duty and begin driving the following morning at 4am. As discussed in the chapter on safety, movement away from a 24 work-cycle is a cause of fatigue and long-term health problems.

The HOS regulations have been recognized as an industry problem for many years. The desire to earn additional income combined with pressures from trucking firms and shippers for fast deliveries provide incentives for drivers to work beyond legal limits. The liability of drivers rather than employers or shippers for violations minimizes any incentive for trucking firms to effectively monitor their drivers. To comply with the HOS regulations, drivers are required to keep paper logs of their hours and there is considerable evidence that drivers have evaded limits. Keeping multiple log-books is a common method of evasion. In a survey of 1,000 drivers conducted between 1997 and 1999, half of drivers reported working at least 60 hours in the prior seven days and 25% reported working 70 hours or more (Belman, Monaco and Brooks, forthcoming). Fifty-five percent of drivers reported violating the HOS regulations at least once in the past 30 days (op. cit). Furthermore, the routing and scheduling software used in the trucking industry typically does not incorporate HOS limits on working time and so treats driving working time as completely flexible.

Responsibility for safety regulation in trucking was transferred from the ICC to the Federal Highway Administration (FHWA) in 1966 as part of the Department of Transportation Act. In 1976 and 1978 the FHWA announced prospective reforms that would have altered HOS regulations including restrictions on night-time driving and driving hours. However, the social costs of these proposals were determined to be prohibitively high and FHWA abandoned the rule changes. The HOS regulations remained unchanged through the deregulation of the late 1970s and 1980s (Federal Register, 2000, p. 25549).

The FHWA was charged with amending the HOS regulations in the ICC Termination Act of 1995 and announced proposed rulemaking in 1996. Three notices of proposed rulemaking followed in 1998, 2000 and 2003. The 1998 NPRM was aimed at requiring firms to maintain accurate records of driver's time (Federal Register, 2003, p. 22458). In 1999 the Federal Motor Carrier Safety Administration (FMCSA) took over responsibility for ensuring safety in trucking and it fell upon them to change the HOS regulations. The 2000 NPRM focused specifically on changing the HOS regulations themselves and engendered considerable controversy. Changes to HOS regulations were specifically prohibited in the transportation appropriations for fiscal years 2001 and 2002 due to concern about the economic and safety implications of the 2000 proposed changes.

The 2003 NPRM outlined significant HOS regulation changes to take effect in January of 2004. These changes included: increasing driving time to 11 hours, decreasing total work time to 14 total hours, and increasing off-duty time to 10 hours. The proposed regulations were a step towards returning drivers to a 24-hour cycle. The shortest the cycle allowable under the proposed changes (assuming full use of the available hours of driving) would be 21 hours. Under the earlier HOS regulations, the shortest allowable cycle was 16 hours. Additionally, the proposed changes prohibited drivers from extending their driving time by going off duty in the middle of the driving cycle. Under the old regulations, drivers could extend their work-day by logging breaks or waiting time as off-duty time. The proposed prohibition would have required drivers to stop driving 11 hours after they started driving and stop working 14 hours after they begin working, regardless of breaks for meals or rest taken. This provision drew criticism from the industry as a whole and from the American Trucking Association in particular (Federal Register, 2003).

The original 60-hour and 70-hour HOS limits remain, however, under the new regulations, drivers are however allowed to "restart" their clock after 34 consecutive hours off-duty. Under the 1937 regulations the 60 hours were determined by any 7 consecutive days. For example, the number of hours a driver could work on a Monday would be constrained by the number of hours they had worked the prior Monday. If a driver had worked eight hours that day and then 52 hours in the following 6 days (for their maximum 60), he could only work eight hours on the next Monday (even if he had taken the weekend off and legally would not reach the daily limit of hours). Under these new provisions, a driver could exhaust his work hours in 4 days and 6 hours, take 34 hours off-duty and then begin driving again after a total cycle of 5 days and 16 hours, rather than the 7 days under the original regulations. This acceleration of the drivers' workweek would increase the total number of hours driven and worked over the course of the year.

In response to this and other safety concerns in the new HOS regulations, Public Citizen led a group of petitioners who sued to block the new HOS regulations. The new regulations went into effect January 4, 2004, but were set aside by the U.S. Court of Appeals for the District of Columbia Circuit on July 16, 2004. In its decision, the Court ruled that the FMCSA had not adequately considered the safety ramifications of increased driving time in a 24-hour period (p. 15) as well as the increased work time resulting from the 34-hour restart (p. 22) (US Court of Appeals, 03-1165, 2004).

Another issue raised in the lawsuit and mentioned by the Court of Appeals was the lack of provision for electronic on-board computers (EOBRs). These are devices that would generate an unalterable record of driving time and might replace paper logbooks. While the original announcement of proposed rulemaking stated that EOBRs would be mandatory under the new HOS regulations, this provision was eliminated in the final NPRM (p. 22488) due to cost concerns raised by trucking firms and concerns as to whether or not the current technology could actually replace logbooks. The U.S. Court of Appeals took issue with this, finding that the FMCSA did not seriously consider whether EOBRs would be effective, focusing on the FMCSA's lack of any cost-benefit analysis of these devices.

At this time, the eventual fate of the revised HOS regulations is uncertain. The FMCSA is currently charged with evaluating the comments of the Court of Appeals and responding to the safety concerns raised. Whether the FMCSA will revise the regulations to meet the concerns of the court, appeal the decision or follow some other course remains to be seen.

Additional Programs to Improve Safety

Concerns over the effects of the 1980 MCA on truck safety led to an increase in the federal funds for state safety programs. The 1982 Motor Carrier Safety Assistance Program (MCSAP) was the first post regulatory reform program of this sort. This program annually provides matching grants to states to fund driver and vehicle roadside inspections, as well as compliance reviews. The MCSAP also provides funding to help states enforce the National Commercial License Program. Minnesota serves as an example of the effectiveness of the MCSAP. The Office of the Legislative Auditor of the State of Minnesota reports that the creation of the Motor Carrier Safety Assistance program in 1982, which Minnesota joined in 1984, was the major impetus behind the growth of state safety regulation. By 1991 the MCSAP had funded 80 percent of the growth in Minnesota's safety regulations from 1982 levels. Annual inspections increased from an average of about 1500 vehicles per year to nearly 390,000 inspections in fiscal year 1991. Moreover, total commercial vehicle crashes dropped from 5.0 per million vehicle miles in 1984 to 2.8 in 1990.

Federal dollars dedicated to safety also helped to fund safe highway construction. In 1991, Congress approved the Intermodal Surface Transportation Efficiency Act (ISTEA), which authorized approximately $120 billion for the fiscal years 1992 through 1997 to fund construction activity aimed at promoting safety including bridge replacement and congestion relief projects. ISTEA funding is awarded to projects that maintain and improve existing highway structure and advance safety goals. Additionally, apportionment is based upon the amount of revenue generated in the state and safeguarding the state's historical funding shares.

The 1998 Transportation Equity Act was built on the initiatives established in the ISTEA. This act combines the continuation and improvement of current programs with new initiatives to meet the challenges of record increases in traffic congestion. For example, the state of Wisconsin used funding to increase signing, install pavement markers, provide better vision centers, and install delineation signs. Upgraded corridors have shown a reduction in fatal and serious crashes. Overall the rate of traffic fatalities per million vehicle miles of travel has declined by 34 percent from 1986-2000. Washington transportation authorities acknowledge that ISTEA and TEA funds have contributed significantly to safer roadways.[5] Nationally, vehicle fatality rates decreased during the post 1980 MCA period and resulting enhancements in safety regulation. Information in Table 6.4 suggest that large truck involvement in fatal crashes per 100 million vehicle miles dropped appreciably during the periods following the 1982 and 1986 acts and remained low thereafter. This fatality rate pattern closely resembles past findings using workdays lost due to injury and illness in the trucking industry (Savage, 2004).

Concerns over national security and terrorism also affect the motor carrier industry because flammable and hazardous materials that could be used in as part of a terrorist attack are regularly shipped in high volume across the country. In response to these concerns the Transportation Security Administration (TSA) revised security requirements for CMV operators who haul hazardous materials. After November 2003 hazardous materials (hazmat) endowment holders are required to submit name-based criminal history checks and checks for citizenship status to the FBI.[6] CMV operators entering the U.S. from Canada or Mexico must also undergo to the same background check and satisfy the same eligibility standards as U.S. based drivers.

Table 6.4   Safety Trend in the Motor Carrier Sector

Year	Large Trucks Involvement in Fatal Crashes Per 100 Million Vehicle Miles
1980	5.0
1990	3.3
1994	2.7
1995	2.5
1996	2.6
1997	2.6
1998	2.5
1999	2.4
2000	2.4
2001	2.3

Source: Bureau of Transportation Statistics.

Economic Theory on Industry Performance Following Regulatory Reform

Since 1980, the combination of economic deregulation and increased safety regulation has successfully limited trucking rate increases and improved road safety. Still, this chapter has not specifically addressed the impact deregulation has had on carriers. The impact of economic deregulation has been the subject of much and varied research, which can only be touched on briefly.

Economic theory suggests that the economic deregulation of an inherently competitive industry should enhance industry productivity as carriers seek competitive advantage through cost saving technology and techniques. Corsi and Grimm (1989) find the use of communications equipment to coordinate haul transfers greatly improved trucking productivity following initial trucking deregulation. Economic theory is less deterministic in predicting the effect of deregulation on industry profits. On the one hand, downward price pressures associated with stepped-up competition should restrict profit gains. On the other hand, carriers' abandonment of unprofitable operations, avoidance of costly backhauls and discontinuance of rent sharing with labor should all raise firm profits.

Table 6.5   Financial Trends in the Trucking Industry

Year	(1) labor	(2) Cost of operations productivity**	(3) Return on as a percent of Net sales#	(4) Operating assets## margin before deducting CEO Compensation###
2000	131	30.0%	7.3%	1.7%
1999	132	30.9%	7.3%	1.3%
1998	130	31.3%	9.7%	2.8%
1997	132	30.7%	9.7%	2.8%
1996	131	32.5%	9.5%	2.4%
1995	125	38.0%	7.4%	1.2%
1994	130	37.8%	7.3%	0.7%
1992	123	36.2%	6.7%	1.0%
1991	117	39.4%	5.9%	0.4%
1990	111	41.0%	8.0%	1.5%
1989	109	42.2%	7.1%	0.7%
1988	105	44.2%	7.9%	1.5%
1987	100	44.0%	9.0%	1.8%
1986	97	45.2%	7.5%	0.2%
1985	94	42.6%	7.1%	NA
1984	97	44.2%	4.4%	NA
1983	94	44.0%	5.3%	NA
1982	74	45.2%	3.0%	NA
1981	81	60.7%	4.4%	NA
1980	78	65.0%	NA	NA
1979	84	64.8%	NA	NA
1978	NA	65.2%	NA	NA
1977	NA	67.0%	NA	NA
1976	NA	65.6%	NA	NA

Sources: Information on cost of operations as a percent of sales, return on assets and operating margins before deducting CEO compensation are taken from Almanac of Business and Financial Ratios (Troy, 2003). Labor productivity indexes are provided by the Bureau of Labor Statistics.
** 1987 is the benchmark year for labor productivity indexes.
 # Cost of operations as a percent of net sales is the ratio of cost incurred in providing carrier service and the gross operating receipts.
Return on assets is the product of the sales to total assets ratio and the profits to total sales ratio.
Operating margin before deducting CEO compensation is the net income before deducting CEO compensation.

Post 1980 changes in safety regulation should also influence the performance of carriers, but the effect is again ambiguous. More stringent HOS regulations may reduce costs by reducing the frequency and costs of accidents and by reducing instances of work related chronic illness resulting from long and irregular hours (Belzer et al., 2002).[7] On the other hand, such regulations may raise operating costs if the reduction in driver working time leads to slower service. The coordination of limits on weight and length should, on the other hand, improve productivity and reduce costs by reducing the number of drivers and equipment needed to handle a given volume of shipments. CDL requirements and federal funding of state highway programs can also lower operating costs. Since the drivers who are adequately trained and informed are also the ones most likely to qualify to obtain the CDL, the costs of asymmetric information employers face in hiring and screening processes are likely to be reduced as a consequence of regulation. Federal funding programs that subsidize state efforts to remove unsafe drivers from the road and that subsidize the maintenance and construction of safe roads help ultimately help to lessen carrier insurance premiums by reducing truck drivers' involvement in fatal crashes. More stringent CDL regulation also creates a challenge to carriers by limiting the pool of applicants who qualify for a CDL. Recent evidence of applicants illegally purchasing CDL's in Illinois and Florida indicates that many applicants encounter significant difficulties in satisfying CDL requirement.[8]

In sum, the effect of safety regulation on carrier performance is not obvious *a priori*. Hence, empirical evidence is needed for a more complete analysis of the effect of recent economic and safety regulatory reform on trucking carrier performance. Information on annual industry performance is presented in Table 6.5. Data on industry productivity is provided by the Bureau of Labor Statistics and data on returns on assets is taken from annual issues of the *Almanac of Business and Industrial Financial Ratios* (Troy 1981-2003). Industry productivity is an index of industry output per worker and annual return on assets and is calculated by taking the product of the sales/total asset ratio and the net profit/sales ratio. Annual information on productivity is reported for each year starting in 1979. The industry source for return on assets in trucking is reported for each year from 1981.

The trucking industry has sustained its initial post deregulation productivity growth rate despite the introduction of more stringent safety regulation in the early and mid 1980s. Contrary to expectations, productivity gains, though, stalled following the 1995 deregulation of intrastate rates and entry. For instance, the findings in column (1) indicate that productivity increased at an annual percentage rate of 3.76 from 1980 to 1995 but annual productivity gains averaged only 0.8 percent from 1995 to 2000, and most of these were the results of a 4.8 percent increase from 1995 to 1996. A graphical depiction of trucking and U.S. productivity trends presented in Figure 6.1 shows that decreasing productivity growth in trucking following the Airport Improvement Act (AIA) is unique to this industry. U.S. productivity increased at a fairly consistent rate during the mid to late 1990s. Figure 6.1 also reveals that other than the recessionary period immediately following the 1980 Motor Carrier Act, pre AIA trucking productivity growth exceeded the U.S. average. This pre-AIA trucking pattern further underscores the effect of intrastate deregulation on productivity, since productivity gains would have been higher if the industry sustained levels reported in preceding years.

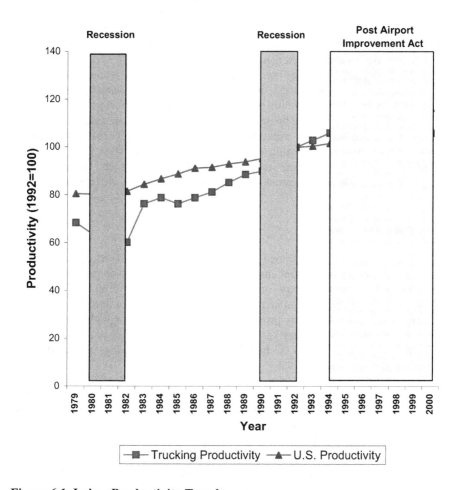

Figure 6.1 Labor Productivity Trends

Even though the trucking industry has not experienced significant productivity gains following 1995 intrastate deregulation, the industry experienced improvements in cost efficiency immediately following this policy change. Lower cost/sales ratios, reported in column (2) of Table 6.5 are indicative of greater operating efficiency as each dollar of sales is generated using fewer resources. Carriers' operating costs as a percent of net sales fell from 38.0 to 32.5 percent after enactment of the AIA and remained below the 32.5 level thereafter. The cost efficient gains arising immediately after 1995 followed five years of relatively minor cost efficiency gains.[9] Interestingly, there was also an immediate cost efficiency effect associated with interstate deregulation in the early 1980s when the cost/sales ratio declined from 60.7 to 45.2 percent from 1981 to 1982, and remained in the low 40s for the succeeding nine years.

The effects of intrastate deregulation on rates of profit are less clear. Carriers have earned relatively high profits following intrastate deregulation. Average returns on assets presented in column (3) vary from 7.3 to 9.7 percent for the 1995-2000 post AIA time-frame. Although the profit rate is higher than in the years immediately prior to 1995, it is only slightly higher than that achieved in 1985-1990. Intrastate deregulation no doubt contributed to robust profit levels after 1995, but this effect cannot be separated from the effect of increased demand consequent to the economic expansion in the mid and late 1990s. Although the series is short, data on operating cost margins support the view that the end of intrastate economic regulation improved industry performance. Operating cost margins rose as high as 2.8 percent, and remained close to historic levels.

Conclusion and Discussion

Regulatory reform has continued to change the business environment in the trucking industry. In the current environment, market forces have greater influence on rates and successful entry into the industry than government regulation. However, government plays an increasingly greater role in promoting safety in this industry. The trucking industry provides a good case study of a highly competitive industry with significant safety regulation. This study contributes an examination of the industry and identifies the beneficiaries of recent trucking deregulation and more stringent safety regulation.

Findings on rate of return trends revealed that the trucking industry has generated single digit profit rates throughout the post 1980 MCA observation period. Carriers, however, were able to take advantage of periods of national prosperity by posting higher profit rates during economic expansions. The evidence on industry productivity is less positive as findings suggest this is an area in which carriers have faced difficulty. Industry productivity growth is actually lower following intra-state deregulation of rates and entry. Attaining high productivity growth was difficult possibly due to legislation that enacted more stringent safety regulation during the same period of economic deregulation. For instance, new CDL requirements limit the number of potential drivers and so carriers may find it difficult to employ an efficient number of drivers. New hours-of-service regulations that lower the number of hours commercial vehicle operators are permitted to drive can make it more difficult for drivers to meet scheduling deadlines. And seemingly outdated weight-length and size regulations create a challenge to carriers as they attempt to reach optimal transport loads, especially during periods of high service demand. Still, there is arguably potential for enhanced productivity gains in the near future given the fact that current economic reforms have removed regulations that stifle the incentive to generate profits through efficiency gains.

This study also found that tougher safety laws have had the intended effect of reducing driver risk. However, further limitations placed on hours of service have created greater scheduling pressure on drivers. It will be interesting to observe whether a more competitive trucking industry can create the necessary incentives for easing work place pressures on drivers. What does seem apparent is the current economic and social regulations have maintained levels of shipper welfare and carrier profitability that are commensurate with a competitive industry.

Notes

1. Taylor (1994) observes that 48 percent of Florida shippers reported a price decline following state deregulation.
2. Evidence of increasing road congestion is reported by the Department of Transportation (2002). Their report shows 40 percent growth in the number of truck drivers from 1983 to 2000.
3. A class-A CDL is required for drivers of any combination of vehicles with a gross of 26,001 or more pounds provided that the gross vehicle weight of the vehicle being towed is in excess of 10,001. A class-B CDL is required for drivers of any single vehicle with a gross vehicle weight of 26, 0001 or more pounds or more pounds or any such vehicle towing a vehicle with gross weight not in excess of 10,000 pounds. Last, a class-C CDL is required for drivers of any single vehicle, or combination of vehicles that does not meet the definition of Class A or Class B, but is either designed to transport 16 or more passengers, including the driver, or is placarded for hazardous materials.
4. CDLs are revoked for operators who are convicted while driving a commercial motor vehicle, who have two or more violations of out-of-service order within a ten year period, who are convicted of driving under the influence, or leaving the scene of an accident.
5. Wisconsin has benefited from the TEA's reapportionments of state contributions, as this state received slightly more than one dollar for every dollar it contributed to the highway trust fund by 1998. In contrast, the vast majority of southern states pay more into the trust than they receive.
6. Hazmat is the shortened version of the term hazardous materials. A hazmat endowment means that CMV operators are permitted to transport highly dangerous materials on U.S. roads.
7. Belzer et al. (2002) argue that market pressures alone might not address high operating cost arising from CMV operators driving long hours if these individuals do not have complete information on the risk associated with such activity. This asymmetric information problem is less likely to pertain to union drivers given the Teamsters' historical success negotiating HOS limits and high pay for their members (Peoples, 1996).
8. Criminal investigation by the US Department of Transportation's Office of Inspector General has charged over 70 defendants in Illinois and Florida with illegally assisting ineligible individuals to fraudulently obtain CDLs in Wisconsin. The defendants typically demand cash payments to assist applicants even though the applicants had not demonstrated an adequate knowledge of operating a commercial vehicle.
9. Increasing employment of low wage non-union drivers is a probable source of cost efficiency gains during the post AIA period of stagnant productivity growth.

References

Belman, Dale, L., Monaco, Kristen, A. and Brooks, Taggert, J. *Sailor of the Concrete Sea: A Portrait of Truck Drivers' Work and Lives, From the 1997 Survey of Truck Drivers,* 2004, Michigan State University Press, East Lansing: Michigan.

Belzer, Michael, Fulton, George, Grimes, Donald, Saltzman, Sedo, Stanley and Schmidt, Lucie, *Proposed Changes in Motor Carrier Hours of Service Regulations: An Assessment,* 2002, University of Michigan, Transportation Research Institute.

Corsi, Thomas and Grimm, Curtis, ATLFs: Driving Owner-Operators into the Sunset. *Transportation Research Forum,* 1989 Vol. 29, pp. 285-290.

Federal Register. "Hours of Service of Drivers; Driver Rest; Sleep for Safe Operations; Final Rule," April 13, 2004, Vol. 68, No. 81, part II, pp. 22540-25611.

Federal Register. "Hours of Service of Drivers; Driver Rest; Sleep for Safe Operations; Proposed Rule," May 2, 2000, Vol. 65, No. 85, part II, pp. 22540-25611.

Moore, Thomas G., Clearing the Track: The Remaining Transportation Regulations, *Regulation,* 1995, Vol. 18.

Peoples, James, "Trucking Deregulation and Union Wages: A Re-Examination." *Applied Economics,* Vol. 28, No. 8 (September 1996), pp. 865-874.

Savage, Ian. "Trends in Transportation Employee Injuries Since Economic Deregulation," in *Transportation Labor Issues and Regulatory Reform* (eds) James Peoples and Wayne Talley, Elsevier Ltd., Amsterdam: The Netherlands, pp. 11-33 (2004).

Taylor, John, C., Regulation of Trucking by the States, *Regulation,* 1994, Vol. 17, No. 2.

Transportation Research Board, *Regulations of Weights, Lengths, and Widths of Commercial Motor Vehicles, Special Report 267,* 2002, Washington, D.C.

Troy, Leo. *Almanac of Business and Industrial Financial Ratios,* Paramus, New Jersey, Prentice Hall, 1981-2003.

U.S. Court of Appeals for the District of Columbia, Public Citizen et al. v. FMCSA, No. 03-1165, July 16, 2004, pp. 1-22.

U.S. Department of Transportation, *Regulatory Impact Analysis and Small Business Analysis for Hours of Service Options* (December 2002) Washington D.C.

Chapter 7

Technology in Trucking

Anuradha Nagarajan, Enrique Canessa, Maciek Nowak,
Will Mitchell and Chelsea C. White III

Introduction

The trucking industry has had to adapt to substantial changes in its competitive environment. Globalization has created supply chains that span international borders. Information technology and the Internet have introduced market opportunities. Increases in productivity and increasing cost pressures from global competition have introduced just-in-time manufacturing and assembly. The trucking industry, which moves over three-quarters of the country's freight, now must meet demands to move freight on time, reliably, and with greater visibility. According to Lahsene, sophisticated product offerings, globalization, and increased customer expectations make logistics – the managed movement of goods – the key to competitiveness of companies and regions.[1] Advances in technology are helping the trucking industry to respond to the imperatives of the new competitive environment.

Technology in Trucking

Throughout history, transportation has attempted to move goods farther and faster. In the 1980s, U.S. industries began adopting just-in-time manufacturing in order to reduce inventory, which led to decreased spoilage and lower costs. In the mid-1990s, supply chain management, or flow management, was introduced to further reduce inventory and help companies purchase only what they need. More recently, since 9/11/2001 and other recent disruptions, companies are starting to look at just-in-case policies that allow for extra inventory just in case something unforeseen or unavoidable happens.[2] "Just in case" and "just in time" have critical implications for the trucking industry since the success of these policies depends to a large extent on the trucking industry's response.

Carriers play an active role in the just-in-time process. Many carriers have become "warehouses on wheels" (WOW). Instead of storing goods close to a factory, WOW actually warehouses them on the trailers that bring goods into the plant, eliminating the need for extra buildings and additional loading and unloading. Most importantly, firms do not hold excess inventory that could go out-of-date or otherwise become unsuitable for sale.

In the "just in time" environment, it is critical that carriers avoid as many delays as possible. Trucks can be delayed by accidents, snarled traffic, bad weather, breakdowns, or the new security procedures being introduced since 9/11. Many of these delays can be prevented with information. In-cab devices help provide instant communication and information, including traffic alerts that help drivers avoid traffic problems in major metropolitan areas. This information can be used to re-route trucks and to alert shippers and receivers of potential delays. Technologies that address internal efficiencies such as route optimization, fuel optimization, driver scheduling, electronic document development, and better integration with shippers' systems are gaining popularity.

This chapter attempts to describe the technological revolution in the trucking industry, addressing important technologies that trucking firms now use or will be available in the near future. We supplement survey data with case studies of implementations that provide glimpses of the key roles that technology plays in the trucking industry. We begin Section A with a discussion of six technologies identified by the American Trucking Associations as the most promising technologies for the industry,[3] while Section B analyzes the adoption of the technologies. Section C discusses how the Internet has affected the industry. Section D presents the current state of technology applications as they relate to security and safety. Section E discusses advances in truck technology. Section F concludes with a discussion of emerging technologies.

A. Information Technologies in Trucking

The American Trucking Associations (ATA) highlight six technologies that have become critical to success in the trucking industry.[4] The six technologies are Mobile Communication Systems (MCS), Decision Support Systems (DSS), Automatic Vehicle/Equipment Identification Systems (AVEIS), Electronic Data Interchange (EDI), Bar Coding (BAR), and Imaging Systems (IMG). These technologies have altered business processes and enabled adopting firms to improve efficiency and productivity.

We begin with a brief description of each of these technologies along with examples of implementation. We follow the descriptions with case studies of technology implementation, focusing on the successful integration of technology products. Finally we present the results of a survey on the use of these technologies in the trucking industry.

A.1. Mobile Communication Systems (MCS)

MCS are interactive communication tools that link fleet vehicles to dispatch centers. MCS send positioning information and messages to a central facility that acts as the communication hub between the dispatch centers and fleet vehicles. Besides cellular communication technologies, MCS can be implemented by Specialized Mobile Radio Systems (SMRS) and Satellite Communication Systems (SATCOMM). The components required to implement MCS vary by the technology deployed and the sophistication of the functionality. Basic system components include mobile terminals, on-board computers, voice communications, network infrastructure, peripheral devices, and software interfaces.

MCS have several common applications: position reporting; estimated time of arrival, out of route (a function warns the driver and/or dispatcher and records instances when the truck is out of the prescribed route), fuel tax mileage reporting, and decision support systems that dynamically optimize parameters such as maximization of contribution per truck per day and driver productivity.

A.2. Decision Support Systems (DSS)

DSS computer systems assist decision-makers by synthesizing data to create information and recommendations for action. Most systems are interactive, helping employees solve difficult, data-intensive problems. While expert systems and artificial intelligence systems are becoming familiar to trucking firms, operations research based systems are most common. In particular, dispatch operations, such as routing and the matching of drivers and loads – which were the most challenging tasks prior to decision support systems – have been gaining popularity.

A simple example illustrates the advantage of computer based decision support systems. A firm with three trucks and three loads to haul faces six different dispatch options. If the firm doubles its size, it faces 720 choices with six trucks and six loads. The number of possible combinations increases into the millions with just 10 trucks and as many loads. Today's load matching and routing software is capable of providing near optimum outcomes quickly, in a variety of situations. Appendix 1 provides an overview of various routing algorithms and software.

DSS evaluations rely on a range of mathematical and computer programming algorithms. Simple DSS aggregates information from one or more sources (generally more than one) based on common attribute dependencies, and presents the information in a useful format. Responsible personnel who can interpret the trends specific to their area of expertise make decisions based on the scenarios. Expert systems apply a set of rules to the decision. The rules are usually in the form of questions in a tree-structure that follow from the data. Artificial intelligence-based systems try to 'learn' to make decisions using the same methodology as humans. Essentially, the system incorporates predicated events, based on the outcome of hypothetical decisions, to make a decision. Over time, the system will use prior information to extrapolate solutions to unrelated problems.

A.3. Automatic Vehicle/Equipment Identification Systems (AVEIS)

AVEIS communication systems consist of a transponder that is programmed with identification, authorization, and other types of information unique to the user, equipment, and application. Three common types of transponders are most common in the industry: Type I transponders that contain fixed data for read only applications, Type II transponders that are capable of read and write operations, and Type III transponders that provide an external interface with on-board devices or smart cards.

An AVEIS is a basic communication system that contains key identification and related information about the vehicle, using radio signals to transfer information to a remote reader. It can identify equipment entering or exiting a yard, equipment available within a yard, trucks passing through toll collection lanes, through a weigh station, or through a border checkpoint, and fuel use and authorization. AVEIS used in conjunction with vehicle-to-roadside communication systems can provide applications to track maintenance histories, service schedules, cargo information, and real time tractor performance characteristics.

A.4. Electronic Data Interchange (EDI)

EDI provides inter-company computer-to-computer communication of data. EDI is used to transmit formatted data that would otherwise be maintained and transferred in a printed standard business document such as a freight bill or bill of lading. Advantages of EDI include reductions in paperwork, telephone calls, postage and handling charges, and duplicated manual data entry. EDI can increase the speed of communication of essential business information, and improve data accuracy, customer satisfaction, and business effectiveness. Examples of information that companies exchange via EDI include shipment information (bill of lading), shipment status and tracking information, freight information and charges, freight payment (remittance advice and bank payment), and loading and route guides.

Competing non-compatible standards in EDI have required each shipper to have a distinct connection with each carrier. Internet based XML technology could soon replace traditional EDI. XML (for Extensible Markup Language) is a computer language that supports exchanging electronic documents and integrating applications running on different operating systems or hardware by using an Internet connection. As the use of the Internet increases, XML is being improved and standardized to encourage widespread adoption.

A.5. Bar Coding

Bar coding consists of an automated reader as an alternative to manual keyboard entry of data into a database. Bar code symbols are a machine-readable form of keyed data. Scanners use a laser beam of light to read the bar code. Historically bar codes have been used in the motor carrier industry since the 1970s. Over the years, there has been increasing standardization of bar code placement on bills of lading and freight bills. The motor carrier industry has been very active in working with other industry associations to develop common standards for shipping labels. Bar codes in the motor carrier industry are now used for a wide variety of applications.

Technological advances in Radio Frequency Identification (RFID) or "smart tags" are threatening to replace barcodes in the near future. These tiny chips emit signals that monitor shipments in real time, unlike barcodes that need to be scanned through a reader. As adoption increases, both in the trucking industry and among shippers, the cost of the smart tags is likely to decrease rapidly making barcodes increasingly obsolete.

A.6. Imaging Systems

Imaging systems enable document imaging and provide an electronic means to store reams of paper. Historically, businesses have stored hard copies of documents, requiring enormous amounts of physical space and highly inefficient methods for retrieving and utilizing information. The advent of microfiche in the 1960s helped cut down the storage space, but it did not make a dent in efficiency. With electronic storage becoming increasingly cheaper and smaller, imaging systems for the use of electronic document management are becoming ubiquitous. The functionality of an imaging system allows easy scanning, storage, and retrieval of business information, including trip sheets, bills of lading, fuel receipts, bill payments, proof of delivery, and claims.

Imaging systems either use a scanner (often connected to a PC) to create an electronic image of a document or can transpose information on a computer system (received either via an EDI or generated internally) to an electronic document. Once the electronic document is generated it is indexed. This index information is critical in the retrieval and utilization of the information through its life cycle.

B. Innovation, Adoption, and Diffusion of Technologies

The complex business processes involved in managing trucking have been a fertile ground for new information and communication technology applications. Over the last decade, products have moved from focusing on a single functionality to providing compatible solutions using multiple technologies. Systems in the market cater to the diverse needs of the trucking market, ranging from simple, low cost solutions to complex, expensive deployments.

The case studies below show that firms are using technology to improve and enhance business processes. The virtuous cycle of information technology innovation and deployment is evident in the industry. The cases represent in-depth applications of information technology, beginning with an example of an owner operator at the forefront of technology adoption. The case studies that follow represent firms from different cross sections of the industry. Since technology is applied primarily to improve processes, the direct impact on the bottom line is hard to measure. The adoption of technology begins for some firms as a means for competitive advantage. Soon, market pressures force other firms to adopt the technology for competitive parity. These case studies illustrate the spectrum of technology adoption in the trucking industry without directly attributing enhanced performance to the phenomenon.

B.1.A Technology Pioneer among Owner Operators

Owner operator Tim Brady is a pioneer in technology use among owner operators. He set up his own home-based company, Driver4PROFITS, in Kenton, Tenn. He contracts with Baystate Moving Systems, a Massachusetts based agent for United

Van lines. Brady and his 77.7 foot tractor-trailer primarily haul exhibits and electronic manufacturing equipment for trade shows throughout the United States. Two cubic feet of Tim Brady's cab are filled with some of his most precious cargo. His in-cab technology center provides the essential communications that keep him in business. The less-than-truckload long hauler has a Pentium computer with a DVD drive, a monitor, scanner, and printer. Brady's set-up also includes a global positioning system and routing software. An 8.5 kilowatt generator runs the computer so that the devices do not drain the truck battery.[5]

Brady uses multiple technologies to co-ordinate and to improve business and personal communications. With wireless Internet access, Brady is able to access loads, get directions, communicate with suppliers and shippers, keep books, and stay in touch with family – all from his cab. Brady also uses a cell phone to keep in touch and for e-mail. While the cell phone and Internet are powerful tools, Brady relies on one other mode of communication that he says is well worth the price tag. His truck sports a Qualcomm satellite communications system that connects him to VanStar, a system used by United Van Lines. United Van Lines paid for the cost of the initial equipment installation, and the company pays half the monthly service fee. Brady lists what space he has available and the system notifies him when a load fits the available proportions and his equipment capabilities. All the details about the load – what, where, when, contact information and special instructions such as required pads, straps or a lift gate are provided – and Brady decides whether to accept the load. Then, once the load is picked up, Brady can document who signed for it. Customers can identify where their shipment is and when they can expect it to be delivered. United Van Lines customers can go to the company's Web site to bring up the location of the truck with their load, based on 30-minutes updates. The truck's TracStar System connects him to Dish Network and transmits instant weather, road conditions and current news.

An in-cab system alerts Brady when a shipper makes a change in a load while he is en route to make a delivery. Brady also has an 800 number that shippers can call which forwards to his cell phone. With constantly updated information, Brady does not waste time going to a pickup or delivery site unprepared. With advance notice, paperwork can be initiated and processed over the Internet, before Brady appears at the dock. Brady's technology toolbox also has routing software (Rand McNally's Route Tools) to list every truck stop along the way and to determine up to date construction information from the Internet. Technology has allowed this owner operator to manage his business and has removed many communication constraints that owner operators traditionally face.[6]

B.2. Managing a Fleet of Owner Operators with Technology

Southern Pride Trucking specializes in the transportation of critical time sensitive, high value airline, aviation, and aerospace related inventories. Satellite communications technology has allowed the company to grow from one owner operator to 70 owner operator teams while enhancing service quality for customers and improving quality of life for employees. The firm is close to being a virtual entity, thanks to advances in communication technologies. With no storage facility, no warehouses, and no maintenance garages, the firm has a handful of employees who manage administrative functions. Dispatchers use the Qualcomm satellite communication and tracking system to manage owner operator teams all over the country. The system tracks the location of the truck, whether the truck is in service, and whether the truck has a load. In the particular niche that Southern Pride has carved out, delays can be expensive. For example, when there is an engine failure, it costs the airlines a quarter of million dollars a day while the plane is grounded. The ability to communicate immediately with customers and drivers twenty-four hours a day helps the firm to respond to customer needs promptly and flexibly. According to the firm's management team and employees, technology has been the cornerstone of the company's success.[7]

B.3. Process Transparency at FedEx

Fed Ex has implemented several technologies as part of the company's drive for process improvement and increased customer satisfaction. In June 2000, Viking, a division of Fedex, completed a rollout of wireless handheld computer devices to approximately 1,200 of its pickup and delivery drivers. The advantage of the handheld devices is in advance planning. Viking dispatchers no longer have to wait until the end of their pickup day to see exact freight volumes. Instead, loads can be planned in advance as pickup drivers enter package specifications throughout their day. Dispatchers monitor pickups and deliveries all day without talking to a driver. Given the fluctuating seasonal and even weekly freight volumes, this enables Viking to allocate its equipment accurately, achieving an industry leading 99% on-time record. The handheld computers work with modeling software that assigns loads to the most efficient truck and driver in the system.[8]

The case studies illustrate how firms in the trucking industry are integrating technology into their business processes. As the next section shows, such examples increasingly are becoming the norm in the industry, as information technology use is becoming widespread.

B.4. Adoption and Diffusion of Technologies: Survey Data

The usefulness and cost-benefit tradeoff of a technology determines its rate of diffusion. Several studies have examined the rate at which technology is being diffused in the trucking industry. A paper by Regan et al. (1995) briefly describes a 1992 survey of about 300 companies that determined carriers' propensity to use new technologies, particularly two-way communication and automatic vehicle location/identification technologies. Primary findings were that interest in technology implementation was closely linked to company size and that carriers believe that the use of communication and information technologies could improve the efficiency of their operations.[9]

Hall and Intihar (1997) report a series of interviews with trucking terminal managers, focus group meetings with representatives of the trucking industry in California, and telephone interviews with technology providers. Their study found that trucking companies were willing to invest and participate in technology implementation as long as the investment required was modest, there were no new taxes or user fees imposed, the technologies promoted operating efficiency, customer service, or safety, and implementation was voluntary.[10]

Several studies of EDI use in the motor carrier industry have been conducted. A study by Crum et al. (1998) compared two surveys of EDI capable carriers that were conducted in 1990 and 1996 and found significant increases in the use of EDI in carrier-shipper transactions during that six year period.[11]

Two studies show the rapid evolution of technology use. The ATA conducted a national survey on technology use in 1994. Four years later, during the spring of 1998, a survey of California-based for-hire trucking companies, private trucking fleets, and large national carriers with operations in California was carried out by a private survey research company for the Institute of Transportation Studies at the University of California, Irvine (UCI).[12] The penetration of technology was significantly higher in the 1998 UCI study than the penetration found by the 1994 ATA study. The ATA study estimated that market penetration for mobile communications, EDI, and AVL was 46 percent, 11 percent and 2 percent, respectively, while the market penetration for companies in the UCI study was 80 percent, 32 percent, and 21 percent.[13] The studies differed slightly, however, as the ATA study defined large fleets as those with more than 100 vehicles, while the University of California, Irvine (UCI) study defined large fleets as those operating 50 or more vehicles (power units) in California at one time.

Recent data is consistent with the notion that technology continues to diffuse in the industry. The data discussed below is based on a mail survey concerning the use and impact of information technology in the trucking industry.[14] Results from 179 respondents (775 surveys mailed) to the survey are summarized, providing information concerning trends in the industry. The information from the survey applies to late 1999 and early 2000. The respondents represent a cross section of the trucking industry, including TL (40%), LTL (71%), logistics services (20%), package express (9%), and private fleet operators (30%). About 55% of the firms participate in two or more of these segments of the industry. There is also a useful size distribution of respondents, with about 65% of the respondents operating 100 or fewer power units and 35% operating more than 100 units.

Findings across the six technologies   It is interesting to compare statistics across the six technologies included in the survey. From the data, one can assess the relative use of each of these systems. Table 7.1 presents the number and percentage adoption of the systems by segment.

Table 7.1 shows that the most prevalent technology is MCS (60%) followed by EDI (43%). High MCS penetration stems from inexpensive acquisition and operation, mainly by using pagers, while EDI penetration results from customer pressure.

Table 7.1   Number of Firms that have Adopted Specific Technology

Segment	MCS	DSS	AVEIS	EDI	BAR	IMG
TL	10	4	4	10	1	6
LTL	22	7	6	17	8	10
Combined	46	10	9	26	14	16
Private	30	11	8	24	15	16
Total	108	32	27	77	38	48
Percent	60%	18%	15%	43%	21%	27%

Table 7.2 reveals similar results for penetration of the technologies between segments. MCS and EDI systems are the most prevalent in all segments of the trucking industry. Note that the adoption of the systems is quite similar within segments except for bar code use (BAR). Since TL firms do not need to frequently transfer loads from one truck to another or consolidate different shipments, the need to track many dispersed shipments is lower than in the rest of the segments.

Table 7.2   Percentage of Firms by Segment that Use Specific Technology

Segment	MCS	DSS	AVEIS	EDI	BAR	IMG
TL	53%	21%	21%	53%	5%	32%
LTL	61%	19%	17%	47%	22%	28%
Combined	67%	14%	13%	38%	20%	23%
Private	55%	20%	15%	44%	27%	29%

Turning now to the question of how successfully the firms have deployed each system, Table 7.3 shows that both between and within segments the success scores are essentially the same. An average score of approximately 4 is indicated, showing that firms believe that the technologies have been successfully deployed.

Table 7.3   Success with Technologies (1 = not successful to 5 = very successful)

Segment	MCS	DSS	AVEIS	EDI	BAR	IMG
All segments	3.8	3.9	3.8	3.9	3.9	4.0
TL	3.5	3.5	3.7	3.8	5.0	4.2
LTL	4.0	4.0	4.2	4.0	4.0	4.2
Combined	3.8	4.0	3.8	3.8	4.0	4.3
Private	3.8	3.8	3.6	3.9	3.7	3.6

The technology trajectory is steep and products are being introduced rapidly. Already, EDI and bar code technology are being replaced by contenders such as web-based EDI and RFID. The challenge for firms is to identify what technology can do effectively. A strong technology base is as important as the ability to move freight. Technology choices can differentiate between survival and extinction.

C. Internet Usage in Trucking[15]

Information is the chain that holds the trucking process together. As the previous section has shown, technologies that enable increased and accurate information throughout the trucking value chain are being widely adopted. The Internet has the potential to improve the efficiency and productivity of firms in the industry due to increased transparency of information for trucking firms and their customers.

Three independent sources confirm that the Internet is widely used in the industry. First, the ATA Foundation and the National Private Truck Council conducted a survey of Internet usage in 1998. The ATA survey found that 51% of TL carriers were using Internet technology in 1998 compared to 11% in 1996. Among the LTL carriers, 61% were using Internet technology in 1998 compared to 14% in 1996.[16] Second, more recent information on Internet use in trucking comes from a mail survey by the University of Michigan Trucking Industry Program (UMTIP) concerning the use and impact of information technology in the trucking industry in early 2000.[17] Based on 179 respondents (775 surveys mailed), 75% of the responding firms use the Internet (79% of the TL firms, 72% of LTL firms, 75% of the firms that participate in more than one segment, and 75% of the private fleets). Third, in August 2000, a web search for public Internet sites of 132 for-hire trucking firms with 1999 Form M data found that 80% had public web-sites (75% of 97 TL firms; 95% of 24 LTL firms; 82% of 11 firms that operated in multiple segments). Thus, the two sources of recent information provide similar estimates of current web-usage rates by trucking firms (75% in the UM survey from early 2000, 80% in the August 2000 web search). As Shulz notes, "the Internet is the new ante needed just to play the freight transport game." [18]

In addition, a Morgan Stanley Dean Witter survey released in October 2000 indicates that 44% of shippers felt that a freight transport provider must have e-commerce connectivity in order to bid for their business. Respondents to the 2000 UMTIP survey indicated that most Internet applications were developed internally by the trucking firms (78%), sometimes in conjunction with consultants. Trucking firm managers believe that they require company specific knowledge to develop effective Internet applications, at least at this early stage of Internet diffusion.

The key reason that the Internet is affecting the industry stems from the availability of more detailed information to customers and competitors about goods and services, prices, and timing. Firms are changing the way they gather, process, and disseminate information. The changes in information result in both a potential for greater efficiency in traditional transportation activities and in the creation of demand for new types of transportation activities. The immediate consequences of increased dissemination of information include greater price pressure and greater incentives for efficiency. In addition to greater efficiency of traditional services, increased information is also leading to more fine-grained market segmentation, as well as to demands for new goods and services by trucking companies.

Section C.1 presents vignettes of how firms in the trucking industry are using the Internet to exploit existing opportunities and to explore new opportunities. Section C.2 presents data on the Internet's impact on firms in the industry based on our survey. As the Internet becomes increasingly ubiquitous in the trucking environment, it is transforming the way firms do business.

C.1. Vignettes of How Firms in the Trucking Industry Are Using the Internet

With the demands for greater speed, reliability, efficiency and innovative services, the Internet is causing substantial pressure on the capabilities of trucking companies. Firms are responding to some demands through incremental expansion of their existing expertise. We illustrate such changes with the example of ABF Freight. The introduction of the Internet has required major changes in business routines and resources.[19] Arnold Industries and UPS are examples of firms that are exploring new opportunities by both building on its existing repertoire of skills and acquiring new skills. In some cases, new skills and opportunities are redefining the business. The freight-broker segment is an example of business transformation. Incumbents such as DAT and Transplace.com have combined existing skills, assets, and intangibles such as reputation with new technology and new skills to dis-intermediate the brokerage business. However, interesting new business models have also emerged. Some such as NetTrans, the Internet Truck Stop, and freightquote.com enable freight brokers and owner operators in their load matching activities. Others such as the industry entrant Nistevo are exploiting latent needs among shippers to create private exchanges to improve transportation outcomes.

Firm level transformation in response to Internet-enabled opportunities – ABF Freight   ABF Freight System is an example of a firm that gradually exploited the web to improve its existing capabilities. Starting in 1994, ABF offered downloadable personal computer rating software, along with routing and zip code directories, and general marketing information. Since then ABF has added a rating guide, shipment tracing, the ability to create bills of lading online, and the ability to request pickups online. ABF also offers customer-specific pricing quotations over the Internet. In 1998, the company introduced an ABF Toolkit to help customers navigate through the site. Customers were able to retrieve shipping documents, as well as review loss and damage claims online. In 1999, ABF introduced "Transparent Direct Links", which enables shippers to incorporate data from ABF's Internet site directly into their own site. In January 2000, ABF introduced the "Shipment Planner", which is a patented program that displays shipment reports on a calendar, and the "Dynamic Rerouting" module, which is a program that allows customers to re-route in-transit shipments. ABF has made the Internet a focal point of their growth strategy. The company has expanded existing capabilities to improve both its interactions with customers and its internal processes.[20] The impact of the actions will be felt primarily by ABF's business customers particularly in the areas of "just in time" and "lean" manufacturing.

Arnold Industries and UPS   Arnold Industries illustrates a trucking company that is exploring the new competitive environment and redefining the boundaries of the services it offers in the Internet-enabled economy. Arnold Industries has long been a profitable LTL company. During the 1990s, the company expanded into the regional TL segment by acquiring TL firms. The company is now combining its trucking and warehouse operations to offer one-stop order fulfillment services for e-tailers and mail-order catalog companies. These services include order processing, inventory management, and small package shipping. In this process, the company has transformed its business to improve its ability to fill orders quickly and precisely. The firm has turned its warehouses into logistics hubs where more than six hundred people are involved in the order fulfillment process. The process involves receiving goods from manufacturers or suppliers, processing, packaging, and delivering to customers. Arnold Logistics, a subsidiary, also provides value-added services by comparing freight rates and handling customer returns. Further, the company takes online orders on behalf of its shippers and provides live-chat and e-mail support for customers.[21]

Several examples involving UPS further illustrate how trucking companies are integrating themselves into the web of Internet activities. UPS dominates shipping from Internet retailers. For instance, UPS delivered 55% of the goods ordered online in the 1998 Christmas season. UPS's relationship with Nike demonstrates the basis of UPS's success. In order to expedite the order-to-delivery process for Nike.com, UPS stocks Nike shoes and warm-ups in its Louisville warehouse and fulfills customer orders hourly. Indeed, UPS plays a direct role in the order process as well as in delivery, because a UPS call center in San Antonio handles Nike.com customer orders. Consequently, Nike saves on overhead costs and achieves quick sales turnaround.

UPS is extending its activities far beyond the traditional movement of goods. Rather than simply being a "package express" shipper, the company is undertaking many business processes, ranging from receiving customer orders, warehousing goods, and coordinating after-sales services. Such business transformations mark changes in the services that companies such as Arnold Industries and UPS offer and also redefine trucking industry boundaries. As the boundaries between transportation services become increasingly blurred, firms that provide logistics and package express services are now central to the industry.

Industry level transformation in response to Internet-enabled opportunities – the freight broker segment The key direct impact that increased electronic information is having on the trucking industry involves load-matching and volume discounts. The strongest challenges are arising for freight brokers, who have provided these services to trucking companies and their customers in the past. In the trucking industry, productivity gains, given legal restrictions on size and weight, come mainly from two sources: (1) fewer empty miles and/or higher cubic space utilization,[22] and (2) less waiting time at the dock. The trucking industry is fragmented and geographically dispersed, so that coordination of disparate fleets and drivers is critically important. Load-matching services provide information that matches available shipments with trucks that have available cargo space, in order to increase trailer utilization and decrease waiting times.

Freight brokers note that the Internet is challenging their business model. In shipper-driven brokerage substitution, the Internet enables shippers to post loads and solicit competitive bids directly from carriers that use the Internet to identify backhauls. This process combines load-matching with competitive pricing. In the process, the shipper receives the advantage of a low bid and the carrier increases productivity by reducing empty miles. Shippers function as their own brokers, dealing directly with freight companies. As Internet business models have matured the Internet has proved to be both a friend and a foe to the freight broker.

The geographical dispersion of the trucking industry makes it a natural application for the integrative powers of the Internet. A number of Web-based exchanges sprung up in the heyday of the Internet boom, all attempting to generate open, efficient spot markets for freight. Mimicking the larger industrial landscape, many of the Internet sites are now defunct, without achieving the critical mass of shipments and carriers needed to become viable and reliable sources of load matching and backhaul freight.

A few sites survived, however, by attracting enough freight to reach critical mass or by evolving into new types of online freight tendering and management systems. The term "online exchange" has come to cover a wide range of business models in trucking. It includes sophisticated systems for developing and managing long-term freight agreements, and private trading groups that offer e-commerce tools for shipper and carrier partners.[23] Simple electronic load posting boards such as freightquote.com also exist. Some trucking industry incumbents are exploiting their existing capabilities and physical assets to extend into the information brokerage segment of the industry, as exemplified by DAT services and Transplace.com, while Nistevo is an example of an industry entrant who is using the Internet to integrate information and conduct e-commerce.

Freight broker enabler – Electronic load boards   The simplest of these exchanges are Web-based load matching operations, providing online access to a backhaul spot market as a single core service. Often known as load boards or freight bulletin boards, those that survived the initial shakeout remain among the most well known Web services for the industry. Contrary to expectations, the freight matching sites have not replaced freight brokers. Instead of being dis-intermediated by online load matching services, freight brokers have become the primary customers for them. According to Darren Brewer, founder of NetTrans, "When we started NetTrans (www.nettrans.com) in 1996, we thought our customers would be shippers and mid- to large-size carriers. But shippers haven't wanted to use [the load board], so virtually all of our freight comes from brokers. Broker freight is less profitable, and our core carriers tend to be smaller fleets with 10 or fewer trucks and owner-operators because they can't afford a sales staff to generate their own backhauls." The Internet Truckstop (www.Internettruckstop.com) is another successful load board that connects smaller fleets to freight offered by brokers and third-party logistics providers. "A freight exchange is a dating service," says founder and President Scott Moscrip "We introduce you to people outside your circle. Small fleets [use an exchange] because they don't have a sales staff. They can't afford to pay someone to make those introductions." These load matching services are suited to owner operators and carriers who do not have contacts in a specific area and would like to use the online exchange to reduce deadhead miles.[24]

Incumbent response to Internet opportunities – a firm effort: DAT Services Incumbents in the load matching business such as DAT Services have had to dramatically alter their business model or face the threat of extinction. DAT Services began load matching services by pinning up printed listings on real bulletin boards located in truck stops. Eventually, they replaced the cork boards with video screens and Internet terminals. Now part of TransCore Inc., the traditional DAT Service is still a leader in load exchanges, with a monthly subscription base of nearly 20,000 users. However, the company has also begun moving beyond simple load matching over the Web to what it calls the TransCore Exchange at www.transportationsoftware.com. With a freight board, the carrier identifies a load online and then negotiates rates over the telephone.

With TransCore Exchange, the Internet is used as a negotiation and confirmation tool. Nearly the entire bill of lading is built online. The advantages of moving to electronic transactions are that the processes are completed quickly and efficiently, while eliminating redundant data entry and decreasing telephone bills, all of which reduces costs. The TransCore Exchange also increases service levels by allowing brokers and other freight intermediaries to create private trading groups. Instead of a load being posted on an open board, the group structure allows users to simultaneously offer it to all their core carriers. Once again, freight brokers are the segment that most directly benefit from the TransCore Exchange. They can identify a group of trusted carriers and offer them loads that meet their requirements. If the core carriers pass on a particular load, it can then be offered to carriers participating in the exchange or posted on the traditional DAT board at truck stops.

Incumbent response to Internet opportunities – a co-operative effort: Transplace.com Cooperation in the trucking industry reached new heights when six of the largest publicly-held TL carriers formed an alliance called Transplace.com to explore new web based business opportunities. Transplace.com is an example of how industry incumbents are combining asset rationalization and the management of information to gain efficiencies. The objective of Transplace.com is to create a high volume freight network that will increase equipment utilization for fleets and reduce waiting time for drivers. Transplace.com serves as an information aggregator in the fragmented truckload sector, with its tens of thousands of competitors, by helping both shippers and carriers to match loads and rationalize capacity. The founding firms hope to leverage their bricks and mortar experience, their physical assets, their industry-specific information technology expertise, their brand equity, and their customer relations in the electronic market-space. The six firms, among the largest publicly-held TL carriers, that combined their expertise in regional and national truckload freight movement include Covenant Transport, J.B. Hunt Transport Services, M.S. Carriers, Swift Transportation, US Xpress, and Werner Enterprises. In addition to providing logistics services, Transplace.com negotiates discounts for fuel, equipment, maintenance and parts, insurance, credit, and other services for its equity partners and other carriers that choose to join the purchasing co-operative.

A new business model exploiting Internet opportunities: Nistevo   The importance of private networks to the trucking industry is evident from the success of Nistevo Corporation. Nistevo sets up collaborative logistics networks for shippers and carriers with existing relationships. It was recently featured as a "Forbes.com Best of the Web" for its unique and successful business model.[25] Headquartered in Minneapolis, the company was formed in 1998 with its first online customer, Monsanto, and has since expanded to provide an Internet infrastructure for shippers who can set up private or semiprivate networks using Nistevo technology. In this sense the Nistevo system differs from other online marketplaces since it specializes in setting up closed marketplaces for individual shippers or groups of shippers. Initial figures show a strong business case for load planning via the online network. The subscription-based service helps ground-transport carriers eliminate "deadhead" miles by matching routes and optimizing truck capacity.

Upon signing with Nistevo, subscribers enter their shipping rules into the system. The database maintains each carrier's agreed-upon rate, committed quantity, service levels, ranking, and equipment usage profile. Based on these parameters, the system enlists its carrier and mode selection engines to determine which carriers are eligible to take a given shipment. In accordance with users' pre-programmed instructions, it then tenders the shipment to a single most appropriate carrier or to multiple carriers. Once a shipment has been assigned, the shipper, carrier and consignee can establish pickup and delivery appointments and track each movement of freight. Shipment status is updated in adherence with subscribers' rules. An "active event notification" alerts transportation managers, customer service representatives, and customers if problems such as late departures, weather delays, or equipment problems occur.

The consumer packaged-goods market is a good fit for the system since players in this sector tend to have long, complex supply chains. An alliance of 12 companies in the consumer packaged-goods business is testing a semiprivate online exchange that enables members to share truck capacity by using the Internet to monitor space availability. The network, which is hosted by Nistevo.com, is a variation on the business-to-business online exchange theme, in that it uses the Internet as a communications infrastructure, but within a trading community that is limited to complementary businesses. The project was initially launched, when General Mills, The Pillsbury Co., Land O'Lakes, Graphics Package Corp. and Fort James Corp. announced an alliance to create the Internet-based logistics exchange. Later, seven more companies joined the group: Nestle USA, Nabisco Inc., ConAgra Inc., McCormack & Co. Inc., Hormel Foods, International Multifoods and IVEX Package Corp. The participants use the exchange to match product shipments and destinations with available trucks. By better utilizing truck capacity, empty backhaul mileage is reduced and the shippers can improve load planning. General Mills estimates that it can achieve total logistics costs savings of 4 percent to 7 percent a year.[26] For example, by combining the freight and the lanes from scattered routes of Georgia Pacific and General Mills, Nistevo was able to create one regular eight day circuit for a truck handling a full load and far less deadhead travel. This combination saved the two companies $731,000 a year, 19% of prior year costs. Further, by making the circuit a dedicated route, drivers were able to work on a more regular, predictable schedule.[27, 28]

The examples in this section illustrate firms that are able to exploit efficiency opportunities because of the information and communication enabled by the Internet. Services that offer to match loads with empty trucks have been around for years, but the rapid spread of Internet communication holds great promise as a cost-effective tool for finding elusive backhauls. Firms in the trucking industry operate in an environment of tight margins. Efficiencies in terms of load matching, reduction of empty backhauls, volume efficiencies in purchasing and negotiating, and other value added services help improve profitability.

C.2. Survey Data on Internet Usage in the Trucking Industry

In order to investigate the most recent Internet technology adoption practices in the trucking industry, the 2000 UMTIP survey on technology adoption also studied Internet penetration. The goal was to identify how the firms are using Internet technology and to gain an understanding of how early Internet usage is affecting firm performance and profitability. Some of the Internet related findings are presented here.

Although 75% of the respondents reported at least minimal Internet activity by early 2000, the impact was at very early stages of both investment and customer activity. The firms on average devoted only about 12% of their investment in new technology on Internet-related projects. Internet sales activity was even lower as the firms with Internet activity procured only about 5% of their shipments through the Internet in 1999. Thus, although Internet applications are diffusing widely among trucking firms, they still account for only small parts of the firms' business activities. Data on the association between Internet use, change of business activities, and firm performance suggest that the Internet is having a greater impact on business activities that enable growth than on cost reduction.

Internet applications   Table 7.4 lists the most frequently used applications of the Internet. Most firms use the Internet to exploit many aspects of their existing capabilities and improve customer relationships and internal processes. In addition, some firms go beyond skill exploitation and look for new ways to identify new markets and customers using the Internet as a springboard.

Table 7.4 Internet Applications available at US Trucking Firms

Internet Application	Firms using (percent)
1. Exploration	
Attracting new customers	72
Service customization	27
2. Exploitation of existing skills: Customer-related	
Marketing your company's services	75
Online shipment orders from existing customers	37
Online pricing and rating software	31
Freight pick up request	29
Dedicated customer service	26
Cargo claims status	16
Offering special discounts	10
3. Exploitation of existing skills: Process-related	
Office communications	61
Recruiting drivers	39
Recruiting personnel other than drivers	37
Real time shipment tracking	30
Forms and permits	30
Online bill of lading and proof of delivery	28
Load viewing and availability	23
Recruiting owner operators	18
Online bill payment	17
Real time routing	14
Real time trailer tracking	12
Posting real time driver schedules	10

Source: UMTIP survey of U.S. trucking firms. The table shows results from 130 respondents who reported at least one Internet application.

Accordingly, the features are classified in one of three categories – "Exploration", "Exploitation of existing skills: Customer-related", and "Exploitation of existing skills: Process-related" – to understand how firms are using the Internet. The two most common *exploration* features in Table 7.4 are attracting new customers (72%), followed by service customization (27%). The four most common *skill exploitation* features that firms use to improve the *customer experience* are marketing services (75%), followed by online shipment orders from existing customers (37%), online pricing and rating software (31%), and freight pick up request (29%). The three most common *skill exploitation* features for *internal process improvement* are office communications (61%), followed by recruiting drivers (39%) and recruiting personnel other than drivers (37%). The central conclusion is that firms are using Internet applications both to enhance many types of existing skills and to explore new opportunities.

Impact on business functions   Trucking firms are using the Internet in many ways. The Internet helps firms explore new opportunities by aggressive sales and marketing. By providing immediate access to routine information and documents, the Internet allows marketing personnel time to offer expedient service to existing customers and to explore venues for new markets and growth. Trucking firms as the physical conduits of e-commerce have access to customer specific data. These firms are combining new data management capabilities, network management capabilities, and existing warehouses and mobile assets to offer integrated transportation services within the supply chain. The Internet allows firms to exploit existing skills by improving the quantity and quality of information available to customers in real time and in a customized manner.

The Internet has also become instrumental in process improvement. The incremental cost of transacting on the Internet is as much as fifteen times less expensive than paper transactions and trucking firms are aggressively moving to the net, in some cases replacing existing systems and in many cases creating new electronic interfaces. For instance, traditional electronic data interchange (EDI) services such as load tendering, status reporting, and invoicing cost thousands and tens of thousands of dollars to set up and run, while also requiring a substantial ongoing effort to maintain inter-firm system compatibility. These costs and difficulties inhibited adoption of EDI systems by small carriers and, in turn, the limited adoption hurt the capability of small carriers to work with large shippers that mandated EDI transactions. Now, some shippers are using systems that allow EDI transactions over an Extranet, which is a secured Internet location that reduces set up costs. Still in its nascent phase, web-based EDI systems require manual entry and have not yet been widely adopted, but the potential low cost and standardized accessibility of EDI over the Internet levels the playing field for carriers that had been excluded from many freight opportunities earlier. Smaller firms are also able to obtain loads and conduct more business due to the freight matching transparency of the Internet.

Table 7.5 reports the use of the Internet for various business functions. The Internet has had the most use for company image enhancement (mean 2.8, on a 1 to 5 scale). The wide reach of the Internet has facilitated the broadcast of information in an environment where all the constituents are geographically dispersed. The connectivity enabled by the Internet also has facilitated the exchange of information with shipper and consignees (2.7), and third parties (2.5). Thus, the Internet has contributed to multiple business functions needed for offering new services, dealing with existing customers, and operating internal processes.

Table 7.5   Use of Internet for Business Functions 1999-2000

Business Activity	Mean effect (1 to 5)
1. Exploration	
Variety of services increase	2.3
Customization of services	2.3
2. Exploitation of existing skills: Customer-related	
Company image enhancement	2.8
Exchanging information with shippers and consignees	2.7
Market share	2.0
3. Exploitation of existing skills: Process-related	
Process improvement	2.6
Exchanging information with third parties	2.5
Exchanging information with other trucking firms	2.1
Service quality improvement	2.1
Security of transactions	1.7

Source: UMTIP survey of U.S. trucking firms (impact of Internet on business functions for 130 respondents; 1= no use 5 = significant use: a higher mean signifies more use).

Table 7.6 reports how the Internet helped firms change their business activities since 1996. Firms were asked about the extent to which changes in different business activities stemmed from their Internet activities. Possible responses were that none of the change arose from the Internet, some of the change is attributable to the Internet, most of the change is attributable to the Internet, and not applicable.

Once again the features are organized in terms of exploration of new opportunities, exploitation of current customers, and process improvement orientation. As Table 7.6 indicates, in the exploration category, 72% of the respondents said that some or most of the change in acquisition of new customers is due to the Internet. In improving services to existing customers, trucking firms respond that the Internet has helped them improve relationships with their shippers (67%) and consignees (63%), as well as provide quicker service (57%). In improving processes, many firms said that the Internet helped facilitate internal process improvements (72%), improve relationships with third-parties (64%), and enhance the management of change (64%). The key conclusion is that the Internet has helped facilitate recent improvement on many dimensions, although the Internet is far from the sole source of improvements.

Table 7.6   Role of Internet in changes of business activity at firms since 1996

Area where change occurred	Firms reporting some change due to Internet
Exploration	
Acquisition of new customers	72%
Addition of new services	51%
Acquisition of new markets	45%
Exploitation of existing skills: Customer-related	
Improved shipper relationships	67%
Improved consignee relationships	63%
Enabled quicker service	57%
Enabled customer analysis	51%
Improved dedicated services	50%
Increased dependability	48%
Improved on-time delivery	46%
Exploitation of existing skills: Process-related	
Quality improvements in internal processes.	72%
Improved third-party relationships	64%
Enhanced the management of change.	64%
Provided time improvements in internal processes.	59%

In summary, the Internet is changing the competitive environment of the trucking industry, both directly in challenges to traditional freight brokers and through changes in trucking company customers' competitive environments that are challenging trucking firms to transform their business services. In this process, the borders of the trucking industry and other transportation-oriented sectors such as package express are becoming increasingly blurred. In addition, traditional trucking companies face incentives to transform their businesses from emphasizing shipment of goods, to providing a broader set of "asset-based transportation management" services. These additional services range from warehousing goods, to order taking, to logistics management, to after-sales services. The connectivity offered by the Internet allows truckers to communicate with shippers and subcontractors. In order to exploit the growing potential of this environment, trucking firms will have to change their business practices in significant ways.

D. Technology Application for HAZMAT and National Security

Since September 11, 2001 homeland security has become an overwhelming concern for the government and trucking firms. Technology is starting to help in the homeland security effort as well as improving the safety of big trucks. The potential threat to truck drivers, especially those with hazardous loads, is immense, and once a truck leaves its terminal, its only safeguard typically is a lone driver.

Several technologies have increased on-board security. Some trucks are now equipped with password access that make hijacking or theft much more difficult. A truck may require a "driver password" to be keyed into the onboard computer, without which it will shut down. Also, a hijacked driver being forced to comply can input a "theft code" that immediately advises company headquarters. Onboard global positioning technology also allows company officials and law enforcement authorities to locate a stolen or diverted vehicle. In May 2002, Qualcomm introduced wireless panic buttons, driver authentication, and tamper detection services. The wireless panic button enables drivers to send a panic message on the OmniTRACS system within 150 feet of their vehicle. For driver authentication, a driver must be authorized to operate the vehicle through use of an ID and password. Approximately 125,000 trucks carrying hazardous materials in the United States have some type of tracking and communications capability on board. These systems provide location, content, and status information to shippers, carriers, and authorized third parties.[29]

A service called the Hazmat Tracking Center tracks the patterns of hazmat shipments, which according to the Department of Transportation amount to roughly 3 billion tons annually. If a driver, unknown to the dispatcher, is suddenly incapacitated, an onboard computer generates an alert message notifying the dispatcher, key trucking company personnel, and authorities of a dangerous situation warranting immediate attention. About 850 hazmat haulers use the services of the Hazmat Tracking Center. The tracking service was developed in cooperation with Qualcomm, a mobile data systems supplier based in San Diego. The response time for state police after being notified of a hazmat spill is 27 minutes according to the Center for Technology Commercialization.[30]

At the heart of the Hazmat Tracking Center is Aries Messenger, a proprietary software that plugs directly into wireless tracking equipment manufactured by Qualcomm and other leading companies via unique connector interfaces. These connectors, which are based on each manufacturer's automated processing interface, allow the automated agent to access data streaming in from mobile transmitting equipment, regardless of vendor. Aries Messenger continuously monitors data transmitted from onboard truck computers and other asset-tracking devices, keeping close tabs on vehicle location, speed, trailer connection, tank valve status, door status and other variables. It predicts problems with freight in transit and identifies possible on-road emergencies or developing incidents by comparing incoming data with data values and patterns that have been programmed into its customized data tables. Matching values trigger automatic alerts to law enforcement agencies, emergency response agencies, and other addresses on client-supplied, customized distribution/notification lists.

Advances in monitoring and communication technologies combined with decision support software are helping to increase truck safety and national security. The trucking industry can look forward to technological advances that will have a significant impact on driver safety and the cost of operating a fleet. Increased adoption of safety related technology will occur when the technology is proven and the benefits of adoption exceed the costs of technology acquisition.

E. Technology for the Truck

The pollution created by the trucking industry has long been a source of concern for the federal government and the public. Recently, the Environmental Protection Agency (EPA) has mandated emission standards for diesel engines in trucks. Further, new solutions are being considered as alternatives to the pollution created by idling trucks at truck stops. This section presents the various alternatives on the horizon that manufacturers are presenting to comply with EPA mandates and to reduce truck idling. We also discuss the new opportunities for efficiency and safety created by tire inflation sensors and electronic brake systems. Together, these new technologies enhance the driving environment for the trucker, provide safety and operational advantages for the business, and a cleaner environment for the public.

E.1. Diesel Engines Face Challenges

Fleets are facing a challenge when they buy new trucks – integrating low-emission engines into their operations. Engines built after October 1, 2002 must meet the EPA's stricter emission standards, bringing new technology into the mix. The standard is also being applied to Mexican trucks, starting in 2004. More stringent standards are expected by 2007.

According to the Diesel Technology Forum, engine makers will have to make changes in four areas in order to meet the 2007 standards. First, there is the need for cleaner diesel fuel. Although the EPA has mandated 15-ppm low-sulfur diesel, several engine manufacturers say 5-ppm fuel is needed to meet the 2007 goals. Second, the advent of electronic engine controls has given diesel engine manufacturers almost pinpoint control of fuel delivery to the combustion chamber. This control of fuel injection systems is necessary to avoid temperature spikes during the combustion process, which create higher levels of nitrous oxide. Third, firms need to focus on air intake management and exhaust gas recirculation. Better air intake management results in better fuel combustion, leaving fewer particles to remove from the exhaust. Exhaust-gas recirculation (EGR) takes it a step further by rerouting exhaust through the high-heat combustion process, literally burning away more hazardous exhaust chemicals. Finally, manufacturers need to invest in after treatment technology. This includes catalysts and particulate traps that either convert or capture emissions before they leave the exhaust pipe.

Engine manufacturers are scrambling to comply with a 2002 consent decree before considering the technology needed to meet 2007 mandates. Most of the manufacturers are using what's called cooled EGR to achieve lower emissions. Although cooled-EGR engines do have drawbacks, the most prominent being a 3% to 6% reduction in fuel economy, they provide drivers with better performance and responsiveness. While fleets have to pay more for the cooled-EGR engines themselves, experts believe that maintenance costs will not be as high as many in the industry have feared. Essentially what happens in engines with cooled EGR is that some of the exhaust air coming out of the engine's combustion chamber is cooled and introduced back into the engine to burn off emissions. Anywhere from 5% to 30% of the exhaust is re-circulated, with between 20% and 60% of the exhaust heat dispersed through the radiator instead of the tailpipe. Overall, cooled-EGR engines will add anywhere from $2,500 to $4,000 to the price of a Class 8 truck. The extra cost of maintaining a Class 8 EGR engine could run about $800 a year, including the cost of new oil and coolant. The reduction in fuel economy must also be taken into consideration. One fleet estimates that there could be an additional $4,000 to $5,000 a year in fuel costs per vehicle although this has not yet been demonstrated in field tests. Cooled-EGR engines will need to use a new grade of engine oil called CI-4, which is designed to handle the higher heat and soot load produced by those engines, as well as new oil filters to remove the higher levels of contaminants produced by the EGR process.[31]

Initially, users were disappointed with the new engines' fuel economy and were uncertain about long-term maintenance and durability. However, while long-term maintenance and durability are still uncertain, most users are experiencing better fuel economy than they expected and driver acceptance has been strong. So far, it appears that engine manufacturers delivered successful technology solutions for the 2002 limits. The 2007 mandates present the next hurdle.

E.2. Technology Alternative to Engine Idling

The deafening hum and illuminated running lights are the mainstay of night at most truck stops. Truck drivers idle their engines to heat/cool the cab or sleeper, and keep the engine warm in the winter so that the engine is easier to start. In addition, truck drivers today need to power communications and computers, in order to keep track of inventory, trip planning, and routes. The need for power has increased as the technology on the truck has increased. Long haul trucks consume more than 838 million gallons of fuel annually while idling overnight, according to the US Department of Energy.[32] With the national average retail diesel price at record highs, idling trucks all over the country are burning a gallon or two of diesel every hour and not producing any revenue. The average long-haul truck idles away up to $1,790 in profits each year.[33]

Idle control technologies provide potential reductions of carbon dioxide of approximately 8.1 million tons a year and the potential reduction of diesel fuel consumption of approximately 1.2 billion gallons per year. Reducing idling would have significant environmental and economic benefits on the national level as well. If all class 7 and 8 long-haul trucks (about 480,000 vehicles) used these devices, the total fuel savings would be as much as 0.6% of all fuel used for surface transportation in the United States.

Furthermore, reducing idling is important for reducing air pollution. Assuming 1,830 hours of idling a year, a *single truck* emits about 22 tons of carbon dioxide, 390 pounds of carbon monoxide, and 1,024 pounds of nitrogen oxide. Several fuel efficient alternatives are emerging through advances in technology. Direct-fired burners for heating, thermal storage devices for heating and cooling and auxiliary power units for heating, cooling, and electrical power are some options. For example, the AuraGen(R) combines a sophisticated mechanical and electronic design, advanced engineering, and break-through electromagnetic technology to produce a highly reliable and flexible mobile power generating system that creates alternating current (AC) and direct current (DC) electricity, both with and without the engine on. Through its Inverter Charger System (ICS), the AuraGen provides engine-off power for any equipment including power to provide heat or air conditioning and electrical power for appliances.[34]

Another proposed solution involves truck stops. A solution to the problems caused by idling is truck stop electrification. Truck stop electrification has been gaining momentum through advances in technology that permit lower costs and the potential for widespread availability. A major privately funded project just began in Atlanta. The Environmental Protection Agency awarded a $200,000 grant under its new SmartWay Transport program to electrify some truck stops. The Petro center located off Interstate 40 was involved with IdleAire Technologies Corp. in a pilot program of electrification.[35] For hourly fees starting at a little over a dollar, drivers are able to access specially designed modules offering electrical hookups, ducts for heat and air-conditioning, and connections for cable television, phone and computer services. Subsequently, IdleAire has been installing module hookups at truck stops across the nation. Many owner operators welcome the idea of truck stop electrification, visualizing fuel savings and reduced wear and tear on the engine. However, company drivers wonder if the company that now pays for the fuel used during idling will pay for the hookups or whether the charges for the services eventually will come out of their pockets. The New York State Thruway Authority has made significant investments in truck stop electrification. They note that idling shortens engine life by about 20 percent, or 100,000 miles over five years and that fuel savings realized by not idling for an 8-hour period could provide truckers with 56 to 64 miles of distance, or about 60 more minutes of travel time before stopping to refuel.[36]

E.3. Tire Inflation Sensor Technology

The tires on the tractor and trailer are often the carriers' largest maintenance cost, and proper inflation is essential to getting the most life out of truck tires. Keeping tire pressures within tolerances is one of the most vexing jobs in maintenance. A Federal Motor Carrier Safety Administration study claims that truck fleet managers may be making a costly mistake in their reluctance to purchase tire pressure monitors and automatic inflation systems. The study found that the managers were having difficulty justifying the cost of the new technology. The average truck fleet loses $750 per tractor-trailer combination every year because of under-inflated tires, according to data collected for the study. Automated pressure monitoring and tire inflation systems on the market today range in price from $500 to $2,000 a truck. Systems that monitor pressure but don't keep tires automatically inflated can be cheaper and average about $30 per tire or $540 per tractor-trailer. FMCSA's study concluded that the cost of automated pressure monitoring and tire inflation systems is paid back in the first or second year.[37] Besides lower maintenance costs, manufacturers state that keeping tires inflated reduces the chance of blowouts and that losing a tire on the side of the road can easily cost $450 or more for emergency help, the cost of the tire, and lost productivity. However, carriers are skeptical about the payback numbers. They are reluctant to invest in technology in the absence of concrete research into the costs of running flat tires.

First generation solutions include sensors attached to the tire or strapped to the wheel rim enabling fleets to read air pressure and tire temperature with hand-held or drive-by short-range radio receivers. Onboard inflation systems constantly monitor each tire's pressure and keep the tire inflated to the optimum level. The "smart" tire is now on the horizon.[38] Radio frequency identification (RFID) – the same wireless technology that shippers rely on to track movement of their goods – is finding a role in monitoring the condition of truck tires. Several manufacturers are placing computer chips on individual tires that read and report air pressure and tire temperature. A short-range radio receiver retrieves the data.

While there are different approaches, the tire monitoring systems have a number of common components. Key components include an in-tire sensor and transponder, which gives the tire a unique electronic "identity," measures air pressure and/or tire temperature and provides a source of low power for transmitting data over very short distances. A hand-held or fixed drive-by receiver to collect the data from tires when a truck returns to a terminal, and/or an onboard receiver to provide the driver with tire information at regular intervals is also needed. Today only one manufacturer, Michelin Tires North America, has made an RFID tire monitoring system commercially available.

Truck operators have many concerns about this new technology. Issues include durability, technological viability, and cost. The price of sensors durable enough to withstand the rigors of heavy vehicles in constant use is above the carriers' willingness to pay at the current state of technological development. The high price level can be attributed to the research manufacturers have had to do to overcome a number of challenges associated with RFID sensors on trucks. They had to find a sensor that can withstand temperatures generated in truck tires, mount the sensor so it can be easily installed on existing tires and not be damaged during tire mounting or removal, counter the radio wave interference created by the large amounts of steel in radial tires without increasing signal strength and still comply with FCC regulations, and eliminate signal crossover when trucks with similar systems are in close proximity.

The sensor for the Michelin's e-tire is mounted in a rubber dock, which is vulcanized to the inside of the tire. The dock is like a rubber mushroom. It allows the sensor to move so the tire can flex without damaging it. The vulcanizing process that attaches the dock to the tire is identical to that used to patch a punctured tire and it can be performed by any maintenance facility equipped to do tire repairs. Since the dock can be fitted to any tire, Michelin expects tire dealers and fleets to attach it to all brands of tires.

E.4. Electronic Braking Systems (EBS)

Traditional brake systems use air signals that travel at the speed of sound. Electronic braking signals, by contrast, travel at or near the speed of light, which will permit implementing braking behavior among trucks that is similar to that of a passenger car. The advantages of EBS range from safety performance to drivability to maintenance costs. Using special software and a kingpin-mounted sensor, tractor-based EBS can maintain the correct braking relationship between the tractor and trailer. The result is safer brakes that last longer. Braking action is both faster and more consistent, whether or not the vehicle is loaded. Potential benefits of EBS include enhanced tractor-trailer compatibility (eliminating brake imbalance); automatic hill-holding (by linking EBS with engine-management systems); blending of engine retarder and service brake actuation (to cut brake wear); incorporation of lining-wear indicators (to rationalize maintenance scheduling); and equalization of lining wear (from left to right on the vehicle).[39]

The durability of valves is the toughest issue facing EBS development. While an ABS valve only has to cycle during emergency braking, an EBS valve goes to work every time the brakes are applied. The durability of these valves is an important concern as manufacturers bring EBS to market. Adding to the design complexity of EBS, the valves must work pneumatically as well as through electronic solenoid actuation. The SAE J1939 electronic data link may serve as a 'skeleton' to support communications interfaces between electronic systems by tying engine or driveline retarders to the braking-control system. Higher retarder application will save on brake wear and increase vehicle safety. As more and more systems become integrated onboard and with engines, retarders, brakes, and other systems working together, a true million-mile truck may be on the horizon.[40]

Brake-system suppliers are working with major vehicle OEMs to make the new technology both practical and cost-effective. For example, AlliedSignal is working with OEMs on how to implement EBS, while Freightliner has been offering an optional electronic braking system supplied by Meritor WABCO on its Century Class line of premium Class 8s. Manufacturers believe that EBS won't see the resistance that ABS did, because fleets have gained experience with the electronics that make antilock brakes work. EBS is gaining wide acceptability in Europe but fleets in North America remain skeptical about the payback.

A major obstacle to EBS acceptance is the way FMVSS-121 – the federal braking safety standard – now stands. Under current federal regulations, an electronic brake system must be backed up by a pneumatic system. Unless the NHTSA relaxes current redundancy requirements, EBS will be an expensive proposition. Thus, the future of EBS lies as much in the hands of policy makers as in the technology trajectory. Brake suppliers, despite the uncertainty in the technological and regulatory environment, continue to work towards offering early versions of EBS. They hope to grab a safety or image edge or simply to gain early experience with a technology they view as arriving inevitably.

Technologies that enhance truck performance and reduce pollution are on the horizon. As new products are introduced, the potential pay-off from these technologies will become more evident. The adoption of these technologies offers the potential for firms to trim costs and improve margins. Innovating firms must satisfy federal regulators including the NHTSA and the EPA while creating products that clearly benefit the trucking industry. Through a combination of federal mandates and voluntary adoption, the trucking industry is headed toward shaping a cleaner, safer, and more efficient environment for the drivers, the business, and the general public.

F. Technology in Trucking – 21st Century Applications

The previous sections have presented the current state of the art in trucking technology. Recent advances and future trajectories are discussed below. The editors of Commercial Carrier Journal, in a recent issue, presented their thoughts on technological applications that are likely to influence the trucking industry the most in the next decades. In addition to the tire inflation systems and electronic brake systems Section E discussed, the Internet enabled EDI and new business models in Sections A and B are on the technology frontier. These technologies are likely to affect the productivity and safety of trucking firms as the technology trajectories advance and the products diffuse throughout the industry. Below are other examples of technological applications that are likely to further advance the performance of the trucking industry.[41]

Weight On the Go Onboard weighing devices will become more widely adopted. For example, in one version of such a system, a microprocessor taps into suspension air pressure to determine and display ground weight, to within a couple of hundred pounds. These systems can reduce or eliminate commercial scale fees, the cost of out-of-route miles to drive to weighing scales, and overweight fines.

Electronic Fuel-Injection/Serial Data Link The ECU (electronic control unit) uses inputs from sensors monitoring accelerator pedal position, engine and road speeds, and other parameters to calculate the on and off signals of proper duration. These signals are then sent to electromechanical injectors to regulate the amount of fuel for given operating conditions. The ECU and the "language" it speaks will open a host of intra-vehicle communications-based applications.

Multiplexing Multiplexing has the potential to drastically reduce the wiring requirements inside a truck. Multiplexing is a system of sending multiple, simultaneous control signals to various devices, along a single wire. As an example, consider that a driver turns on his left turn signal. The turn signal is a smart device that sends a coded message to the flasher, along the same wire that is used to signal all other electrical devices on the truck. The flasher, itself a smart device, recognizes the one signal and ignores all others. It then "knows" to send a message to the left turning lights. In turn, the smart lights recognize their unique signal and start flashing. All this happens almost instantaneously.

E-training　　While face-to-face training is still the most popular, technicians are supplementing traditional training via computer-based CD-ROM and Internet-based training. With electronic training, the technicians not only receive bite-sized on demand training but also gain valuable and marketable computer literacy skills.

Conclusion

Advances in information technology, communications, and digital technology provide the trucking industry with the means to cope with challenges presented by the new competitive environment. Trucking firms continue to struggle to conform to new and upcoming regulations and standards in emissions, ergonomics, and diesel fuel. The operating environments for the driver, the fleet manager, and the firm, are undergoing tremendous shifts as new technologies are offered in all facets of the business process. These technologies are coming faster than fleets can adopt and utilize them. Adopting a technology before the fleet and the firm is ready for it is just as bad as waiting too long to adopt it. The challenge of the future for the trucking industry is to incorporate technological advances at the right time.

　　　　The rapid diffusion of technology may be good for economies, but companies derive the greatest advantage from innovations when competitors can not adopt them quickly. Once many companies in a sector have implemented a set of IT applications, they become just another cost of doing business, not sources of competitive advantage. Competitive advantage arises from technologies that substantially extend a company's existing advantages or generate new products, processes, and services. These advantages are accentuated when technology adoption is accompanied by broader changes in business processes and organizational structure.[42] Technology is presenting new opportunities for excellence in the trucking industry. Survival and success will depend on the rate at which firms initiate and accept the technology driven challenge of the new competitive landscape.

Appendix 1 – The Vehicle Routing Problem and Some Solutions

Decision Support Systems are based on various routing problems that have arisen due to the needs of the trucking community. The most commonly known routing problem is the Traveling Salesman Problem (TSP). The TSP may be described as follows: "A salesman is required to visit a set of locations, visiting each at least once, starting from any location and ending at the original place of departure." An example of the TSP in trucking can be found in the package delivery service, where a vehicle must visit a number of stops to make deliveries.

　　　　A generalization of the TSP is the Vehicle Routing Problem (VRP), in which the objective is to design a set of pickup or delivery routes such that:

1)   each route starts and ends at the depot
2)   each customer is visited exactly once by exactly one vehicle
3)   the total amount picked up or delivered does not exceed the capacity of the vehicle
4)   the duration of each route does not exceed a preset limit
5)   the total routing cost is minimized.

The VRP is the most commonly found problem in the trucking industry, particularly as reflected in the focus of software developed for determining solutions to this problem.

Over the years, as dictated by real life practices, modifications and additions have been made to the VRP. One important addition involves the use of time windows in determining pickups or deliveries. This problem is commonly referred to as the vehicle routing problem with time windows (VRPTW). A time window can indicate the earliest time that a driver can make a pickup or delivery, the latest time, or both. Time windows are used for a variety of reasons, such as ensuring a consistent production schedule, keeping inventory at a desired level, or minimizing wait times for truckers at a dock. They are particularly important in the world of just-in-time production, where deliveries must be made as scheduled to avoid delays in production or overstocks in inventory. The majority of routing software available allows for the use of time windows.

Another modification involves determining an optimal strategy with only some information available prior to making routing decisions. This is called the Stochastic Vehicle Routing Problem (SVRP). Information that becomes available only after routing decisions are made can include travel times, load sizes, and pickup and delivery locations. In these situations, decisions are made based on the probability of a set of circumstances occurring. For example, the number of parts to be delivered to a production facility may vary depending on the production schedule, which is unknown prior to the vehicle's departure. Therefore, the solution to the routing problem must take into account this randomness. This problem is significantly more complicated than the standard VRP, with only small instances solved to optimality.

Additional extensions include the use of split deliveries, where multiple vehicles can service the same destination, backhaul pickups, which allow for vehicle to make pickups on the return trip to the depot, and real-time information, which enables a route to be modified at any time in response to various events, such as traffic, and new transportation requests. Each of these extensions allows for the VRP to adapt to real world circumstances, but each also adds to the complexity of the problem and difficulty in finding an optimal solution.

Solution Methods

The complexity of the VRP prohibits the exact solution of any realistically sized problem in a reasonable length of time. Therefore, researchers have turned to heuristics for help in approximating good solutions. Cordeau, et al. provide a thorough review of various VRP heuristics, with some of their work summarized here.[43] VRP heuristics have steadily evolved over the last 40 years. "Classical" heuristics put an emphasis on quickly obtaining a feasible solution with the possibility of using a post optimization procedure to improve the solution. One of these heuristics is the well-known Clarke and Wright Savings algorithm. This algorithm remains widely used in practice despite shortcomings involving accuracy and flexibility. It creates an initial feasible solution by dedicating an individual route to each customer back and forth from the depot. At each iteration, two routes are merged into a single route whenever this is feasible, thus generating a cost saving. Another classical heuristic is the sweep algorithm. This heuristic creates feasible routes by rotating a ray centered at the depot and gradually including customers on a route until the capacity or route length constraint is attained.

Recent research has focused more heavily on "metaheuristics" that use two main principles: local search and population search. Local search intensively explores the solution space by moving at each step from the current solution to another promising solution in its neighborhood. The neighborhood is all those solutions that can be reached from the original solution by making a slight modification to that solution. Population search utilizes a pool of good parent solutions from which it selects certain traits to create offspring solutions. Simulated annealing and tabu search are two heuristics that use local search, while genetic search is an example of population search. Each of these methods implements some process that prevents the solution from becoming fixed at a local minimum. That is, they allow steps that are detrimental to the objective function, moving the solution away from a local minimum to test other possibilities.

Simulated annealing is analogous to the annealing process in which metals are initially melted at very high temperatures, and then slowly cooled to an ordered "frozen" state. The algorithm begins with an initial solution and holding certain parameters (or the "temperature") constant, perturbs the solution, accepting the changes if the objective function (or the "energy") goes down or accepting them with some probability if the value goes up. This is repeated several times at the same temperature with different perturbations, after which the temperature is decremented. This continues until the temperature reaches a base state.

Tabu search performs a local search by moving at each iteration from the current solution to a neighboring solution. This move may be inferior, causing a depreciation of the objective function, so an anti-cycling mechanism is utilized to prevent a return to the original solution. This mechanism declares certain attributes of the original solution as tabu, or forbidden, for a number of iterations. Therefore, the algorithm forces a move away from the local minimum.

The adaptive memory procedure is a generalization of genetic search that is finding use in solving the VRP. In this procedure, a heuristic is used to create a pool of good solutions. This pool is then dynamically updated by adding new improved solution characteristics and removing elements of lower quality. Recombining good solutions from the pool then generates new solutions. This procedure is heavily dependent on the quality of solutions created by the underlying heuristic.

With the advent of these highly effective algorithms, larger problems can now be solved to optimality or near-optimality with minimal computing effort. However, for several reasons, many commercial software and several in-house computer programs used by trucking companies utilize overly simple and outdated methodologies. Many of the heuristics available for solving the VRP lack necessary attributes that the trucking companies require for implementation. Certain methods do well in solving some problem instances, but perform poorly on others, lacking the robustness needed in real world situations. Many algorithms are overly complicated, with practitioners unable to decipher the process and write applicable code. Also, the optimization component of the routing software is only one part of the overall product, and until recently, most effort was focused on data management and user interfaces. The trucking industry is beginning to recognize the benefit of some of the more easily applied algorithms and making the appropriate changes to their software.

Vehicle Routing Software Survey

As the complexity of routing problems has increased and the algorithms developed to solve those problems have become more robust, and the trucking industry pursues new methods for reducing transportation costs, routing software developers must continually make improvements to their products. They must also adapt to and utilize the ever-increasing technological tools available to the industry. The use of the Internet is becoming less of an option for survival in trucking, rather more of a requirement. Because of this, Internet-based routing applications have grown significantly in usage. Similarly, new developments in areas such as wireless data communication and genetic algorithms have led to an improvement in the level of service as well as an increase in the number of offerings available from routing software companies. The following analysis of a variety of those companies heavily draws from a vehicle routing software survey conducted by Hall in 2002.[44]

The primary growth in routing software can be found in the areas of wireless communication/vehicle tracking, integrated order processing/routing systems and web-based applications. Descarte's "Mobile Link Freight" and "Mobile Link Tracker" software permit a driver to transfer real-time data from a pocket PC to the routing system. This allows for re-planning of routes, scheduling of tighter time windows, and the combination of orders located close to one another.

GeoCom USA follows the Microsoft ".NET" structure to allow for a client-server architecture that permits each client to access server-based routing applications without having to maintain and update the software on each client workstation. GeoCom is also using genetic algorithms to improve the quality of routes, as well as real-time data for re-planning of routes. Meanwhile, UPS Logistics has made their Mobilecast available on the Web so that customers know exactly when orders can be placed.

On the software development side, ESRI and ILOG have made libraries of routing code available for customization through software licensing arrangements. ILOG Dispatcher is a C++ library built on top of the ILOG Solver, using constraints commonly found in vehicle routing problems, as well as search techniques effective in routing. ESRI's NetEngine product provides a family of network-based algorithms, while MapObjects can be used for creating GIS interfaces.

The vehicle routing software survey by Hall consisted of a questionnaire covering algorithmic capabilities, interfaces and features, and applications. Responses were collected from twenty-four software vendors. All responses were self-reported and unverified. The following is a brief summary of key results.

Algorithmic Capabilities   Each package has the capability to sequence stops on a route, and almost all are able to assign stops to routes and to terminals. Most vendors claim that assignment and sequencing are simultaneous, and not sequential, with these decisions based on actual street distances (some approximation of street distances can be helpful in reducing the computational effort in distance calculations).

Node routing is the process of assigning and sequencing discrete stops, while arc routing involves the assignment and sequencing of street segments. The former is needed more often, and occurs when the driver visits 100 or fewer locations per day. This feature was offered by the majority of products. Arc routing occurs when vehicles must visit a significant number of stops on a block segment, as in meter reading, mail delivery and garbage pickup. It is more specialized, and is correspondingly offered by fewer products. Some software also allows for routing in real time (while vehicles are in motion) and on a daily basis.

Interfaces and Features   Each product can display routes and stops on maps, and most allow the user to edit these routes with the "drag-and-drop" feature (i.e., click on a stop, and move it to whichever route you desire). This allows a dispatcher to make changes to the routes produced by the algorithm in order to satisfy customer constraints. A digital map underlies each of these products, such as the commercial products from Navigation Technologies and GDT, as well as low-cost Tiger maps available from the U.S. government. These maps are generally selected by customers based on their requirements in terms of accuracy, pricing and coverage. Software that is compatible with multiple map products can be extremely useful, particularly for companies that operate in many regions.

Applications   While a few vendors design their products to serve a variety of applications, most have specialized in an industry sector. Specialization is largely driven by interface requirements – both in terms of presenting information in a manner that is useful to the target user and in terms of interfacing with business software systems. For example, companies like Trapeze, RouteLogic (Compass) and VersaTrans serve the transit industry, UPS Logistics serves the beverage and food distribution industry, and CAPS Logistics has been strong in distributing manufactured products. On the other hand, MicroAnalytics (TruckSTOPS) and

ESRI (Arc Logistics Route) attract a broader market with a more generic and lower-priced product. ILOG has established a unique position, providing a library of solvers rather than a family of interfaces.

Notes

1. Lahsene, Susie. *New Economy, New Vision for Transportation.* TR News. September 2001, pp. 9-11.
2. Farrell, Diana, Terra Terwilliger, and Allen P. Webb. Getting IT spending right this time. The McKinsey Quarterly, 2003 Number 2 available at http://www.mckinseyquarterly.com/article_page.asp?ar=1285&L2=13&L3=13&srid=2 7&gp=0.
3. American Trucking Associations (1999). *Understanding the Trucking Industry: Technology in Trucking series.* Alexandria, VA.
4. American Trucking Associations (1999). *Understanding the Trucking Industry: Technology in Trucking.* Alexandria, VA.
5. Howells-Tierney, Janet. The Connected Man. *Transport Topics.* Alexandria: August/September, 2002, pp. S12-13.
6. Ibid.
7. DeMarco, Tony. Technology drives the growth of Southern Pride Trucking. *Owner Operator.* March 1998, pp. 32-36.
8. Schulz John. D. 'Brand' new system *Traffic World.* Washington: June 12, 2000. Vol. 262, No. 11; pp. 25-26.
9. Regan Amelia. C., H.S. Mahmassani, and P. Jaillet (1995). Improving efficiency of commercial vehicle operations using real-time information: potential uses and assignment strategies. *Transportation Research Record.* Vol. 1493; pp. 188-198.
10. Hall, R.W. and C. Intihar. Commercial Vehicle Operations: Government Interfaces and Intelligent Transportation Systems. *California PATH Research Report UCB-ITS-PRR-97-12.* (Institute of Transportation Studies, University of California, Berkeley) 1997.
11. Crum, M.R, D.A. Johnson, and B.F. Allen (1998). A longitudinal assessment of EDI use in the U.S. Motor Carrier Industry. *Transportation Journal.* Vol. 38, No. 1; pp. 15-28.
12. Regan, Amelia C., Thomas F Golob (1999). Freight operators' perceptions of congestion problems and the application of advanced technologies: Results from a 1998 survey of 1200 companies operating in California *Transportation Journal.* Spring 1999, Vol. 38, No. 3; pp. 57-68.
13. American Trucking Associations (1996). *Assessment of Intelligent Transportation Systems/Commercial Vehicle User Services; ITS/CVO Qualitative Benefit and Cost Analysis.* Alexandria, VA.
14. We conducted the survey during early 2000, with the sponsorship of the University of Michigan Trucking Industry Program (UMTIP). UMTIP receives generous support from the Sloan Foundation and from trucking industry corporations.
15. This section draws from two earlier publications by the authors: Nagarajan, A., E. Canessa, W. Mitchell, and C.C. White III. "Trucking Industry: Challenges to Keep Pace". In *The Economic Payoff from the Internet Revolution.* Eds. Robert E. Litan and Alice M. Rivlin. Washington D.C.: Brookings Institution Press 2001 and Nagarajan, A., E. Canessa, W. Mitchell, and C.C. White III. "e-Commerce and Competitive Change in the trucking industry". In *Tracking a Transformation: e-Commerce and the terms of competition in industries.* BRIE-IGCC E-conomy project. Washington D.C.: Brookings Institution Press 2001.

16. Daniel P. Bearth. Industry Use of Internet Blossoms. *Transport Topics*. July 31, 2000, p. 18.
17. We conducted the survey during early 2000, with the sponsorship of the University of Michigan Trucking Industry Program (UMTIP). UMTIP receives generous support from the Sloan Foundation and from trucking industry corporations.
18. Schulz John D. It's Adult Swim Time. *Traffic World.* October 30, 2000, p. 31.
19. Karim, S. and W. Mitchell. (2000). Reconfiguring business resources following acquisitions in the US Medical Sector, 1978-1995. *Strategic Management Journal* (special issue on the Evolution of Business Capabilities). Vol. 21, Nos. 10-11; pp. 1061-1081.
20. Bearth, Daniel P. "ABF Website wins Kudos" Transport Topics, July 31, 2000, p. 16.
21. Bearth, Daniel. "Arnold Industries hits vein in logistics" *Transport Topics*. January 24, 2000, pp. 10-12.
22. Space utilization is particularly important for LTL shipments, but also applies to TL carriers. The need to eliminate empty miles applies to both segments.
23. Mele Jim. Surfing for freight *Fleet Owner*. June 2002, Vol. 97, No. 6; pp. 84-87.
24. Ibid.
25. Forbes.com Best of the Web Summer 2003 B2B directory Logistics and Transportation available at http://www.forbes.com/bow/b2b/industry.jhtml?id=13.
26. Ibid.
27. Reiskin, Jonathan S. Trucking Firms tout their products as able to boost trucking productivity. *Transport Topics*. May 28, 2001, pp. 2, 31.
28. Ross Julie Ritzer A shipper connects to the Internet. *Transport Topics*. March 10, 2003, No. 3527; pp. S14-17.
29. Joey Ledford. High-Tech Systems Work To Keep Big Rigs Secure *Atlanta Journal Constitution*, March 5, 2003, available at http://www.accessatlanta.com/ajc/metro/0303/05ranger.html.
30. Ritzer Ross, Julie. Hazmat haulers: On being prepared *Transport Topics* Alexandria: January 13, 2003, No. 3519; pp. S14-15.
31. Kilcarr, Sean. Making '02 work. Overland Park. September 2002, Vol. 97, No. 9; pp. 49-51.
32. Vise, Avery. Money for Nothing. Commercial Carrier Journal. March 2003. Available at http://www.etrucker.com/apps/news/article.asp?id=34989.
33. www.ipd.anl.gov/ttrdc/idling.html.
34. Aura Systems Press Release. U.S. Environmental Protection Agency Study Lists AuraGen as Technology to Reduce Emissions and Save Fuel. April 7, 2003.
35. Charlier, Tom. 18-wheeled comfort – lot hookups save fuel, money, environment. The Commercial Appeal. Memphis, TN. June 12, 2003, p. B1.
36. Scruton, Bruce A. *Less idling, fewer fumes: New ideas are aimed at reducing air pollution at truck stops*. Albany NY: The Times Union. April 7, 2002, p. B1.
37. Johnson, Jeff. Study urges adoption of tire technology. *Transport Topics*. February 10, 2003, No. 3523; pp. S1-2.
38. Ryder, Andrew. Dial up signals from sensors to see what your tires are doing. *Transport Topics*. February 10, 2003, No. 3523; pp. S1-5.
39. Cullen, David. Smart brakes Fleet Owner. Overland Park: August 1999, Vol. 94, No. 8; pp. 58-62.
40. Ibid.
41. Editorial staff. Technologies that will advance trucking in the 21st century. *Commercial Carrier Journal*. January 2000, pp. 34-42.
42. Nagarajan, A.; E. Canessa, W. Mitchell, and C.C. White III. (2001). E-Commerce and competitive change in the trucking industry. In *Tracking a Transformation: E-*

commerce and the terms of competition in industries. BRIE – IGCC E-conomy project. Washington D.C.: Brookings Institution Press.

43. Cordeau, J-F, Gendreau, M., Laporte, G., Potvin, J-Y., and Semet, F. (2002) A guide to vehicle routing heuristics. *Journal of the Operational Research Society.* Vol. 53; pp. 512-522.
44. Hall, R.W. (2002) Change of direction. *OR/MS Today.* Vol. 29, No. 1.

Chapter 8

Truck Drivers in the Age of Information: Transformation without Gain

Dale L. Belman, Francine Lafontaine and Kristen A. Monaco

Introduction

In contrast to the declining role, and employment, of blue-collar workers in many sectors of the economy, truck drivers continue to play a central role in their firms and the trucking industry. Despite technological and business innovation in the industry, a driver still is needed to move each load from the shipper to the consignee. Improved scheduling, larger trailers and real-time communication between drivers and dispatchers have improved driver productivity, but these improvements have been modest compared to those in other industries where automation and IT have replaced entirely some portion of the blue collar labor force. In part because of the slow pace of technological change in this industry, truck driving is now among the largest and fastest growing occupations in the United States. The number of drivers, three million employees and owner-operators, is only surpassed by the number employed as retail salespersons and cashiers. The 100 percent growth in the number of truck drivers from 1975 to 2000 is substantially higher than the 59 percent growth of the employed labor force. Truck driving is also distinctive in its exemption from many of the provisions of the Fair Labor Standards Act. Moreover, it is unique in its working conditions, particularly the long hours and time away from home required of many drivers, and the importance of the self-employed segment of the labor force. Finally, technologically driven skills upgrading has been minimal in this occupation over the last several decades. In contrast with many other blue-collar jobs, a driver from 1975 or even 1950 would quickly recognize and master the job of today's driver.

While the work of truck drivers has remained relatively unchanged, the trucking labor markets have been affected by a number of forces, including deregulation, the implementation of new technologies in the industry – especially logistics and communications technologies – globalization, just-in-time production processes and business cycles. These forces have affected the demand for drivers, the intensity of use of labor, the supply of labor, and firms' perceived ability to pay for labor.

This chapter begins with a description of the changes that have occurred in trucking labor markets over the last quarter century. In section III, we rely on the survey data from the Sloan Foundation Trucking Industry Program to develop a more detailed portrait of drivers' work lives today. In Section IV, we investigate four specific trucking labor market issues, namely 1- the effect of deregulation on driver earnings, 2- whether, as is often alleged, there is a shortage of drivers, 3- whether truck drivers are underpaid and, finally, 4- the role that owner operators play in this market. We provide some concluding remarks in Section V.

Changes in Trucking Labor Markets: 1975-2000

Employment

The work life of truck drivers is very different from that of most blue-collar employees. As celebrated in song and film, drivers benefit from a greater degree of independence than most blue-collar workers. They also work longer hours, spend extended periods of time away from home, often are not directly compensated for certain components of their work, receive relatively few fringe benefits given their age and experience, and experience high levels of turnover. This work life reflects both the particular needs of, and competitive pressures faced by, the motor-freight industry, as well as the regulatory framework that controls much of a driver's work.

Following deregulation and the 1980-1982 recession the growth of the motor-carrier industry spurred a rapid increase in the number of truck drivers. In this section, we draw on the Current Population Survey, a monthly survey of 50,000 households by the U.S. Census Bureau, to assess the evolution of the driver workforce between 1975 and 2000.

The employment of truck drivers has risen by slightly more than 100 percent, from 1,495,607 in 1975 to 3,013,664 drivers in 2000 (see Figure 8.1).[1] Although the number of drivers declined between 1980 and 1983 due to the concurrent impact of deregulation and recession and again, but less severely, in the early 1990s due to another recession, annual employment growth averaged 3.85 percent over the entire period. Not all types of drivers saw the same rapid growth in employment. The trucking industry has historically been divided between for-hire firms, firms which provide trucking services to other firms, and private carriage, non-trucking firms which engage in trucking services for their own purposes. Although employment grew substantially in both for-hire and private carriage, growth was greater in for-hire (127 percent) than in private carriage (81 percent). For-hire was the smaller employer of drivers in 1975, with 669,311 drivers against the 826,296 drivers in private carriage. By 2000, it was the larger of the two segments, with 1,518,615 drivers versus the 1,495,049 in private carriage.[2]

Drivers may either be employees or self-employed workers (owner operators), in which case they will own at least one tractor. Owner-operators comprise a relatively small portion of all drivers, approximately 10 percent. Although small in absolute terms, this proportion is higher than the proportion of self-employed in the majority of occupations.[3] While the percentage of owner-operators has remained a fairly constant ten percent, their numbers have risen rather steadily from 153,234 in 1975 to 315,166 in 2000.

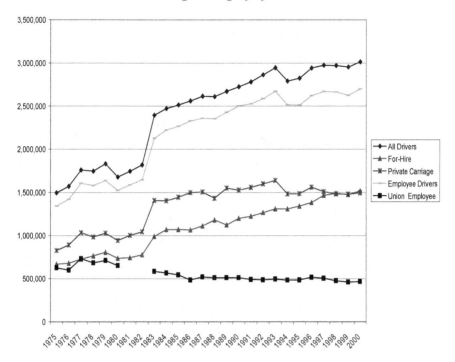

Figure 8.1 Trends in the Number of Drivers

Although there is a substantial break in the union membership data available from the CPS between 1979 and 1983, and some discontinuities because of the change in the sample used for union membership between these years, the CPS data indicate that the Teamsters had a substantial presence among employee truck drivers prior to deregulation.[4] In 1975, slightly less than half of employee drivers, 627,388 out of 1,342,373, reported being union members.[5] By 2000, the number of union employee drivers had declined to 467,347, or 26 percent of the then larger driver work force.

Demographics

The American workforce has changed dramatically over the last quarter century. Immigration and an increased labor participation rate of women have contributed to enlarging the labor force, while declining birthrates and improved public education have produced a labor force that is older but better educated. We examine the impact of these and other forces on the driver labor force using the 1975 May CPS and the 1985 and 2000 CPS ORG. Our inquiry is limited to drivers employed in for-hire as they are more likely to be engaged in motor freight carriage rather than local carriage. We begin with data on race, gender, education, marital status, unionization, region, and age for all for-hire drivers, and then separately for employees and owner operators (Table 8.1).

Table 8.1   For-Hire Driver Demographics from the CPS

		ALL FOR-HIRE DRIVERS		FOR-HIRE EMPLOYEE DRIVERS		FOR-HIRE OWNER OPERATORS	
	year	1975	2000	1975	2000	1975	2000
	n	401	2039	326	1631	75	408
RACE	black	7.2%	12.6%	6.7%	13.2%	9.3%	10.0%
	other	0.2%	1.7%	0.3%	1.8%	0.0%	1.2%
	hispanic	4.0%	10.0%	3.7%	10.1%	5.3%	9.3%
GENDER	female	1.0%	4.4%	0.6%	4.7%	2.7%	3.2%
EDUCATION	less than high school	50.1%	18.8%	48.5%	18.5%	57.3%	20.1%
	high school	39.6%	51.5%	40.2%	50.8%	37.3%	54.7%
	some college	8.7%	19.0%	9.5%	20.1%	5.3%	14.7%
	associates degree		1.9%		2.1%		1.0%
	vocational or technical		3.8%		3.4%		5.4%
	college or higher	1.5%	5.0%	1.8%	5.2%	0.0%	4.2%
MARITAL	married	92.8%	67.6%	93.6%	66.3%	89.3%	72.8%
STATUS	separated, divorced, widowed	6.0%	16.6%	4.9%	17.0%	10.7%	15.2%
	single	3.7%	15.8%	3.7%	17.0%	4.0%	12.0%
OTHER	veteran	54.6%	23.9%	56.1%	24.5%	48.0%	21.8%
	union		55.5%	21.2%			
REGION	Northeast	20.4%	15.8%	21.5%	16.0%	16.0%	15.0%
	Midwest	28.2%	26.5%	27.6%	25.8%	30.7%	29.2%
	South	33.2%	36.1%	32.5%	36.8%	36.0%	33.6%
	West	18.2%	21.6%	18.4%	21.4%	17.3%	22.3%
AGE	21-25	7.7%	5.5%	8.0%	6.1%	6.7%	3.2%
	26-39	46.6%	35.5%	48.5%	37.1%	38.7%	29.2%
	40-54	34.9%	42.5%	35.0%	41.9%	34.7%	44.9%
	55-65	10.7%	16.2%	8.6%	14.8%	20.0%	22.8%

Although women, racial and ethnic minorities remain a small part of the driver labor force, each has become a more important part of that labor force over time. In 1975, slightly less than one percent of drivers were female. By 2000, this proportion had increased to 4.4 percent. In 1975 there were slightly more female owner operators (2.7 percent) than employee drivers (0.6 percent). Twenty-five years later we find the opposite pattern with women comprising 4.7 percent of employee drivers versus 3.2 percent of owner operators. African-Americans and Hispanics also have increased their presence, from 7.2 percent in 1975 to 12.6 percent in 2000 for African Americans and from 4 to 10 percent for Hispanics. The relative racial and ethnic composition of employee drivers and owner-operators has however remained constant.

As in most of the economy, there has been educational upgrading among truck drivers. The proportion of drivers with less than a high school education has declined, from 50.1 percent in 1975 to 18.8 percent in 2000. The proportion of drivers with a high school degree rose from 39.6 to 51.5 percent while the proportion of drivers that report post high-school education other than a college degree rose from 8.7 to 24.7 percent over this period. Although the number of drivers with a college education remains low, it too rose, from 1.5 to 5.0 percent.

The driver labor force is aging. Less than half, 45.6 percent, of the driver labor force was age 40 or older in 1975. By 2000, this group comprised 58.7 percent of drivers. The proportion of drivers aged 55 or older meanwhile increased from 10.7 to 16.2 percent. Not surprisingly given financial requirements, owner operators tend to be older than employee drivers. In 2000, over two-thirds of owner operators were 40 years old, versus 56.7 percent of employee drivers. Similar to the workforce as a whole, the proportion of drivers who report being married has declined considerably. In 1975, 92.8 percent of drivers reported being married. By 2000 this proportion had fallen to 67.6 percent.

Driver Pay

Over the last 25 years, deregulation, de-unionization, and a flow of workers from declining industries into trucking have placed downward pressure on driver compensation. These have been at least partially counterbalanced by the growth in labor demand that has gone unabated after deregulation despite recessionary periods. Drawing on CPS data, we examine the net effect of these forces on employee drivers' annual and weekly earnings for the period 1975-2000. Our analysis of owner-operators is limited to annual earnings as the only CPS data on the earnings of the self-employed is the retrospective annual earnings data in the March files.

Nominal annual earnings of drivers working at least 35 hours per week rose by 185 percent, from $10,264 to $29,234, from 1975 to 2000. However, nominal earnings exaggerate increases in purchasing power as they do not allow for increases in the cost of living. We adjust nominal earnings to year 2000 dollar equivalents using the CPI-U-X1 consumer price index for this period (Figure 8.2). With this adjustment, we find that drivers earned $32,603 in 2000 dollar equivalents in 1975. Following deregulation and recession, employee drivers' mean annual earnings declined to $28,917 in 1984 but then slowly recovered through the balance of the 1980s and 1990s. By 2000, employee drivers' mean annual earnings stood at $31,633, almost $1000 below the 1975 real earnings, and five percentage points below the 1979 earnings of $33,116. Owner-operators have done better than employee drivers over this period as their earnings net of expenses have risen from $32,603 in 1975 to $36,792 in 2000.[6]

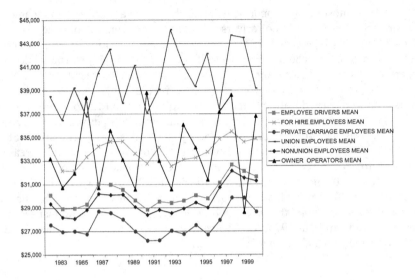

Figure 8.2 Trends in Annual Earnings

Annual income differs substantially by industry segment and union membership. For-hire drivers earn substantially more than drivers in private carriage, but changes in real income for the two groups display similar patterns. In 1975 drivers in for-hire earned $36,647 compared to $28,217 in private carriage. Real annual earnings were sensitive to business cycle factors and deregulation, as the earnings of both groups peaked in the late 1970s at $40,038 and $29,985 respectively for for-hire and private carriage. Both reached their minima, $32,144 in for-hire and $26,754 in private carriage, in 1985. By 2000, drivers in for-hire averaged $34,862 and drivers in private carriage averaged $28,634, close to their 1975 levels but substantially below the peak of their earnings immediately before deregulation. The sustained difference in earnings between the two groups likely reflects the different composition of the driver labor force in these two segments, with many private carriage drivers involved in light truck local delivery. Finally, union drivers earn consistently more than nonunion drivers. Unfortunately, as the question on union membership was only added to the March CPS in 1983, we cannot examine the effect of deregulation on annual earnings by union status. The annual real earnings of union drivers rose only slightly from $38,507 in 1983 to $39,159 in 2000 (Figure 8.2). Non-union annual income also grew modestly over this same period.

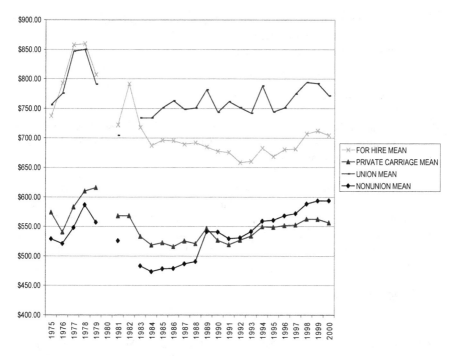

Figure 8.3 Trends in Weekly Earnings

Considerably larger samples of data on weekly and hourly earnings are available from the May and ORG files of the CPS, though these include only employee drivers. Figure 8.3 displays the evolution of real weekly earnings of drivers, broken down between private and for-hire, and union and non-union employee drivers.

Average weekly earnings for all employee drivers were $635 in 1975, peaked at $705 in 1978, reached a post deregulation minimum of $571 in 1986 and subsequently returned to $627 by 2000. The differential in weekly earnings between for-hire and private carriage narrowed somewhat through this period but remains large. In 1975, for-hire drivers earned $737 per week, those in private carriage $574. Weekly earnings in the two sectors both peaked in the late 1970s, declined substantially in the 1980s recession following deregulation and then rose somewhat unsteadily toward their year 2000 endpoints of $704 and $556 in for-hire and private carriage respectively. Wages for union and non-union employed drivers peaked in 1978 at $850 and $587 per week respectively, bottomed out in 1984 at $734 and $473 respectively, and then rebounded to $772 for union drivers and $594 for nonunion drivers by 2000.

To summarize, data on income suggests that truck drivers' real earnings in 2000 were no higher, and in some instances were lower, than they were a quarter century ago. The strong demand for transportation services, and thus labor, in the late 1980s and through the 1990s has helped drivers by raising their real wages from their low levels immediately after deregulation to levels that are now approaching their pre-deregulation levels.

Driver Survey Results

Although national data informs us about trends in the driver labor force over time, they tell us little about the work and life of truck drivers. Fortunately, the Sloan Trucking Industry Program (TIP) Survey of Drivers provides detailed information on drivers' work, pay, and benefits. Drivers were asked questions about were asked questions about their work history; their current work; the structure of compensation; time spent working, waiting, and resting; and their use of technology at randomly selected truck stops in the Midwest between 1997 and 1999.[7] The survey was administered at truck stops because it was meant to focus mostly on over-the-road, as opposed to local, drivers. And indeed 90.6 percent of the respondents were over-the-road drivers.

Driver Characteristics

Table 8.2 summarizes demographic and other characteristics of the 850 full-time over-the-road drivers who responded to the survey, broken down by type of carriage and between owner operators and employee drivers.[8] We find that the demographic characteristics of the TIP drivers overall are quite similar to those reported in the CPS data generally.

One exception is the proportion of African-Americans which is below the national average in the TIP data, likely because the survey was conducted in the Midwest. The typical driver in the TIP data is 42 years old, started driving at 26 and has spent 14.6 years in this occupation. Owner operators are somewhat older than company drivers, and so it is not too surprising to find that they also have higher levels of experience as drivers (16.8 instead of 13.8 years). Drivers in private carriage also report more years of driving experience than those in the for-hire industry, with 16.4 and 14.3 years respectively. The educational background of drivers in the TIP survey is also very similar to that found in the CPS data, with about one-fifth of drivers reporting less than a high school degree, one-half having completed high school, and one-fifth again reporting some college education.

Drivers were asked where they learned to drive and how long they have been with their current employer. We find that a majority of drivers learned their occupation "on the job". One-fifth report learning from a private truck driving school, while another fifth learned from a friend or family member. Only one out of ten drivers learned from a trucking company program. Drivers have worked with their current employer for a modest 5.4 years, with median tenure less than half this at two years. While most of the demographic characteristics of drivers are reasonably similar between the CPS and TIP data, Table 8.2 shows that one fourth of the drivers in the TIP survey are owner operators, much above the 10 percent found in the overall population of drivers, and only 10 percent of the drivers are unionized, much below the 20 percent we found in the CPS data in 2000. Finally, 84 percent of respondents in the TIP survey work for for-hire common carriers while only one half of all drivers do according to the CPS data.

Table 8.2 Driver Survey Demographics

	All Drivers	Employee Drivers	Owner Operators	For-Hire	Private Carriage
Age, Experience, Tenure:					
Age	42.21	41.7	43.63	42.03	43.19
Age When Started	26.07	26.46	25	26.13	25.78
Years as Driver	14.6	13.8	16.82	14.27	16.36
Months with Current Firm	5.4	5.39	na	5.34	5.69
How Learned to Drive:					
Private School	17.1%	18.8%	12.6%	17.3%	16.4%
Public or Tech. School	8.3%	9.9%	4.0%	9.1%	4.5%
Trucking Company	9.4%	9.7%	8.5%	9.6%	8.2%
Military	6.5%	7.3%	4.5%	6.5%	6.7%
Other, Family Member	20.7%	18.5%	26.9%	21.5%	16.4%
Personal Characteristics:					
Female	2.6%	2.1%	4.0%	2.8%	1.5%
Male	97.4%	97.9%	96.0%	97.2%	98.5%
White	87.0%	86.9%	87.5%	85.7%	94.1%
Black	7.8%	7.7%	8.0%	8.5%	3.7%
Native American	2.7%	2.7%	2.7%	3.1%	0.7%
Hispanic	2.5%	2.7%	1.8%	2.7%	1.5%
Married	64.6%	62.1%	71.6%	63.1%	72.4%
Separated, Divorced, Widowed	22.7%	23.2%	21.3%	24.0%	15.7%
Single	12.7%	14.7%	7.1%	12.9%	11.9%
Union	8.59%	10.4%	3.56%	7.12%	16.42%
Private Carriage	15.76%	16.8%	12.89%		
Education:					
Less Than H. S.	19.8%	19.4%	20.9%	20.3%	17.2%
H.S. Diploma	44.1%	45.3%	40.9%	43.2%	49.3%
Voc. or Tech. School	5.8%	5.9%	5.3%	6.3%	3.0%
Some College	20.8%	20.6%	21.3%	20.5%	22.4%
Associate's Degree	3.8%	3.4%	4.9%	3.8%	3.7%
College Degree Plus	5.7%	5.3%	6.7%	5.9%	4.5%
Number of Observations	850	625	225	716	134

All of these differences are explained by the focus of the TIP survey on over-the-road drivers. Indeed, owner operators are found almost exclusively in over-the-road carriage. Thus what the TIP data indicate is that within over-the-road haulage, owner operators represent 25 percent of all drivers. Union membership is highest among local employee drivers (13.9 percent) and especially low among over-the-road owner operators (3.2%). Finally, the large proportion of TIP drivers involved in for-hire is due to the fact that a disproportionate amount of private haulage is local. Nearly half of the local drivers work in private carriage while only 13.5 percent of over-the-road employee drivers, and only 11.1 percent of owner operators, are involved in such haulage.[9]

Drivers' Work

Drivers' work typically requires driving long distances and working long hours. Tables 8.3 and 8.4 respectively describe the number of miles and hours worked by all the TIP surveyed drivers over the last 24 hours, last seven days, and, in the case of mileage, the last full year of driving. Respondents overall averaged 113,278 miles in the last year. The distribution of miles over the past year is nearly identical for over-the-road employees and owner operators, with 25 percent of employees reporting 135,000 or more miles driven and 25 percent of owner operators reporting 130,000 miles or more in the year prior to the interview. Local drivers tend to drive fewer miles, averaging 82,775 miles annually. The same patterns are found for miles driven in the seven days prior to the interview, though the weekly information displays somewhat greater dispersion in mileage for owner operators than employee drivers. Finally, over the last 24 hours, the median employee driver had driven 446 miles but a number of drivers reported substantially higher mileage. Over-the-road employees in the 75th percentile for mileage drove 600 miles while the 75th percentile owner-operator covered 570 miles. Ten percent of employees report driving 800 miles or more in the previous 24 hours, while a similar percentage of owner operators report 700 or more miles.

Driving is only one aspect of the work of truck drivers. In the 24 hours prior to their interview, drivers averaged 8.7 hours of driving time and an additional 2.9 hours of non-driving work time (Table 8.4). The division between driving time and non-driving work time, which includes activities such as waiting to be loaded and unloaded, actual loading and unloading time, and waiting for a dispatch, differs by type of driver. Local drivers tend to spend less time driving (7.8 hours) and more time involved in non-driving work (3.9 hours). Drivers averaged 60 hours of work in a five-day work week. There is considerable variation in weekly hours of work by type of employee, with owner-operators reporting the least amount, 55 hours, while drivers in private carriage along with over-the-road employee drivers reported an average of 62 hours.

Table 8.3   Miles in the Last Year, Week, and 24 Hours

		All Drivers	Local Employees	Over the Road Employees	Over the Road Owner Operators	For-Hire	Private Carriage
Last Year	n	850	79	554	216	716	134
	mean	113,278	82,775	117,034	115,038	114,410	107,235
	10th percentile	60,000	25,000	72,000	70,000	65,000	50,000
	25th percentile	100,000	60,000	100,000	100,000	100,000	80,000
	50th percentile	115,000	80,000	120,000	112,250	120,000	100,000
	75th percentile	130,000	113,000	135,000	130,000	131,000	130,000
	90th percentile	150,000	130,000	156,000	150,000	150,000	150,000
Last 7 Days	n	813	77	524	211	683	130
	mean	2144	1468	2255	2121	2191	1895
	10th percentile	1000	500	1100	940	1000	750
	25th percentile	1500	1000	1800	1500	1600	1250
	50th percentile	2200	1500	2300	2100	2200	2000
	75th percentile	2800	2000	2900	2800	2800	2500
	90th percentile	3200	2700	3200	3400	3200	3000
Last 24 Hours	n	849	79	553	216	715	134
	mean	446	322	474	420	454	405
	10th percentile	100	70	150	70	110	70
	25th percentile	300	180	325	264	300	212
	50th percentile	450	300	476	400	450	400
	75th percentile	600	425	600	570	600	548
	90th percentile	750	560	800	700	762	700

Table 8.4   Picture of the Last 24 Hours and Last Week of Work

		All Drivers	Local Employees	Over the Road Employees	Over the Road Owner Operators	For-Hire	Private Carriage
Last 24 Hours	n	848	79	553	216	712	133
	Miles	446.14	321.73	474.44	419.86	453.86	404.97
	Hours of Sleep	8.39	7.80	8.43	8.52	8.40	8.33
	Hours Driving	8.68	7.77	8.96	8.28	8.70	8.56
	Hours Non-Driving	2.93	3.91	2.78	2.95	2.76	3.85
Last 7 Days	n	783	75.00	501.00	206.00	662	121
	Days Worked	5.20	5.10	5.28	5.04	5.21	5.16
	Hours Worked	60.06	60.68	61.99	55.19	59.69	62.11
	Miles Driven	2143.81	1467.58	2255.06	2120.69	2191.27	1894.51

Prior to 2004, and thus at the time at which the TIP surveys were conducted, the Federal Hours of Service (HOS) Regulations limited drivers to 60 hours of work time in seven days period and 70 hours in eight days.[10] Drivers were also limited to 10 hours driving and 15 hours of total work time before taking an eight-hour break. With an average of 60 hours of work reported among truck drivers, and twenty-five percent of drivers reporting seventy or more hours, the data from the TIP survey confirms the widely held view that the system of regulating drivers working time has become ineffective. Respondents were queried directly about their adherence to the 10-hour rule. Not only did many report exceeding the limit in their last week of work, but almost sixty percent of drivers reported working more than indicated in their legally mandated log books in the month prior to the interview (see Table 8.5). This number was lowest for local drivers (37.3 percent) and highest for over-the-road owner operators (61.3 percent). Drivers reported driving more than ten hours without an eight-hour break an average of 8 times in the 30 days prior to the interview.

Drivers also were asked a number of related questions on safety (Table 8.5). More than one-quarter of drivers reported receiving a moving violation in the last year. Fourteen percent of drivers report being involved in an accident in that time. Finally, over one-third of drivers report dozing or falling asleep at the wheel while driving at least once in the prior 30 days.

Table 8.5   Regulations and Safety

		All Drivers	Local Employees	Over the Road Employees	Over the Road Owner Operators	For-Hire	Private Carriage
Work More Than Logged	n	762	51	511	199	649	113
	mean	57.1%	37.3%	57.5%	61.3%	57.9%	52.2%
Involved in Accident in Last Year	n	849	79	553	216	715	134
	mean	14.0%	16.5%	14.5%	12.0%	13.3%	17.9%
Received a Moving Citation in Last Year	n	848	79	552	216	714	134
	mean	27.7%	24.1%	26.6%	31.9%	28.6%	23.1%
Dozed While Driving in Last 30 Days	n	850	79	554	216	716	134
	mean	34.8%	40.5%	34.7%	33.3%	34.8%	35.1%

Drivers' Compensation

Driving is a difficult occupation, but one that allows individuals with modest levels of education and occupation-specific training to earn enough to place them solidly in the middle class as indicated by the mean annual earnings of $38,830 (in 2000 dollars) for respondents. Moreover, earnings differ only modestly by type of employment.

Table 8.6   Holidays, Sick Days, and Benefits

		All Drivers		Non-Union Employees		"Union Employees"		"Non-union Owner Operators"	
		n	mean	n	mean	n	mean	n	mean
Vacation Days	holiday	829	2.938	543	3.57	65	6.615	213	0.314
	sick days	120	0.108	91	0.011	6	3.5	22	0
Deferred Compensation	have	849	44.3%	559	56.7%	65	44.6%	217	12.9%
	firm provided	850	40.6%	560	54.6%	65	44.6%	217	3.7%
	firm pay	850	5.5%	560	7.0%	65	10.8%	217	0.5%
Pension Plan	have	847	25.4%	558	21.9%	65	73.9%	216	19.0%
	firm provided	850	14.6%	560	13.0%	65	69.2%	217	1.4%
	firm pay	850	7.7%	560	6.3%	65	40.0%	217	0.5%
IRA	have	847	21.5%	557	15.1%	65	26.2%	217	35.5%
Health Insurance	have	845	83.7%	555	87.8%	65	100.0%	217	68.2%
	firm provided	850	58.0%	560	71.3%	65	93.9%	217	12.9%
	spouse	850	10.0%	560	8.4%	65	6.2%	217	15.7%
	private	850	12.1%	560	5.7%	65	1.5%	217	31.8%
	military	850	2.6%	560	2.9%	65	0.0%	217	2.8%
	firm pay	850	17.8%	560	18.8%	65	58.5%	217	3.2%

The majority of drivers, 62.1 percent, are paid by the bureau mile, others are paid a percent of trip revenue, and others still by the hour. Local drivers are most likely to be paid by the hour (53.2 percent). On average, drivers paid this way earn $13.05 per hour.[11] Over-the-road employee drivers are most likely to be paid by the mile (73.1 percent) – these drivers on average receive $0.32 per bureau mile.[12] Finally, owner operators are most likely to be paid a percent of haul revenue (57.2 percent). On average, owner-operators paid mileage rates obtain $0.98 per bureau mile. Percentage of freight rates are 26.8 percent on average for company drivers and 68.4 percent for owner operators. Survey results suggest that annual earnings are highest for those who are paid by the hour or by the mile, $40,182 and $40,055, respectively, and substantially lower for those who are paid a percent of revenue, $36,377. However, the large number of owner operators among this last group, and the possibility that these business owners can account for various costs in different ways, complicates direct earnings comparisons with employed drivers. On average, owner operators who responded to the survey earned $38,127 net of all their expenses last year.[13]

Although drivers' earnings place them in the middle class, their non-wage compensation is relatively paltry. On average, drivers reported having three paid holidays and no sick days in their last year (Table 8.6). However, union employees reported 6.6 paid holidays and 3.5 paid sick days per year. Not surprisingly given the nature of their relationship with carriers, owner operators have no paid holidays or sick days, and they report lower levels of other benefits as well. Fifty-seven percent of non-union employee drivers, and forty-four percent of union drivers report having some form of deferred compensation plan through their employer, however firms contribute to these plans in only seven and eleven percent of cases respectively (Table 8.6). Nearly three-fourths of union employee drivers (73.9 percent) and 21.9 percent of nonunion employee drivers indicated that they participate in a conventional pension plan. Thirty-five percent of owner operators, 26 percent of union employees, and 15 percent of nonunion employees reported having an IRA. Though most drivers (84 percent) report having some form of health insurance, and all union employees have this type of insurance, it is noteworthy that only 68 percent of owner operators have such insurance.

A Look at Four Labor Market Issues

Deregulation and Driver Pay

The Motor Carrier Act of 1935 regulated the for-hire trucking industry with controls on entry and the establishment of rate bureaus to set prices. Union density in trucking peaked in the 1960s with nearly two-thirds of drivers covered by a collective bargaining agreement. Rose (1987) and Hirsch (1988) have established that firms earned monopoly rent under regulation, rent that they shared with their union drivers. Rose (1987), however, finds no evidence of spillover effects between the union and non-union labor segments.

Deregulation at the federal level, which culminated with the Motor Carrier Act of 1980, was followed by considerable industry upheaval with many established incumbents leaving the market, replaced by large numbers of small carriers. The labor market was impacted by this change. Union density declined significantly and so did driver wages (see Figure 8.3). However, as nonunion drivers did not receive rents under regulation, authors such as Rose (1987) and Hirsch (1988) have hypothesized that we should find smaller wage declines following deregulation for non-union drivers compared to their union counterparts. Using data from the CPS from the 1970s through mid-1980s, these authors found support for this hypothesis.

Belman and Monaco (2001) use a different estimation technique and additional years of data to revisit this issue and find that nonunion drivers experienced larger wage declines following deregulation than did union drivers. The estimates, which correct for the quasi-panel structure of the data and adjust for heteroskedasticity implicit in the data structure, show that nonunion wages fell by between 11.7 and 15.0 percent following deregulation, while union wages declined by between 7.6 and 8.3 percent. The larger decline of nonunion wages is attributed to two factors. First, deregulation was followed by the de-unionization of the truckload (TL) segment and the withdrawal of the union into the less-than-truckload (LTL) and local cartage. LTL firms are somewhat protected from the competitive forces that characterize the TL sector because the complexity of their systems creates a barrier to entry. As a result, the Teamsters were able to maintain some of their bargaining power and the union wage differential.

Deregulation's larger effect on nonunion earnings is also attributable to differences in the laws governing working hours for truck drivers and other blue collar workers. The syllogism used to argue that deregulation could not affect the earnings of nonunion workers presumes that any 'rents' earned by nonunion drivers, would be arbitraged away by the movement of workers seeking economic advantage between truck driving and other work. However, as data from the TIP driver survey indicates, the typical driver, whose work time is governed by the Hours of Service regulations, worked more than 60 hours per week. In contrast, the typical blue-collar worker was working between 40 and 41 hours. The driver who moved from a job in trucking to a typical blue-collar job would, absent an increase in pay, suffer a one-third decline in income. This potential loss of income limited driver mobility and, by weakening the arbitrage mechanism, permitted carriers to pass part of the loss of rents caused by deregulation to drivers in the form of large reductions in pay. The finding that nonunion wage reductions were larger than union reductions is then consistent with economic theory as it plays out in this specific institutional context.

Is There a Driver Shortage?

A more recent, and in fact continuing, labor market controversy in trucking concerns the reputed "driver shortage," a popular theme of the trucking industry press over the last decade. Carriers, especially truckload carriers, typically point to their ongoing need to recruit and train drivers as evidence of this shortage. But what carriers are really referring to when they mention a driver shortage is that they are not able to recruit sufficient numbers of workers at the *going wage*. If there were an ongoing shortage of drivers, the excess of labor demand over labor supply should result in an increase in the earnings of drivers. This, in turn, would attract new drivers into the market and reduce the imbalance of supply and demand. In the presence of ongoing increases in labor demand, we would expect to observe large increases in earnings as carriers also would attempt to poach drivers from one another.

Data on wage movements provide limited support for the view that there has been an ongoing shortage of drivers over the last decade. The driver labor force has grown rapidly with only brief periods of slower growth since 1983. In contrast, annual and weekly earnings have remained relatively stable since the end of deregulation (recall Figures 8.2 and 8.3). The strongest growth in earnings occurred in the late 1990s when the United States achieved the lowest levels of unemployment in the prior thirty years. Even at that time the growth was relatively modest: real annual earnings rose from $27,296 in 1995 to $29,234 in 2000. This increase in earnings parallels that of most low-wage labor markets in the same period and is far smaller than that experienced by occupations, such as IT, where rapid wage growth occurred in response to widely recognized labor shortages. Additional evidence that the driver shortage was of modest proportions may be found in the observation by Louis Uchitelle who notes that shippers had no real trouble getting loads delivered and that there was no evidence that large numbers if tractors were left idle by a shortage of drivers (New York Times, August 29, 1999, p. C3).

Our research suggests that what firms interpret as a labor shortage is mainly an issue of rapid turnover among drivers. As previously noted, the TIP driver survey found that the median driver had been with his current employer for only 24 months. It is regularly reported that some larger firms have experienced 100 percent turnover in their driver labor force each year.[14] The rapid turnover of drivers presents carriers with problems similar to those faced by firms during a labor shortage; the carriers must expend significant resources recruiting, screening and training new drivers. But labor turnover issues differ from labor shortage situations in that there are a sufficient number of workers for the available work and there is little upward pressure on wages. Note that inter-firm turnover problems are likely to be particularly severe in the trucking industry because very little ties drivers to firms: neither pay nor benefit plans are affected by drivers' decisions to remain longer with their firm. Firms looking to reduce the cost of driver turnover thus might benefit from instituting labor practices that address this lack of long-term benefit from remaining with one's firm.

Are Drivers Underpaid?

In combination with the long hours of work and demanding working conditions, the post-deregulation decline in driver's real earnings, has fueled discussion over whether drivers are adequately compensated for their work. The view that drivers' pay is too low is common currency among those who drive, but such views are not limited to those immediately involved in driving. Belzer (2000) argues that since deregulation the non-union sector in trucking has taken on many of the characteristics of sweatshops: below subsistence wages, overwork and unpleasant and unhealthy working conditions. Corsi (2001) argues against such conclusions and Beilock (2001, 2003) finds that drivers' earnings are consonant with those of individuals with similar educations.

Economic theory suggests that wages are largely determined by an individual's productivity; several decades of empirical research have established a strong link between individuals' human capital and innate abilities, their productivity and pay. But pay is not determined solely by productivity. The theory of compensating differentials also implies that pay is influenced by working conditions. Employers who provide substandard working conditions will be unable to attract a sufficient supply of workers at the going wage rate. The operation of markets compels them to offer an increment to pay, a "compensating differential," to attract workers who would otherwise choose jobs with better conditions. As there is some fluidity across occupations and industries, this "compensating differential" applies not only to similar jobs within an industry but across industries and occupations. Holding other wage determinants, particularly human capital, constant, wages in less desirable industries and occupations should be higher than wages offered for similar jobs in industries and occupations that provide better working conditions. Given truck drivers' working conditions, we would expect that if truck drivers were underpaid, their wages would resemble those of workers with similar human capital working under better conditions.

One way to determine whether the market is compensating drivers for their working conditions is to isolate the component of individuals' wages that is associated with their occupation and compare this occupational component to that of similar occupations.[15] This is done by estimating a wage model with an indicator variable for each occupation but no overall intercept. The coefficient on the occupation indicator variable is the 'occupational wage component', which reflects the market valuation of the advantages and disadvantages of that occupation. The estimated magnitudes of the occupation components can be compared between occupations and judgments made about the appropriateness of the implied wage differentials. For example, the occupational wage component of truck drivers in the trucking industry can be compared with that of drivers outside of the trucking industry. Similar comparisons can be made with other motor transportation occupations, with manual occupations that require similar levels of education and training, and with other manual occupations that involve more advanced training than truck driving. This approach is somewhat judgmental as there is seldom a perfect correspondence between the occupation of interest and other occupations. It nevertheless provides a means of exploring the underpay issue.[16]

We use data from the year 2000 CPS ORG files to estimate a conventional human capital model for private sector employees with controls for educational attainment, age, gender, race and ethnicity, union membership, region of residence and residence in a metropolitan area. The 99,821 individuals in the resulting data were engaged in 484 three-digit private sector CPS occupations. The model includes indicator variables for each of these occupations. To better understand the occupational effects of employment in trucking, we separate drivers employed in the for-hire trucking industry from those in private haulage. Owner operators are excluded as the CPS lacks data on their earnings. We estimate models using log hourly earnings and log weekly earnings as the dependent variable.[17] We use the log wage estimates to construct predictions of the hourly wage by occupation, and report these in Table 8.7. The predictions are standardized for human capital by calculating the predicted wage at sample mean human capital characteristics.

Table 8.7 is divided between hourly earnings (left hand side) and weekly earnings estimates. Turning first to hourly earnings estimates, the occupational title is in column one, the CPS occupation code is in column 2, actual mean hourly earnings by occupation unadjusted for individual characteristics) in dollars is in column 3, and the earnings predicted by the regression (calculated at the mean human capital characteristics), also in dollars, is in column 4. The difference between the earnings of drivers in the trucking industry and each of the other occupations is in column 5. The t-statistic for the difference is in column 6. The last column is the number of individuals in the sample for the occupation. We limit the estimates to occupations with at least 80 observations. The occupations included in Table 8.7 are a subset of the blue-collar occupations which represent the patterns found in the full set of occupations. The sample mean hourly earnings for truck drivers employed in the trucking industry is $15.67; the earnings predicted at sample mean human capital characteristics are $13.64 (Table 8.7).

A natural initial comparison is with truck drivers employed outside of the motor freight industry. This "occupation" is comprised of drivers whose work is similar to that of drivers within motor freight, but it also includes local delivery drivers in light trucks, construction drivers and others whose work and working conditions are different from that of freight drivers. Average hourly earnings for these drivers are $13.11, while the predicted hourly earnings are $12.06, $1.57 less per hour than drivers in motor freight. This difference in pay is statistically significant. Motor freight drivers earn a premium of 13.1% on average over drivers with similar skills doing similar work but who are less likely to work extended hours or be away from home for extended periods.

Comparing the earnings of drivers in motor freight with those of other motor vehicle operatives again indicates that motor freight drivers earn a premium over other drivers. Drivers in motor freight earn $1.40 (11.4%) more than driver-sales workers, $2.27 (20.1%) per hour more than bus drivers, and $3.70 (37.2%) more than taxi drivers; each difference is significant at the 5 percent or better level.[18]

The balance of Table 8.7 compares drivers in motor freight with non-transportation blue-collar occupations. Individuals in the first group, production operatives, are engaged in repetitive operations, typically in a factory or other production facility. Similar to truck driving, these jobs require no more than a high-school degree and no more than a few months of occupation-specific training and on-the-job experience. They provide better working conditions, at least with respect to hours of work and time spent at home. The predicted wages indicate that the hourly earnings of truck drivers in motor freight are similar to those of printing machine operators but significantly higher than that of sewing machine and punch press operators. The educational and training requirements for laborers, manual workers involved in operations such as stock and freight handling, are similar to those of truck drivers but laborers are less likely to control expensive or powerful machinery.[19] Although laborers' duties often involve heavy work, they are not characterized by extended working time and time away from home. Consistent with the lesser requirements of the laborers' position, most laborers are paid between $2.34 and $4.03 per hour less than truck drivers. The differences are statistically significant.

Table 8.7 Comparing Hourly Earnings Across Occupations

	Hourly Earnings				Weekly Earnings				No. of Obs.
		Adjusted for Human Capital				Adjusted for Human Capital			
	Hourly Earnings	Predicted Earnings	Diff. from Truck Drivers	t-stat for Diff.	Weekly Earnings	Predicted Earnings	Diff. from Truck Drivers	t-stat for Diff.	
Motor Vehicle Operators									
Truck driver-trucking ind.	$15.67	$13.64			$708.54	$603.01			1,986
Truck driver-other ind.	$13.11	$12.06	$1.57	2.910	$554.77	$501.88	$101.13	4.105	2,032
Transportation Operatives									
Motor vehicle supervisor	$17.29	$13.98	-$0.34	-0.374	$779.94	$615.26	-$12.25	-0.289	106
Driver-sales workers	$14.35	$12.24	$1.40	1.948	$614.17	$527.76	$75.25	2.245	206
Bus drivers	$12.08	$11.36	$2.27	3.677	$421.40	$457.35	$145.67	5.300	383
Taxi cab drivers	$11.21	$9.94	$3.70	6.063	$484.80	$422.20	$180.82	6.438	362
Operatives									
Punching & stamping op.	$12.33	$11.86	$1.78	2.200	$496.27	$468.49	$134.52	3.793	118
Printing machine op.	$14.99	$13.42	$0.21	0.319	$617.18	$536.87	$66.14	2.234	370
Textile sewing machine op.	$8.56	$10.14	$3.49	6.400	$418.27	$184.74		7.455	
Laborers									
Stock handlers and baggers	$9.39	$9.61	$4.03	7.872	$346.87	$377.27	$225.74	9.947	1,555
Freight & material handler	$11.81	$11.30	$2.34	4.157	$454.71	$445.31	$157.71	6.306	856
Material Moving Operators									
Operating engineers	$17.53	$15.75	-$2.11	-2.778	$709.83	$635.73	-$32.72	-0.962	289
Excavating machine op.	$16.38	$15.50	-$1.87	-2.042	$645.86	$618.52	-$15.51	-0.383	151
Industrial truck op.	$12.58	$11.93	$1.70	2.927	$519.41	$471.80	$131.21	5.093	642
Precision Production									
Automobile mechanics	$15.08	$13.77	-$0.13	-0.220	$634.97	$552.78	$50.24	1.849	1,104
Aircraft engine mechanics	$18.74	$15.11	-$1.47	-1.716	$806.37	$610.29	-$7.28	-0.188	130
Carpenters	$16.38	$14.85	-$1.22	-1.990	$634.02	$563.90	$39.11	1.470	1,890
Electricians	$19.46	$16.42	-$2.79	-4.231	$815.32	$645.98	-$42.97	-1.4769	987
Roofers	$15.89	$14.58	-$0.94	-1.172	$557.59	$558.77	$44.24	1.269	254
Machinists	$16.57	$14.53	-$0.90	-1.411	$680.48	$577.62	$25.39	0.893	599
Butchers/ meat cutters	$12.38	$12.57	$1.07	1.658	$508.31	$511.01	$92.00	3.179	370

Source: Earnings estimates constructed from a log wage equation estimated with the 2000 Outgoing Rotation of the Current Population Survey. The wage difference is calculated as (estimated earnings of drivers – estimated earnings of other occupation).

Material moving occupations involve the operation of heavy equipment, often on construction sites. Proficiency in these occupations may require extended formal and on-the-job training; they also involve exposure to weather and hazardous conditions and may require time away from home. Our estimates suggest that these occupations are paid more than drivers. In contrast, industrial truck and tractor equipment operators, individuals who operate trucks and other moving equipment on factory premises and whose jobs involve skills similar to those of truck drivers, are paid $1.70 per hour less than drivers. The lower pay is consistent with a downward adjustment for the better conditions of industrial truck operators.

Finally, precision production occupations are blue-collar jobs that require advanced vocational training, often three or four year apprenticeships. Some, particularly construction occupations, involve exposure to weather, hazards at job sites, and may also require spending time away from home. The predicted earnings of most of these occupations are $1.00 to $2.00 per hour more than those of truck drivers, and most are statistically significant. The occupations for which earnings are not significantly higher than those of drivers are those that do not involve extended advanced vocational training (roofers) or trades that have evolved into production jobs in factories (butchers and some machinists).

In sum, the hourly wage data indicates that truck drivers earn more, sometimes considerably more, than workers in manual occupations with similar training requirements that do not entail the hours or working conditions associated with truck driving. In contrast, drivers often earn less than manual occupations that involve advanced vocational training and that may involve less favorable working conditions.

The pattern that emerges from estimates based on weekly earnings is quite different (Table 8.7, right hand side). The favorable position of truck drivers relative to occupations with similar training requirements is more pronounced. Drivers in motor freight earn considerably more per week than drivers outside of motor freight, transportation operatives, and laborers. Drivers' weekly pay is similar to that of material moving operatives, including operating engineers and excavating machine operators, and of precision production workers including aircraft engine mechanics, plumbers and carpenters. On a weekly basis, the earnings of drivers approach those of electricians.

Consistent with the theory of compensating differentials, these results suggest that truck drivers are paid more per hour than those employed in occupations with similar skill requirements but better working conditions. The longer weekly work hours of truck drivers allow them to earn as much per week as blue-collar workers in occupations requiring greater skills and occupational training. One interpretation is that drivers engage in a Faustian bargain in which they accept long hours of work in return for earning as much as manual workers with more training and skills.

It remains possible that markets do not compensate drivers for the full value of the disutility of their working conditions. Economic theory proposes that compensating differentials are driven by the movement of marginal workers out of employment with worse conditions and into employment with better conditions.

This mechanism relies on ease of movement between markets. Movement from a sixty-hour week in trucking to a job with similar pay and somewhat better conditions outside of trucking would result in a one third reduction in weekly take home pay. Such a reduction in income would restrain the arbitraging of pay and working conditions. Although our results suggest that driver pay is not greatly out of line with the nature of their job, the impediments to the smooth functioning of the market may permit moderate underpay to persist.

The Role of Owner Operators in U.S. Trucking

As noted in Section II, owner operators are independent contractors who bring to the firm not only their labor and experience, but also the capital needed to do their work. The vast majority of owner operators own a single tractor: in its 1998 Owner-Operator Profile Survey, the Owner-Operator Independent Drivers Association (OOIDA) found that 705 of the 873 respondents (81 percent) owned only one tractor. Only 21 owner operators, or 2.4 percent, operated small fleets with five tractors or more. Belman, Monaco and Brooks (forthcoming) document similar tractor ownership patterns. About half of all owner operators own a trailer in addition to a tractor – in the OOIDA survey, 481 (53.6 percent) of the 873 respondents said they owned one or more trailers, with 324 indicating they own only one.

Based on the CPS data, we estimate that there were 315,166 owner operators in the U.S. in 2000. The vast majority of them operate in the truckload segment of the for-hire trucking industry – very few are found in private haulage or the less-than-truckload segment.[20] So while owner operators represent only 10% of the overall driver population, within the for-hire truckload segment they comprise about 30% of all drivers.[21]

Most owner operators obtain their loads through established carriers to whom they provide their equipment under a "permanent" lease, usually with themselves as drivers.[22] The lease stipulates the type of equipment to be used, working conditions, and, of course, the way in which the owner-operator is to be compensated. These contracts are exclusive but typically terminable at will with 30 days notice. In the OOIDA (1998) survey, 78 percent of respondents operated under a permanent lease to a carrier, while 21 percent operated under their own authority, meaning that they obtained their loads through brokers or directly from shippers.

According to company officials, most carriers offer the same loads and give the same priority to giving loads to owner operators and company drivers. However, in most companies, owner operators can refuse loads, and the right to do so is an important aspect of owner operator independence relative to company drivers for whom "forced dispatch" is the norm. Still, some carriers indicate that they can "force dispatch" owner operators as well by imposing penalties for refusing hauls, such as loss of priority in the dispatching queue or no pay for empty back hauls resulting from haul refusal. Frequent refusals to take loads also may be grounds for termination.

It has been argued that owner-operators are really employees in disguise, and that firms use them rather than employee drivers to circumvent the legal protections afforded employees, including the payment of benefits (see e.g.

Hamelin, 2000).[23] Owner operators sometimes also are associated with persistent low wages in the truckload trucking industry because, some argue, they do not correctly assess their costs or they are willing to pay a price for their independence, and hence set low prices (see e.g. Peoples and Peteraf, 1995). Finally, owner operators are sometimes described as a flexible source of labor that carriers mostly rely on during periods of higher than usual demand (see e.g. Garrod and Milkius, 1984).

In Table 8.6, we saw that relative to other drivers, owner-operators indeed do not receive many benefits. Carriers could therefore realize savings by using owner-operators presuming that these drivers are not compensated in some other way for their low benefits. The comparable annual earnings of owner operators and employee drivers suggest that owner operators do not obtain direct monetary compensation in return for not receiving benefits. Mean annual earnings for employees in the TIP data set are $39,084, slightly higher than the $38,187 earned by owner operators. Indeed, aside from any benefits issues, Peoples and Peteraf (1999) found that owner operators earned less than company drivers even post deregulation. Of course, their lower total compensation (earnings plus benefits) is consistent with the argument that they set prices too low. However, from the driver survey, we find that they work somewhat less hours per week (55 hours on average compared to 62 for company drivers – see Table 8.4), which also could explain some – if not most – of the differences in the sum of yearly earnings and benefits.

The fact that the number of owner operators has increased throughout the 1980s and 1990s, and that these drivers have remained a stable proportion of all drivers, as shown in Figure 8.1, moreover, challenges all these claims. After all, if owner operators do not do well relative to company drivers, either in terms of net earnings or overall benefits, we should not see increasing numbers of individuals joining their ranks. Nothing prevents most of them from selling their truck and becoming company drivers, particularly in an industry in which there has been a steady rising demand for drivers. Of course, there is the issue of independence and the price they may be willing to pay for that. In other words, here again compensating differentials may be playing a role: drivers may be willing to receive lower total compensation if they find their working conditions are better when they own their own truck. Consistent with this view, Peoples and Peteraf (1995) found that annual earnings of owner operators were lower than those of company drivers both before and after deregulation, but the difference narrowed after deregulation and this lead to an increase in the proportion of owner operators. Specifically, they estimated that a "representative driver with mean characteristics is 155.6 percent more likely to choose employment as an owner operator in the deregulated environment."[24] Thus drivers find it beneficial to be owner operators even if they get paid less, suggesting they do value their independence (including perhaps their option to work fewer hours). The stable proportion of owner operators in the overall driver population also clearly poses a problem for the notion that owner operators are just a source of peak-demand capacity for established carriers. If this were the case, we should find relatively high proportions of owner operators during booms and low proportions of such drivers during slumps, yet no such pattern arises in the data.

Table 8.8 shows the proportion of tractors provided by owner operators in each of the largest 20 TL firms in 2003. This table shows that most of the largest TL firms rely on a combination of owner-operators and company drivers, but this reliance varies from zero for firms such as Crete Carrier Corp. and Contract Freighters to 100 percent for example at Dart and Landstar. Thus carriers are able to compete despite very different ways of organizing their relations with their drivers. In other words, whatever the differences in costs and benefits that may be associated with the use of these two types of drivers must either be very small or cancel each other out in some way. After all, if there were systematic differences in costs or benefits from one type of driver over the other, then the firms that use the most efficient organizational form would have lower costs and the others would have to switch to the same.

Table 8.8   Top 20 TL Firms and Percent of Owner Operator Tractors

Carrier	2003 Revenues (in $000)	2003 Company Tractors	2003 Owner Operator Tractors	Percent Owner Operators
Schneider National	2,900,000	10,500	3100	22.8%
J.B. Hunt Transport	2,433,469	9880	1009	9.3%
Swift Transportation	2,397,655	14,344	3692	20.5%
Landstar System†	1,548,998	0	8573	100%
Werner Express	1,457,766	7430	920	11.0%
U.S. Express	930,509	5244	950	15.3%
Covenant Transport	582,457	3339	413	11.0%
CRST International	525,362	1245	1627	56.7%
Crete Carrier Corp.	521,946	5348	0	0%
Comcar Industries††	215,600	2556	1028	28.7%
NFI Industries	476,960	1493	141	8.6%
Heartland Express	405,116	0	NA	100%
Interstate Distributors	368,592	1750	250	12.5%
Celadon Group	367,105	2491	417	14.3%
Contract Freighters, Inc.	362,100	2347	0	0%
Anderson Trucking Service	359,931	545	1330	70.9%
Dart Transit	351,345	0	2100	100%
Knight Transportation	326,856	2165	253	10.5%
Gainey Corp. †††	311,137	2350	50	2.1%
Day & Ross Transportation Group	307,297	1121	2340	67.6%
Average	857,510.1	3707.4	1483.8	28.5%

Source: Transport Topics 100 Top For-Hire Carriers.
† - Landstar System is comprised of Landstar Ranger, Landstar Inway, Landstar Ligon, and Landstar Gemini.
†† - Comcar Industry is comprised of Commercial Carrier Corp., Midwest Coast Transport, and Coastal Transport.
††† - Gainey Corp. is comprised of Gainey Transportation Services, Super Service, LCT Transportation Services.

In fact, while owner operators may cost less directly – which remains to be established given accounting and hours of work issues – there is another reason to expect that owner operators should be the preferred type of driver in TL haulage. The effort expended by over-the-road truck drivers is costly to monitor directly;

their work takes drivers large distances at all times of day, making it difficult for carriers to assess their driving behavior. If the truck belongs to the carrier, in which case the carrier also normally pays for fuel, the driver may have low incentives to minimize damage to the truck and fuel consumption. Nickerson and Silverman (2003), whose paper's title appropriately begins with "Why Aren't all Drivers Owner Operators?," note that drivers in long distance haulage can increase the length of their breaks by driving faster. But the faster speeds are more damaging to the truck and lead to higher fuel consumption. Of course, the carrier observes the total fuel consumption but it may be difficult to ascertain whether high fuel consumption is due to driver behavior or to some other factor such as traffic in some regions or a problem with the tractor. When the truck driver owns his truck, however, and pays for the fuel, he will have every incentive to minimize the damage to the truck and the cost of fuel. Thus the question posed by Nickerson and Silverman.

The answer, they suggest, lies in part in the cost of coordinating loads across drivers in LTL. But this does not explain why TL firms do not all rely on only owner operators. The authors further propose that certain loads, namely those that are more time sensitive or those requiring particular truck configurations, may give rise to more hold up potential. This in turn would increase carriers' desire to vertically integrate and own the trucks. Baker and Hubbard (2005) argue instead that carriers trade off the benefits associated with the high-powered incentives of owner operators with the cost associated with their greater capacity to refuse loads. Consistent with their theory, they find that carriers' reliance on owner operators is lower in the type of haulage where the driver is more likely to be able to find backhauls. For hauls with low backhaul opportunities, such as those associated with dump or log trailers, they note that the driver is unlikely to find his own backhaul and thus haggle over the work that the carrier wants him to do. This in turn makes the use of owner operators more attractive. Also consistent with their theory they find that the use of owner operators was lower for firms that, by 1992, had adopted On Board Computers (OBCs). OBCs allow carriers to get very detailed information on some aspects of driver behavior and thus reduce monitoring costs, making it less costly to rely on company drivers instead of owner operators.

The point that owner operators have better incentives to treat the truck better but potentially impose costs on carriers due to their tendency to be more independent is, we believe, an important insight. But Baker and Hubbard's (2005) data end in 1992. Projecting their results forward, one would expect that OBC adoption would continue to reduce the proportion of drivers that are owner operators and would show significant impact by the end of our data, in 2002. Yet we see no reduction. Of course it is not possible to tell without a much more detailed analysis whether in the absence of OBC adoption there might have been much higher growth in the number of owner operators, growth that would have been spurred by some other changes in the trucking industry. Still, the fact that we see continuous growth in the number of owner operators at a rate consistent with the growth in the number of drivers generally casts some doubt on the overall impact of OBC adoption on the use of owner operators in the industry. Moreover, we find that some of the large 100% owner operators TL firms such as Dart transit already have fully adopted the type of satellite communication systems that allows real time messaging and position reporting, yet they have retained their focus on owner operators.[25]

Owner operators exist in trucking in part because there are individuals who want to be owner operators. Of course there must also be opportunities for them in the market otherwise this option would not be feasible. And while Nickerson and Silverman (2003) and Baker and Hubbard (2005) provide useful insights concerning what drives the demand for owner operators, Peoples and Peteraf (1995) illustrate the importance of the supply of owner operators in this market. In addition, Lafontaine and Masten (2002) use the TIP driver survey data to find what determines the status of owner operator among the respondents. They find that haul characteristics captured by different trailer types have no capacity to explain owner operator status in these data, but driver characteristics such as age or experience, marital status, and non-driving family income play a large and significant role in determining who becomes an owner operator. This again suggests that the supply side of the market for owner operators matters: people with more human (older or more experience) and financial capital (non-driving family income) are more likely to become self-employed within the driving occupation. These results accord well with Peoples and Peteraf's (1995) findings and with results from the self-employment literature generally.[26]

Summary and Conclusions

In this chapter, we have described the changes that have occurred in trucking labor markets in the U.S. over the last quarter century using data from the Current Population Survey (CPS) and developed a more detailed portrait of drivers' work lives today using the Trucking Industry Program (TIP) driver survey data. We showed that the number of drivers in the U.S. has increased steadily over this period. We also showed that although owner operators have maintained their place in the industry, the number of employees in private carriage and the number of union members has declined. Further, as with many other blue collar occupations, truck drivers have not faired well over the last twenty-five years. Real earnings peaked in the late 1970s and only regained much of the loss suffered during deregulation and recession of the early 1980s in the tight labor markets of the late 1990s.

We have also used the TIP driver survey to document aspects of drivers' work and work lives in detail. We showed that most drivers obtained their training from informal sources or on the job. Despite modest educational attainment, truck drivers earn a 'middle class' income, with mean earnings of $38,830 in 2000 dollars, but often do not have the benefits typically associated with full time employment. The relatively high income is earned by working long hours, at times in violation of limits established by the hours of service regulations. The demands of the job, and the absence of institutions tying the driver to the firm, result in high turnover rates; the median driver has been with their employer for less than two years.

Finally, we investigated four specific trucking labor market issues, namely 1- the effect of deregulation on driver earnings, 2- whether, as is often alleged, there is a shortage of drivers, 3- whether truck drivers are underpaid and, finally, 4- the role that owner operators play in this market. Not surprisingly, consistent with prior studies, we found that deregulation had a detrimental effect on driver earnings. We found no evidence, however, of a driver shortage even in the late 1990s, when the claims of such shortage in TL were most frequent. We showed that what was perceived as a shortage most likely was the consequence of the high level of turnover found in most TL firms. We also compared the pay of truck drivers overall and found that they are paid somewhat more than other workers with similar skills. This is to be expected given the difficult working conditions that drivers face. We showed, however, that drivers are able to earn substantially (50 percent) more than most workers with similar skills on a weekly basis given that they usually work 60 hours per week. Finally, we noted that owner operators are an important segment of the population of drivers, representing about 10% of drivers, and 30% of over-the-road drivers in the truckload segment of the for-hire industry. These drivers are used to varying degrees by most firms in the TL industry. We argued that both demand and supply factors matter in determining the number of such drivers. As for most forms of self-employment, it is the more experienced older driver, and the driver with more financial resources, who is most likely to become an owner operator.

Notes

1. The number of drivers in trucking is estimated using the May Current Population Survey for 1975-1982 and the Outgoing Rotation Groups (ORG) Current Population Survey for 1983-2000. Samples are limited to individuals age 21 to 65 as drivers have to be 21 to hold a commercial drivers license. Inferences about the total number of drivers are constructed using sampling weights provided in the files.
2. Current CPS questionnaires do not differentiate drivers of heavy and light trucks. As light trucks are more common in Private Carriage, the equal division of drivers between private and for-hire trucking found in the CPS over-estimates the number of drivers of heavy trucks in private carriage. Contrary to this, data sources such as the VIUS suggest more private haulage than the CPS. This presumably results from drivers in non-trucking firms not describing themselves as truck drivers in the CPS.
3. Based on the CPS the proportion of self-employed in the U.S. in 2000 was 5.26 percent overall.
4. The International Brotherhood of Teamsters is the dominant union representing truck drivers.
5. As the CPS does ask about the union status of the self employed, our calculations are limited to employees.
6. The annual earnings of owner-operators have much greater annual variation than do employee earnings because of the small size of the owner-operator sample. The apparent gains of owner-operators may be due to sampling variation. Further, the net earnings for the self-employed are affected by individual's calculations of their business expenses. Earnings data for the self-employed are, as a result, less reliable than those for employees.

7. Detailed discussion of the survey methods and findings may be found in *Sailors of the Concrete Sea: The Work and Life of Truck Drivers* (Belman, Monaco and Brooks, forthcoming).
8. The survey included 1009 drivers. This study was limited to full-time drivers who had driven a truck for at least a portion of the preceding year. Observations with annual miles or income that exceed realistic levels were also omitted, leaving 850 drivers in the sample.
9. Because of the small sample sizes, in the remainder of this section we omit responses from owner-operators from data on local drivers and union members from data on owner-operators.
10. The new rules – in effect since January 4, 2004, now permit 11 hours of driving in a 14-hour on duty period following 10 consecutive hours off. Drivers are also limited to 60 hours in seven consecutive days or 70 hours in eight consecutive days after which they must be off duty for at least 34 consecutive hours. Perhaps the most important change is that drivers cannot extend their workday by taking short breaks, logged as off-duty time. Many carriers are reacting to this last change by imposing new penalties for shipper-caused delays.
11. Only 92 employee drivers and 4 owner operators reported being paid by the hour. The average pay of these employees was $12.48 per hour.
12. The industry does not use actual, but rather bureau miles as a compensation basis.
13. In particular, the net earnings reported by owner operators may be low because these drivers are allowed to deduct a variety of expenses in their calculation of profits.
14. A 100 percent turnover rate does not imply that all drivers have worked for the firm for less than a year. Rather, most firms have a core workforce with relatively low turnover and a peripheral workforce that turnover frequently, sometimes several times a year. Firms with high turnover have a relatively small core and a large peripheral workforce.
15. An alternative approach would be to incorporate measures of working conditions into a conventional human capital model of wages. The difference between the average predicted and actual wage of drivers would measure over or under pay.
16. See Belman, Heywood and Voos (2002) for further explanation and an example.
17. Hourly earnings are calculated as the ratio of average weekly earnings to actual hours last week. Actual rather than average hours were used as it is not possible to calculate an hourly rate for employees who work irregular schedules. As many truck drivers work irregular schedules, use of average hours would exclude large numbers of truck drivers.
18. A driver sales worker is a truck driver, such as a soft drink or bakery driver, who delivers and positions goods.
19. Information on occupations is obtained from O*NET, the successor to the dictionary of occupational titles.
20. See Peoples and Peteraf (1999) and Nickerson and Silverman (1997) for more on this. The latter argue that the differential reliance on owner operators in truckload and less-than-truckload is due to the greater need for coordination and time specificity of investments in less-than-truckload carriage.
21. Per Figure 8.1, the for-hire segment employs half of all drivers, and the truckload segment accounts for about 60% of the for-hire industry (at least in terms of revenues according to the U.S. Census Bureau's Motor Freight Transportation and Warehousing Survey, 1997, Tables 3,5, and 6).
22. Owner operator leases were also the norm prior to deregulation. Owner-operators then were not allowed to obtain their own operating authority. Besides working with ICC Carriers, owner-operators could only haul exempt commodities, primarily agricultural goods. See Wyckoff and Maister (1975).

23. The status of leased owner-operators is also controversial in the European Community. Tax authorities would like to classify them as employees. National and European registration authorities are faced with the question of whether the individual driver or the transportation company should be the owner of the operating licenses and authorizations. Trade unions are concerned about the loss of social benefits if leased drivers are treated as self-employed. The European Parliament has temporarily excluded the owner-driver from the scope of the directive that governs working times for mobile workers and has given itself until 2007 to evaluate the role of the owner-driver in Europe.

24. See Rose (1987) for evidence that monopoly rents were earned in the trucking industry under regulation, and shared with unionized company-drivers, but not with non-union drivers or owner-operators.

25. See www.cancomtracking.com/attachment/9025842546_qualcomm_secure_the_big_fleets. pdf.

26. See e.g. Dunn and Holtz-Eakin, 2000; Evans and Leighton, 1989; and Holtz-Eakin, Joulfaian, and Rosen, 1994; among others. Note that the prevalence of carrier-operated lease purchase and rent-to-own programs in the industry is consistent with our "supply side" argument (see The National Survey of Driver Wages, 2001, p. 6).

References

Baker, G.P. and T.N. Hubbard (2005), "Contractibility and Asset Ownership: On-Board Computers and Governance in U.S. Trucking," forthcoming, *Quarterly Journal of Economics*.

Beilock, R. (2003) "The Elusive Sweatshop," *Journal of the Transportation Research Forum*, 153-165.

Beilock, R. (2001) "Review of: Sweatshops on Wheels: Winners and Losers in Trucking Deregulation," *American Economic Review*, 39, 1264-1265.

Belman, D.L., K.A. Monaco, and T.J. Brooks, "Sailors of the Concrete Sea: A Portrait of Truck Drivers' Work and Lives," forthcoming, Michigan State University Press.

Belman, D.L., J.S. Heywood and P. Voos (2002) "Public Sector Earnings Comparability: Alternative Estimates for the U.S. Postal Service," *Relations Industrielles-Industrial Relations*, 57, 687-711.

Belman, D.L. and K.A. Monaco (2001) "The Effects of Deregulation, De-unionization, Technology, and Human Capital on the Work and Work Lives of Truck Drivers," *Industrial and Labor Relations Review*, 54, 502-524.

Belzer, M.H. (2000) *Sweatshops on Wheels: Winners and Losers in Tricking Deregulation*, Oxford: Oxford University Press.

Camerer, C., L. Babcock, G. Loewenstein and R. Thaler (1997) "Labor Supply of New York City Cabdrivers: One Day at A Time," *Quarterly Journal of Economics*, 112, 407-441.

Corsi, T.M. (2001) "Book Review: Sweatshops on Wheels: Winners and Losers in Trucking Deregulation," *Journal of the Transportation Research Forum*, 40, 147-149.

Corsi, T.M. and C.M. Grimm (1987). "Changes in owner-operator use 1977-1985: Implications for management strategy," *Transportation Journal*, 26, 4-16.

Dunn, T. and D. Holtz-Eakin (2000), "Financial Capital, Human Capital, and the Transition to Self-Employment: Evidence from Intergenerational Links," *Journal of Labor Economics*, 18, 282-305.

Evans, D.S. and L.S. Leighton (1989) "Some Empirical Aspects of Entrepreneurship," *American Economic Review*, 79, 519-535.

Garrod, P.V. and W. Milkius (1984), "Owner-Operators, Demand Fluctuations and the Choice of Technology," *Journal of Transport Economics and Policy*, 18, 293-302.

Hamelin, P. (1999), "Social Aspects of Road Transport Drivers' Working Hours," *Social Aspects of Road Transport*, Paris and Washington, D.C.: Organisation for Economic Co-operation and Development, 67-88.

Hirsch, B.T., M.L. Wachter, and J.W. Gillula (1999) "Postal Service Compensation and the Comparability Standard," in *Research in Labor Economics*, Volume 18, Stamford, CT: JAI Press, 243-279.

Hirsch, B.T. (1988) "Trucking Regulations, Unionization, and Labor Earnings: 1973-1985," *Journal of Human Resources*, 23, 296-319.

Holtz-Eakin, D., D. Joulfaian and H.S. Rosen (1994) "Entrepreneurial Decisions and Liquidity Constraints," *RAND Journal of Economics*, 25, 334-347.

Nickerson, J.A. and B.S. Silverman (2003), "Why Aren't All Truck Drivers Owner-Operators? Asset Ownership and the Employment Relation in Interstate For-Hire Trucking" *Journal of Economics and Management Strategy*, 12, 91-118.

Nickerson, J.A. and B.S. Silverman (1997), "Profitability, Transactional Alignment, and Organizational Mortality in the US Trucking Industry," *Strategic Management Journal*, 18, 31-52.

Peoples, J. and M. Peteraf (1999) "The Effects of Regulatory Reform on Company Drivers and Owner-Operators in the For-Hire and Private Sectors," *Transportation Journal*, 38, 5-17.

Peoples, J. and M. Peteraf (1995) "Deregulation and the Competitive Fringe: Owner-Operators in the Trucking Industry," *Journal of Regulatory Economics*, 7, 27-42.

Rose, N. L. (1987) "Labor Rent Sharing and Regulation: Evidence from the Trucking Industry," *Journal of Political Economy*, 95, 1146-1178.

SignPost Inc. (1997) "Carriers Open Door to Owner Operators," *The National Survey of Driver Wages: A Newsletter of Labor Costs for the Trucking Industry*, 2(2), 3.

"The 2004 Transport Topics 100 Top For-Hire Carriers," *Transport Topics*, July 19, 2004.

Uchitelle, L. "In Truckers' Pay, A Lesson About the Inflation That Isn't," *New York Times*, August 29, 1999, p. C3.

U.S. Department of Commerce (1999), U.S. Census Bureau, *1997 Commodity Flow Survey*, December.

Victor (1998), "Widening Pay Gap," The National Survey of Driver Wages, A Newsletter of Labor Costs for the Trucking Industry, 3(2), 1.

Wyckoff, D.D. and David H. Maister (1975), *The Owner-operator: Independent Trucker*, Lexington MA: Lexington Books.

Chapter 9

Just-in-Time and Trucking Logistics: The Lean Learning Enterprise

Jennifer N. Karlin and Jeffrey K. Liker

The Pressure for Lead Time Reduction

Over the past three decades, "Just-in-time" has become the battle cry in many American industries, as the Internet raises consumer expectations and mass customization requires an increasingly flexible production base. Consumers want their grocery stores to have the freshest produce available regardless of the local growing season. Automobile owners needing to repair their vehicles are no longer willing to wait an indefinite amount of time for their parts to arrive. Home remodelers expect to purchase a dishwasher that exactly matches their cupboards today and have it delivered tomorrow. Online shoppers assume whatever they order is sitting in a warehouse ready to be shipped. The trucking industry, and the distribution networks it runs, has had to make, and continues to anticipate, changes due to these demands.

Many customers need goods delivered just-in-time, including manufacturing companies, the high-tech industry, retail, fashion, and food. Whether to cut inventory costs of spoilage or obsolescence or to be more flexible and have a shorter lead time, just-in-time delivery saves companies money. To support this, they are increasingly looking to the trucking industry to supply more than carrier service. Customers, who recognize that logistics is not part of their core competence, want both logistics and transportation provided by a single third party provider. For example, CAMI Automotive, the General Motors – Suzuki joint venture, began operations in Ingersoll, Ontario, in the early 1990s. One of the key points required of CAMI's logistics partner is that the company be able to offer more than simple transportation. CAMI searched for, and found, a logistics partner to provide small, mixed loads of material from suppliers spread out over a region, sequencing and re-crating of some parts, seamless transportation of palletized material as well as lineside racks of varying dimensions, and other customized services.

These changing business needs and pressure to cut lead times have led the trucking industry to respond differently to their customers, who desire coordinated management of moving and storage activities. Toyota Motor Manufacturing is a prominent example of a customer demanding that their inbound parts follow a short lead time while requiring small, mixed loads of parts delivered frequently to their plants.

The purpose of this chapter is to clarify what we mean by lean logistics and provide a detailed example based on Toyota's logistics network in North America and a logistics partner, Transfreight. To clarify what we mean by lean logistics we contrast it with alternative approaches by developing a classification system of logistics approaches. We define the highest level of lean logistics as the creation of a "lean learning enterprise" (Liker, 2004). A lean learning enterprise focuses on eliminating waste in the total value stream through a process of continuous learning. The relationship between Toyota and Transfreight is an excellent example of an evolving lean learning enterprise as a work in progress.

Traditional Approaches to Lead Time in Logistics Systems

Whether provided by a group within the customer organization or by a third party, logistics management comprises all of the activities necessary to pick up freight from the supplier and deliver it to the customer – in the form desired by the customer, at the time desired by the customer, and in the quantity desired by the customer. Ballou (1999) separates the components of a logistics system into key and supporting activities. Key activities, which occur in most, if not all, supply chains, are customer service, transportation, inventory management, and information flows and order processing. The support activities, which only happen as needed by the circumstances of the logistics provider and customer, are warehousing, materials handling, purchasing, protective packaging, working with production/operations, and information maintenance. Logistics management has grown among firms in the trucking industry, particularly in the supporting activities. These firms are expanding their knowledge in techniques such as sequencing material and the design of packaging that were previously not in their domain. The Motor Carrier Act of 1980 opened up new avenues for the trucking industry to create business by deregulating the interstate trucking industry. This section briefly identifies how logistics activities have been traditionally used to shorten lead time in logistics systems since deregulation. The traditional approaches are 1) the use of truck load shipments; 2) inserting break bulk facilities; and 3) picking up material in "milk runs." Each of these three approaches will be described in turn.

When a single facility fills an entire trailer and that trailer is shipped to a single location, it is called a truckload shipment. In some situations, this is very convenient. For example, when shipping aluminum cans to be filled at the bottling facility the volume of cans needed on a daily basis combined with the ease of packing the cans in standard pallets allow cost-effective shipment on trucks in which every cubic foot of space is used. Problems with truck load shipments occur when the volume, packaging, and speed requirements are not met. If the customer facility does not use the entire truck load of material in a short period of time, they will have to store the extra material somewhere on their grounds. This becomes an even greater problem when aggregated over multiple suppliers. When the material is not packaged in square, stackable pallets which are designed to fit the trailer, there is empty space on the truck that is wasted. The increasing use of line side racks by assembly manufacturers is adding non-standard sized containers to a mix that already includes items such as office chairs, which are often not crated, making them difficult to stack. Finally, even if storage is not a problem, some items become obsolete or go bad before an entire truck load of the item will be used. There are many examples of this in the food industry, such as sending a truck load of a single produce item to a single grocery store. But it is also an issue in other industries such as electronics and fashion. The other two traditional approaches address these limitations of full truck load shipments.

A break bulk facility is a facility where a shipment is brought in and redistributed among other outgoing shipments. Break bulk facilities are often used by trucking firms who ship less than truck-load trailers to redistribute the material for more efficient delivery. The FedEx airfreight hub in Memphis, Tennessee, is an example of this. All of the packages shipped by FedEx are brought into the hub, sorted by place of delivery, and then sent back out to be delivered. Another type of a break bulk facility is called a cross-dock, in which the majority of the pallets are not "broken," or divided into individual cases or items. Rather, the material enters the cross-dock in pallets and goes out with the pallets still intact but divided among different outgoing shipments. A pick and pack warehouse is another type of break bulk facility in which the individual items or cases on a pallet are picked for each customer's order. The major wastes associated with break bulk facilities are the extra time required and the double handling placed in the system. The extra time required to route the material through the break bulk increases the time the material spends in the logistics system over the truck-load approach. The double, and sometimes triple or more, handling adds cost in the form of labor and/or technology.

The third traditional approach is to use milk runs. A milk run is a truck route in which the driver picks up and/or drops off material at multiple facilities on the same route, like the milk trucks of old. We all do this when we group our errands together – visiting the pharmacy, dry cleaner, and post office in the same trip. Another example is when an assembly manufacturer sends a truck on a single route to pick up small amounts of material from several suppliers; often, the route repeats multiple times in a day or week. With this approach, there is little need to store the material before it is used without the extra time and handling needed in a break bulk facility. The problems with milk runs are when the trucks are not filled and when the suppliers are a great distance from each other or the customer. When the trucks are not filled to full capacity, then additional trucks are required to be in the system in comparison to truck load shipment. Additional trucks means additional costs in equipment, labor, as well as costs to the environment. When the suppliers are a great distance from each other or the customer, the milk run truck is not as efficient because the material must still spend so much time sitting in the truck as it goes between stops.

All three of these approaches – truck load shipments, break bulk facilities, and milk runs – are used in practice. All three of the approaches as traditionally practiced have limitations and weaknesses, so using these approaches is a matter of managing tradeoffs. This chapter builds a model to help explain how firms can overcome these weaknesses by implementing the approaches as part of a broader value stream focus.

What is Lean Logistics?

This chapter focuses on how firms can overcome the limitations of logistics' traditional approaches, yet achieve the short lead times demanded by the market. The term "lean logistics" will be used to denote a logistics system in which short lead times and high quality are achieved through eliminating waste throughout the value stream. A lean logistics system will use the same pieces of the system as a traditional logistics system, however a lean logistics system puts the pieces together in such a way as to eliminate waste and manages the pieces from a system-wide philosophy, rather than managing each piece separately. The model for lean logistics is the Toyota Production system.

As the trucking industry continues along the learning curve of logistics for short lead times, private fleets and third party providers must develop and manage a total logistics system for each customer that will get the material to the right place, at the right time, in the right quantity and packaging, and for the right price. In order to provide this service, firms must offer a service that uses innovative means to cut costs and lead time.

Over the past century, Toyota has developed and honed an operations philosophy which cuts costs and lead time within their factories leading to exceptional quality and excellent customer service. Many manufacturing firms, envious of Toyota's quality, productivity, and profit margin (Garsten, 2002; Harbor 1999, 2000, 2001, 2002; Womack, Jones, and Roos,1990) have attempted to implement the Toyota Production System, also called lean manufacturing, on their shop floors with varying levels of success (Liker, Fruin, and Adler, 1999; Liker, 1997). The primary goal of the Toyota Production System is to increase profit by reducing cost and increasing productivity; this is achieved through the elimination of all the waste in the system (Monden, 1998). Waste is "anything other than the minimum amount of equipment, materials, parts, space, and worker's time, which are absolutely essential to add value to the product (Suzaki, 1987: 8)." The seven wastes plus one defined by Toyota are described below (Liker, 2004). Note we have added an eighth waste – unused employee creativity.

1.   *Overproduction*: Producing items for which there are no orders – producing more than is needed generates other wastes such as over-staffing, storage and transportation costs because of excess inventory.
2.   *Waiting (time on hand)*: Workers merely serving as a watch person for an automated machine, or having to stand around waiting for the next processing step, tool, supply, part, etc., or just plain having no work because of stock outs, lot processing delays, equipment downtime, and capacity bottlenecks.
3.   *Unnecessary transport or conveyance*: Carrying work in progress (WIP) long distances or creating inefficient transport. Or having to move materials, parts or finished goods into or out of storage or between processes.
4.   *Over processing or incorrect processing*: Taking unneeded steps to process the parts. Inefficiently processing due to poor tool and product

design, causing unnecessary motion and producing defects. Waste is generated when providing higher quality products than is necessary.

5.   *Excess inventory*: Excess raw material, WIP, or finished goods causing longer lead times, obsolescence, damaged goods, transportation and storage costs, and delay. Also extra inventory hides problems such as production imbalances, late deliveries from suppliers, defects, equipment downtime, and long setup times.

6.   *Unnecessary movement*: Any wasted motion employees have to perform during the course of their work, such as reaching for, looking for, or stacking parts, tools, etc. Also walking is waste.

7.   *Defects*: Production of defective parts or correction. Repairing of rework scrap, replacement production, and inspection means wasteful handling, time, and effort.

8.   *Unused employee creativity*: Losing time, ideas, skills, improvements and learning opportunities by not engaging or listening to your employees.

Since transporting material or storing material in a warehouse is not adding value to the material, it is, by definition, waste. Therefore, shortening the lead time in a logistics system removes waste from the system. Also, the creators of the Toyota Production System recognize that its value is in the implementation and discipline of the whole system rather than picking bits and pieces (Ohno, 1988; Shingo, 1981). The logistics system is viewed as providing the right parts, at the right time, in the right amount and right sized containers to value-added workers who manufacture and assemble automobiles. A few cents saved on logistics can mean over-sized containers which add waste to the value-added workers in their factories who must walk and reach for parts.

From this ideological basis, Toyota desired a logistics system integrated into their overall operations philosophy that would offer just-in-time delivery to Toyota in North America with the lead time for the supplier parts kept to a minimum. Toyota did not find what they wanted already in existence, so a joint-venture, called Transfreight, was formed at Toyota's behest to provide in-bound parts logistics using Toyota's operating philosophy. The lean logistics system developed at Transfreight is discussed later in this chapter.

The Toyota Production System is called "lean manufacturing" because it seeks to do more with less, or tighten the belt on production operations (Womack and Jones, 1996). Similarly, we call the logistics system operated on the principles of the Toyota Production System "lean logistics" because it seeks to shorten lead time and tighten the belt on logistics operations.

A Sociotechnical Model of Lean Logistics

In the last section, we defined lean logistics, and suggested Toyota's logistics partner Transfreight exemplifies this. But where does lean logistics fit into the broader picture of approaches to supply chain improvement? In this chapter we step back and create a framework and place Transfreight and six other examples in this framework. These cases were selected because they all used some form of break bulk facility and all claimed some type of logistics innovation.

There are many ways to look at a logistics system, whether lean or traditional. When investigating the case studies summarized later in this chapter, it became clear that while each logistics system used some sort of break bulk facility to organize the deliveries and trucks as the mode of transportation, the resulting systems were not the same. For example, some of the logistics systems contained more waste than others. Some of the logistics systems performed standard procedures every time while others did not. Thus, a conceptual model was formed to consider why logistics systems which seem to use similar approaches to moving the material can be implemented in such different forms. The model was built with two dimensions: the scope of the value chain (the number of links) the organization considers when optimizing the supply chain and whether the organization focuses on building their technological systems or jointly optimizes their people systems along with the technological systems.

Individual Process versus Multi-Link Supply Chains

First, we consider the scope that an organization considers when optimizing the supply chain. Consider a supply chain as a simple network diagram of boxes connected by arrows. The boxes, which we call "nodes", can represent factories, warehouses, storefronts, or raw material producers. The arrows, which we call "links", are methods of transporting goods between nodes, such as trucks, airplanes, ships, and rail roads. Using this supply chain view, we further define a process in a supply chain as *either* one node *or* one link. This means that a warehouse and all of the operations that happen within its doors count as a single process. Similarly, an entire factory is one process and the transportation from the warehouse to the factory is one process.

As seen in Figure 9.1, once we begin connecting processes, we create supply chains of different sizes. A "one link" supply chain consists of one link and two nodes. For example, if we consider a supplier which ships by truck to a final assembly plant, we have a supply chain with one link – the trucks, and two nodes – the supplier factory and the assembly plant.

While there are some simple value streams which are complete as one link supply chains, such as purchasing produce directly from the farmer, driving it home, and eating it for dinner, most industry supply chains in practice are multi-link supply chains. A multi-link supply chain contains at least two links and at least three nodes. An example of a three link, four node supply chain is pictured in Figure 9.2. Here, there is a parts producer who delivers the subcomponents via rail to a warehouse. A truck picks up the parts at the warehouse and takes them to a sequencing station where the parts are put into lineside racks in the order in which the final assembly line will need the particular parts. Another truck then takes the sequenced parts to the final assembly plant where they are placed on the line.

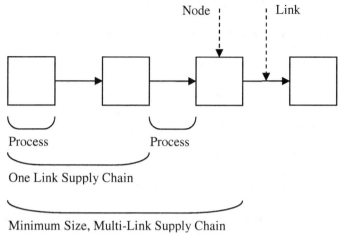

Figure 9.1 **Defining the Levels of a Supply Chain**

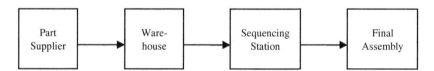

Figure 9.2 **Example Three Link, Four Node Supply Chain**

If a firm considers either a single node or a single link in the chain when making improvements or optimizing the network, then we say the firm is focusing on an *individual process*. An example of this is Haughton's (2002) study of truck route optimization. This study focuses on the individual process as the link between a warehouse or supplier and a customer. Similarly, Achuthan et al. (2003) consider only the vehicle routing problem for truck load carriers, though their model does take into account the constraints of time windows at the docks and the cost of having trucks sit and wait to be loaded or unloaded.

Rother and Shook (1999) begin to lay out a road map for moving the firm's focus from one link into a multi-link supply chain focus. They begin by teaching the reader to look at the level of their factory – one node – and draw value stream maps of each product family. These maps define the material and information flow within the facility and as they reach out to a key supplier and customer. Once that is accomplished, they suggest that the reader continue to branch out, eventually building value stream maps that link the suppliers back multiple tiers and the customers to the end consumer. Jones and Womack (2002) pick up this thread with "extended value stream mapping," or macro-mapping, and attempt to give a method for mapping a product family from raw material to end consumer, including the transportation and warehousing links along the way. They admit that taking this to the extreme, i.e. beginning with the "molecules in the ground" is unwieldy, but encourage the reader to extend as close to that ideal as is practical (Jones and Womack, 2002: 4-5). Both Rother and Shook and Jones and Womack are concerned with optimizing the entire supply chain, rather than bettering parts of the chain at the expense of the whole, though the practical approach suggested it to start at a node – inside the plant.

Once the firm begins to consider multiple links – modes of transportation – and the nodes they connect, the firm is focused on a *multi-link supply chain*. Schwarz and Weng (2000) consider a multi-link supply chain with their study of safety stock in a two link, two node supply chain operating on a just-in-time philosophy. The supply chain in their study consists of a supplier, the transportation from the supplier to the customer, the customer, and the transportation from the customer to the point of purchase.

The number of links and nodes a company considers when it designs its supply chain defines the scope of optimization external to the firm. Firms that consider only a single link in their supply chain close off opportunities to gather ideas from and implement improvements with the rest of their supply chains. They also risk sub-optimizing a link or process at the expense of the whole.

Technical versus Sociotechnical Systems

Technology is important in any logistics system. While some may consider only the computers and the trucks, Daft defines *technology* as the "tools, techniques, and actions used to transform organizational inputs into outputs (1998: 119)." This broader definition of technology includes all of the tooling, processes, and information needed to move the material through the logistics system. These include items typically considered technology, such as bar code readers, radio frequency tags, and warehouse automation, as well as the processes and operational procedures used by both the people in the logistics system and to control the physical assets.

When the needs of the people in the system are considered mutually inter-dependent with the needs of the technology and both must be met in order for the firm to be efficient, we call this a *sociotechnical systems* approach. In a sociotechnical system design, the people, or social systems are simultaneously optimized with the technical systems and both are designed to function together. This means that the people systems and the technical systems are so entwined that removing or harming one has a detrimental effect on the other. Further, social, psychological, environmental, and technological systems must be assessed as a whole, rather than optimizing one to the possible detriment of the others (Trist and Bamforth, 1951).

This differentiation of technical and sociotechnical is not to say that technical studies lack value. To the contrary, technical studies are important to fully understand all of the systems that exist for any given organization. Much of the literature, however, is dominated by technical studies. The problem occurs when managers in practice work from a technical systems-only paradigm. These managers need the technical studies to inform their decisions, however they need more than just the technical information to make good decisions.

A Two by Two Model

The previous two subsections considered external and internal influences to optimality in a logistics system. When we put together the two dimensions – the scope of the supply chain considered and a technical systems or socio-technical systems perspective, we create a two by two model of logistics systems. This is a conceptual model and, in reality, the dimensions are not discrete but continuous. The perspectives found at the intersections of the two dimensions of the model, as seen in Figure 9.3, are given the names: 1) process improvement tools; 2) STS Organization; 3) supply chain tools; and 4) learning enterprise. Each of the four perspectives is discussed in turn below. It is important to note that, by definition, all logistics systems contain both sociotechnical systems and cover multiple links. This model reflects a management focus, or the way in which the logistics system is organized and improved.

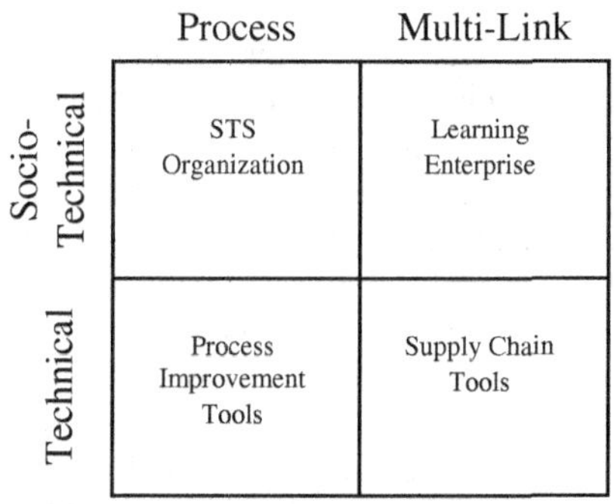

	Process	Multi-Link
Socio-Technical	STS Organization	Learning Enterprise
Technical	Process Improvement Tools	Supply Chain Tools

Figure 9.3 The Two by Two Model

Process Improvement Tools   When a logistics system looks at the technical tools in a single process, we call this a Process Improvement Tools focus. This focus may be the most frequent in trucking and logistics literature. One example is the way in which trucking firms determine the pricing structure for their customers. Pricing structures used by trucking firms are still as complex as before the trucking industry was deregulated under the Motor Carrier Act of 1980 (Richardson, 1998). This is partly because many carriers, especially in the less-than-truckload (LTL) segment of the industry, continue to play by the rules of regulation rather than exercising their freedom to create new rate structures and shipping terms (Schulz, 1997). The Surface Transportation Board has taken up rate bureaus, rate classification, and discounts in an effort to ease the minds of shippers while encouraging competition between carriers (Schulz, 2001). This is a single process technical perspective because the literature looks only at one link in the supply chain, the transportation, and the technical systems, in this case the processes by which rates are determined.

STS Organization   When a supply chain looks at a single process – either a link or a node, but considers both the social and technical systems, we call is an STS Organization approach. Much of the socio-technical systems literature focuses on the systems within an operation like a manufacturing plant (e.g., Taylor, 1986; Marty, 2000; Jacobs et al., 2000). The majority of the literature asks how does one best design a social-technical system for a single system or company? Much of the lean manufacturing literature also focuses on multiple processes in the plant, mostly linking process within the plant (Rother and Shook, 1999). Ohno (1988), Monden (1998), Shingo (1981), Suzaki (1987), Womack and Jones (1996) and others describe in detail how lean manufacturing, a sociotechnical philosophy, applies to and is implemented on the shop floor within a single factory. In the scope of a supply chain, the factory is a node and thus a single process, though at a more micro-level there are multiple-linked processes within the plant.

It is important to note that an organization can have a sociotechnical design while not using a lean philosophy, while the reverse is not true. For example, Adler and Cole (1993) studied Volvo's Uddevalla assembly plant and NUMMI, the Toyota and General Motors joint venture. Both plants used a sociotechnical systems design, however only the NUMMI plant also used lean manufacturing. The Volvo plant was centered on work teams building an entire car with a great deal of autonomy. The layout of the plant and even design of the vehicle were designed to support the autonomous work group structure. But just-in-time, standardized work, and the related set of lean tools were not part of the system. NUMMI also had a high involvement work team structure but still in short cycle, highly standardized jobs linked to the broader Toyota Production System. There was an intimate connection between the technical systems of standardized work, pull systems, and stop the line system and the social system. So lean is sociotechnical, but sociotechnical is not always using the lean approach. By lean being sociotechnical we mean that any complete implementation of the Toyota Production System must involve the development of work groups and involve people in continuous improvement. It is not purely a technical system.

Supply Chain Tools   A firm with a technical systems perspective and which also considers one or more links when defining its supply chain is referred to here as a "Supply Chain Tools" focused logistics system. The Supply Chain Tools approach characterizes most of the trucking and logistics industry literature that is multi-link in focus.

For example, the food industry, in the mid-1990s, began a push called Efficient Consumer Response (ECR), which is most often described as a multiple link supply chain. Following the footsteps of the apparel industry the decade before, ECR is a response to club stores and mass marketers, such as Wal-mart (McGovern, 1998). The components desired in an ECR system are Electronic Data Interchange (EDI), category management, continuous replenishment based on point of sale information, reduced touch distribution such as cross docking, and partnerships throughout the supply chain (Knill, 1997). Many of these "partnerships" use scorecards to benchmark against one another. One of the most comprehensive is the partnership between Proctor and Gamble and Kroger (Matthews, 1996). Proctor and Gamble went so far as to publicize the scorecard in order to receive feedback from the industry (Matthews, 1995). The growth of online grocery shopping is also forcing the industry to rework and reconsider ECR to lift it to full efficiency (McGovern, 1998). The literature on ECR falls under Supply Chain Tools because it does not consider the people systems as compliments to the machine systems, while it does focus on more than one link in the supply chain.

Learning Enterprise   A Learning Enterprise describes a supply chain covering multiple links through a socio-technical systems perspective. While actual studies and implementation are still rare compared to the Buyer-Supplier Partnership approach, the Learning Enterprise is receiving increasing attention in the literature. Both Monden (1998) and Ohno (1988) observe that extending the Toyota Production System philosophy into multiple links and nodes in the supply chain is necessary for the entire chain to be optimized. This is echoed in Jones and Womack's (2002) work which attempts to teach industry how to create a picture of their entire supply chain, or a macro map, and then use this picture to inform cross-organization improvement efforts.

For generations teachers have tried to induce in their students a desire to continue learning through their lives. The idea being that as long as a person is learning new ideas they are moving forward and not getting stale or closed minded. But what does it mean for an organization to learn? The conceptual basis for the learning organization is in systems theory (Senge, 1990). A machine-like organization tends to have fixed specialized parts and learning is slow and cumbersome. More "organic" organizational forms tend to be adaptive with the parts interrelated and changing as the organization's purpose and environment change (Senge, 1990).

As the research into the learning organization is relatively new, there is not yet a single accepted definition. There is agreement that for an organization to have the title of learning, it must have the underlying belief that learning is valuable, happens continuously, and broad involvement of people in the learning activities (Calvert et al., 1994; Watkins and Marsick, 1993). Some say that learning organizations conduct a continual process of finding and solving problems in order to improve (Daft and Marcic, 1998). Others see learning as creating new routines in the organization (Levitt and March, 1988). Still others consider a learning organization as one in which the organization changes its way of processing and evaluating information when presented with new ideas (McGill et al., 1992). Cole (1995) distinguishes between individual learning, or the "continuous development of the skills necessary to perform changing job demands," and organizational learning. He warns that a focus on individual learning will not aggregate to organizational learning on its own. He cites as a distinct competency of the best Japanese companies the capacity for organizational learning starting at the work group level while Western companies have been traditionally stronger at individual learning.

For this chapter, we will use Garvin's (1993) definition: "a learning organization is an organization skilled at creating, acquiring, and transferring knowledge, and at modifying its behavior to reflect new knowledge and insights." We choose this definition because it contains both the knowledge management process common in many definitions but also includes the necessity of an organization to use the knowledge to modify its behavior. Also, Garvin's knowledge management component includes both knowledge created within the organization and knowledge distilled from outside the organization (Levitt and March, 1988).

The enterprise contains all of the firms which are part of the value stream for the product and often contains a leader, who emerges to coordinate the learning among the other organizations in the enterprise (Womack and Jones, 1996). Therefore, if learning is the basis of competitive advantage, then learning must be expanded from the organizational level to the enterprise, or multiple organization, level. From this perspective, we must expand the definition of a learning organization beyond the firm boundary. We will denote a learning enterprise as a chain of organizations which are not only learning organizations themselves, but which are skilled at, as a group, creating, acquiring, and transferring knowledge, and at modifying the behavior of all of the organizations to reflect the new knowledge and insights.

Placing the Cases

To fully understand how the two by two conceptual model can be used to characterize logistics systems innovations, data is included from five case studies: MediumProduce, InternetGrocery, BigFurniture, Ford, and Toyota/Transfreight. In this section, each of the case studies is described, and then fit into the model.

MediumProduce – Process Improvement Tools

Family-owned for four generations, MediumProduce states that their top concern is delivering high quality produce to the end consumers. The distributor delivers directly to local grocery stores as well as cross docks in other supermarket distribution centers. To deliver the best produce every time, MediumProduce takes delivery of the produce orders in their warehouse, processes the produce, and then ships it to their customers, as mapped in Figure 9.4.

Figure 9.4 MediumProduce Process Map

MediumProduce moves produce from their warehouse to their customers using a captive fleet of trucks. Depending on the customer, they deliver either daily or twice per week. A portion of their trailers are dual-temperature. These trailers split length-wise to ease loading and unloading. The roof, however, is lower on these trailers, lessening the amount of stock that can be fit on each truck. The power units are kept on all the refrigerated trailers unless they are under repair. They run on about half as many power units as other, similarly sized produce distributors. Overall, MediumProduce has a tractor/trailer ratio of three. This is higher than the ratio of two they would prefer because they use a portion of their trailers for additional storage.

While MediumProduce does some drop shipping and have a few truck load orders, most of the outgoing trucks contain multiple orders. Drop shipping is where the MediumProduce quality inspector grades the produce and immediately sends it on. A multiple order truck averages four customers in the winter and three in the summer, with a practical maximum of ten customers on a truck. This is due to space on the truck, minimum order requirements, and route design. MediumProduce prefers trucks with fewer stops because these trucks pick faster as they contain more whole pallets and customized pallets. While the warehouse staff tries to load the trailers in stop order, it is not always possible as they have very limited staging room and the outgoing trucks peak overnight.

After they are loaded, the trucks leave to deliver the produce to the stores. MediumProduce wants their trucks to keep moving as much as possible on their routes. This goal frequently leads the drivers to simply drop the inventory at the stores and leave. This exacerbates the problem of stores claiming a miss-ship when they cannot find food that has been delivered to their back room. Other problems faced by the truck drivers include employees at the stores slipping a box or more off the back of the truck while the driver is in the store. The truck drivers unload their own trucks at the stores, but rarely load their own trucks. While the drivers are unionized and paid by the hour, there is an option in their contract that allows MediumProduce to pay by the mile for longer runs. Longer runs are generally defined as those that leave the city. Often, the drivers make more than one cycle, or run, per shift.

Fit into the Model   MediumProduce optimizes a *single process* when they look at their supply chain. In this case, the process, a node, is their distribution center. They do not look outside their own distribution center for improvements as evidenced by their concentration on remedial measures when incoming trucks arrive so late that the produce must be loaded directly from the incoming truck to the outgoing truck – bypassing the internal procedures. They do not look at how they can work with their suppliers to find the root causes of the problem and fix them. Because MediumProduce does not control any part of the supply chain beyond their own warehouse, they consequently work to optimize only their own warehouse.

The *technical* systems perspective at MediumProduce is seen in their concentration on creating a set of procedures to move produce through their warehouse before the produce is past the point where its level of ripeness makes it impossible to sell. The fact that the workers in the warehouse forgo a portion of the procedures whenever the produce must make a shorter-than-planned turnaround in the system implies that the procedures where created to optimize not the people, but solely the techniques and actions. When the two dimensions of the model are put together, we see that MediumProduce employs a *Process Improvement Tools* focus.

There are many examples of waste in the MediumProduce system. One example is the "warehouse on wheels," or the full trailers dropped off in the yard. This is the waste of overproduction because they are receiving material too early and their process is not ready to bring in the material. It is also waste because the produce, which is at a very high risk of spoilage by nature, sits in inventory, especially since while in the trailers the workers cannot see if the produce is spoiling. Additionally, the "warehouse on wheels" is a symbol of processes that are not keeping up with the material flow through the logistics system.

Another example of waste at MediumProduce is in item ageing. Item ageing is the result of purchasing planning one season ahead of actual customer orders combined with customer variability. Item ageing is a waste because it results in produce that must be sold at a discount to the customers or produce that spoils before it can be sold.

Correction is another example of waste at MediumProduce. The order fulfillment process only verifies the pick sheets and thus does not find some errors, such as miss-bills and miss-picks. Not only can these lead to significant monetary loss, but since produce is, by nature, perishable, it is difficult or, in most cases, impossible to re-ship an incorrectly picked order.

Finally, the lack of visual systems severely limits the effectiveness of the processes in place at MediumProduce. There are no visual systems in the "warehouse on wheels," or full trailer waiting in the yard. Also, there is no visual system to assure that the right produce is picked for each order or that the oldest produce of a type is moved first. Where the visual systems do exist, such as the bay signs, the systems are not kept current as the produce is picked and new produce is placed in that bay. Also, the signs rarely specify type within a category. For example, all grapes are placed in bays marked with the same signs, whether the grapes are seedless or seeded. MediumProduce does not involve employees in continuous improvement.

InternetGrocery – STS Organization

Customers place orders on InternetGrocery's web site which are delivered to the customers' homes. All receiving and order picking occurs at a central warehouse, which is the hub in their hub and spoke delivery system, diagrammed in Figure 9.5. The spokes in this system are the sub-warehouses, which are centrally located in the midst of residential areas of the city. Picked orders are delivered to the sub-warehouses where they are divided onto the trucks by route. Some routes leave directly from the central warehouse.

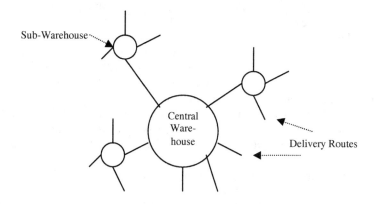

Figure 9.5 InternetGrocery's Hub and Spoke Delivery System

The routes are designed so that each neighborhood is entered by a InternetGrocery truck at least two times each week. Since the orders are placed on computer or via telephone, the truck drivers are the major customer contact. Therefore, the drivers are paid as a professional position receiving a base salary plus a commission of two percent of the orders they deliver, plus a bonus of ten dollars for every new customer on their routes who orders at least three times. The drivers are sales people for the company. As they are building their routes, they have the time to talk to the neighbors of their customers and recruit new customers. As the routes mature, the drivers have less time to talk up InternetGrocery during their working day.

In overview, the InternetGrocery process begins with receiving items from the suppliers (Figure 9.6). The customer orders are then picked from the stock in the pick and pack warehouse. The completed customer orders are sent out to the sub-warehouses which function as cross-docks to move the customer orders to the delivery trucks. The delivery trucks take the orders to the customers.

Figure 9.6 InternetGrocery Process Map

Fit into the Model InternetGrocery takes a *process* view to the scope of the supply chain because their effort and focus for improvements is rooted in the warehouse, not extending beyond, which is a single process. Even though InternetGrocery owns two nodes: the central warehouse and the sub-warehouses, they focus their optimization efforts on the central warehouse. The sub-warehouses are treated like necessary evils and dismissed from most consideration.

The *sociotechnical systems* viewpoint employed by InternetGrocery is evident in the way the picking systems are designed to jointly optimize the efforts and skills of the people performing the picks and the technology available to assist the people. For both the pack to light grocery system and the pick to light frozen and perishable system, the people are seen as compliments to, rather than extensions of, the mechanisms used to deliver the picked orders. This is evidenced by the consideration of the people's language skills as a constraint to overcome rather than an impediment to a smoothly running system. The original warehouse operated by InternetGrocery did not have either the pick to light or the pack to light systems. The management of InternetGrocery worked with their employees to choose the systems for the current warehouse and continues to improve their systems with feedback from the workers. When the two dimensions of the model are put together, InternetGrocery uses a *STS Organization* focus.

An example of waste in the InternetGrocery logistics system is the waste of correction. Under the above described process, InternetGrocery conducts a random check of the picked orders before the orders leave the central warehouse. Approximately ten percent of the double checked orders contain an accuracy error. The waste here is in the resources required to inspect the orders, the rework required to fix the orders, and the goodwill that is lost when the incorrect orders reach the customers.

There are several limitations to the InternetGrocery logistics system. One of the limitations is the difficulty the InternetGrocery process has in dealing with a sudden spike in customer demand for a single product. While some spikes can be expected, such as increased ice cream sales in the hottest parts of the summer, others may not be expected. Should this happen, InternetGrocery would either stock out of an item or have to pick up the item at a local supermarket, at much higher prices.

A similar limitation is the manufacturers' use of exception packaging. InternetGrocery defines exception packaging as anything other than the standard packaging for an item. Examples of this include special offers of a certain percentage more of a product in the box, like cookies or noodles, or an additional item packaged in with regular item, such as a travel size container of deodorant packaged with a regular sized container. The InternetGrocery processes are not designed to be able to handle exception packaging. The physical space allocations to the different items in the warehouse prevent some of the exception packing from working within the InternetGrocery system. Another reason they attempt to avoid exception packaging is that their customers have an expectation of what will appear when the customer places the order. Since the customer is not choosing the items off the shelves for themselves, InternetGrocery must be very careful to provide standard responses to orders.

Another example of a limitation to the InternetGrocery logistics system is the high amount of computer control and lack of non-computerized visual systems. The computer controls all of the picking directions in the frozen foods, perishable foods, and grocery, as well as directing the picked orders to the appropriate trucks.

The bays in the central warehouse are not labeled by what item goes in that slot, but solely by an alphanumeric code. This is a limitation because if anything happens to the computer system, it would be very difficult to continue fulfilling the customer orders.

BigFurniture – Supply Chain Tools

BigFurniture[1] is a large manufacturer of office furniture. One of their goals is to make the supply chain transparent to the BigFurniture dealer network, and therefore transparent to the individual customers. One reason this is important to BigFurniture is because some products are integrated into the BigFurniture supply chain after they are made by other manufacturers. These items complement the BigFurniture product lines and are sold together as sets. Part of the transparency is in packaging – the vendors put BigFurniture stickers on the vendor packing to blend all the items together.

    The BigFurniture-produced items and the out-sourced items are brought together and processed by customer order in the cross-docks, called distribution centers at BigFurniture (Figure 9.7). The orders are then shipped to the customers.

Figure 9.7 BigFurniture Process Map

    Thirty-three percent of the loads shipped by BigFurniture go out on Fridays for two reasons: because BigFurniture delivers to the 48 contiguous states while the distribution centers do not work on Saturday and Sunday, so the over the road drivers need the weekend to drive the long distance to their customer; and because of the way the computer system groups the orders.

Fit into the Model   BigFurniture works with a supply chain scope of *one link* and two processes as evidenced by the orientation of their system which concentrates on the distribution center, transportation link to the customer, and then customer facility. The extremely tight – often two to three minutes – time windows, along with the needs of some customers to schedule elevator time and other building resources forces BigFurniture to consider the customer in any improvement activities. The importance of meeting these time windows combined with the personal interaction necessary to complete a delivery have led BigFurniture to form an unusual relationship with their unionized truck drivers. The BigFurniture truck drivers are paid by the route rather than the mile. Also, the drivers have a council formed of representatives of each seniority classification which sets and enforces many policies, such as dress and grooming codes. BigFurniture considers the truck drivers an important part of their sales staff, even giving the drivers business cards.

BigFurniture uses a *technical systems* perspective within the distribution center in relying so completely on the computer system to tell them which grid to place material in and where to find that material again when the checking teams need to stage the material. The computer runs the system and therefore must be optimized, not considering the people using the computer system. When the two dimensions of the model are combined, we see that the BigFurniture logistics services has a *Supply Chain Tools* focus. In the trucking portion of the system the drivers are clearly treated like valued team members and their input is solicited so one could argue this portion reflects a STS organization approach. On the other hand, the treatment of drivers is really independent of what goes on in the distribution center where workers are subservient to the computer systems.

One of the wastes in the BigFurniture logistics system is the waste of motion. As the material enters the distribution center, the computer assigns the items to different spaces in the grid based on which order the items are part of and what grid spaces are open. The trucks are filled based on the geographic location of customers, the promised delivery day and time, and the amount of material that fits on a truck. The combination of these two means that the dock employees may have to travel to many different areas of the distribution center to gather the items which leave on a single truck, wasting time and motion.

Another waste in the BigFurniture logistics system is the lack of leveling in the processing of orders. Thirty-three percent of all orders leave the distribution center on Fridays. This means that the dock operators have more work on Fridays than on the other days of the week – thus they are either over-burdened on Fridays or under-burdened on Mondays through Thursdays.

One of the limitations of the BigFurniture logistics system is the lack of visual systems and the over-reliance on the central computer system for direction. The only labeling of the grids in the distribution center is the alphanumeric code that indicates the row and column of the grid. Also, different material is placed in each grid space each time it is filled. The only list of what material is placed in each grid location, when that material leaves, and to which customer is located in the centralized computer system. This is a limitation because if anything happens to the computer system, it would be very difficult to find what material is placed in each grid and to continue fulfilling the customer orders. Moreover, the workers have no way of telling by looking whether or not materials are in the correct place.

Another limitation of the BigFurniture logistics system is the number of uncrated pieces of furniture which they move through the distribution center. The uncrated pieces are a limitation because they require different handling within the distribution center and decreased the cube utility of the trucks. A material handling device which grabs the material without proper padding could cause breaks or scratches to the furniture pieces. Even though BigFurniture does try to better the cube utility, or volume usage, in their trucks, the uncrated furniture still leaves some volume unused and requires extra work by the dock operators and truck drivers to load and unload.

Old Ford – Supply Chain Tools

The Ford[2] inbound parts delivery network before Ford's approach to just-in-time, was operated by a group of sub-contractors, all of which where considered tier one suppliers to Ford. Most of the sub-contracted firms focused on trucking and other modes of transportation, while the remaining few maintained the five pooling centers, or cross-dock warehouses. The largest of the pooling centers was located in Romulus, Michigan, and handled five percent of Ford's North American inbound parts orders and 80 percent of all Ford freight sent through a pooling center. This system remained intact until Ford began a major JIT Project in 1999.

The Old Ford approach consisted of incoming material from the suppliers brought to the yard of the cross-dock, called a pooling center at Ford. The inventory stored in the yard was brought to the cross-dock where it was processed. The material was sent on to the Ford plants either on regular truck routes or on scheduled expedite routes (Figure 9.8).

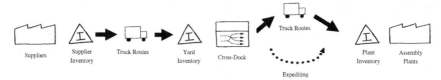

Figure 9.8 Ford Process Map

The Process   According to the manager of the largest of the pooling centers, the goal of the system was to get the right parts to the right factories "before they need it." To accomplish this, the pooling center worked seven days a week, 24 hours per day. Most of the freight arrived over the weekend or at the beginning of the week, was processed, and sent out to the factories beginning with Monday deliveries. Tuesday and Wednesday were peak working days for the pooling center, while the workload on Fridays was generally light.

Normal trailers, or cold trailers, contained no emergency freight. The earliest time any of the freight on a cold trailer was needed at the factory was 36 hours after the trailer was released. A red ball trailer was used by Ford to expedite shipments which would usually have traveled by air or other higher priced methods. At 6:00 A.M. and 6:00 P.M. every weekday, the nerve center decided which red ball trailers needed to be cut and sent the trailers on their way. The exception to this was the trailers headed to Mexico. For example, there were two doors designated for Hermissillo, Mexico. One door, the cold trailer, loaded mostly on Saturday and was released on Monday. The weekly, scheduled red ball trailer was loaded all week and released every Saturday morning at 10:00 A.M.

Fit into the Model   The Ford logistics system does consider *multiple links* in the supply chain, beginning the scope of their chain with the supplier plans, providing the transportation link between the suppliers and the pooling center, the node of the pooling center itself, the second transportation link from the pooling center to the Ford plants, and finally the Ford plants themselves.

Logistics at Ford optimizes the *technical systems* without consideration for the people systems, as seen in their reliance on a bar code scanning technology as the solution to all of their process problems. The workers in the system are considered merely extensions of the computer system. The Ford logistics system is an example of the Supply Chain Tools focus.

One of the wastes in the Ford logistics system is the waste of overproduction. The management stated that it is their goal to get the material to the plant "before they need it." This means that rather than moving the material through the logistics system to reach the final assembly plants just in time to put it on the line, the Ford logistics system stacks up inventory at the final assembly plants that must wait to be used.

Another waste in the Ford logistics system is the inventory sitting in the full trailers in the yard of the pooling center. The logistics system is dependent on the computer system to alert the dock workers which trailer to bring in next in the unload process. However, the sub-contracted drivers must give the exactly right information to the nerve center, and the person in the nerve center must enter the information exactly right for the dock workers to be able to find the correct trailer at the correct time. Since the yard is mixed with both trailers full of material and empty trailers, there is no quick visual system to see if a trailer is overlooked. Also, there is no visual first in, first out system with the material and the central computer's first in, first out algorithm may changed by a manual override by the nerve center workers.

Another example of waste in the Ford logistics system is the lack of a process to return containers to the suppliers. Since there is no process in place to take empty returnable, reusable containers from the final assembly plants to the supplier plants, the suppliers are forced to use cardboard boxes. The cardboard boxes are disposed of upon use.

The regularly scheduled expedites and assigned expedite doors are the symptoms of additional waste in the Ford logistics system. The Ford logistics system knows in advance that it will have to expedite certain material to the final assembly plants and has built its processes to allow for this. This is a symptom of waste because they are not finding the root causes of the problem and fixing them, but allowing the problems to continue.

A limitation of the Ford logistics system is the complacency and desire to maintain the status quo. One example of this is in the expediting mentioned above. Another example is the error rate. The manager of the largest of the Ford pooling center claimed that they had reduced their error rate to three percent. He was quite proud of this fact and did not have any plans to continue decreasing their error rate. In six sigma terms, this is 30,000 parts per millions defects – far from the single digits that are world class.

Toyota/Transfreight – Learning Enterprise

Transfreight[3] was formed in 1987 as a joint venture between TNT Logistics and Mitsui Trading Company to provide sole support for all inbound parts logistics to the North America Toyota assembly plants. To accomplish their goal of increasing quality and decreasing cost, Transfreight uses the Toyota Production System principles of small lot sizes, high frequency of delivery, first in first out, and level flow. The bottom line is to be accurate, quick, and cheap. Transfreight is so tightly linked to Toyota that the Canadian corporate headquarters of Transfreight is across the street from the Cambridge, Ontario, Toyota assembly plant and the U.S. headquarters are within three miles of the Georgetown, Kentucky, Toyota complex. In the words of one Transfreight manager on the Toyota contract, "We are basically an extension of Toyota."

Transfreight maintains two cross-docking facilities for the Toyota contract: one in Georgetown, Kentucky, and one in Romulus, Michigan. Both cross-docks deliver to Toyota's manufacturing centers in Ontario, Kentucky, and Indiana, as well as Toyota's engine plant in West Virginia, NUMMI – the Toyota and General Motors joint venture in California, and Toyota's aftermarket parts distribution network. Freight is brought in to the cross-dock via Transfreight's own fleet of trucks and, for expedites and certain long haul routes, sub-contracted LTL carriers.

Material ordered mostly daily by Toyota is picked up from the suppliers and delivered to the cross-dock. The material is processed in the cross-dock and shipped out to the Toyota plants multiple times daily. Reusable containers are returned to the suppliers in the same system by the reverse process (Figure 9.9).

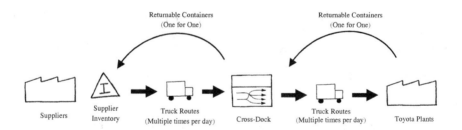

Figure 9.9 Transfreight Process Map

Fit into the Model Transfreight has a *multi-link* scope when considering their supply chain because they attempt to optimize a network that not only consists of the suppliers, the customers, and the direct transportation links, but also multiple cross-docking facilities and switching yards between them.

Transfreight concentrates on *sociotechnical systems* as evidenced by the way the multi-functional dock workers and the truck drivers are considered integral parts of the system; parts without which the system would fail. There are numerous quality check points in the Transfreight logistics system all performed by people, requiring and respecting the knowledge of the people to keep the system running smoothly. The machines in the system are seen as tools to support the people and processes and no new information technology or procedure change is introduced to the system without first considering the impact on the people and how both the people and the technology can be jointly optimized. Additionally, the people in the system are actively involved in improving their work as well as the overall system through continuous improvement suggestions and group problem solving.

	Process	Multi-Link
Socio-Technical	Internet Grocery	Toyota/ Transfreight
Technical	Medium Produce	BigFurniture OldFord

Figure 9.10 The Cases Placed in the Model

When the two dimensions of the model are put together, the Transfreight logistics system displays a *Learning Enterprise* focus. All of the cases are placed in the model in Figure 9.10. Only Toyota/Transfreight fits our definition of a lean learning enterprise so we will discuss this system in greater detail in the next section.

A Lean Logistics Learning Enterprise: Toyota and Transfreight

In 1985, Toyota announced their plans to build a vehicle assembly plant in Cambridge, Ontario – the first non-joint venture Toyota assembly plant in North America. Shortly after the announcement, TNT Canada – an established trucking and logistics firm, and Mitsui and Company – a Japanese trading company with close ties to Toyota, began discussions with the goal of together winning the transportation contract with the new Toyota plant in Canada. Mitsui had no previous experience in logistics and was linked to TNT by Toyota for this project. Toyota realized that traversing the great distances of North America would require something other than the milk runs characteristic of Toyota City in Japan where suppliers are within a short drive of the assembly plant. A cross-dock would be needed and they wanted a third-party logistics provider to operate the external logistics process. At the same time they were not willing to cut loose an outside contractor and wanted a high degree of control over the process at a very detailed level as we will see.

In 1988, the same year the first car was produced at the Toyota plant in Cambridge, TNT and Mitsui formed a joint venture called Transfreight. Unlike many joint ventures, Transfreight was formed as a 50/50 partnership; both TNT and Mitsui had an equal stake in the new company. The Transfreight president came from the TNT side and the vice-president came from the Mitsui side. Transfreight did, indeed, win the Toyota transportation business and immediately began operations as the sole logistics partner of Toyota Motor Manufacturing Canada.

From Transfreight's conception, Toyota worked tirelessly to teach Transfreight how to operate using the Toyota Production System. Teachers, called "coordinators," were sent from Toyota in Japan to educate the Transfreight management on how to provide the just-in-time delivery mandated by Toyota without just pushing inventory up stream. Like any good teacher, the coordinators did not walk in to the Transfreight offices when the company first opened and hand them the final answer. The job of the coordinators was not to remove the learning curve from the growth of Transfreight, but to accelerate it.

As Toyota continued ramping up North American operations, Transfreight continued winning much of the transportation and logistics business. Soon after Toyota opened their truck plant in Princeton, Indiana, in 1997 and awarded the logistics business to Transfreight, the drop point in Lexington, Kentucky, was expanded to 31,800 square feet and began cross-docking operations. That same year, Toyota presented Transfreight with the Toyota Cost Reduction Award. By the end of 1997, the level of material flow through the Lexington cross-dock to Toyota had increased so much that Transfreight relocated it to an 81,000 square foot building in Georgetown, Kentucky. Transfreight custom built this cross-dock to fit Toyota's needs. Transfreight has continued to expand globally to serve Toyota and other customers and continues to win Toyota awards for excellence.

The material and information flow from supplier to Transfreight internally to Toyota has been thought through and refined over time. Each step of the process has been planned to a great level of detail with visual management and quality checkpoints throughout the process. The system summarized here (described in detail in Karlin, 2004) has evolved over years through a process of continuous improvement with extensive involvement of associates who work in the cross-dock. While the process is very similar across cross-docks we draw mainly on the Romulus, Michigan cross-dock in our discussion here.

The process is broken into inbound parts coming from suppliers, called the "sub route process," and shipments from the cross-dock to Toyota assembly plants, called the "main route process." The sub route process begins when the production control office at the cross-dock receives a copy of the EDI parts order releases sent to the supplier plants and prints these manifests out in a form called a checksheet. The different Toyota manufacturing centers have different formats for their checksheets, but all include the supplier information for that order, dock location of delivery, day to be delivered, and inventory number of the part. The checksheets are placed in clear plastic pouches and held in the production control office until shortly before the truck leaves to pick up the material on that checksheet.

The pouches for a particular sub route are placed in the sub route basket for that route. The sub route basket is a hanging file box with a handle and the sub route information attached to the outside of the basket. This information includes: the sub route number, the time the sub route leaves the cross-dock, the time the truck is expected to arrive at each of the suppliers on the sub route, and whether or not the supplier uses returnable containers. Posting the information clearly on the sub route basket is a visual tool to reduce driver error.

The driver, sub route basket, and any empty returnable containers bound for suppliers on this route leave in the truck for the sub route. As the truck arrives at each supplier in that supplier's time window, the returnable containers are unloaded, if appropriate, and the driver compares the checksheets to supplier's prepared pallets or lineside racks of parts. If the checksheets and freight match, the freight is loaded on the truck and the driver has a supplier representative sign the checksheet. This is the first checkpoint to assure the customer receives the required material and only that material. If the supplier is not ready in that supplier's time window, it is the supplier's responsibility to get the freight to the cross-dock prior to the main route departure.

After the driver visits all the suppliers on the sub route, the truck, loaded with material, returns to the cross-dock. The driver fills out the necessary paperwork and updates his/her log book. The cross-dock has the capability to unload multiple sub route trucks simultaneously. The window times for door utilization are tightly managed to avoid the pile up of fill trailers in the yard.

Prior to unloading the material, the dock operator, or team member, gathers the freight tickets for that sub route. The tickets are kept in the sub route ticket board when not attached to material. The labels on the ticket boxes tell the team member which ticket should be in which slot. There are exactly as many slots as there should be tickets when the truck is ready to be unloaded. The ticket boxes are labeled with the sub route number and unloading time. The second checkpoint in the system happens when the team member verifies that all of the tickets for the sub route he is about to unload are present and accounted for in the ticket box.

The team member unloads the freight from the truck and attaches the proper ticket to each skid by matching it to the information on the supplier label found on the material. Every skid must have a ticket while inside the cross-dock. The freight tickets at Transfreight are like tickets at a movie theater. When a patron attends the movies, the ticket states which movie he has paid to see, at what time, and in which theater. This is the only time and place the patron is allowed. Similarly, the freight ticket at Transfreight, lists the sub route number on which the material arrived, the frequency with which this part number arrives at the cross-dock, the name of the supplier, the information on the main route on which the material will leave the cross-dock, and the time windows for staging and loading the material onto the main route truck. The third checkpoint occurs when the team member unloads the freight from the truck and attaches the tickets to the skids. A ticket left in the ticket box or a pallet of freight without a ticket requires additional verification and problem solving. When a supplier has no freight to send that would be matched to a particular ticket, the ticket is placed in the "no pick" box, filed by main route, so the team member can find it later.

After the freight is unloaded and ticketed, it is put away in the place listed on the ticket. The tickets are color coded by where the material moves from the dock door. Yellow tickets go to the wait area. This material comes from suppliers who are significantly distant from the cross-dock and thus pick ups are daily or less often. The material waits for a day or so and then is moved, at a scheduled time, to the appropriate main lane, as described below. Green tickets are placed on parts from repack suppliers and are moved to the repack area stored by main route. A repack supplier ships material that is less than one skid on any given truck to the customer (main route). This small amount of material is picked up less often than it is delivered to the customer and kept in the cross-dock. Repack allows for increased cube utilization on the sub route trucks and better mileage design on the routes. The rest of the freight, with pink tickets, is moved to the appropriate main route lane.

After the team member has unloaded the material, ticketed it, and put it away, the trailer is now empty. Since nearly all of the Toyota suppliers picked up by Transfreight use returnable containers purchased by Toyota, there are no empty backhauls in this system. The team member loads the empty returnable containers for that sub route's suppliers into the trailer. The trailer is then moved to the yard, ending the sub route process. The main route process begins when it is time to prepare a load for main route shipment. The first segment is called the setting the load and is the process of gathering the freight and documentation for a particular main route.

As the team member moves the material from the main route lane to the set lane, the tickets are removed from the material and placed in the clear box. The clear box is a slotted plastic box, similar to the sub route ticket board, with velcro on the face. The team member attaches a laminated strip of paper to the velcro that lists the different suppliers for the particular main route he is clearing. As the number of suppliers in each main route varies, some slots are not labeled, meaning no ticket belongs in that slot. The detached tickets from the material are placed in that supplier's slot in the clear box. There should be one and only one ticket in each labeled slot in the box. This is the seventh checkpoint. Two tickets in one slot imply a bad connection. A missing ticket is first looked for in the "no pick" board. The no pick board is the holding place for tickets when the supplier has no freight to send. If there is a ticket in the no pick board for that supplier for that main route, the team member pulls it from the board and puts the ticket in its slot of the clear box. If a team member can not find a solution to too many or too few tickets, he or she immediately gets help from a team leader.

As the material is moved to the set lane, it is arranged as it will be on the truck. The dimensions of the trailer are painted on the ground and a sign hanging above the set lane marks the height of the trailer. The team member checks for best cube, but the truck is almost never at full cube, though it is very close. The use of the set lanes means that, in contrast to a traditional cross-dock, the team members never have to unload the freight when it doesn't fit in the first time and try again to fit it in to the trailer. One reason Transfreight works with less than full trucks is so that they have the flexibility of adding an additional order to their regular main route runs when their customer requests one. This is a contingency plan so just-in-time delivery can still handle the additional material movement when suppliers have quality problems or other issues. While there is extra space in the trailer planned in to the route, it is not much. For example, the Toyota contract allows only an extra three percent of demand planned to accommodate this extra material.

When all the material is moved to the set lane and the clear box is full, the team member pulls the checksheets from the control board and takes the checksheets and the clear box to the table. The team member verifies that the tickets and checksheets match. This is the final checkpoint. Once the verification is complete, the checksheets are removed from the pouches and placed in the clear basket where the driver will retrieve them prior to driving that main route to the customer. The checksheets become the manifests needed by the driver to deliver the freight. The pouches return to production control office to be reused. The returnable containers from the customer's plant are unloaded from the main route truck and stored by supplier in the returnables area until loaded on an appropriate sub route. Finally, the truck is loaded from the set lane and the driver is ready to go.

Clearly a lot of thought has been given to this very detailed process. All jobs are standardized with standard steps and checkpoints for doing the jobs. Workers are all carefully trained and organized in small teams with a team leader. Continuous improvement is ongoing with small improvements taking place week to week. Is it worth it?

Grading Lean Logistics: Transfreight Metrics

Transfreight has implemented the entire lean logistics philosophy in their operations. They have done so with 1) minimal floor space, 2) high accuracy, and 3) truck drivers compensated to show that they are integral to the system. This section describes a set of performance metrics which suggest Transfreight's efficacy in these three areas.

Productivity

One of the extraordinary accomplishments of the Transfreight cross-docks is the amount of material handled with a small amount of floor space. The Transfreight cross-dock in Romulus, Michigan, is 44,160 square feet in size, or 4102 square meters. In April, 1998, the Romulus cross-dock released 16 main routes per day to the Toyota vehicle assembly plant in Cambridge, Ontario (TMMC). Two years later, August of 2000, the Romulus cross-dock increased its output to 34 main routes per day, shipping to three locations: TMMC, Toyota's vehicle assembly facility in Princeton, Indiana (TMMI), and Toyota's engine assembly facility in West Virginia (TMMWV). By the end of 2002, the Romulus cross-dock released

42 main routes each day to TMMC, TMMI, TMMWV, Toyota's vehicle assembly facility in Georgetown, Kentucky (TMMK), the GM and Toyota joint venture in Fremont, California (NUMMI), Toyota's aftermarket parts division (TMS), and export to Toyota facilities in other parts of the world. The operations numbers for the Romulus cross-dock are summarized in Table 9.1.

What makes this increase in material so remarkable is that Transfreight accomplished it without any increase in floor space. In fact, Transfreight increased its throughput at the Romulus cross-dock from 16 main routes to 34 main routes without increasing the number of dock operators handling the freight, ten people over two shifts. Transfreight managed to increase their main routes leaving per day by 162.5 percent while remaining in the same size facility. Rather than increase floor space or add people every time they increased business, Transfreight chose first to eliminate waste, making itself more efficient.

Table 9.1   Transfreight Romulus Cross-Dock Operations Over Time

	April 1998	August 2000	December 2002	Increase (1998 to 2002)
Dock operators	10	10	22	120.0 %
Number of main routes per day	16	34	42	162.5 %
Main Route Destinations	TMMC	TMMC, TMMI, TMMWV	TMMC, TMMI, TMMWV, TMMK, NUMMI, TMS, Export	700.0 %
Number of sub routes per day	14	18	36	157.1 %
Number of suppliers	65	74	129	98.5 %

While logistics systems do not report many productivity measures in any public place, the following measures of equipment usage are clearly very good. On the corporate level, Transfreight maintains high cube utility in the trucks and a low tractor/trailer ratio. Cube utility is the percent of cubic space in the trailer that is occupied by freight. In their standard, 53 foot trailers, Transfreight maintains a cube utility of over 90 percent. The tractor/trailer ratio is the number of trailers in the system divided by the number of tractors in the system. Transfreight has maintained a tractor/trailer ratio of less than 2 during the entire period of study. The Ford logistics system running in 1998 had an average cube utility between 80 and 90 percent and a tractor/trailer ratio of 5.5.

Another metric used in the trucking and logistics industry is the percent of the day the average truck tractor is used. At Transfreight, this rate of tractor utility is over 90 percent. A concern about operating a just-in-time system firms have in practice is that the new system will result in extra trucks on the road and floating in storage yards. The Transfreight cube utility, tractor/trailer ratio, and other equipment usage measures, summarized in Table 9.2, show that Transfreight manages a lean logistics system, which includes just-in-time delivery, for Toyota without giving in to the temptation to just add trucks.

Table 9.2   Transfreight Equipment Usage Metrics

Metric	Transfreight
Cube utility	> 90 %
Tractor/Trailer Ratio	< 2
Tractor Utility	> 90 %

Customer Service

The second area of performance is accuracy. To Toyota, Transfreight is accurate when the right material arrives at the right dock of the facility within its assigned time window. The number of orders *not* delivered to Toyota accurately the first time, or the defective parts per million, is 3.6 parts per million. Again comparing to the Ford logistics system running in 1998, the manager of their largest distribution center was proud that they had decreased their error rate to three percent, or 30,000 defective parts per million. Transfreight's results are remarkable because Toyota expects material to arrive in time windows of approximately 45 minutes, while the old Ford system had time windows of 12 to 24 hours. These metrics are summarized in Table 9.3.

Table 9.3   Customer Service Metrics at Transfreight and Old Ford

	Transfreight	Old Ford Partner
Defective Orders Per Million	3.6	30,000
Length of Time Windows	45 minutes	12 to 24 hours

Truck Driver Quality of Work Life

If the lean logistics system was efficient at the expense of the work force it would not be classified as an effective sociotechnical system. Truck drivers at Transfreight are compensated in such a way as to show that they are integral to the system, rather than unimportant cogs which are easily replaced. Transfreight is paying their drivers for their knowledge and part of the check points in the system as much as their ability to drive the truck. The drivers are paid by the route. All of their working time is considered on the clock and thus paid for, including the 15 minute pre-trip truck inspection, driving time, and waiting time. The Transfreight truck drivers are also paid for their lunch break. Similar to the cross-dock employees, the drivers receive health insurance from Transfreight and have a 401K deferred compensation plan. Transfreight matches 50 cents to every dollar invested by the driver, up to six percent of the driver's gross income. They also receive paid vacation days based on their tenure with the firm and all employees receive nine scheduled paid holidays and three floating paid holidays each year. This system of compensation remained the same throughout the study period.

Belman, Monaco and Brooks (2004) conducted a national survey of truck drivers. They found that, in contrast to Transfreight, only ten percent of truck drivers nationally are paid by the hour; the remaining drivers are paid by the mile (55.8 percent) or by a percent of the revenue they haul (30 percent). The survey results also show that 20 percent of the average truck driver's work day is occupied with non-driving activities. About half of the non-driving time is spent in waiting tasks, such as waiting for the truck to be loaded, waiting for the truck to be unloaded, and waiting for dispatch, while the remaining non-driving time is occupied with working tasks, such as loading the truck, unloading the truck, dropping, hooking, and tarping the truck.

Payment for non-driving working tasks is uncommon. Belman (2004) found that 44.7 percent of drivers are paid for loading and unloading their trucks while 21.2 percent of drivers are paid for dropping and hooking their trucks. Pay for waiting tasks is even less common, with only 33 percent of drivers paid for waiting while their truck is loaded or unloaded and 24.1 percent of drivers paid for waiting for dispatch. Only 13.8 percent of drivers are paid for any other type of waiting, and of those 18.3 percent are paid for breakdowns. When the average truck driver is paid for time spent waiting, there is usually a detention period of 5 to 24 hours before the payment begins, similar to having a deductible as part of your auto insurance. In contrast, Transfreight not only pays their drivers for waiting time as part of their route, but also compensates the drivers for unplanned waiting time. Drivers receive extra compensation for every hour spent on their route beginning one hour after the route ends. Drivers do not take advantage of this system because they know how important it is to meet all of their time windows if at all possible and because most days they finish their routes early. Once all of their driving and non-driving tasks are completed, the drivers are allowed to go home, even if they are still technically being paid for that time.

The average truck driver, as describe by Belman et al. (1997) also has considerably fewer fringe benefits as part of their compensation plan as a Transfreight driver. Eighty-three point four percent of truck drivers do have health insurance and 92.6 percent of drivers have some sort of retirement plan. Only about half of the truck drivers with a retirement plan have a deferred compensation plan, like the Transfreight drivers. Of those, 65 percent of the drivers report that the company pays a portion of the investment. Paid holidays are much less common, with the average truck driver taking off only four days per year for holidays – none of which are paid.

Transfreight designed their compensation plan for the truck drivers to prove with their pocketbook that the drivers are important to the lean logistics process. The drivers are paid like salaried people who are valued for their knowledge and encouraged to use that knowledge to meet the customer's demands. In contrast, the average truck driver is rewarded to drive material as fast as they can get away with from the origin to the destination.

Table 9.4 Transfreight Truck Drivers Compared to the Average Truck Driver described by Belman et al. (1997)

	Transfreight Truck Drivers	Average Truck Driver
Driver pay is based on route or mile?	Route	Mile
Driver paid for time spent waiting for the truck?	Yes	No
Driver is paid for time spent not moving but not waiting, e.g. lunch?	Yes	No
Driver provided paid vacation days?	Yes	No
Holidays taken off last year?	12 paid	4 *not* paid

Conclusions

The difference between Transfreight-Toyota and the other cases was striking as we carried out the case studies. It was not a matter of a particular tool or technique. It was a matter of philosophy. Toyota views people facilitating the material and information flow as the backbone of their manufacturing process. "The chain is as strong as the weakest link" and every link in the chain has been thought through to the finest detail. By contrast, to the other companies a warehouse is a warehouse, a truck is a truck, and drivers are there to drive the truck or operate the forklift. In many cases it is not too severe to say that the humans in the system are a necessary evil that could not be automated out of the process.

Transfreight views themselves as an extension of the assembly line. They are an integral part of the process of making cars. Toyota also sees it that way and therefore would not consider outsourcing this vital transportation and logistics service to the highest bidder. The logistics system is something that needed to be developed and evolve into a learning organization to complement the overall lean learning enterprise. The joint venture was set up to give Toyota the control it needed to build a continually improving learning organization that was an organic part of the lean value stream. A non-lean transportation and logistics system would be rejected by the organism like an organ of the wrong blood type. Interestingly, over time TNT Logistics had an opportunity to learn from Transfreight how to do lean logistics but never really adopted the lessons of its joint venture offspring. Ultimately, TNT sold off the whole of the joint venture to Mitsui and business has to Toyota and other customers has continued to grow.

Since Mitsui is part of the closely held family of Toyota suppliers in Japan, the *keiretsu*, this further cemented Toyota's control. The result was a living organization that learns along with the rest of Toyota. And costs have continued to come down while quality has gone up. Toyota-Transfreight is one of the best examples we have seen of a high performance lean learning enterprise.

Notes

1. The data in the BigFurniture case study is from March, 2000.
2. The data in the Ford case study is from September, 1999.
3. The data in the Transfreight case study is from June, 1999, through January, 2003.

References

Achuthan, N. R., L. Caccetta, and S. P. Hill. "An Improved Branch-and-Cut Algorithm for the Capacitated Vehicle Routing Problem," *Transportation Science*. Volume 37, Number 2, 2003: 250-269.

Adler, P. S. and R. E. Cole. "Designed for Learning: A Tale of Two Auto Plants," *Sloan Management Review*. Spring 1993: 85-94.

Ballou, R. H. *Business Logistics Management*. Upper Saddle River, NJ: Prentice Hall, 1999.

Belman, D., K. Monaco, and T. J. Brooks, *Sailors of the Concrete Sea: A Portrait of Truck Drivers' Work and Lives*, East Lansing, MI: MSU Press, 2004.

Calvert, G., S. Mobley, and L. Marshall. "Grasping the Learning Organization," *Training*, Volume 48, Number 6, 1994: 38-43.

Cole, R. E., "Reflections on Organizational Learning in U.S. and Japanese Industry," in *Engineered in Japan: Japanese Technology-Management Practices*. New York, NY: Oxford University Press: 365-379.

Daft, R. L. *Organization Theory and Design*. Cincinnati, OH: South-Western College Publishing, 1998.

Daft, R. L. and D. Marcic. *Understanding Management*. Fort Worth, TX: The Dryden Press, 1998.

Garsten, E. "Japanese cars most reliable," *Detroit News*, March 13, 2002.

Garvin, D. A., "Building a Learning Organization," *Harvard Business Review*. July-August 1993, 78-91.

Harbour and Associates, Inc. *The Harbour Report 2002*. Troy, MI: Harbour and Associates, Inc., 2002.

Harbour and Associates, Inc. *The Harbour Report 2001*. Troy, MI: Harbour and Associates, Inc., 2001.

Harbour and Associates, Inc. *The Harbour Report 2000*. Troy, MI: Harbour and Associates, Inc., 2000.

Harbour and Associates, Inc. *The Harbour Report 1999*. Troy, MI: Harbour and Associates, Inc., 1999.

Haughton, M. A. "Measuring and Managing the Learning Requirements of Route Reoptimization of Delivery Vehicle Drivers." *Journal of Business Logistics*. Volume 23, Number 2, 2002: 45-66.

Jacobs, D. A., A. A. Fernandez, and C. B. Keating. "Analyzing complex processes with a sociotechnical systems tool," *Research and Technology Management*. Volume 43, Number 2, March/April 2000: 8-12.

Jones, D. and J. Womack. *Seeing the Whole*, Brookline, MA: The Lean Enterprise Institute, 2002.

Karlin, J. N. *Defining the Lean Logistics Enterprise: Examples from Toyota's North American Supply Chain.* Unpublished Ph.D. dissertation, Ann Arbor: University of Michigan, 2004.

Knill, B., "Information Pulls Food Distribution," *Material Handling Engineering*, Volume 52, July 1997: 4-8.

Levitt, B. and J. G. March. "Organizational Learning," *Annual Review of Sociology*. Volume 14, 1988: 319-340.

Liker, J. K. *Becoming Lean: Experience of U.S. Manufacturers*. Portland, OR: Productivity Press, 1997.

Liker, J.K. *The Toyota Way*, N.Y.: McGraw-Hill, 2004.

Liker, J. K., W. M. Fruin, and P. S. Adler. *Remade in America: Transplanting and Transforming Japanese Management Systems*. New York, NY: Oxford University Press, 1999.

Marty, P.F. "Museum informatics: sociotechnical information infrastructures in museums at the Spurlock Museum," *Bulletin of the American Society for Information Science*. Volume 26, Number 3, February/March 2000: 22-24.

Matthews, R., "Know the Score," *Progressive Grocer*, Volume 74, May 1995: 77.

Matthews, R., Trying to Score: Scorecarding Offers Potential and Danger to Trading Partners," *Progressive Grocer*, Volume 75, October 1996: 59-60.

McGill, M. E., J. W. Slocum, Jr. and D. Lei, "Management Practices in Learning Organizations," *Organizational Dynamics*. Volume 21, Number 1, Summer 1992: 4-14.

McGovern, J. M., "One-Stop Shopping," *Transportation and Distribution*, Volume 39, Number 5, May 1998: 39-40.

Monden, Y. *Toyota Production System: An Integrated Approach to Just-In-Time*. Norcross, GA: Engineering Management Press, 1998.

Ohno, T. *Toyota Production System: Beyond Large-Scale Production*. Portland, OR: Productivity Press, 1988.

Richardson, H. L., "Simplify! Simplify! Simplify!: Motor Carrier Pricing," *Transportation and Distribution*, Volume 39, Number 10, October 1998: 111, 114, 116-117.

Rother, M. and J. Shook. *Learning to See*. Brookline, MA: The Lean Enterprise Institute, 1999.

Schulz, J.D. "LTL Revolution Brewing: Carriers Trying to 'Think Outside the Box,' Want End to Discount-Off-Class Rates," *Traffic World*, April 14, 1997: 9-10.

Schulz, J.D. "Full Disclosure: Discounts Offered by Rate Bureaus", *Traffic World*, December 3, 2001: 9-10.

Schwarz, L. B. and K. Weng. "The Design of a JIT Supply Chain: The Effect of Leadtime Uncertainty on Safety Stock," *Journal of Business Logistics*. Volume 21, Issue 2, 2000: 231-253.

Senge, P. M. *The Fifth Discipline: The Art and Practice of the Learning Organization*. New York, NY: Currency Doubleday: 1990.

Shingo, S. *A Study of the Toyota Production System*. Portland, OR: Productivity Press, 1981.

Suzaki, K. *The New Manufacturing Challenge: Techniques for Continuous Improvement*. New York, NY: The Free Press, 1987.

Taylor, J. C. "Long-term sociotechnical systems change in a computer operations department," *The Journal of Applied Behavioral Science*. Volume 22, Number 3, 1986: 303-313.

Trist, E.L., and K.W. Bamforth, "Some Social and Psychological Consequences of the Long-Wall Method of Coal-Getting," *Human Relations*, Volume 4, 1951: 3-38.

Watkins, K. and V. Marsick. *Sculpting the Learning Organization: Lessons in the Art and Science of Systemic Change*. San Francisco, CA: Jossey-Bass, 1993.

Womack, J., D. Jones, and D. Roos. *The Machine that Changed the World.* New York, NY: HarperCollins Publishers, 1990.

Womack, J. and D. Jones. *Lean Thinking*. New York, NY: Simon and Schuster, 1996.

Chapter 10

Truck Safety in the Age of Information

Lee Husting and Elyce A. Biddle

Introduction

It is near dusk. An 80,000 pound tractor-trailer on a limited-access interstate makes an ascending left turn while climbing a grade in hilly terrain. The driver has been traveling all day and must maintain the maximum legal speed to reach the terminal before exceeding Federal Hours of Service Regulations. To maintain speed, the driver is forced to downshift repeatedly as the truck loses momentum on the rising grade. A call from dispatch flashes on the internal monitor. The setting sun flashes across the windshield, briefly obscuring vision, as the vehicle moves in and out of the shadows of the higher-elevation foothills. While the driver reflexively reaches for his sunglasses, a low–fuel light comes on. The truck builds up speed to climb the next rise. The road ahead curves more sharply as the truck rapidly approaches a turn that overloads the outside wheels. Over that rise, not yet visible, is a disaster in the making: Twelve car lengths ahead, an older van with weak rear lights and a nearly flat tire is struggling up the grade, at well below the minimum legal speed. Under a traditional scenario, the tractor-trailer would have struck the van in the next minute at best causing vehicular damage, at worst, losing lives.

A more palatable conclusion is possible using information and communication technologies developed in the last decade. A number of things occur in microsecond sequence: The on-board data manager recognizes time-functional hazards, suppresses the fuel warning light and dispatch call, allowing the driver to pay full attention, adjusts the windshield polarization to maximum visibility, records a hazard-data sequence from the sensor embedded in the highway, reduces the speed of the truck and adjusts the calibrators for the shock absorbers to prevent a rollover, and activates the Collision Warning System (CWS) indicators, flashing visual warnings and audible alerts to the driver.

The operator, now with the vehicle fully under control and with full visibility, brakes, downshifts, and steers the rig toward the break-down lane. The van is now immediately before him. The driver is unable to avoid contact, and the left front bumper strikes the van, forcing it across and off the road, where it comes to a halt. The truck maneuvers farther to the right and stops. Braking and vehicle status are captured in the on-board data recorder. No one in the van is seriously injured, but several of the passengers, none wearing seat belts, are shaken. The driver unbuckles the seat belt, sends a message describing the situation to the fleet dispatcher (who has already been electronically informed of the event and the location, along with the state police). Upon incident reconstruction, using data from the "black box," it is determined that the truck driver took immediate action to slow and to avoid a crash. The fortuitous outcome of this scenario could only happen with modern information technology used to improve roadway safety.

Trucks have been integral to the nation's transportation for decades. Commercial trucking safety and health have been affected both positively and negatively by new information and communication technologies. Although larger, more streamlined, and more powerful, the trucks of today remain recognizably similar to the earliest trucks. The internal systems and components have changed dramatically. The technological developments and innovations of the past century have transformed trucks from straightforward internal combustion driven vehicles with simple mechanical systems to sophisticated integrated systems with electro-mechanical, fuel, suspension, and transmission components dependent on advanced technologies. More recently, optimization routines, sophisticated relational databases, and advances in telecommunications have made trucks integral components of advanced transportation delivery systems.

Within the commercial trucking industry, the changes brought on by "The Age of Information" include advances in vehicle technology, systems integration, electronic communications, control technologies and scientific knowledge of human physiology have resulted in profound changes, affecting the way that commercial motor vehicles are operated, dispatched, tracked and managed. The ongoing evolution of these systems influences how driver safety and health is studied as well as the interventions which can be undertaken. Driver work/rest cycles can now be understood through data on human performance and fatigue. New information and communication technologies enable professional truck drivers and fleet managers to access data on the location, status, and overall functioning of vehicles, which can prove to be particularly helpful in the event of a crash. Drivers can plan, control, and adjust their routes and stops to coincide with traffic movement and to access available rest stops. Dispatchers can work more effectively with drivers to schedule arrivals and departures and load allocation. Newer information technologies can provide feedback on the physical status of the driver that can be used to help to prevent excessive fatigue or drowsy driving. Using these technologies directly impact the health and safety of truck drivers and indirectly improve safety for other vehicle drivers.

Improving the safety and health environment for the trucking industry requires multidisciplinary collaboration. Engineering, epidemiology, statistics, as well as the medical and social sciences provide necessary expertise. Implementing new technologies relies on the trucking community including drivers, fleets, government agencies, researchers and others. Measuring and monitoring the progress toward improved safety and health benefits from a structured process analysis. A scientific model employed by many public health agencies is referred to as The Public Health Model. It address issues from initial knowledge through effective solutions in five stages: Identification and prioritization of problems (surveillance), quantification and prioritization of risk factors (analytic research), identification of existing or development of strategies to prevent injuries (prevention and control), implementation of the most effective injury control measures (communication/dissemination/technology transfer) and monitoring the results of intervention efforts (evaluation).

Identify and Prioritize Problems (Surveillance)

Motor vehicle safety has been recognized as an important public health problem affecting both truck drivers and those in other vehicles for much of the last century. Identifying and prioritizing problems through analyzing surveillance data is the first step to reducing the occurrence of fatal and nonfatal trucking incidents.

Surveillance programs on truck crashes are maintained by state or federal government entities. The predominant federal agencies are the Federal Motor Carrier Safety Administration (FMCSA) and National Highway Traffic Safety Administration (NHTSA) within the Department of Transportation (DOT), the Bureau of Labor Statistics (BLS) within the Department of Labor (DOL), and the National Research Council (NRC). Although this data can be used to measure changes in the safety and health experience in trucking, differences in the missions of the organizations with surveillance programs, with consequent differences in purpose, jurisdiction and audiences, structural formats, and computer platforms result in incompatibility among programs and gaps in our information.

In 2001 there were more than 6.3 million police-reported motor vehicle traffic crashes, resulting in over 4.28 million property-damage-only crashes, over 3 million people injured, and more than 42 thousand people killed (NHTSA, 2002). With an average of 105 fatalities daily, motor vehicle crashes are the leading cause of death from unintentional injury in the general population (NHTSA, 2004). Moreover, deaths and injuries resulting from motor vehicle crashes disproportionately affected the younger population; they were the leading cause of death for ages 2 through 33 years (NHTSA, 2003).

Large trucks contribute substantially to motor vehicle crashes, well over 400,000 were involved in traffic crashes during 2002 (NHTSA, 2004). Almost 10%, or 4,542, of all vehicles involved in fatal crashes were large trucks. Drivers and passengers involved in these crashes accounted for nearly 5,000 deaths, 11% of all traffic fatalities in 2002. The numbers of large trucks involved in fatal crashes increased from 4,035 to 4,542 between 1992 and 2002; but, as the number of large trucks increased from 6 million to over 8 million, the crash experience decreased from 67 to 61 per 100,000 trucks between 1991 and 2001. The rate for fatal crashes dropped from 3 to 2, per million miles traveled between 1991 and 2002 (NHTSA, 2003).

Four per cent of all vehicles involved in nonfatal injury crashes were large trucks (NHTSA, 2004). The number of trucks involved in non-fatal injury crashes declined from 95,000 in 1992, to 94,000 in 2002, while the rate dropped from 62 to 43 per 100 million miles (NHTSA, 2003).

Detailed information on fatal and nonfatal work-related incidents is available from the Census of Fatal Occupational Injuries (CFOI) and the Survey of Occupational Injuries and Illnesses of the BLS. Despite annual fluctuations, highway incidents account for nearly one-fourth of fatal work injuries. From 1992 to 2001, highway transportation incidents were the leading cause of workplace death, with over 13,500 workers killed, an average of three worker deaths daily. Occupants of trucks accounted for nearly 60% of fatalities; almost half of these were semi-truck occupants (Pratt, 2003). During this period, trucks were involved in just over 7,700 or 58% of work-related incidents increasing from 50% to 64% between 1992 and 2001. Just under 50% of these trucks were identified as tractor-trailers (BLS, 2003).

Truck drivers accounted for 40%, of the fatal work-related highway incidents in the United States. Nearly two-thirds of the truck driver fatalities reported by CFOI were highway incidents. An additional 14% of driver fatalities were attributed to other transportation events such as railroad incidents, 8% were attributed to contact with objects and equipment, and 3% were assaults and violent acts.

Moreover, truck drivers are subject to frequent and serious injuries at work. Drivers had more lost-time workplace injuries and illnesses than any other occupation for each year from 1993 to 2001. In 2002 they experienced 129,000 work-related injuries and illnesses that required recuperation beyond the day of the incident. Drivers' incidents also tend to be severe. Nearly one-third resulted in missing 31 or more days. Truck drivers' median 10 days away from work compared unfavorably to the 6 days for all occupations (BLS, 2003).

Nearly 30%, of work-related truck driver incidents with days away from work were associated with overexertion. Falls were responsible for 20% of all truck driver incidents, just over 18% involved contact with objects and equipment while transportation incidents accounted for 13% of incidents. Musculoskeletal disorders, including sprains, strains, and tears comprised well over half of all truck driver incidents when categorized by the nature of injury or illness (BLS, 2003).

Despite the volume of surveillance data regarding motor vehicle and trucking incidents, each data system presents only a partial picture of the problem. Absent some means of linking these systems, it will be difficult to accurately quantify the safety benefits of technological advances or policy interventions on safety and health.

Quantify and Prioritize Risk Factors

The second step in the Public Health Model is to quantify and prioritize risk factors. This entails analytic research to determine the risk factors – the elements that cause or contribute to an incident – that identify areas for developing and implementing intervention strategies. In trucking, the identified risk factors relate to truck drivers, other drivers, vehicles, fleet and management characteristics, and the physical environment. Current interventions and those under development attempt to target and mitigate one or more risk factors. Interventions can address driver training, education, physical fitness programs, and by acceptance and appropriate use of the new technologies individually or some combination.

Truck Driver Factors

A number of risk factors are associated with truck drivers. In the preliminary evaluation from the Large Truck Crash Causation Study fatigue, speeding, distraction/inattention, aggressive driving, and motor carrier dispatching were found to be primary reasons for 286 of 1000 crashes (NHTSA, 2002; Craft and Blower, 2004). The critical event was attributed to the truck driver actions in 29%, of two vehicle crashes; other driver reasons included non-performance, recognition errors, and decision errors. Driver decision errors were most common in single truck crashes. Surveys of commercial motor vehicle (CMV) fleet safety managers and experts in motor carrier safety conducted by the Commercial Truck and Bus Safety Synthesis Program identified insufficient driver training, risk taking behaviors, fatigue, driver health and wellness, and driver turnover as important risk factors (Knipling, 2003).

Lack of seat belt usage has been identified as an important risk factor for drivers. The "Safety Belt Usage by Commercial Motor Vehicle (CMV) Drivers" study observed only 48% of the drivers of 3,909 trucks at 117 sites in 12 states using seat belts (FMCSA, 2003). Usage rate for units identified as a major regional or national fleet was 55% but only 44% for trucks that were either independent or part of local fleets. The highest usage rate was found in single tankers (61%), and the lowest usage was found in single-trailer dump truck (26%). Subsequently an industry partnership to encourage seat belt use by commercial drivers has been formed by FMCSA, the National Private Truck Council (NPTC), Owner-Operator Independent Drivers Association (OOIDA), American Trucking Associations (ATA), the Motor Freight Carriers Association (MFCA) and others.

Fatigue has long been recognized as a risk factor in truck crashes. A 1990 study of 182 heavy truck crashes involving truck driver fatalities identified the most frequently cited probable cause as fatigue, with a 31% incidence (NTSB, 1990). Fatigue was found to be a related factor for at least one truck driver in 1.6.7% of 3,169 fatal accidents involving 3,311 heavy trucks (NTSB, 1995). The NTSB suggested that driver fatigue was underestimated by Fatality Analysis Reporting System (FARS) data in general and specifically with regard to truck drivers. Further, truck driver fatigue may be a contributing factor in 30% to 40% of heavy truck accidents (NTSB, 2002).

Drivers may face a trade-off between rest and driving schedules. Using physiological and self-reported measures from 188 commercial drivers, Filiatrault found a significant correlation between sleep quality and schedule based priorities. Drivers' attitude toward maintaining a schedule versus insuring proper rest was the most important predictor of sleep quality (Filiatrault, 2002).

FMCSA TechBriefs summarize studies of matters such as sleep schedules, stress, fatigue, alertness, and driver wellness training. One brief reported on a study comparing drivers in two tractor trailers equipped to monitor the driver's face, driving performance, sleeper berth environmental conditions, and subjective driver alertness ratings. It concluded that road and travel disturbances detrimentally affected the quality of sleep of truck drivers, particularly of those driving in teams (Carroll, 2002).

Long haul commercial drivers who are obese or who have sleep-related breathing disorders may be at higher risk for traffic accidents. A study of 90 commercial long-haul truck drivers 20-64 years of age found that drivers identified with sleep-disordered breathing had a two-fold higher accident rate per mile than drivers without sleep-disordered breathing. Obese drivers presented a two-fold higher accident rate than non-obese drivers (Stoohs et al., 1994). A subsequent study reported that drivers with sleep apnea perform as poorly as persons who are legally intoxicated (Alvarez, 2002).

A study of 593 randomly selected long-distance truck drivers interviewed with regard to their typical work and rest patterns at public and private rest areas indicated that almost one-half reported falling asleep while driving a truck and one-fourth had fallen asleep at the wheel in the past year. Factor analysis identified greater daytime sleepiness; more arduous schedules; older drivers; poorer sleep on road; symptoms of sleep disorder; and a greater tendency to night-time drowsy driving as predictive factors. Interventions that limited work hours, enabled drivers to get sufficient rest, and identified drivers with sleep disorders were suggested to reduce the likelihood that drivers would fall asleep while driving (McCartt et al., 2000).

Finally, the Trucks Involved in Fatal Accidents Report for 2000 (TIFA) reported 2% of truck drivers as drowsy or asleep. However, driving too fast (7.6%), ran off the road (6.9%), and inattention were the most common truck driver factors reported. Only 2.2% had been drinking alcohol before a fatal crash, and drug use was less than 1%. Almost two-thirds of incidents reported no driver factors (Matteson, 2001).

Other Drivers

Drivers of other vehicles are frequently responsible for crashes involving large trucks. The Automobile Association of America Foundation reported that in 80% of passenger car-truck crashes with passenger car fatalities, the car driver was driving dangerously. Of 94 factors identified with crashes, only 27% of truck drivers had at least one unsafe driving act (AAA Foundation for Traffic Safety, 2002). A preliminary evaluation of 286 of 1,000 crash investigations from the Large Truck Crash Causation Study indicated that, for two vehicle crashes, the critical event was attributed to the truck driver actions in only 29%, of crashes, compared with 60% to the actions of the other vehicle driver (Craft, 2004).

A study of unsafe driving acts (UDAs) by motorists driving near large trucks found common UDAs included tailgating, speeding, and driver distraction and less common factors including failure to obey traffic controls, reckless driving, driving into opposing traffic, and disregard for poor weather or visibility conditions (Stuster, 1999; Office of Motor Carriers, 1999). A report of heavy truck collisions from Kentucky found that the most common cause of a car-truck incident was another vehicle crossing the centerline or turning into the path of a truck – accounting for about one-third of crashes (Pigman, 1999). Matteson reported similar findings; the other vehicle crossed the center-line and hit the truck head on in about 10% of fatal collisions (Matteson, 2003).

To address the risk factors associated with drivers of other vehicles, the FMCSA suggests that drivers of other vehicles need to be educated on how to share the road with commercial trucks. *Share the Road Safely* Program and web site of FMCSA is intended to improve the knowledge of all highway users in order to reduce the likelihood of a crash with a large truck, and to minimize the consequences of those that do occur.

Vehicle Factors

In addition to driver behaviors, the type, number and interaction of vehicles are important to understanding the causes of trucking incidents. Eighty-four percent of the large trucks in fatal crashes are in multiple vehicle crashes, compared with only 61% of passenger vehicles. Only 5% of large truck occupant fatalities, and 11% of large truck occupant injuries, occur in multiple vehicle crashes (NHTSA, 2004). Of fatal crashes involving large trucks, nearly 77% involved a collision with another vehicle compared with only 5% involving a rollover (FMCSA, 2003). In two-vehicle fatal crashes involving a large truck and another type of vehicle, both vehicles were impacted in the front 29% of the time, suggesting head-on collisions. Trucks were impacted from the rear almost twice as often as other vehicles, 16% compared with 7% (NHTSA, 2002).

Fleet Factors

Fleet factors also influence safety performance in the trucking industry. The TIFA 2000 study indicated that 49.1% of the trucks in fatal crashes were driven by for-hire interstate carriers, nearly one-fifth by privately owned interstate carriers. Only 17% were privately owned intrastate carriers. About one-third were on local haul trips within 50 miles of their home base (Matteson, 2001).

The FMCSA conducted a study of safety performance by trucking industry segments using 1992 to 1998 data from the Motor Carrier Management Information System (MCMIS) and the Motor Carrier Safety Status Measurement System (SafeStat). The performance of 11 for-hire and 10 private commodity segments was evaluated on nine standard safety measures related to driver performance, vehicle scores, accident history, crash rates, and safety management. The passenger segment and the less-than-truckload segment were the safest of the for-hire segments, while refrigerated foods and produce segments were least safe. Among private commodity carriers, the safest groups were the tank and household goods transporters, while general freight and large machinery segments had lower safety ratings. Overall, private commodity carriers displayed significantly safer ratings than those carriers in the for-hire segments (FMCSA, 2002). Although studies have demonstrated that fleet factors influence safety performance, little is known of the underlying reasons for such influence.

Physical Environmental Factors

Environmental conditions also contribute to the safety and health experience of trucking. The frequency of fatal crashes involving trucks varied by time of day and year, as well as by weather conditions. There is seasonal variation with most fatal crashes occurring in June, and the fewest in April. About two-thirds occurred in rural areas, the same proportion occurred in daylight. More than 80% took place on dry roads, and in normal weather conditions (Matteson, 2003).

Availability of space to rest is important, particularly with increasing truck traffic. In a study of more than 2,000 truck drivers from Canada and the U.S., drivers indicated that they decide where they will park and make that decision while driving. Safety, convenience and the availability of basic amenities were listed as important considerations. Drivers preferred well-lighted lots to the presence of security personnel for safety. Drivers favored rest areas for short stops. A universal comment from drivers was the need for more spaces (Chen et al., 2002).

Management Practices

Management practices are another area that affect driver safety behavior. Management support is critical in developing a positive safety culture, management practices can also compel drivers to push themselves physically and mentally with consequent adverse effects.

Arboleda's (2003) study of management practices at 116 trucking firms found that strong safety cultures resulted in fewer incidents. Using data on perceptions of safety training, driver autonomy, opportunity for input, and management commitment collected from drivers, dispatchers, and safety directors, the study found that driver scheduling autonomy was not a predictor of a positive safety culture but that driver fatigue training and driver opportunity for safety input were significant predictors for safety. Top management commitment to safety was a significant predictor for all three occupation groups; the effect on drivers was strongest.

Effective Commercial Truck and Bus Safety Management Techniques (Knipling, 2003), part of the FMCSA's *Commercial Truck and Bus Safety Synthesis* documents addressed 20 distinct safety problems such as driver knowledge of safety and behaviors and vehicle maintenance, and 28 management methods, including driver certification, evaluation and recruiting, and scheduling. Based on a review of literature, interviews with industry experts, and suggestions from the TRB Synthesis Panel, Knipling concludes that effective safety management results from multiple factors, and that more rigorous evaluation studies to improve qualitative and quantitative risk factor knowledge are needed.

Prevention and Control (Intervention)

Prevention and control (intervention) strategies are developed using the findings from surveillance and analytic research steps of the Public Health Model.

Intervention efforts generally target the subsystems: 1) behavioral (driver), 2) physical, (vehicle) or 3) managerial/work organization subsystems. Interventions are typically most effective when they address multiple subsystems. Prevention and control of occupational injury and illness requires a multi-dimensional approach applying the principles of disciplines including data management, economics, education, engineering, and psychology. The complexity of intervention strategies in trucking is best understood through examples.

Behavioral – Driver Factors

Although intervention strategies intended to influence behavior include pre- and post-employee selection, and disciplinary controls, the trucking industry has focused on driver training. Training is used to modify behavior to lessen the occurrence of undesirable driving actions such as speeding and aggressive driving, and to reduce the number of fatal and nonfatal incidents. Factors that can be addressed in training include vehicle maneuvering and control, operation in adverse conditions, operation under fatigued conditions, and avoiding negative health outcomes.

Historically the Federal government has not regulated driver training. The Federal Highway Administration developed a *Model Curriculum for Training Tractor-Trailer Drivers* (1985, GPO Stock No. 050–001–00293–1), which incorporated recommendations for training standards for CMV drivers including minimum training guidelines, specifications for vehicles and facilities, instructor hiring practices, and graduation information, but use of the curriculum was discretionary. A later study mandated by the Intermodal Surface Transportation Efficiency Act (ISTEA) found private sector training of entry-level drivers in the heavy truck, motor coach, and school bus industries was inadequate. In 1991 Congress required Federal entry-level training requirements be established for CMV drivers. The positive effect of commercial drivers licensing (CDL) on trucking safety inclined the FMSCA to take a basic licensing approach to improve safety performance. The current Federal and State CDL license programs do not however mandate training to obtain a license.

Although there are differing views on when and who to train, and the effectiveness of training, the FMCSA initiated federal regulation of CMV driver training in May 2004 by issuing a final rule establishing "Minimum Training Requirements for Entry-Level Commercial Motor Vehicle Operators." An entry-level driver is defined as "a person with less than two years experience operating a CMV that required a CDL." The rules apply to drivers in the heavy truck, motor-coach, and school bus industries, and those in interstate commerce. The agency also proposed training topics be expanded in traditional CDL requirements covering subjects such as medical qualifications; substance abuse; driver well-being; and whistleblower protection.

Although entry-level training is usually accepted as improving safety, the measured effects are too desperate to dependably predict the effect of training programs or of the new requirements. For example, case studies suggest that driver training programs reduced truck related incidents, but the results vary drastically, ranging from 2 to 40 percent. FMCSA's a preliminary regulatory economic evaluation, which considered the costs of medical and emergency services, property damage, lost productivity, as well estimates of pain, suffering, and quality of life-losses determined that the new training rules would have to reduce truck related crashes by entry level drivers by 5 percent – 201 crashes – annually to be cost beneficial (*Costs of Large Truck- and Bus-Involved Crashes*, (Zaloshnja et al., 2000 and 2004). Because the effects of training programs on safety performance are not certain, not all critics agree that training programs or the new rules will be effective safety interventions.

Commercial driver training programs of varying costs and duration are available from trucking firms, specialized providers and community colleges. The courses are structured to meet the requirements to obtain the CDL. Traditional methods combine textbooks, classroom and hands-on training. Emerging information technologies have expanded training modalities to include driving simulation, computer and internet based instruction and self-paced instructional videos.

Several public-private partnerships involving the FMCSA, the American Trucking Associations (ATA), the American Trucking Associations Foundation (ATAF) and the National Private Truck Council (NPTC) have served to develop driver education programs addressing driver fatigue, wellness, health, and fitness. The *Awake at the Wheel* program included public service announcements, brochures and a video on the alert driver. It also provided a 4-hour train-the trainer course, and a 1 to 3 hour course for trucking executives. The *Gettin' in Gear* Program was intended for commercial vehicle drivers, their employers and their families. The program emphasizes the importance of driver health to safe driving; highway safety; and preserving the workforce. It addresses the numerous health risks affecting commercial drivers, including smoking, obesity, and poor dietary habits, and overall fitness and encourages adopting a healthier lifestyle (Krueger, 2002).

Countries differ in their approaches to training. In both Canada and the U.S., the employer is responsible for evaluating drivers and determining their training needs, and is at liberty to decide the specifics of any training. Training is available from a variety of sources; there is no universal accreditation to standardize and evaluate the effectiveness of training programs. In contrast, European programs are regulated by the European Agreement concerning the International Carriage of Dangerous Goods by Road; programs must be certificated and accredited. Countries verify programs differently; for example, the Netherlands requires examination of those attending training while Sweden has standards for accreditation that individual training companies must adhere to during business conduct (Kuncyte et al., 2003).

Training in simulators is safer and generally less expensive than behind-the-wheel training. Simulators can present trainees with crisis situations, such as a pedestrian entering the roadway in front of the vehicle, which are difficult to recreate in with real trucks. Simulators however provide a less realistic experience with loss of vehicle control and recovery than training programs using full size trucks with stabilizers on skid pads. The degree of realism varies by system. Some simulators mount truck cabs to re-create the motions, noises, and actions of driving with 180 degree virtual reality scenarios. Others are little more than a simulated steering wheel and gear-shift with a simple computerized display. Intuitively, more elaborate simulators provide more effective training, but elaborate simulators are costly to use and mainly reserved for research.

Drivers of vehicles that may be in proximity to large trucks in traffic also need education to appreciate the realities of trucks with large mass, heavy loads, and limitations on maneuverability. There have been campaigns to publicize the *No-Zone*, area behind large trucks that other vehicles cannot safely enter.

Selection of employees using defined work characteristics or later screening of unsafe drivers may also serve to improve safety performance. In the trucking industry, the CDL, which establishes baseline standards for operators of large commercial vehicles, serves as both an ex-ante and ex-post selection mechanism. Minimum standards are established by the FMCSA (http://www.fmcsa.dot.gov/rulesregs/fmcsr/regs/383.htm) but CDLs are issued by the states according to Federal regulations that govern the State programs. CDLs are required for vehicles weighing 10,001 pounds gross vehicle weight rating (GVWR) or more. Operators may be subject to other business regulations or regulations for hauling hazardous waste.

The physical qualifications of commercial motor vehicle drivers are also regulated by the Federal government. For example, Title 49 CFR Part 391.41 stipulates physical, medical and psychiatric disorders including a loss of extremity that would interfere with driving, diabetes under treatment with insulin or current alcoholism, and conditions such as epilepsy, that disqualify an individual from operating a CMW. Vision and hearing must also meet specified standards (NTSB, 2002).

Physical – Vehicle Factors

Changes in the physical work environment may also improve safety and health. This section will focus on electronic interventions that have evolved during the Age of Information. In general these interventions are intended to provide a more comfortable environment and information useful in operating the vehicle. The latter may include information about the status and performance of the vehicle systems. However, the same technologies may result in complex and distracting array of visual and audible information about the vehicle and roadway.

The Department of Transportation's Intelligent Vehicle Initiative (IVI) provides valuable insight into the types and benefits of these electronic interventions. Established in 1998, the IVI is intended to prevent driver distraction, and facilitate the development and deployment of crash-avoidance systems (Resendes, 2003). The IVI focuses on improving driver activity related to safety performance under normal conditions, degraded driving conditions, and imminent crash conditions for several types of vehicles. The IVI addresses four areas related to collision avoidance – from the rear, during lane changes or merges, during road departure, or at intersections and two areas related to the driver – enhancing vision, and providing the driver with condition warnings. Field tests of a rear-end Collision Warning System (CWS) that includes Adaptive Cruise Control and Advanced Cruise Control are underway on 100 new commercial trucks.

Preliminary results indicate positive results, particularly in driver acceptance of the device. In another study, the viability of electronically controlled braking systems is also being explored (Resendes, 2003). The United States Department of Transportation's Joint Program Office (JPO) for Intelligent Transportation Systems (ITS) has been actively collecting information regarding the impact of ITS projects on the surface transportation network and on ITS costs since 1994. The resulting database provides estimates of ITS costs to be used for policy analyses, benefit/cost analyses, and project planning. The range of applications extends from advanced traffic control systems to ramp meters, to CWS. Technologies are rated in terms of the impact on safety, mobility, customer satisfaction, productivity, and impact on energy and environment. A recent report has compared the relative benefits and costs of Intelligent Transportation Systems as of 2003 (Maccubin, 2003). The most recent annual summary of benefits by program area and by benefit measure is available at: http://www.benefitcost.its.dot.gov.

There are a number of safety information technologies in use inside vehicles that provide immediate feedback to the driver or store information for later review. These on-board devices are in contrast to the more common warning devices placed outside the vehicle, such as stationary intersection alerts. Some devices, for example the CWS, are in limited use and also are being evaluated in field operational trials. Although some of these technologies were developed for other purposes, they have the potential to improve vehicle safety. Definitive quantitative data regarding their effects on preventing collisions are generally not publicly available.

CWS for commercial vehicles are usually radar-based devices located on the front or sides of commercial vehicles. They emit an audible or visible signal as other vehicles or objects are being approached and speed drivers' response to an imminent collision. They may also distract drivers or affect team drivers' ability to get berth-sleep. Trucking trade journals suggest that CWS are effective in preventing or mitigating collisions. In 2000, a manufacturer of CWS released a summary of three years of data from an evaluation study that indicated an 80% reduction in collisions. Six of eight fleets reported 100% reductions, one fleet reduced lane change and rear-end collisions from 0.33 per million vehicle miles traveled to zero. Other fleets also reported substantial reductions in fixed object collisions, and lane change and rear-end collisions (Roadranger, 2000). CWS may be used in combination with technologies such as antilock braking systems (ABS), Adaptive Cruise Control, and various information storage devices. Information collected during the use of such systems can be used in driver education, evaluation of driving patterns, or crash reconstruction. A survey of truck drivers' attitudes toward feedback by technology found that CWS was among the most frequently mentioned technologies (Roetting, 2003).

Global Positioning Systems (GPS) devices can accurately determine and provide information on vehicle location. This is useful to the driver in navigating, and can be used by dispatchers to track driver movements. The use of this technology by emergency responders to located accidents has shortened their response time, a potential critical element in victim survival. GPS can also be used to locate stolen vehicles or vehicles that have deviated from a projected route. GPS might also be used to track vehicles with hazardous materials in a security crisis.

Event Data Recorders and feedback systems are electronic devices that monitor and record events such as hard-braking incidents that may reflect driver behavior. Similar to CWS, Event Data Recorders may be used in combination with devices such as Adaptive Cruise Controls. Data collected may be used in reconstructing a crash and determining the contributions to cause (NHTSA, 2002).

Other technologies such as Fatigue Tracking Systems are currently being tested for commercial use. One device measures the percent of driver eye closure time. These systems could be used to provide a warning to drivers, or slow or control the vehicle. These devices are undergoing tests and their effectiveness is not established.

Some fleets are installing speed control devices on trucks to ensure that drivers remain within a prescribed speed. Speed control devices are unpopular with drivers as they limit the driver's ability to accelerate to pass another vehicle or to avert a collision. Their impact on safety will not be clear until there is more experience with these devices.

Cell phones and other communication devices are controversial. Studies of cell phone use suggest that they may be a major distraction if not a potential driving hazard. A review of nine studies that suggested mobile communications can increase the risk of collisions by causing delayed reactions. "Drivers using cell phones were found to have braking reaction time three times longer than drivers under the influence of alcohol, and a four-fold increase in risk compared to not using a cell phone." http://www.occupationalhazards.com/articles/12035. Responding to the perception of cell phone hazards, the City Council of Washington D.C. passed an ordinance in 2004 which made any vehicle driver, including truck drivers, using a cellular phone without a hands-free device subject to a fine of $100.00 and 1 point. Exxon Mobil Corporation banned cell phone use by drivers while working in June 2004. In spite of any risk associated with hand-on cell phone usage, the cell phone is of positive value to truckers in finding rest stops, arranging schedules, and communicating road problems. Like many technologies, the benefits are substantial when properly used.

Managerial or Work Organization

Managers, regulators and customers of the trucking industry affect safety and health through their control of work organization. Trucking managers can play a central role in creating a culture in which safety is a priority for drivers through personal contact, incentives, training, and by sanctioning unsafe acts. For example, the Owner-Operator Independent Drivers Association has sponsored campaigns, such as the Safe Driver Awards Program, encouraging individual members to drive safely (OOIDA, 2003). However, the tension between scheduling for profitability and promotion of safe practices creates ambiguity in mangers role in the safety process. Management practices can reduce driver fatigue, and improve safety, but may also force drivers to push themselves physically and mentally with adverse effects. Drivers respond to pressure from dispatchers to continue driving, even when aware of their own fatigue (Filiatrault, 2002). Scheduling may limit driver's ability to recover from fatigue. Focus groups of industry representatives assembled by the FHWA suggested that shipper and motor carrier personnel are unaware or unconcerned about pressures on drivers. Firms accept unrealistic deadlines to obtain business and then pressures drivers to exceed Hours of Service (HOS) limits and safe speeds as well as inappropriately load or unload freight to make timely deliveries. Dispatchers were crucial in any effort to reduce fatigue as they are directly involved in setting schedules. Managers have leverage to improve safety by enforcing existing regulations. Fleet managers can ensure that drivers have credentials for their vehicle. Despite revisions of the CDL to incorporate data on driving violations, 8% of commercial drivers of large trucks in fatal crashes had no CDL, only 86% had a valid CDL and of these, only 92% had a CDL for the class of vehicle they were driving (FMCSA, 2002).

Managerial support for the HOS of the Federal Motor Carriers Safety Administration might also improve safety and reduce fatigue. The legislative and administrative history of the HOS regulations is given extensive discussion in the chapter on regulation in this volume; we limit ourselves to a brief summary of the recent changes and the safety issues raised by these changes. The regulations in force from 1962 until 2004 established an 18 to 23 hour work schedule with 10 hours driving and up to 5 hours of non-driving work before a mandatory 8 hours rest. Drivers could extend the length time over which work could be done by inserting non-working time breaks into this schedule. Drivers were also limited to 60 hours of work in seven days and 70 hours in eight days.

In order to provide drivers with necessary rest and sleep within the realities of commercial driving, the FMCSA promulgated new HOS rules in April 2003 with a compliance date of January 4, 2004. The revisions are estimated to prevent between 24 and 75 driver deaths per year, prevent over 1,300 fatigue related injuries and 6,900 damage only crashes, with a national annual savings of $628 million.

The new rules create a 21 hour drive-rest cycle. Drivers of property-carrying CMVs may not drive for more than 11 hours after 10 consecutive hours off duty, or for any period of time after having been "on duty" 14 hours following 10 consecutive hours off duty. Non-driving and break time is, with few exceptions, counted against the 14 hours, resulting in a hard shut down 14 hours after a driver starts to work without regards to the nature of the driver's activities. If drivers use a sleeper berth required off-duty hours may be divided into 2 periods, neither of which may be less than 2 hours. The new regulations retained the 60 and 70 hour rules but allow drivers to begin a new 7- and 8-day cycle after they have been off duty for 34 consecutive hours. Drivers are still required to maintain duty logs for each 24-hour period but those who are out of compliance will now be declared out of service until they go off duty for the required number of hours.

Although the revised HOS regulations may be a positive direction for improving safety, on July 16, 2004, the U.S. Court of Appeals in Washington, D.C. rejected the new HOS rules and sent them back to the FMCSA for reconsideration. The court indicated concerns with several aspects of the regulation, but its central concern was the failure of the agency to consider "the statutorily mandated factor of drivers' health in the slightest." The court raised specific concerns about the effects of vibration, noise, and the 11th hour of driving. The unknown effect of restarting the weekly log after 34 hours off duty, the ability of drivers to split the required 10 hours off duty into shorter periods if using a sleeper berth, and the failure of the FMCSA to mandate the use of electronic on-board recorders (EOBR) to monitor compliance were also raised. The court mandated a limited period of consideration, the new hours-of-service rules remain in effect through this period. Issues surrounding HOS have stimulated new research but it is unlikely that much new information regarding driver health that can be obtained in the time available.

Driver fatigue appears to be influenced by fatigue inducing factors and management safety practices. To reduce fatigue and the occurrence of incidents, research suggests management practices such as encouraging a safer environment, designing manageable schedules and shifts, and assisting drivers with tiring tasks (Morrow, 2004). Training drivers to recognize fatigue is a marker of a strong fleet safety culture for employees (Arboleda, 2003). Managers have the opportunity to create a safety conscious culture and to lead by example. If safety is perceived to be a priority by management, drivers will be more likely to drive safely.

Discussion

The term Age of Information has many possible interpretations and implications as it applies to trucking. It refers not just to the exponential explosion in the amount and quality of data available, but to the recent technologies that make it possible to store, screen, integrate, interpret, access, and utilize information for operations of single vehicles and fleets. While empowering truck owners and drivers with tools for managing and driving their vehicles, information has also made the task of managing vehicles more complex. Because of this, the commercial drivers and vehicles in the context of information should be viewed as complex interactive systems operating in a complex external environment.

There are numerous levels or layers of information. One level of information involves cumulative epidemiological statistics on large truck crashes that have been consistent in highlighting this problem over many years. Data on truck crashes, costs, and possible interventions inform regulatory decisions such as Hours of Service rules or rules regulating training for entry level drivers. A relatively new development is the sharing of information between primary sources – public health and transportation agencies – to better manage trucking safety (TRB 2004). Data on individual drivers are potentially available through CDL records, state police crash records, and other sources. Individual companies maintain detailed fleet data, including records on specific vehicles.

In addition to the fundamental economic importance of commercial trucking, the important public health implications of commercial trucking are well known and thoroughly documented in published national statistics. Numerous fatalities, injuries, and damages result from crashes involving large trucks that extend beyond the trucking industry as they frequently involve drivers of other vehicles and their vehicles.

Although truck safety information is available from the numerous sources described in this chapter and others, no single source or combination of sources permit accurate calculations of risk. One problem in estimation of risk is that good denominator metrics relating truck and driver exposure to adverse outcomes are lacking. Various surrogate indices, such as million-miles traveled, offer crude substitutes for true exposure measures.

Many of the risk factors which influence the occurrence of crashes are relatively well known. Some of these are environmental factors, such as road conditions, weather, time of day, and visibility. Other factors relate to the physical configuration and condition of vehicles. Human risk factors clearly play an important role as well. Some of these relate to truck drivers, while factors influencing drivers of other vehicles are also important. Again, there is a scarcity of quantitative information on the contributions of these factors. Studies such as the Large Truck Crash Causation Study conducted by the National Highway Traffic Safety Administration will do much to clarify these risk-related issues.

Interventions are not always well defined and many are in the trial or evaluation stage. Much of the discussion about training is anecdotal and based on personal experience of safety personnel. The numerous commercial training courses available focus on preparing the driver to understand and competently drive a large truck in most common traffic situations. These courses prepare the driver to obtain a CDL and to find employment. The courses range widely in terms of cost, duration, and content. One commercial company combined classroom training with realistic simulator training in a full-size truck cab, behind the wheel training in a large truck on a slippery skid pad with a rain curtain, and physical fitness training. The program was discontinued, prior to conducting a robust evaluative study.

As recently as May 2004 there is a lack of stakeholder consensus on the effectiveness of driver training programs. In the comments on the FMCSA Final Rule on training for entry level drivers, estimates of crash reduction from driver training ranged from two to 40 percent. The FMCSA justified the rule in terms of cost benefit using various assumptions about crash reduction and also about crash costs.

Despite the lack of agreement regarding the effectiveness as well as the lack of evaluative studies, training has been a prominent intervention in trucking. The lack of evaluative studies can be partly attributed to a number of inherent difficulties in evaluating the effects of driver training on driving performance. One problem is that such evaluations would ideally be conducted prospectively over extended periods of time, preferably years of driving history. Another problem is to relate training to improvements in driving performance, for example, there is difficulty in measuring crashes avoided or prevented. The FMCSA Research and Technology Stakeholder Forums have clearly identified various aspects of driver training as important. However, there is not agreement on when to train, how often, training content, who should train, and how to evaluate training.

Perhaps most impressive in the Age of Information are the technological advances that appear promising to improving the safety and health experience. Electronic transmission of information between driver and dispatcher, between driver and the physical environment, and between driver and the truck are changing how the industry operates. With technology changing rapidly, the safety and health community can expect many new methods to protect the worker and improve productivity.

A number of activities are underway to identify research gaps and needs. These include activities of the Transportation Research Board (TRB) including the Truck and Bus Safety Committee and Task Forces, a National Institute for Occupational Safety and Health's Motor Vehicle Research Program with two projects focusing on commercial truck drivers, and the FMCSA Commercial Truck and Bus Safety Synthesis Program. Over 125 specific research recommendations are outlined in the FMCSA sponsored report on *Results from the Fall 2003 Research and Technology Stakeholder Forums* (FMCSA, 2004). These recommendations fall into the general areas of research related to the Driver, the Vehicle, the Carrier/Shipper, and the Roadside/Environment. Approximately one-fourth of the total research recommendations focused on driver factors, highlighting insurance company statistics that 95% of crashes are related to driver factors and error. The majority of the driver-related research centered on training, seen as the best way to improve driver performance (FMCSA, 2004). This confirms that priorities are being defined, but research on trucking information has a long road ahead.

In summary, there are abundant sources of trucking related information but at present these have not been linked to form a composite overview of trucking health and safety. There are initiatives underway to improve information collection, linkage, and utilization and these advances promise great future accomplishments for trucking health and safety. Also, the evaluation of interventions to improve trucking health and safety is expanding rapidly as of 2005. We are hopeful that these initiatives will improve our knowledge of the factors affecting safety and health in commercial trucking, point the way to more effective interventions and, most important, result in truck driving becoming a safer occupation and improved safety on the public highways.

References

AAA Foundation for Traffic Safety. Identifying Unsafe Driver Actions that Lead to Fatal Car-Truck Crashes. Washington, DC, 2002, April.

Adams-Guppy, J. and A. Guppy. Truck driver fatigue risk assessment and management: a multinational survey.

AHAS. The Dangers of Large Trucks. Advocates for Highway and Auto Safety (AHAS). FACT SHEET. 2003.

Alvarez, Albert. A Study of Prevalence of Sleep Apnea Among Commercial Truck Drivers. Federal Motor Carrier Safety Administration, U.S. Department of Transportation, FMCSA TechBrief No. RT-02-080, -2002 Jul.

American Association of State Highway and Transportation Officials. AASHTO Transportation Security Task Force. Website.Pdf. 2002.

Anderson, DG. Workplace violence in long haul trucking: occupational health nursing update. 2004 Jan 1; 52(1).

Arboleda, A. P. C. Morrow M. R. Crum and M. C. Shelley II. Management Practices as antecedents of safety culture within the trucking industry: similarities and differences by hierarchical level. Journal of Safety Research. 2003 Apr; 34(2), pp. 189-197.

Beilock, Richard. Schedule-induced hours-of-service and speed limit violations among tractor-trailer drivers. Accident Analysis and Prevention. 1995 Feb; 27(1), pp. 33-42.

Blincoe L., E. Seay, E. Zaloshna, T. Miller, E. Romano, S. Luchter, and R. Spicer. The Economic Impact of Motor Crashes 2000. National Highway Traffic Safety Administration, U.S. Department of Transportation. NHTSA Technical Report No. DOT HS 809 446. 2002 May.

Braver, Elisa R.; Preusser, Carol W., and Ulmer, Robert G. How Long-Haul Motor Carriers Determine Truck Driver Work Schedules: The Role of Shipper Demands. Journal of Safety Research. 1999; 30(3).

Bureau of Labor Statistics. Case and Demographic Characteristics for work-related injuries and illnesses involving days away from work. 2002.

Bureau of Labor Statistics. Census of Fatal Occupational Injuries Summary-2001. 2002.

Bureau of Labor Statistics. Census of Fatal Occupational Injuries Summary-2002. 2003 Sep 17.

Bureau of Labor Statistics Jobs with the most lost time injuries. Monthly Labor Review. 2003 Mar 28.

Bureau of Labor Statistics. Outdoor Occupations Exhibit High Rates of Fatal Injuries. Issues in Labor Statistics. 1995 Mar.

Bureau of Labor Statistics. Truck Drivers Again Have the Most Lost time Injuries. Monthly Labor Review. 2002 Apr 24.

Carroll, Robert. Impact of Sleeper Berth Usage on Driver Fatigue: Final Report, Federal Motor Carrier Safety Administration, U.S. Department of Transportation. FMCSA TechBrief No. MCRT-02-070. 2002 Aug.

Chen, G. X., Jenkins E. L., and E. L. Husting. Truck crash experiences of for-hire motor carriers in the United States: 2000-2001. Proceedings of The 3rd National Occupational Injury Research Symposium (NOIRS). 2003.

Chen, K. J. K. K. Pecheux J. Farbry Jr. and S. A. Fleger. Commercial Vehicle Driver Survey: Assessment of Parking Needs and Preferences. 2002 Mar.

Craft, R. and D. Blower. The Large Truck Crash Causation Study. Preliminary Report. Presented to Association of Traffic Safety. Professionals September 2004 Available at ATSIP website, www.atsip.org.

Department of Transportation. Intelligent Transportation Systems Benefits and Costs 2003 Summary Desk Reference. Department of Transportation. Statement of purpose. http://www.Dot.Gov/DOTagencies.htm.

Donaldson, Gerald. Comment on HOS rule: September 29, 2003. BNA Occupational Safety and Health Reporter. 2003 Oct 9.

Federal Motor Carrier Safety Administration. Large Truck Crash Facts-2000. U.S. Department of Transportation, FMCSA Document No.-RI-02-011. 2003 January.

Federal Motor Carrier Safety Administration. The Revised Hours-of Service Regulations. FMCSA Website. 2003 Oct.

Federal Motor Carrier Safety Administration. Minimum Training Requirements for Entry-Level Commercial Motor Vehicle Operators. http://www.fmcsa.dot.gov/rulesregs/fmcsr/final/04-1475EntryLevel.pdf.

Federal Motor Carrier Safety Administration. Model Curriculum for Training Tractor-Trailer Drivers. 1985. GPO Stock No. 050-001-00293-1.

Federal Motor Carrier Safety Administration. Motor Carrier Safety Programs- Home Page. 2003; 6(1).

Federal Motor Carrier Safety Administration. Portfolio of FMCSA Research and Technology Programs. Research and Technology Forum, Transportation Research Board's 83rd Annual Meeting. 2004 Jan 11.

Federal Motor Carrier Safety Administration. Results from the Fall 2003 Research and Technology Stakeholder Forums. 2004 Feb.

Federal Motor Carrier Safety Administration. Safety Belt Usage by Commercial Motor Vehicle (CMV) Drivers-FMCSA. Final Report. 2003 Nov; Purchase Order DTMC-01-P-00071.

Filiatrault, Daniel. Vavrick J. Kuzeljevic B. and P. J. Cooper. The Effect of Rest-Schedule Orientation on Sleep Quality of Commercial Drivers. Traffic Injury Prevention. 2002; 3(1), pp. 13-18.

Husting, E. L. and Biddle E. A. Costs to Society of Fatal Truck Injuries. Proceedings of the 3rd National Occupational Injury Research Agenda (NOIRS), 2003.

Keane, T. T. Corsi and K. Braaten. Motor Carrier Industry Profile Study: Evaluating Safety Performance by Motor Carrier Industry Segment. International Truck and Bus Safety Research and Policy Symposium. 2002.

Kisner, S. and L. Jenkins. Preventing Worker Injuries and Deaths from Traffic-Related Motor Vehicle Crashes. National Institute for Occupational Safety and Health, DHHS (NIOSH) Publication N0. 98-142.

Knipling, R. R., J. S. Hickman, and G. Bergoffen. Commercial Truck and Bus Safety Synthesis Program. Effective Commercial Truck and Bus Safety Management Techniques. Transportation Research Board, 2003.

Krueger, G. P., R. M. Brewster, and A. Alvarez. Gettin' in Gear, A commercial driver training program for wellness, health and fitness: Precursors to mastering driving alertness and managing driver fatigue. International Truck and Bus Safety Symposium, 2002.

Kuncyte, R; C. Laberge-Nadeau, T. Crainic, T. Gabriel, and J. A. Read. Organisation of truck-driver training for the transportation of dangerous goods in Europe and North America. Accident Analysis and Prevention. 2003 Mar; 35(2), pp. 191-200.

Lantz, Brenda M. and M. W. Blevins. An analysis of commercial vehicle driver traffic conviction data to identify high safety risk motor carriers. International Truck and Bus Safety Research and Policy Symposium. 2001, Sep.

Lin, L-J and H. Harvey Cohen. Accidents in the Trucking Industry. Industrial Ergonomics. 1997; 20, pp. 287-300.

Lyman, Stephen and E. Braver. Occupant deaths in large truck crashes in the United States: 25 years of experience. Accident Analysis and Prevention. 2003 Sep; 35(5).

Maccubin, R. P., B. L. Staples, and M. R. Mercer. Intelligent Transportation Systems Benefits and Costs 2003 Update. Department of Transportation, FHWA Document No. OP-03-075. 2003 May.

Matteson, Anne and D. Blower. Trucks Involved in Fatal Accidents Factbook 2000. The University of Michigan Transportation Research Institute, Center for National Truck Statistics; 2003 July.

McCartt, A. T.; Rohrbaugh, J. W.; Hammer, M. C., and Fuller SZ. Factors associated with falling asleep at the wheel among long-distance truck drivers. Accident Analysis and Prevention. 2000 Jul; 32(4), pp. 493-504.

McKillip, J. L. Fleet Safety- Protecting Drivers and The Bottom Line. Professional Safety. 2003 Oct.

MMWR. Achievements in Public Health, 1900-1999. Motor Vehicle Safety: A 20th century public health achievement. Morbidity and Mortality Weekly Reports. 1999; 48(18).

Morrow, Paula C. and M. R. Crum. Antecedents of fatigue, close calls, and crashes among commercial motor-vehicle drivers. Journal of Safety Research. 2004; 35(1), pp. 59-69.

NHTSA. Event Data Recorders; Summary of Findings by the NHTSA EDR Working Group; Volume II, Supplemental Findings for Trucks, Motorcoaches, and School Buses. 2002 May; National Highway Traffic Safety Administration, Department of Transportation Report No. DOT HS 809 432 Washington, D.C.

NHTSA. Large Truck Crash Causation Study. – National Highway Traffic Safety Administration, Department of Transportation Report No Interim Rep. DOT HS 809 527. 2002 Sep., Washington, D.C.

NHTSA. Traffic Safety Facts 2001- Large Trucks.; National Highway Traffic Safety Administration, Department of Transportation Report No Publication DOT HS 809 472. 2002, Washington, D.C.

NHTSA. Traffic Safety Facts 2001- Overview. National Highway Traffic Safety Administration, Department of Transportation Report No DOT HS 809 476. 2002, Washington, D.C.

NHTSA. Traffic Safety Facts 2002. National Highway Traffic Safety Administration, Department of Transportation Report No DOT HS 809 620. 2004 Jan., Washington, D.C.

NHTSA. Traffic Safety Facts 2002- Large Trucks. 2003; National Highway Traffic Safety Administration, Department of Transportation Report No DOT HS 809 608, Washington, D.C.

NHTSA. Traffic Safety Facts 2002- Overview. National Highway Traffic Safety Administration, Department of Transportation Report No DOT HS 809 612. 2003.

NHTSA. Traffic Safety Facts- a Compilation of Motor Vehicle Crash Data from the Fatality Analysis Reporting System and the General Estimates System.

NTSB. Safety Study: Fatigue, Alcohol, Other Drugs, and Medical Factors in Fatal to the Driver Heavy Truck Crashes: Volume 2. NTSB/SS-90/02, NTIS Number: PB90-917003, 1990, February. National Transportation Safety Board, Washington, D.C.

NTSB. Safety Study: Factors that Affect Fatigue in Heavy Truck Accidents Volume 2: Case Summaries. NTSB/SS-95/02, NTIS Number: PB95-917002, 1995, January. National Transportation Safety Board, Washington, D.C.

NTSB. Safety Report- Analysis of Intrastate Trucking Operations. NTSB/SR-02-01PB2002-917001Notation 7448. 2002 Mar 28. National Transportation Safety Board, Washington, D.C.

NTSB. Safety Report: Transportation Safety Databases. NTSB Number NTSB/SR-02/02 NTIS Number PB2002-917004. 2002 Sep 11. National Transportation Safety Board, Washington, D.C.

Office of Motor Carrier Safety. The Unsafe Driving Acts of Motorists in the Vicinity of Large Trucks. Department of Transportation Report No. MCRT-00-002, 1999, Nov., Washington, D.C.

Pigman, J. G. and K. R. Agent. Heavy Truck Involvement in Traffic Accidents and Related Countermeasures. Research Report KTC -99-20. 1999 Mar.

Pratt, Stephanie G. Work-Related Roadway Crashes: Challenges and Opportunities for Prevention. National Institute for Occupational Safety and Health, Department of Health and Human Services, Publication No. 2003-119, 2003 Sep., Cincinnati, OH.

Reed, D. B. and Cronin JS. Health on the road: issues faced by female truck drivers. AAOHN J. 2003 Mar; 51(3).

Resendes, R. and Martin K. H. Saving Lives Through Advanced Vehicle Safety Tech, Intelligent Vehicle Initiative Annual Report-2002. 2003 May 15; FHWA-OP-03-101. Washington, D.C.

Roadrunner. New Statistics Demonstrate Conclusively That Collision Warning Systems Significantly Reduce Accidents. Accessed www.roadrunner.com, November, 2003.

Roetting, M. Y. Huange, J. McDevitt, and D. Melton. When Technology Tells You How You Drive – Truck Drivers' Attitudes Towards Feedback by Technology. Transportation Research Part F Vol. 6, No. 4, 2003, Dec. pp. 275-287.

Saltzman, G. M. and M. H. Belzer. Truck Driver Occupational Safety and Health: A Conference Report and Selective Literature Review (DRAFT). 2003 Dec.

Steenland, N. K. D. T. Silverman and R. W. Hornung. Case-control study of lung cancer and truck driving in the Teamsters Union. American Journal of Public Health. 1990.

Stoohs, R A; Guilleminault, C; Itoi, A, and Dement, W C. Traffic accidents in commercial long-haul truck drivers: the influence of sleep-disordered breathing and obesity. Sleep. 1994 Oct; 17(7).

Stuster, J. The Unsafe Driving Acts of Motorists in the Vicinity of Large Trucks. 1999. Technology and Maintenance Council, American Trucking Associations. Securing Corporate Infrastructure. Technical Journal of TMC's 2002 Annual Meeting. 2002 Mar 5-2002 Mar 8.

Thakuriah, Vonu. Data Linkage Issues: Some Considerations and Applications. Presentation at the Bureau of Transportation Statistics, USDOT, Washington, D.C. 2002 Jun 11.

TRB. National Cooperative Highway Research Program (NCHRP 520). Sharing Information between Public Safety and Transportation Agencies for Traffic Incident Management. Transportation Research Board, Washington, D.C. 2004.

TRB. TRB Trucking- Related Activities and Publications. Available at: www.trb.org/ publications/Transportation Research Board, Washington DC 2003.

Yiin, H-C. Exposure to diesel exhaust and risk of lung cancer in the trucking industry. Dissertation. 2003 Dec.

Zaloshnja, E., Miller, T., and Spicer, R. Costs of Large Truck- and Bus-Involved Crashes, FMCSA, Washington, D.C., Nov. 2000.

Zaloshnja, E. and T. R. Miller Costs of Large Truck Involved Crashes in the United States. Accident Analysis and Prevention, Vol. 36 No. 5, 2004, Sep.

Chapter 11

Future Truck Drivers: Where will they Come From, Why would they Take the Job?

Michael E. Conyngham

Introduction

The trucking industry has evolved rapidly over the last twenty years. Driven by the needs of an ever more complex system of global production, and facilitated by the efforts of supply chain management (SCM) theorists and software engineers, the system has developed to meet the demands for faster inventory turns while recognizing the constraints required to provide greater homeland security. To the industry's credit, tremendous technological advances have been made in recent years to reduce cycle times for transportation of both raw and finished materials within and across the expanding international marketplace.

Although the pursuit of a sleek, multi-modal shipping system responsive to ever-tightening supply chains has steadily driven down expenses and cut transit times, the structural transformation of the global supply chain has been accompanied by significant social costs. As such, the failure to consider the impact of changes in the transportation system on individual truck drivers, a link of the supply chain often overlooked by the creators and users of the sophisticated SCM software, has increasingly acted as a brake upon the operations of large motor carriers and on the industry as a whole.

Navigating the landscape of modern trucking is a daily challenge for the millions of Americans who derive their livelihood moving domestic and international goods between shippers, receivers and retailers. Truck drivers, who comprise nearly one-third of the trucking industry's nine million workers,[1] directly experience the harsh realities of the modern supply chain system. What were once predictable work schedules based on a regular route system of inter-city transportation have been largely replaced by an operating environment that stresses driver flexibility and the capacity to meet irregular, customer-driven service demands. Tractor-trailer drivers also face an increasingly congested inter-state highway system combined with increasingly intrusive federal and state regulation and monitoring by their employer. In addition to these trying conditions, the typical general freight driver in the truckload sector spent nearly six months on the road away from home in 2003 to earn a modest \$36,940.[2]

This deterioration of occupational conditions belie the fact that truck driving has historically been considered a good job for a large number of workers in the United States, with advantages that appealed to these "knights of the road." Truck driving provided a stable, albeit moderate, income that was valuable to workers of ordinary educational background and opportunity. In addition, the truck cab was well suited to individuals, some of who had troubled work histories, who preferred less direct supervision and valued personal freedom and independence to a traditional office or factory setting. Dispatch practices allowed considerable flexibility to OTR drivers on where they started their tour of duty, thereby reducing their need to move or uproot their families if they needed to find work or pursue a better job. Truck driving has never been an easy job, but it has been, and continues to be, a job suited to the needs and abilities of a substantial segment of the labor force.

Despite these potential attractions of truck-driving occupations, many of the economic and lifestyle incentives that once lured workers to the profession are disappearing from the industry, thus affecting the number and quality of drivers available. Fewer and fewer individuals, even those facing difficult economic conditions due to loss of employment or low wages, view truck driving as a desirable career. Even in rural areas where the traditional industrial employment base has been eroded by international trade and other changes, truck driving is increasingly viewed as a temporary occupation for a hard-working individual willing to travel to make a living. Current research suggests the stint behind the wheel of a large rig may be less indicative of a career choice and more a sign of temporary employment on the way to a more desirable job.[3]

This change in the attractiveness of truck driving affects not only the trucking industry but also the nation as whole. The U.S economy is critically dependent on trucking services, as the for-hire and private trucking industry hauled $6.2 trillion worth of goods in 2002. This is nearly 60 percent of the $10.5 trillion Gross Domestic Product that year and a 25 percent increase in the value of goods hauled since from 1997.[4] Given the centrality of trucking to American commerce, structural defects in the surface transportation system can interfere with commerce within and between industries. The shrinking pool of committed, qualified drivers hampers the trucking industry's ability to meet the growing demands for freight transport, a condition referred to in the trucking press as the "capacity crunch."[5] The negative impact on the economy has been especially severe over the last several years as other modes of transport, most notably railroads, have also experienced operational problems such that shippers are increasingly seeking to utilize OTR trucking solutions.

A slowdown of economic activity originating in the transportation system will not just affect domestic freight flows; the international flow of commerce is also being slowed by port congestion. Inadequate infrastructure and the exponential growth of trade with Asia account for much of the congestion, however the inadequacies of the ports are increasingly exacerbated by the economic plight of owner-operator port drivers on both coasts. Low pay per trip, rising fuel costs, and an inability to make multiple daily trips due to congestion and poor organization of transportation in the ports has provoked drivers to stage protests and, eventually, abandon their tractors.[6]

Although any solution to the emerging problems in freight transportation will need to address issues ranging from the adequacy of the current interstate system to the reconsideration of current regulatory framework, the most immediate and possibly the most important issue is the maintenance and expansion of the driver labor force. Much has been written about the effect of trucking deregulation on driver's pay, benefits, and work duties, and its subsequent evolution of truck driving into an increasingly unattractive career over the last quarter century (Belzer, 2000; Belman, Monaco, and Brooks, 2005). Rather than revisit a topic ably addressed by others, this chapter will discuss emerging issues that affect the professional driver and could amplify current problems in the future. Few of the matters addressed in this chapter are inherently bad for drivers, as advances in in-cab comforts and new pay structures, as well as more scientifically-based regulations of working time, have the potential to enhance the lives of over-the-road drivers. What will be argued in this chapter is that, in a context of highly competitive markets, efforts by motor carriers to obtain reasonable returns on their investments in human and physical capital often causes them to use these improvements to push over-the-road tractor-trailer drivers beyond legal and physical limits to the detriment of the industry.

These demands for greater driver productivity has led to longer hours on duty (Belzer, 2000), more time away from home, and more in-cab responsibility. Personal freedoms that once drew people to the driving profession are frequently encroached upon by the aggressive implementation of in-cab technologies that indiscriminately monitor driver behavior even when they are not on duty. Coupled with regulations that heighten scrutiny of one's off-duty behavior, these actions have reduced the rewards for current drivers and made the job less attractive to prospective drivers. As such, this chapter additionally postulates that the deterioration in drivers' work and work life originates from their declining ability to control their work environment that originates in the absence of a forum for collective discussion. Consequently, this study advances a new paradigm in which employers, unions and driver associations address drivers' chronic issues by working cooperatively to solve these dilemmas.

The Need for Drivers

Every month provides additional evidence that too few US citizens are willing to enter driving professions to meet the growing need of the modern trucking industry. Whether the evidence is in the form of reports of large truckload employers flying in squads of drivers from foreign lands, or the latest corporate push for easing DOT's amendments to NAFTA's trucking provisions, it is obvious that the US's largest trucking companies are nervous about their driver pools and their continued ability to move large volumes of freight.[7] Although most acute in the truckload sector, the problem is present throughout the industry.

The US Department of Labor has regularly found that tractor-trailer, heavy truck driving to be among the fastest growing occupations on both absolute numbers and its rate of increase. The number of heavy truck driving positions is predicted to increase by almost 600,000 by 2012; moreover, it is fifth among all occupations when ranked by its expected rate of growth.[8] These projected needs are especially daunting because large numbers of current drivers are approaching retirement and there is not an obvious pool of new entrants willing to adopt the lifestyle of an OTR driver.

In an effort to obtain new drivers to meet shipper's tightening demands, motor carriers have increasingly turned to mergers and acquisitions. The two largest motor carriers in the less-than-truckload (L-T-L) and truckload sectors, Yellow-Roadway and Swift Transportation,[9] are the end product of mergers driven in part by the need to increase the driver pool and improve utilization of drivers. Both Yellow-Roadway and Swift doubled their driver pool through their mergers.[10] Even Schneider National, the largest truckload carrier on a revenue basis in the US, broke its longstanding strategy of growing its driver complement only through organic and internal means when it purchased three motor carriers in 1998 in response to a pronounced driver shortage that year.[11]

The need for drivers is not just a concern for participants and affiliates of the trucking industry. Continued expansion of the US economy and global trade will be hampered by what are already historically low complements of drivers at most large national carriers. For example, the Federal Reserve Board's Beige Book on local economic activity recurringly cites the inadequate supply of truck drivers as an impediment to economic expansion.[12] Much of this problem rests not in a lack of potential workers, but in the demands of the occupation. The economic position of OTR truck drivers has not improved in the two decades following the deregulation of the trucking industry (Belzer 2000), and the increasingly negative effects of technological change and regulation on drivers' work and home lives place the prospect of a sustainable and active domestic driver pool in jeopardy. Absent significant improvements in the perception among younger workers of truck driving as a career occupation, thousands of tractor-trailers will remain idle in terminal yards into the foreseeable future.

Technology and its Consequences

Long-haul truck drivers have long rationalized their low pay and impersonal employer relationships by the freedom enjoyed in what has been a largely unsupervised workday routine. A common refrain has been "I may be married to the truck but at least I don't have a boss looking over my shoulder." However, information technologies increasingly encroach on this freedom, as the modern OTR truck is equipped to monitor truck and driver performance, pinpoint a driver's location within a few yards and communicate this information to the firm in real-time not only when the driver is on duty, but when their workday is over. The lure of the unobserved life is becoming a thing of the past when drivers are almost as closely monitored as the clerical whose computer counts keystrokes and idle time.

For much of the industry's history, trucking companies were unable to communicate with drivers in trucks on the road or exchange real-time information about road conditions or delivery status. The driver was mostly alone with their load and relied on pay phones to call dispatchers and others for daily instructions and updates. Revolutions in cellular, hardware and software technologies in the last ten years, however, have resulted in increased communications and dispatching capacities that demand a new level of sophistication of drivers.

One important change has been the deployment of on-board computers that observe drivers' operating practices by monitoring engine and driver performance. These computers can monitor average and instant speed, wheel time and idling practices along with other performance data. Even drivers' sleep patterns can be examined with these systems.[13] They also allow ex-post monitoring of a driver's actions, and in combination with mobile communications devices, permit real-time monitoring of drivers. Although this can be advantageous to drivers, it also places their boss over their shoulder, potentially watching their every action. Cell phones and other communications devices also result in closer monitoring of drivers, as the occasional check call – the requirement that drivers' periodically call their dispatcher – has evolved into an ability to interrogate drivers about their actions and decisions at any time.

Global Positioning System (GPS) devices also reduce drivers' control over their work. The system uses a constellation of US Air Force satellites orbiting about 12,000 miles above the earth's surface. Unaffected by weather conditions, GPS satellite communications allow firms to determine the longitude and latitude of a signal receiver within a few yards. Whether the tracking is by GPS-enabled cell phone or the latest trailer tracking device, these devices provide companies with real-time information about truck locations and permit firms to compel drivers to remain on their routes and follow schedules that may not be to the driver's preference. Diversion to a preferred rest stop or diner becomes a thing of the past when the driver has to justify the action or the length of time spent away from the truck and is subject to discipline on the evidence provided by GPS systems.[14] Although these devices have multiple positive uses in an industry that regularly transports high value and hazardous materials, devices are regularly used to monitor a driver's on and off-duty activity, placing the driver under the watchful eye of the firm on every moment of a three-week trip.[15]

Another technology that may be introduced into the tractor cab, with large consequences for the driver's work life, is the mandatory use of on-board recording devices. Following the dramatic revision of the hours-of-service regulations in early 2004, the Federal Motor Carrier Safety Administration (FMCSA) issued a formal call for comments on the use of electronic on-board recorders, or EOBRs, to document compliance with the federal hours-of-service rules. As stated in the Federal Register, EOBRs "must be integrally synchronized with specific operations of the commercial motor vehicle in which it is installed. At a minimum, the device must record engine use, road speed, miles driven, the date, and the time of the day."[16] Although it may be argued that EOBRs can be used to keep bad operators off the highway and give regulators and safety advocates a better look at the cause and effect of large truck crashes, the technology is expensive and still suffers from a number of technological problems.[17] The mandatory use of this evolving technology would result in further reductions in drivers' control over their time and privacy.

Not all technological innovations and applications in trucking have a negative effect on the OTR driver. Many of the more tech savvy long-distance operators welcome the ability to communicate via e-mail with friends and family and conduct personal business such as banking or online research and purchasing (albeit at a usage fee charged by the employer) to make the weeks away from home a little more tolerable.[18] Mobile communications systems can be used to monitor instances when shippers or receivers impose unreasonable holds on a driver, potentially protecting the driver against excessive waiting time. Owner-operators may get more lucrative loads more rapidly by utilizing the new speed of information technology and features of internet freight load boards. Whether it is Wi-Fi connections at truck stops that allow drivers to access the internet without leaving the cab to the latest collision warning systems keeping them alert, drivers who embrace technology will find that the most recent advances can improve their work life, as these benefits may outweigh the inevitable intrusion on privacy. For many other drivers, the positive attributes of a laptop computer or on board recorder must be demonstrated if it is to be received as something other than a needless invasion of the cab.

Although technology has improved some aspects of drivers' work, new information technologies are increasingly used to monitor drivers and to eliminate valued features of the job. For older and experienced drivers, these devices represent unwanted intrusions into an over-examined daily routine and provide another reason to exit the industry. The discretionary ability of a driver to control their work time, whether ducking off the highway for a moment to get some extra rest, visit a favorite restaurant, or even divert to a fishing hole for a break, has been an important and valuable aspect of a truck driver's working life. On-board technology and the derivative metrics that employers use to evaluate drivers have started to eliminate trade-off of hard work for independence and left little favorable in its place.

Changing Role of the Driver as a Logistics Professional

The physical conditions faced by the three million surface transportation professionals who navigate this country's major metropolitan areas are deteriorating. The number of commercial vehicles registered for business purposes is staggering – over 85 million trucks of all sizes, including 1.5 million large tractor-trailers,[19] with numbers only predicted to increase rapidly into the future.

The problems of an increasingly overloaded and deteriorating infrastructure of roads results in steadily rising time lost to congestion and delays. Performance measure data from 1982 to 2002 indicates that total hours of delay ballooned from 700 million hours to 3.5 billion hours with the total cost of congestion increasing from $14.2 billion to $63.2 billion in the two-decade period.[20] In addition, peak period travel for all persons using motorized transport grew from 16 hours in 1982 to 46 hours in 2002 for the 85 urban areas studied recently by the Texas Transportation Institute. Additional measures calculated by the Federal Highway Administration (FHWA) indicate that urban areas with populations greater than three million have seen the greatest increases in congestion, with 40.4 percent of daily travel in 2000 occurring under congested conditions, requiring 78 percent more travel time than the same trip did in 1987.[21] Assuming only modest growth in the density of metropolitan populations and the freight tonnage needed to serve them, and absent any improvement in the National Highway system, both urban and rural highway system truck traffic will more than double by 2020.[22] The problem facing the country, but particularly those who drive for a living, was well summarized by the Texas Transportation Institute:

> The problem can be simply stated – *congestion has grown everywhere in areas of all sizes. Congestion occurs during longer portions of the day and delays more travelers and goods than ever before.*[23] (emphasis in original)

Part of the problem is found in the lack of growth in the US interstate highway system, which has seen little expansion to its current 45,000 miles over the past 30 years. But it is not only the increasing volume of traffic on a limited system that poses a problem. The infrastructure of the US transportation system, most notably our highways, bridges, and tunnels is also in such disrepair and so far behind the scheduled capital expense necessary to maintain them that partial and total shutdowns of major arteries are becoming the norm rather than the exception. In its Report to Congress, the DOT found that "27.9% of the Nation's bridge deck area was on bridges that were classified as structurally deficient or functionally obsolete."[24] Although this number had declined since 1996, the numbers for urban bridges was significantly higher than this average. It would require average annual investments of $76 billion, considerably more than is currently spent by all levels of government, to simply maintain existing highways and bridges through 2020.[25]

The nation's OTR drivers, the individuals ultimately responsible for negotiating and completing the millions of transportation transactions occurring daily, shoulder the brunt of these conditions. As the only actors with real-time navigation information *and* the discretion to make critical decisions essential to insuring the safe and timely delivery of product, drivers are accountable for more than merely satisfactory time management practices. Driving decisions are increasingly dependent on on-board computers and hand held, wireless devices that provide the latest traffic and weather information. The proper use of information technology when driving requires skill and training, demanding discretionary calculations, especially with multiple shipment loads, in difficult operating environments. Although the problems facing drivers may be mitigated by emerging systems that relay real-time information about the location and status of shipments in transit, these systems are not a complete replacement for driver knowledge, discretion, and effort, nor will they be universal throughout the freight system in the foreseeable future.

More important, despite the improvements in driver information brought about through IT, the central factor in drivers' decision-making remains the dependence of their income on the speed with which they can complete their tasks. The industry is dominated by compensation systems, such as mileage pay and pay as a percentage of freight bill revenue, that are intended to motivate the driver to move freight as rapidly as possible. But these systems also have the effect of imposing the cost for delays and other scheduling problems on drivers. Estimates of non-highway driver waiting time, sitting at a shipper or receiver's dock waiting to get loaded or unloaded, are close to the standard workweek full-time workweek of 40 hours. This translates into more than $1.5 billion in lost productivity annually.[26] It also places the driver in the position of regularly needing to run hard, violate laws and take chances to earn a decent income.

Overworked Drivers

Even the most tightly integrated supply chain systems must be able to adjust to rapidly changing conditions including weather, traffic, shipper and consignee schedules, and more recently, security concerns. In the two decades following the deregulation of the industry, the buffer in sophisticated logistics operations, where movements are speeded up or delayed to meet shipment deadlines, has been the driver. Prior to the new hours-of-service rules, drivers were expected to manipulate their driving logs, including reporting waiting time as "off duty", so that problems in transit would not delay deliveries. This attitude was reflected in routing software that did not incorporate constraints for legal limitations on hours of work. The driver was, in programming terminology, a "non-binding" constraint. Add in shippers' demands for repetitive and uncompensated services and the financial pressure on a driver becomes enormous, often pushing drivers into unsafe decisions. The ongoing necessity of handling floor loads, 'unfriendly freight', driving in difficult regions of the country and having to wait long hours without compensatory pay has often caused the otherwise committed driver to leave the industry.

With the drying up of applicant pools and the rising expense of recruiting experienced drivers, transportation employers are ever more anxious to stretch the limits of productivity for existing workers. The result is longer working hours and increased driver fatigue. A 2001 DOT Office of the Inspector General report stated:

> Driver hours-of-service violations and falsified driver logs continue to pose significant safety concerns. Research has shown fatigue is a major factor in commercial vehicle crashes. During roadside safety inspection, the most frequent violation cited for removing a driver from operation is exceeding allowed hours of service.[27]

The overtime provisions of the Fair Labor Standards Act do not cover truck drivers in interstate commerce and, as their average earnings are above the minimum wage, the US Department of Labor does not require that drivers be paid for time spent waiting or other activities that are not directly compensated. As a result, absent a union agreement, longer hours often mean more work for little or no additional money. If one is typically paid by the mile or as a percentage of the load's revenue, that is, a predetermined value, waiting time at the shipper or receiver is typically uncompensated. Although recent changes to federal hour-of-service laws now require employers and drivers to count wait time during a shift as part of daily and weekly hours worked, these hours do not have to be paid. In addition, although trucking companies are now able to extract surcharges from customers who delay drivers, there is no assurance that this additional revenue will be shared with the driver.

In addition to directly uncompensated time, excessive waiting can also introduce delays into a driver's schedules and reduce their earnings unless they "run hard" once released to make up for lost time and income.[28] This phenomenon, which occurs daily in the industrial parks and shipping docks of America's largest retailers and manufacturers, contributes to the stress and fatigue experienced by over-the-road drivers.[29] The consequent overtime and extended work shifts are associated with poorer perceived general health, as well as increased injury and illness rates or increased mortality in 16 of the 22 studies reviewed by the Center for Disease Control.[30] Stress doubles the risk of accidents and injuries and is compounded when pressure to perform additional tasks are mandated by employers.[31] Employee fatigue and job stress costs all US employers in increased health expenses, absenteeism, employee turnover and other less tangible costs including lower productivity. Estimates of these costs vary from $150 billion to $300 billion annually.[32] The problems caused by stress-related illness and injury are compounded for transportation workers such as drivers who often face health issues while away from home and without a local or familiar medical care systems. Although it remains to be seen if the recent changes to hours-of-service regulations will reduce highway accidents and fatalities involving large commercial vehicles, it is counter-intuitive to expect that the move from ten to eleven hours of actual driving time allowed per day under increasingly difficult conditions would achieve improved safety performance.

Driver Safety: A Growing Concern

With almost 43,000 deaths annually on the nation's highways in the last two years, the US Department of Transportation is renewing its emphasis on reducing the number and severity of highway crashes.[33] Although the majority of these accidents do not involve commercial vehicles, accidents, injuries, and fatalities affect the attractiveness of the profession to current and future drivers. According to the National Highway Traffic Safety Administration, employees' occupational and non-occupational wage and benefit losses due to crashes was $61 billion in 2000. Another $5 billion can be added if the employer's costs of employee's lost time are included.[34] Today's congested and deteriorating urban infrastructure makes operating a commercial motor vehicle on the highway system more dangerous than most other occupations, further contributing to the relegation of truck driving to an occupation of last resort.

Although trucking industry safety data is given an extensive treatment in chapter nine of this volume, it is appropriate to review the data that establishes trucking among the most dangerous occupations in the United States. Forty-two percent of all workplace fatalities occurred in transportation incidents in 2003,[35] with deaths among transportation and material moving occupations accounting for more fatalities (1,388) than any other major occupational group.[36] The transportation and warehousing industry trails only agriculture and mining in fatality rates; the rate for transportation and warehousing is 17.5 per 100,000 employees while the latter two have rates of 31.2 and 26.9 per 100,000 respectively.

The dangers of truck driving are not limited to fatalities, as 94,000 large trucks were involved in crashes involving personal injuries in 2002, with another 336,000 involved in property damage-only accidents.[37] Injuries also are sustained off the road, as most truck drivers are required to load and unload their vehicles – strenuous, non-driving activity that cans stress and strain the body. It is not surprising then that truck drivers are second among all occupations in terms of musculoskeletal disorders and the number of serious illnesses and injuries, as truck drivers reported 112,200 such cases of the latter in 2002.[38] Half of these injuries were strains and sprains, often to the back or lower extremities, stemming from over exertion, contacts with objects or equipment, or falls. Although the safety and health performance of some firms have improved recently as firms have begun to address escalating worker's compensation expenses,[39] these efforts have yet to appear in industry statistics for truck drivers.

Employee turnover further adds to the hazards faced by drivers. Recent FMCSA research concludes "that a significant relationship exists between job change rate and crash involvement."[40] Additional evidence of a relationship between turnover and crashes is provided in a second FMCSA report that finds the sectors with the highest crash rates per power unit are the general freight TL carriers and the bulk carriers – sectors with very high turnover rates.[41] In an industry in which most large carriers have turnover rates in excess of 100 percent, such evidence suggests poor safety outcomes of human resource policies that do little to bind the driver to the firm.

The combination of a stressful, strenuous occupation and a dangerous operating environment has made a career as a professional over-the-road driver a hazardous choice. Compared to almost any other service occupation, truck drivers rank at or near the top of every index measuring occupational discomfort or danger. High illness and injury rates are one of the less acknowledged factors underlying high turnover among long haul drivers – injured drivers either run out of disability benefits, wear themselves out of the industry, or draw such attention from their employers they are terminated.

Homeland Security Impact on Drivers' Rights

Prior to September 11, 2001, the trucking industry viewed the theft of a big rig or its contents as an issue for the carrier's loss prevention department. Likewise, while a catastrophic trucking accident or hazardous material spill might create unwanted publicity and make future insurance negotiations more difficult, the consequences were largely economic. Responsibly addressing safety issues and abiding by hazardous material regulations in the name of insurance requirements and environmental safety were part of doing business.

However, the terrorist acts of September 11, 2001, and the subsequent events, have profoundly altered employers' views of their employee, client and vendor relationships, rippling through the entire supply chain with expensive and far-reaching implications. While OTR drivers were initially asked to serve as another set of eyes and ears on the lookout for potential terrorist threats in programs such as Highway Watch, the lens was soon turned around on the drivers themselves. The prospect of further terrorist acts has caused the federal government and Congress to require criminal history record checks for many workers assigned to security sensitive areas, including airline employees, drivers of hazardous materials (hazmat), and port workers.

The USA PATRIOT Act (Public Law 107-56, Section 1012) and the Safe Explosives Act (Public Law 107-296, Sections 1121-1123), which placed certain requirements on states issuing Commercial Drivers Licenses (CDLs) with a hazardous material endorsement (HME), are having a marked impact on the trucking sector. After some reworking, the final rule issued by the Transportation Security Administration (TSA) and US Department of Homeland Security in May 2003 requires a criminal background check on commercial drivers certified to transport HAZMAT, including the collection of an individual's fingerprints if warranted.[42] In 2004, the TSA conducted name-based, terrorist-focused check on drivers authorized to transport hazardous materials and made a "security threat assessment" of those individuals through mandated self-disclosure, background checks and fingerprints. The second phase was in place in all states in January 2005 and requires a fingerprint-based check on all new HME applicants. The final phase in which all HME drivers seeking to renew or transfer their CDL endorsement will have their biographical information collected and fingerprints analyzed will be implemented by May 31, 2005. The culmination of this process will be to remove tens of thousands of drivers and further exacerbate the driver shortage.

The Patriot Act does not require a showing of a relationship between a conviction and a security threat; the inference is absolute by statute. The result is a dramatic shake out among the 3.5 million drivers who haul even small amounts of hazardous materials, affecting thousands of drivers whose previous convictions on charges unrelated to their driving record may now cause them to lose their HME and, consequently, their job. This hazmat endorsement is often a vital component of one's CDL and is especially necessary for over 150,000 L-T-L drivers who haul diverse shipments that may contain hazardous materials, such as chlorine and gasoline, in addition to non-hazmat materials in a single trailer on a daily basis. Although most drivers outside the tank, haul, and munitions sectors rarely transport large loads of chemicals or explosives, an L-T-L driver's value to their firm comes from their ability to haul small shipments, including hazmat, on short notice.

The changes set in motion by the response to 9/11 are becoming steadily stricter and affecting a broader cross section of drivers. Once operational, it is to be expected that the HME vetting process, initially limited to new applicants, will eliminate significant numbers of CDL-qualified drivers. Many who previously would have entered a driving school or company-sponsored training program will be disqualified from driving a large truck because of a serious encounter with the law in the past seven years or having been released from prison for a similar offense in the past five years. Disqualification from a HME endorsement can be imposed for a number of criminal convictions and may be interim or permanent. Most of the crimes eligible for permanent disqualification are severe and obvious, such as sedition, terrorism, and treason.[43] However, other TSA disqualifiers leave industry participants questioning the logic behind the rules and guidelines. Although murder was not initially classified as a permanently disqualifying offense, simple drug possession was sufficient cause of driver to lose their HME or become ineligible to obtain an HME.[44] TSA later added unlawful purchase, receipt and transfer of a firearm or explosive to the offenses that would cause a driver to lose their HAZMAT certification. Drivers can also be disqualified for rather ambiguous offenses such as "dishonesty, fraud or misrepresentation", crimes that are defined differently in each state.

Drivers who lose, or fail to qualify for, their hazardous materials certification can accept non-hazmat driving positions. In reality, they will be consigned to a more limited set of driving positions and stigmatized as they seek alternate employment or wait their case on appeal. Since FMCSA also recently began requiring companies to provide information about former drivers who become drivers for new employers, including accidents, drug and alcohol violations and other employment data, the ability of drivers with questionable events or backgrounds to escape their past has all but vanished.

Putting aside the specific disqualifying offenses, there is reason for concern about the potential effect of full criminal and security checks on an employer's treatment of its employees and contractors. Any federally-mandated information sharing system that covers millions of workers whose records reside and remain in databases under state control, as they do in the CDL certification system, brings with it issues of accuracy and confidentiality. As a program of this magnitude requires the review and of biographical and driving records on millions of workers, it requires the TSA to coordinate with agencies including the FBI and Immigration and Naturalization Service, agencies with purposes and operating procedures very different from those of the TSA, there will undoubtedly be coordination problems, including inaccurate information and false identification. Assurances that this evolving driver identification process has adequate measures to address issues of incorrect information and false identification are essential if the nation expects to keep its existing and future driving labor force. Between the cost of the hazmat driver check ($94 borne by the driver) and the month-long wait the program takes, it is estimated that as many as 500,000 drivers, or 20 percent of the driver labor force, will forego the endorsement process, further eroding the pool of drivers available to haul both chemicals and general freight.[45]

The changes to the HAZMAT endorsement process come on the heels of even more significant revisions to the commercial driver's licensing program. Under final rules of the Motor Carrier Safety Improvement Act (MCSIA) of 1999, FMCSA issued significant changes including the expansion of the definition of "serious traffic violations", extension of the driver record check, further mandates on notification requirements, and the disqualification of commercial drivers for violations obtained while driving a non-commercial motor vehicle.[46] Regulations in place in 2004 delineated new minimum training requirements for entry-level CMV operators and mandated sharing of drivers' records and history between employers.[47]

These may be more significant for current drivers or potential entrants than the homeland security-driven rules, as non-work related behavior was previously mostly exempt from government and employer scrutiny. The final rules of the MCSIA allow CDL drivers to be disqualified if they have been convicted of traffic offenses while operating non-CMV including infractions that only result in a suspension. Alcohol or drug-related offenses are treated similarly along with new disqualifying offenses, such as driving a CMV after one's CDL was revoked or suspended or causing a fatality through the negligent operation of a CMV. While no one should defend the illegal acts of drivers of large trucks, the economic consequences for a one-time, off-duty violation may be disproportionate to the offense. Further, the termination is under the control of the employer. A driver may now be terminated on the basis of inaccurate records provided by a prior employer without the knowledge, notification or consent of the driver.

These new regulations can have devastating consequences for many drivers. Those whose past does not conform to these new requirements will either be limited to positions which do not require hazmat certification or will be pushed out of the industry entirely. As motor carrier employers have indicated a strong desire to access any personal information uncovered by the security threat assessment process and fingerprint-based background check for use in their personnel processes, drivers will increasingly be tracked in permanent records that exist in a netherworld between the government and employers.[48] Black marks in such records, even those that do not result in a driver's disqualification, would permanently tarnish his or her work history and restrict future employment opportunities. Many will become "tagged" in these databases by offenses that predate their trucking careers, are unrelated to their performance as truck drivers, or are simply erroneous. This will result in drivers being forced from their current position and reluctantly exiting the industry.

Although TSA has attempted to strike a balance between security and the rights of drivers, establishing certain basic principles would go along way to insuring the screening and review process is fair and provides due process for drivers.[49] First, the background check process should involve the driver and state and federal agencies, and not provide a new source of information about a driver to the employer beyond a "pass/fail" level. Second, Canadian and Mexican drivers should undergo an identical screening process before they can haul HAZMAT in the United States. The TSA should also establish a mechanism for workers to file privacy complaints regarding the handling of their personal information and threat assessment results. In addition, indictments should not be treated as convictions and drivers should be able to challenge the characterization of an offense in the appeal or waiver process. The TSA should not be the agency where appeals or waivers are adjudicated, as it is the agency that determines if a driver is a security threat. Finally, the TSA should not allow states to impose additional security threat assessments on drivers beyond those imposed by the federal government.

As these systems have been developed in response to federal mandates, legislation is needed to secure due process, the correction of errors, mitigation for circumstances and a list of criminal acts that define security risks as well as protection from summary dismissal by employers. Even with such rights, truck drivers, particularly those not represented by a union or employee or owner-operator organization, are typically unfamiliar administrative processes and generally lack the knowledge and funds to obtain effective representation. This places them at a disadvantage in protecting their rights and their economic well-being. It may then be appropriate for the federal government to provide advocates or an ombudsman to represent drivers in this system

Regardless of one's views about the possible infringement on a driver's civil liberties and the ongoing penalization for offenses committed long in the past, this vetting process will further erode the pool of active drivers and workers available to the industry. This is particularly daunting for an industry facing a historically unique driver shortage and a multimodal capacity crunch.[50]

In summary, the professional truck driver's role and expectations in the modern transportation industry have shifted dramatically in the deregulated environment of the past 25 years. While the introduction of new technology and compensation schemes to reward high-revenue drivers keeps some tethered to the seat, most view their employment as temporary, always hoping the next driving job pays better and gets them home more often, with future occupational sights set on leaving the industry. Clearly, operating environments are getting more difficult for those who remain in the industry and only further exacerbate the driver shortage. Equally importantly to raising the profile and status of drivers will be long-term improvements in their work environment. This includes those conditions imposed on them daily by their employer, the stresses of an ever more competitive global economy and increased government regulations in a post 9/11 world.

From Port to Highway

Increasing demand for goods from overseas, particularly from China, has made port operations and the movement of freight to and from the ports increasingly important to the American economy. Despite their centrality to the operations of ports, the drivers who move overseas freight containers in and out of the ports are among the worst paid and most poorly treated truck drivers. Their plight illustrates the problems that have accompanied the new economy and globalization of commerce.

Given the recent surge in international trade over the last 20 years, and the lack of infrastructure improvements by the rail industry, truck transportation has become ever more essential to the movement of overseas freight. The work of the drivers who pick up and deliver containers at the ports inherently differs from that of over-the-road trucks and their drivers. Rather than picking up a container and delivering it to the final destination, port drivers provide short-haul drayage, delivering the containers to warehouses and distribution centers within fifty to one hundred miles of the port.

The relationship between the shipper, the ocean freight carrier, and drayage firms operates to the disadvantage of the drayage firm and port drivers. When freight is shipped into the US, the shipper is typically quoted a rate from the ocean carrier that includes the cost of the haul to the shipper's warehouse or distribution center. The ocean freight firms then contract this movement with a local drayage company that specialize in this service. There are hundreds of these port drayage companies in the major ports across the US. Because of the large number of drayage firms, and the small number of ocean freight firms, the drayage companies are at a disadvantage in negotiating rates for their services. The exemption of the ocean freight firms from antitrust laws only exacerbates this imbalance in market power.

Operational characteristics at the ports result in time-consuming inefficiency in port drayage, particularly the lack of space. Unloaded containers destined for trucks can be handled in one of two ways. Containers can be placed directly on the chassis, lessening delay time as the load is waiting at the terminal when the driver arrives. This requires considerable space, a rare commodity in most ports. More common is for containers to be stacked in the terminal facility and then placed on a chassis only when the driver arrives at the terminal with the paperwork. This can involve a significant time cost in locating the proper load and placing it on a chassis. In addition, while ships are unloaded 24 hours per day, the terminals are not typically open for pickups and deliveries for more than 12-14 hours per day, further creating congestions and delays.

These conditions work to the disadvantage of port drivers. Most drivers are owner-operators, self-employed workers who provide both their labor and a tractor to the drayage firms. As independent contractors, they enjoy none of the protections of labor law. Instead they are paid flat rates, an average of $94 per trip in the port of Los Angeles/Long Beach, for hauling containers and pay their own fuel costs as well as the costs of the tractors (Monaco, 2005). The inefficiencies in port drayage result in drivers spending considerable portion of their potential working time waiting to get in and out of the port. The waiting time problem is exacerbated by the poor condition of many of the container chassis; drivers often have to wait for chassis repairs after waiting to get their load. In neither case are the drivers compensated for waiting time. Long waiting times limit drivers to an average of three trips per eleven hour day in Los Angeles. As a result, average daily earnings are $235 for their labor and truck expenses, including fuel, insurance, permits, etc. Port drivers average $29,900 annually, and median earnings are $25,000.[51] As might be expected given the low pay and poor working conditions, the majority of port drivers on the West Coast are non-native, as many are recent Hispanic immigrants.

The problems with the physical and economic structure of the ports are not just for drivers. The lack of physical facilities to handle trucks effectively result in long backups and congestion in the areas near the port. The low pay of port drivers compels them to drive older trucks with high mileage. In concert with the long waiting time to get loads, the age of the trucks, in causes considerable air pollution in the metropolitan areas around the ports.

Although port drivers' predicament is an extreme example of financial and operating pressures experienced by drivers throughout the industry, its extremity reveals the deleterious effects of a system with unequal power that plays drivers off against one another.

Representing Those who Need it Most: A New Paradigm for Truck Drivers and their Employers

One of the more troubling developments of the last 15 years is that the over-the-road driver population that would benefit most from union representation, a truckload driver in the for-hire dry van segment, is the least likely to carry a union card. While estimates vary, it is generally accepted that fewer than 10 percent of all TL drivers in the for-hire segment are union members (Belzer, 2002). Although the Teamsters represent thousands of short-haul TL drivers working in private fleets, the sector of the industry born out of deregulation in the early 1980s, the for-hire, long-haul TL sector, remains largely unorganized and diffuse.

The working lives of OTR, TL drivers have been well documented in recent years in research covering topics ranging from drivers' declining earning power to triple-digit turnover rates (Belman, Monaco and Brooks 2005; Belzer, 2000). Despite this plethora of information, little attention has been paid to developing constructive solutions to drivers' issues. Most would be hard pressed to dispute that the vast majority of drivers lead isolated work lives characterized by low pay, low benefits and low prestige. And although a few motor carriers, most notably J.B. Hunt, have used wage rates above industry norms to lure experienced drivers and reward tenure with positive effects on their firm's safety record and possibly their bottom line, the rest of the industry remains mired in a low-pay/high-turnover conundrum.

What the balance of this article explores is the potential for labor agreements as a vehicle for alleviating the common problems of the parties in the trucking industry. The industry currently lacks institutions that bring drivers, employers, shippers, and regulators together to reconcile their interests. Indeed, the only parties currently trying to manage these relationships are third-party logistics providers and freight brokers whose personal interests do not encourage them to address the foundational issues facing the trucking industry.

For solo drivers, whose only physical contact with other company employees might be a passing meal with a driver at a truck stop, some greater level of personal attachment in the employment relationship may reduce the personal distance of the road. In reality, the only contact a driver may have with any co-worker is the occasional phone call or e-mail from the company dispatcher.[52] In this scenario, where both drivers and their employers are often separated by more than just physical distance, a labor agreement jointly negotiated by the parties may work to everyone's advantage. It can facilitate a tripartite dialogue between drivers, employers and the government about the real concerns and experiences of the OTR drivers. Properly arranged, a contract can bridge the unforgiving and increasingly difficult operating workplace on the American highway.

What a Labor Agreement Offers

The fundamental problem facing most drivers is that they lack an effective forum to discuss and resolve their issues with employers, the regulators, the industry and the shipping public. Lacking such a forum, or any mutual means of resolving pressing issues, drivers exercise the other available solution, leaving the industry, or, in the case of those who are not yet drivers, deciding against a driving career. Although economic theory suggests that the market should, in light of the increasing need for drivers, act to resolve the economic and working condition issues, the experience of the last two decades suggests that the market is failing to adequately address these issues to eliminate persistent labor shortages in the industry. The lack of driver representation in political and administrative forums exacerbates this dilemma, as regulators and employer representatives tend to develop solutions that do not adequately address the situation of drivers, particularly those lacking union representation.

A collective bargaining agreement that defines the terms and conditions of employment is an important mechanism for ensuring worker's rights in a traditional setting, such as a factory or shop floor, but it is also particularly useful to long-haul truckload drivers and provides benefits to the industry. The terms of a labor agreement and the resources of an effective local union provide the driver with clear standards, an advocate, and due process rights. These give the driver some latitude to discuss situations in which they are potentially at odds with shippers or employers. Such rights provide the driver with a means of avoiding the overwork, and consequent safety and health issues, faced by most drivers. Most labor agreements for truckload drivers give meaningful avenues and timeframes for addressing grievances that relate to pay, hours worked, and equipment problems.

For example, drivers need the right to review company records to ascertain if proper dispatch procedures were followed in a particular situation. They may not quit in frustration over a missed load knowing that a formal process, possibly a grievance in this case, can be invoked to investigate and adjudicate their concerns. In the best case, employers live by codified work and dispatch rules that will standardize the treatment of drivers and, when necessary, appropriately compensate drivers who are excessively dispatched. In addition, if the negotiated contract demands that drivers get back to their domicile every ten days, employers will likely devise routing plans that necessitate such action. With the industry consolidation that has occurred over the past five years in this sector, and its largest employers having driver pools that are measured in the tens of thousands, scheduling and routing drivers home more frequently should be less troublesome. Such efforts are unlikely absent a collective means of asserting their importance to employers.

Collective agreements also reduce the rewards to turnover. Where there is bargaining, drivers are able to anticipate pay and benefits improvements over the three to four years of a standard contract. Changing employers to obtain modestly superior pay or signing bonuses is thus less attractive given that the immediately better pay is seldom accompanied by assurances of further regular increases as wrought by a collective bargaining agreement. The standardization of pay across firms that comes with extensive systems of collective bargaining thus reduces the economic gains from job-hopping.

Essentially what the collective bargaining agreement provides are additional tethers to the job, often highlighted by the fact that a work history with a common employer is rewarded over the course of a lifetime through the agreement rather than over a matter of months or years otherwise. Virtually every labor agreement is structured such that paid time off, including vacations, holidays, and sick leave, will improve significantly with each passing year. Many truckload carriers currently provide only minimal time off and only marginal improvements in benefits over time since most drivers change employers so frequently. By design, the nature of this relationship has become controlled by short-term economics which itself identifies the occupation as one of temporary value.

Further, collective bargaining agreements can help facilitate new developments in the ever-shifting sea of regulatory and technological change for transportation companies. Although frequently underutilized by both parties, many contracts have labor-management committees that provide forums to anticipate and structure needed changes in the workplace. As the lines blur between the freight services provided by large transportation companies, the Teamsters Union has placed enabling language in its National Master Agreements that provide for joint negotiations on new and emerging services and ways of constructing agreements that benefit all parties. As a process, bargaining allows for the orderly introduction of change, such as in-cab technology and communication systems, where its purposes are known, its uses are negotiated and understood, and the system is established in a manner that is fair to all parties.

Most unions are particularly adept at representing the privacy interests of its members and defending against the intrusion of unnecessary employer and government monitoring when appropriate. For example, although Teamsters drivers have the lowest violations rates for drug and alcohol offenses and virtually all other traffic violations, the union is studying how new employee identification systems, such as biometric cards, can be used to improve security for shippers and receivers without providing employers and third parties unnecessary personal information.[53] The union has similarly been able to limit the ability of employers such as UPS to use Qualcomm or other GPS-based systems to discipline a driver regarding activities unrelated to work performance. Unless a collective bargaining agreement is present to address such issues, drivers are at the mercy of their employers. Although each situation involves thorny issues for the union, the outcome of a joint process will certainly be superior to unilateral decision-making by firms that undervalue employee concerns. The experience of the last twenty years suggests that changes are easier and more successful when unions are integrated into the decision-making process.

Especially when viewed in the context of a less adversarial bargaining relationship, labor contracts have the capacity to bridge and rationalize the relationship between employers and employees that are seldom in contact with one another. In the case of truckload drivers, a labor contract adds stability and resources for both labor and management to improve what are often very temporary employment relationships. More importantly, once longevity is rewarded and lasting economic and life-style improvements arrive for over-the-road drivers in the truckload market, the industry will be spending less capital on the training and recruitment of drivers and enjoying more stable relationships with the drivers who serve it. In an industry where profit margins are thin and dramatic pay and benefit improvements are unlikely, the quality of life issues that collective bargaining agreements are uniquely situated to address can empower drivers and effectuate change for the positive.

This is not to suggest that the reorganization of the industry will be easy. There are multiple barriers to organizing OTR-TL drivers. Operating few terminals over an irregular route structure, truckload carriers are adept at balancing a mix of so-called "owner-operators" and company drivers with schedules that vary tremendously from week to week. Not only difficult to locate when driving, true owner-operators are exempt from collective bargaining laws and company drivers, when home for the relatively few brief periods, are generally uninterested in spending time with union organizers. In addition, the drivers in this sector tend to be the new entrants in trucking, often younger drivers, who faced with limited employment opportunities, have sought the open road as an occupational way station. Without experience with unions, these new employees often buy into the negative myths and stereotypes of unions that employers present, or follow the perceptions carried forward from a previous work experience. Nevertheless, a properly conducted campaign, free of malignant rhetoric on both sides, can overcome these cultural and institutional barriers and allow the free exercise of an employee's choice in representation.

An Example of What Can Be Done

Historically fractured by political and ethnic concerns, many port drivers are seeing their common plight as more important than their respective differences. Similar to other drivers handling brokered freight, port drivers are uniting against the low pay and long hours they must endure to eke out a living. Initially a campaign focused on economic and social justice, Teamsters efforts in the ports have resulted in tangible improvements for this underclass of tractor-trailer drivers through coordinated legislation that improves pay and shortens wait times for loads, illustrating the potential of organizing and embracing a new paradigm.

A particular hurdle for port drivers effort to improve their situation has been their classification as owner-operators. This has not only denied them many of the protections of labor law, but has also barred them from engaging in collective activity. In response to shipping companies' efforts to disenfranchise port drivers' collective efforts, the Teamsters Union has opposed legislation to make it easier for employers to classify workers as independent contractors or leased employees, thereby eliminating the employer's obligation to pay workers' social security, pensions, overtime, vacation, health insurance, sick-leave and workers' compensation coverage, and depriving these workers of vital health and safety, anti-discrimination, and workers' rights protections. The issue of "who is the employer?", long a debate confined to truck stops throughout the nation, is central to port driver organizing, as the nation's port operators have long endeavored to keep its drivers from organizing and collective bargaining.

The legal impediments to port truckers' ability to discuss rates and coordinate activity may be also be changing because of their increased importance in moving global traffic and the union's ability to coordinate their advocacy. For the first time in history, port truckers, Teamsters and others have advanced legislation in California in 2005 that would exempt port drivers from federal anti-trust laws. This would allow port drivers to form an association to negotiate rates and undertake collective action.[54] While the opponents of such legislation are powerful and unlikely to concern themselves with the condition of drayage operators, the legislative action to establish rights for "independent contractors" that recognize the similarity of their circumstances to those of employees is a significant step toward improving their conditions.

The safety campaign recently spearheaded by the union with regards to liability issues related to unsafe intermodal chassis is another example of the role a coordinated advocate can play for drivers, particularly the unrepresented owner-operators. Working with the International Longshoremen's Association, the International Longshore and Warehouse Union and the American Trucking Associations, the Teamsters have been able to pass legislation affecting operations in major ports throughout the US. In addressing the basic economic and safety issues of chassis maintenance, roadability and equipment interchange liability, the alliance has been able to focus the attention of harbor regulators and terminal operators on safe and efficient drayage practices to the betterment of the port trucker and traveling public. With this example of an alliance between a diverse group of industry representatives and drivers, the potential for other groups of heavy truck drivers to work beneficially with the union and their employers needs to be taken seriously.

Conclusion

The truck driver is a largely unacknowledged but central actor in the modern freight industry, as the evolution of the industry over the last twenty years has been particularly disadvantageous to drivers. The purchasing power of drivers has fallen sharply since the early 1980s and working conditions have not improved. Recent technological and regulatory changes have continued the trend toward making the job more difficult and scrutinized without increasing the rewards for drivers. The predictable consequences of these factors, a shortage of drivers and consequence drag on the US economy, have begun to appear. As such, there is no evidence of countervailing forces, be they the actions of the impersonal market or of industry players or regulators, that will reverse these trends in the next decade. Rather, the continued deterioration of the job will likely lead to a steadily more severe capacity crunch.

These issues will not be addressed until the driver has effective representation at the industry and regulatory tables. Absent such presence, the concerns of the other players, particularly trucking firms, shippers, and regulators, will always be placed ahead of drivers' concerns. The experience of American workers over the last two centuries suggests that the only way for workers to take their place at the table is through collective action, typically by way of unions or other types of employee associations. What is clear is that, absent better representation in whatever forms it takes, the problems faced by drivers will spill over more and more into the wider economy, with consequences for the nation as a whole.

Notes

1. American Trucking Trends: 2003, American Trucking Associations, Inc. Alexandria, VA 2003.
2. Occupational Employment and Wages, November, 2003, 53-3032 Truck Drivers, Heavy and Tractor Trailer, Bureau of Labor Statistics, Occupational Employment Statistics, www.bls.gov/oes/current/oes533032.htm.
3. "Driver Availability Problems Begin to Surface in LTL Sector", Transport Topics, ATA, August 16, 2004, p. 3.
4. 2002 Commodity Flow Survey – United States (Final), US Department of Census and Bureau of Transportation Statistics, USDOT December, 2004.
5. "Execs Push Driver Hiring Issues", Transport Topics, ATA, October 18, 2004 p. 2.
6. "Truckers Protest Fuel Costs", Transport Topics, ATA, May 10, 2004, p. 1.
7. The use of foreign drivers has declined since 9/11 as homeland security rules have made it steadily more difficult to bring foreign drivers into the United States.
8. Occupational Outlook Quarterly, Spring 2004, Bureau of Labor Statistics, USDOL, Vol. 48, No. 1 pp. 46 and 56.
9. Top For-Hire Carriers, 2004 Transport Topics Report, ATA, 2004.
10. Form M Annual Reports, Motor Carrier Financial and Operating Statistics Program, Federal Motor Carrier Safety Administration, USDOT (1999-2003).
11. "Schneider trucking poised to buy firm", *Milwaukee Journal-Sentinel*, July 3, 1998, Business p. 3.
12. The Beige Book, Federal Reserve Board, 10/27/04, www.federalreserve.gov/ FOMC?BeigeBook/2004/20041027/FullReport.htm.
13. "New technology helps distributors track drivers", Central Penn Business Journal, August 23, 1996, Vol. 12, No. 34, p. 20.
14. "On Your Tracks: GPS Tracking in the Workplace", National Workrights Institute, Princeton, N.J., 2004.
15. One motor freight carrier was confronted with the issue of whether it should release GPS information that showed when a married driver was visiting the house of an alleged girlfriend, even though the visits were during off duty hours.
16. Federal Register, Vol. 69, No. 169, Wednesday, September 1, 2004 "Proposed Rules, p 53387 citing Federal Motor Carrier Safety Regulations, Part 395, 53 FR 38666 September 30, 1988.
17. "Electronic Cost Barriers", *Traffic World*, December 13, 2004, p. 23.
18. Schneider National, *TouchHome* Program (January, 2005) as outlined at www.schneider.com/drivers/specialPrograms.html.
19. 2002 Economic Census: Vehicle Inventory and Use Survey, Economics and Statistics Administration, US Census Bureau, US Department of Commerce, December 2004.

20. The 2004 Urban Mobility Report, Texas Transportation Institute, The Texas A and M University System, September, 2004, http://mobility.tamu.edu.

21. 2002 Status of the Nation's Highways, Bridges, and Transit, Conditions and Performance, Report to Congress, Executive Summary, Federal Transit Administration and Federal Highway Administration, Pub. No. FHWA-PL-03-004.

22. Traffic Congestion and Reliability: Linking Solutions to Problems. Office of Operations, Federal Highway Administration, US Department of Transportation, revised September, 2004 p. 8, www.ops.fhwa.dot.gov/congestion_report/chapter3.htm.

23. The 2004 Urban Mobility Report, Texas Transportation Institute, The Texas A and M University System, September, 2004, p. 1 http://mobility.tamu.edu.

24. 2002 Status of the Nation's Highways, Bridges, and Transit: Conditions and Performance, Report to Congress, Executive Summary, Federal Transit Administration and Federal Highway Administration, Pub. No. FHWA-PL-03-004, p. ES-4.

25. 2002 Status of the Nation's Highways, Bridges, and Transit: Conditions and Performance, Report to Congress, Executive Summary, Federal Transit Administration and Federal Highway Administration, Pub. No. FHWA-PL-03-004, p. ES-12.

26. Dry Van Drivers' Survey, Truckload Carriers Association, conducted by Martin Labbe Associates, Press Release, TCA, June 22, 1999.

27. Top Ten Management Issues, Report Number PT-2001-017, January 18, 2001, p. 27.

28. "Just in Time to Wait: An Examination of Best Practices for Streamlining Loading and Unloading Practices", Truckload Carriers Association, Alexandria, VA August 2000.

29. Dry Van Drivers Survey, Truckload Carriers Association, Alexandria, VA, June 1999.

30. Overtime and Extended Work Shifts: Recent Findings on Illnesses, Injuries, and Health Behaviors. National Institute for Occupational Safety and Health, Centers for Disease Control and Prevention, Department of Health and Human Services, Publication No. 2004-143, April 2004.

31. Work-related Roadway Crashes, Prevention Strategies for Employers, Centers for Disease Control and Prevention, National Institutes for Occupational Safety and Health, Pub No. 2004-136, March 2004.

32. "Sick of Work: The Stress Explosion", *New York Times*, September 5, 2004, p. 1.

33. "Targeting Highway Fatalities", FHWA Office of Safety, USDOT, January 2004.

34. Work-related Roadway Crashes, Prevention Strategies for Employers, Centers for Disease Control and Prevention, National Institutes for Occupational Safety and Health, Pub No. 2004-136, March 2004.

35. Census of Fatal Occupational Injuries, Information on Deadly Work Hazards, 2003 Data, Bureau of Labor Statistics, US Department of Labor.

36. "Occupational Injuries and Illnesses: Counts, Rates, and Characteristics, 2002", BLS, USDOL, September, 2004, Bulletin 2566.

37. "Large Truck Crash Facts, 2002, Federal Motor Carrier Safety Administration", Analysis Division, US Department of Transportation, April, 2004, p. 39.

38. "Lost-Worktime Injuries and Illnesses: Characteristics and Resulting Days Away From Work, 2002", BLS, USDOL, March 25, 2004 USDL 04-460.

39. "Carriers Say Workers' Comp Premium Increase Cutting into Profit Margins", Transport Topics, ATA, November 24, 2003, p. 1.

40. "Commercial Motor Vehicle Driver Retention and Safety", Technical Brief, FMCSA, USDOL, FMSCA–RT-04-002, October 2003.

41. Motor Carrier Safety Performance Profile, Analysis Division, Office of Information Management, Thomas M. Corsi, Marius Stefan, February 2004, p. 17.

42. Security Threat Assessment for Individuals Applying for A Hazardous Materials Endorsement for a Commercial Drivers License, Federal Register, TSA, Department of Homeland Security, 49 CFR Parts 1570 and 1572, May 5, 2003.

43. Hazmat Disqualifying Crimes, Transportation Security Administration, www.tsa.gov/ pubilc/display.

44. 49 CFR Part 1572, Security Threat Assessment for Individuals Applying for a Hazardous Materials Endorsement for a Commercial Driver's License; Final Rule, Federal Register, Vol. 69, No. 226, p. 68723, Nov 24, 2004.

45. Driving Out Hazmat Drivers? *Traffic World*, January 24, 2005, p. 28.

46. Summary of the Motor Carrier Safety Improvement Act of 1999, P.L. 106-159, Federal Motor Carrier Safety Administration, December 9, 1999, USDOT website and Federal Register, Vol. 67, No. 147 July 31, 2002, Part 383 – Commercial Driver's License Standards: Requirements and Penalties.

47. Minimum Training Requirements for Entry-Level CMV Operators, Federal Register, FMSCA, USDOT, 49 CFR Part 380, May 21, 2004.

48. Testimony of American Trucking Associations, Re: Docket No. TSA-2003-14610: Security Threat Assessment for Individuals Applying for A Hazardous Materials Endorsement for a Commercial Drivers License and Docket No. FMCSA-2001-11117 "Limitations on the Issuance of Commercial Driver's Licenses with A Hazardous Materials Endorsement" July 7, 2003, p. 6.

49. Comments of the International Brotherhood of Teamsters before the US Department of Homeland Security, TSA, regarding Docket No. TSA-2003-14610; Amendment No. 1572-4, December 21, 2004.

50. See transcripts of The Freight Transportation Capacity Crisis Summit held at the Logistics Institute at Georgia Tech, October 11-12, 2004, www.tli.gatech.edu/tcs/a.

51. Op. cit., p. 4.

52. Belman, Monaco and Brooks, 2005, pp. 126-127.

53. Issue Briefs, Motor Freight Carriers Association website, www.mfca.org/ eissues/eissues.html.

54. "Teamsters Take a Different Tack", The Journal of Commerce, January 24, 2005 p. 12.

References

Belman, Dale, Monaco, Kristen, and Brooks, *Sailors of the Concrete Sea: The Work and Life of Truck Drivers*, Michigan State University Press, East Lansing, Mich., 2005.

Belzer, Michael H., *Sweatshop on Wheels*, Oxford University Press, New York, New York, 2000, p. 94.

Belzer, Michael H., "Trucking: Collective Bargaining Takes a Rocky Road", Collective Bargaining in the Private Sector, Industrial Relations Research Association, Champaign, IL, 2002 and International Brotherhood of Teamsters, Internal Records, 2004.

Monaco, Kristen, "Wages and Working Conditions of Truck Drivers in the Port of Long Beach", paper given at the 84th Annual Meeting of the Transportation Research Board, Washington, D.C., January, 2005. Professor Monaco provided additional data to the author.

Index

Printed in the United States
by Baker & Taylor Publisher Services